WHITE AND NEGRO SCHOOLS IN THE SOUTH

WHITE AND NEGRO SCHOOLS

Truman M. Pierce

James B. Kincheloe

R. Edgar Moore

Galen N. Drewry

Bennie E. Carmichael

PRENTICE-HALL, INC.

IN THE SOUTH:

An analysis of biracial education

Dean of the School of Education, Alabama Polytechnic Institute, and Director, Southern States Cooperative Program in Educational Administration

Coordinator, Program in the Administration of Local School Systems, Southern States Cooperative Program in Educational Administration

Coordinator, Communication and Evaluation, Southern States Cooperative Program in Educational Administration

Coordinator, Program in State Educational Administration, Southern States Cooperative Program in Educational Administration

Coordinator, Program in the Administration of Local School Systems, Southern States Cooperative Program in Educational Administration

ENGLEWOOD CLIFFS, N.J.   1955

PRENTICE-HALL EDUCATION SERIES

John S. Brubacher, Editor

Library of Congress
Catalog Card No.: 55-11346

PRINTED IN THE UNITED STATES OF AMERICA

95721

Preface

In one sense it is a curious fact that at no time in the history of the biracial school systems of the South has it been possible to say with certainty what their precise status was on either a local, state, or regional basis. To be sure, many studies of schools in the region have been made. But heretofore there has appeared no region-wide study comprehensive or penetrating enough to reveal the full scope of true conditions in Negro schools as compared to those in white schools. Much of the data that have been gathered on Negro schools has been for use in arguments for or against segregation. Despite this lack of thorough study, even simple observation has always been enough to show that Negro schools have in general been inferior to white schools.

In another sense, failure adequately to understand Negro education is simply a normal reflection of the feeling on the part of many Southerners that the Negro belongs to an inferior race and, therefore, particular knowledge of his educational needs, and provisions for meeting them, are of minor consequence. To Southerners who hold to this belief, the inferiority of the Negro is a patent fact and there has been simply no reason to study the degree to which his inferior status is reflected in Negro schools or in any other aspect of Negro life. As a result, educational statistics have often been of such nature as to meet only prudential requirements rather than to provide data for the objective analysis of differences in the dual school systems of the South. Furthermore, the way education is organized and administered in the region has complicated the problem of determining the actual differences between schools of the two races. Although there are separate schools, separate faculties, and separate facilities for each race, there has been a single administration and a single budget for both races in school districts.

The necessity for a comprehensive body of facts about Negro schools was not generally recognized until court decisions made it mandatory for states with dual school systems to give serious attention to the "equal" phase of the "separate but equal" doctrine on which public education in the South has been so long predicated. When the courts were used as an instrument for a direct attack on segregation itself, it became obvious that necessary judgments regarding the future of schools in the region could not be made on the basis of existing knowledge.

The Fund for the Advancement of Education clearly perceived the need for an objective and far-reaching study of the facts concerning public education in the region; after extensive consultation with Southern leaders of both races, the Fund decided in the summer of 1953 to provide necessary financial support for the needed research. A large staff of Southerners who were familiar with the educational scene in the region was quickly assembled, and the most searching study of education on a regional level ever undertaken was launched. The staff of the Southern States Cooperative Program in Educational Administration accepted the responsibility for conducting the research on the dual school systems. Research of this nature was in keeping with the Program's general purpose, which is to contribute in every way possible to the stimulation and strengthening of educational leadership in the region. Both the Fund for the Advancement of Education and the Cooperative Program made explicit in the beginning the nature of their interest in the project. Stated simply, each agency declined the role of a protagonist in the segregation issue and sought only to provide, in as objective a fashion as possible, data essential to those in whose hands policy determination is lodged—essential if they are to make wise decisions concerning the future of Southern education.

The historic decision of the Supreme Court in May, 1954, ruling that racial segregation in public education as a matter of public policy was unconstitutional, greatly increased the importance of the inquiry.

The purposes of this book are to set forth, analyze, and interpret facts concerning the dual school systems of the South to the end that the findings may be useful in efforts to deal intelligently with the segregation issue and other problems in Southern education during the years immediately ahead. In Chapters 1, 10, and 11, the authors go one step beyond the original research objective of simple-fact-finding and analysis, and suggest both a point of view and somewhat specific approaches consistent with American values and ideals in dealing with educational problems.

The decision of the Supreme Court, which undoubtedly will accelerate the rapid improvement in educational opportunities for

Negroes that has been underway for several years, calls for certain
knowledge and understanding of the general racial and cultural background of the South that reach beyond the mere presentation of facts
concerning Negro and white schools. The psychological, sociological, and philosophical foundations of the South, particularly as they
bear on segregation, cannot be overlooked in any realistic effort to
understand the region and to project the most sensible course of action
in the face of issues that must be met.

Hence, Part One of this book is designed to show that the evolutionary nature of American value patterns has produced a society of
change which constantly reaches out for its ideals and, in so doing,
has brought about the present crisis in education in the Southern
region. As a part of this analysis, the historical context of biracial
education is reviewed and interpreted in order that attitudes and
beliefs prevalent in the region may be more clearly understood. The
last of the three chapters in Part One is an analysis of the organization
and administration of education in the Southern region with emphasis
on how they reflect the traditional concept in the South concerning
the role of the Negro.

In Part Two a comprehensive report is made of the major facts
concerning public education in the region with particular attention
directed at the biracial aspects of education. School population, enrollment, and attendance are analyzed with respect to the educational
tasks they impose. This analysis is followed by an evaluation of the
wealth of the region and a consideration of the financial support
needed to educate the existing school population. Next, an analysis
of school revenues and school expenditures is presented. Data on
teaching personnel and school facilities follow. The last chapter in
Part Two deals with certain parts of the school program itself, and
an inquiry into their adequacy is made. Somewhat lavish use of
statistical treatment is relied upon in this section, as the purpose
of these chapters is to present a factual analysis of schools in the
region. This kind of analysis inescapably involves comparisons of
white and Negro schools and seems fundamental to wise policy-
making.

Part Three is composed of two chapters. The first consists of generalizations drawn from the body of facts presented in Part Two,
generalizations stated as great unfinished tasks in Southern education.
The tasks are considered in the light of conditions in the region which
may determine how these tasks are approached. The second chap-

ter in this section seeks to define and evaluate a point of view for looking at school issues in the region and the segregation issue in particular; the point of view is subjected to rigid examination for consistency with the American value pattern. This is followed by suggested guides for consideration in resolving the issues faced by the public schools of the region.

States covered by the investigation were Alabama, Arkansas, Florida, Georgia, Kentucky, Louisiana, Mississippi, North Carolina, Oklahoma, South Carolina, Tennessee, Texas, and Virginia. In these writings, reference is to these states when the terms "the South" and the "Southern region" are used.

This book is the work of hands too numerous to list in this space. Special appreciation is due Dr. A. D. Albright, Associate Director of the Southern States Cooperative Program in Educational Administration, and Dr. Glen Robinson and Dr. Fred Gupton, Staff Associates, for their important roles in the research project. Dr. Louis Swanson, Director of Instruction, Public Schools, Chattanooga, Tennessee; Mr. Amos Trotter, Assistant Superintendent, Marlboro County Schools, Bennettsville, South Carolina; Mr. Oren B. Wilder, Assistant Director, Division of Teacher Education and Certification, State Department of Education, Kentucky; and Dr. Edward C. Merrill, Staff Associate, Southern States Cooperative Program in Educational Administration, provided invaluable assistance in various phases of the inquiry. Mr. Harry Ashmore, Executive Editor, *Arkansas Gazette,* Little Rock, Arkansas, who was director of the entire project financed by the Fund for the Advancement of Education; Mr. Philip Hammer, Atlanta, Georgia, research director of the project; Dr. Ernst Swanson, Emory University; and Dr. John Maclachlan, University of Florida, have made substantial contributions for which our sincere thanks are expressed. The materials for the study could not have been collected without the active cooperation of the chief state school officers of the Southern states and members of their staffs; we are deeply grateful for their help. Finally, we are indebted to the authors and publishers who generously consented to the use of copyrighted materials in certain portions of this volume.

TRUMAN M. PIERCE
JAMES B. KINCHELOE
R. EDGAR MOORE
GALEN N. DREWRY
BENNIE E. CARMICHAEL

Table of Contents

SECTION I

The Issues—

Their Setting and Development

ONE

Public Education
and American Society

It is scarcely possible to understand the schools of a nation, region, state, or community without first taking a look at the cultural environment which fosters and gives sustenance to education. What education seeks to do and the means used to achieve its goals are a part of the entire society. An essential step, therefore, in the consideration of white and Negro schools of the South is a brief treatment of the basic drives which make American society what it is. As a setting for this volume, such a treatment makes it necessary to summarize the American value system; to trace some of its effects as shown by recent societal changes; and to analyze ways American values may be expressed in the character of schools, with special reference to the current segregation issue as an example of the interrelationships characteristic of American society. All of this is necessarily done in very broad and very brief strokes, but the treatment inescapably points to the necessity for perspective as educational issues are faced.

What people believe, the things that are important to them, their hopes, aspirations, and loyalties go far toward shaping the nature of their nation or region. A simple comparison serves as an illustration. Where ancestor worship is practiced, people are afraid of changing their beliefs and behavior because to do so is to threaten the security they derive from the conviction that reliable guides to living are found only in the past. On the other hand, people who believe that man has intelligence which he should use to solve his own problems regard the past as only one source of understanding and guidance, and they in no sense offer the past blind allegiance. Societies developed under these conflicting beliefs will obviously differ in numerous important respects.

People of any society have many kinds of beliefs, ideals, and aspirations which, however, have a fairly common core. This common core of values gives a society its unity. Without such basic values there would be nothing to hold the parts of the society, nation, or region together. A people's beliefs and dedications possess, at the philosophical level at least, a comprehensiveness and unity which determine a society's goals. These goals, in turn, are the means of setting the directions in which a society will move; thus, a measure of harmony among the various parts of a society is attained.

It is, therefore, necessary to look beyond the bare facts evident in the contemporary scene of American democracy in order to understand its sources of strength. If societies can be characterized by the values to which their peoples are dedicated and the ideals toward which their labors are directed, it is important to this inquiry to examine the basic beliefs which make the American society what it is and to note their influence on the schools.

AMERICAN VALUE-DEDICATIONS

Much has been written about the value commitments which characterize the American society. In a provocative interpretation of the American spirit, George Counts brilliantly summarizes the ideological wellsprings of its strength as follows:

> *The Hebraic-Christian Ethic.* It proclaims, without qualification, the supreme worth and dignity of the individual human being. Every man is precious simply because he is a man. . . . Here, then, according to this ethic, is the source of all values. . . . Recognition of the supreme worth of the individual leads inevitably to the principle of equality among the members of society.
>
> *The Humanistic Spirit.* . . . it declares that man is endowed with the capacity of choice and that his chances of salvation depend on his own powers, efforts, and decisions.
>
> *Science and Scientific Method.* Science is knowledge, and knowledge is power. But science is far more than knowledge. In its essence it is a method of obtaining knowledge about the world of nature and man — the only truly reliable method man has ever discovered or devised.
>
> *The Rule of Law.* . . . guarantees to the citizen freedom of political and civil assembly . . . freedom of speech, press, and religious worship. . . . freedom from arbitrary arrest, trial, and imprisonment, . . . freedom of movement, occupation, and property.
>
> *The Democratic Faith.* . . . affirms the worth and dignity of the individual. . . . that . . . all men are created equal. . . . regards political and civil liberty as the only dependable guardian of individual worth and equality. . . . [It] rests on law and orderly process. . . . [it] rests on basic morality. . . . [it] rests on individual opportunity. . . . [it] rests on individual responsibility.[1]

---

[1] George S. Counts, *Education and American Civilization* (New York: Bureau of Publications, Teachers College, Columbia University, 1952), pp. 220–291.

The eminent sociologist, Charles S. Johnson, identifies certain basic assumptions or commitments of the American culture which he defines in these words:

> *The Political Assumption* . . . under which men can choose their rulers and give free expression to dissent.
>
> *The Social Assumption* . . . all men can and in the long run will voluntarily choose those courses of action that are most advantageous to them, individually and collectively, if all are given full opportunity to choose, and if the consequences of the alternatives are explained in terms the choosers understand.
>
> *The [Economic] Assumption* . . . the individual is free in his economic activity to follow the incentive of the profit motive, and that prices are controlled by effective demand.
>
> *The [Philosophical] Assumption* . . . every human personality is of equal worth and dignity.
>
> *The Ethical and Religious Assumption* of basic and inalienable human rights, freedom of conscience, belief in Deity, belief in the possibility of personal salvation through overcoming worldly sin and evil and the further belief that moral values in human relationships transcend purely secular codes and customs.[2]

The great humanitarian, Franklin D. Roosevelt, saw American value commitments as even more specific aspirations of her people. In his message to Congress on January 6, 1941, he said:

> In the future days which we seek to make secure, we look forward to a world founded upon four essential human freedoms.
>
> The first is freedom of speech and expression. . . .
>
> The second is freedom of every person to worship God in his own way. . . .
>
> The third is freedom from want. . . .
>
> The fourth is freedom from fear. . . .[3]

The National Resources Planning Board, in a report issued in 1943, offered a more comprehensive and pointed analysis of the aspirations and goals which are characteristic of the American value commitments. The Board presented nine rights in the following language:

> 1. *The right to work,* usefully and creatively through the productive years;

---

[2] Charles S. Johnson, "The Culture Affecting Education," in *Forces Affecting American Education,* 1953 Yearbook of the Association for Supervision and Curriculum Development, ed. by William Van Til (Washington: National Education Association, 1953), pp. 23–24. [Italics added.]

[3] *Congressional Digest,* January to December 1942. A. G. and N. T. N. Robinson (Washington: Congressional Digest Corporation, 1942), p. 228.

2. *The right to fair play,* adequate to command the necessities and amenities of life in exchange for work, ideas, thrift, and other socially valuable service;

3. *The right to adequate food, clothing, shelter, and medical care;*

4. *The right to security,* with freedom from fear of old age, want, dependency, sickness, unemployment, and accident;

5. *The right to live in a system of free enterprise,* free from compulsory labor, irresponsible private power, arbitrary public authority, and unregulated monopolies;

6. *The right to come and go, to speak or to be silent,* free from the spying of secret political police;

7. *The right to equality before the law,* with equal access to justice in fact;

8. *The right to education,* for work, for citizenship, and for personal growth and happiness;

9. *The right to rest, recreation, and adventure,* the opportunity to enjoy life and take part in an advancing civilization.[4]

The foregoing quotations may be said to define the great beliefs which are characteristic of American society and to express them in terms of specific aspirations of the people who make up this society. They are, then, the dynamics of social action, and they are the sources upon which choices rest.

The several definitions clearly place the American culture in an evolutionary setting. Each of the five great sources of power which Counts identified has behind it many centuries of development. The experience of man has constantly brought about new definitions of the meanings of these streams of influence and more penetrating understandings of their significance for human behavior. Johnson, looking perhaps more directly at the contemporary scene, discerns the assumptions he has enunciated as springboards whence social and economic action in American society should arise. Roosevelt, in his statement of the four freedoms, interprets man's restless quest for a society in which he can find the security and opportunities for self-achievement which he has a right to expect if the forces pointed out by Counts are expressed in the behaviors of this society. The more specific elaboration of aims in the National Resources Planning Board report are the simple and direct objectives toward which individual and social efforts are to be directed. These definitions of the American civilization, taken together, may be said to constitute an expression of what has come to be known as the American spirit. This expression is in terms of the goals toward which American society is striving and, at the same time, it suggests means whereby the goals may be pursued.

[4] R. Freeman Butts, *A Cultural History of Education* (New York: McGraw-Hill Book Co., Inc., 1947), pp. 585–586.

A society which is dedicated to this spirit can never become static or decadent; whereas a culture the values of which fail to provide their own source of constant refinement and improvement is likely eventually to fall. This spirit will not create a society of deadening uniformity because the values which give it strength are inherently dynamic in quality. These values give birth to the forces which shape the destinies of Americans as individuals and as a people; these values are the source of the many aspirations and drives which harness energies. The translation of these drives and aspirations into behavior results in choices of specific ends to be sought and the selection of appropriate means for achieving the desired ends.

Change in a democracy is, therefore, inevitable. In a democratic society man is always striving for something, striving to create new wealth, to compose a new symphony, to right a wrong. Although change is essential to a democracy, it falls within limits which are determined by the beliefs, values, and goals which define individual and social behavior. This means that conflicts can be minimized and that they may be held within healthy bounds. Under these conditions, change is the normal state of a democracy and is its lifeblood. It is always present and its sweep is as broad as the society itself.

The impact of change is upon the whole of society, although change itself may be made up of many parts which can be analyzed separately. Components of change rarely if ever act independently of one another. Rather, they tend to interact in a way to bring about some unity and balance in the over-all configuration of the pattern of social change. At times, however, forces producing change may act in opposition to one another, thus accentuating differences and creating conflicts. But the American system of values is such that it prevents change from flying off in all directions at once, and somehow creates of it a measure of unity which moves society forward toward its goals. New horizons open up at each forward step.

The development and progress of this nation are, of course, products of the influence of foundational ideals and beliefs expressed in various patterns of change. At one time major concerns may be for the creation of new wealth; at another time emphasis may be upon achieving social justice through a more equitable distribution of wealth, equitable as determined by the extent to which the ideals of respect for the dignity and worth of every individual require a measure of economic freedom. Another type of emphasis may be that of redefining in the experience of a people the meaning of an established value. An example is afforded by the current struggle of the South to redefine the role of the Negro so that his role will be more consistent with American allegiance to democratic values.

Not only does the character of change vary from time to time but its tempo and vitality vary also. When conflicting objectives develop, choices as to emphasis are required. The choices made determine both the kind of change which is to develop and its relative degree.

Change is sometimes superinduced, as is the case when forces from without a country threaten it. The two world wars fought during the first half of the twentieth century serve as examples of external forces being brought to bear upon American society.

These wars also illustrate the complex interrelatedness of various forces which produce change and the crises which may be created by these forces. Both wars were a product and a cause of tremendous developments in technology and of conflicting social ideologies. They occurred partly because of great advances made in the physical sciences and the inability to harness them exclusively for socially useful purposes due to opposing social theories. The failure to use technological advances for goals more creative than the waging of war can be charged to the fact that these conflicting social philosophies could not coexist in peace. Technology, through the employment of media of mass communications, was used as never before to gain control of the minds of men. These two wars did not solve, but rather aggravated the complex problems which brought them into being, with the result that the world at mid-twentieth century is still a world of unresolved conflicts and a world which is in the throes of forces which are bringing about changes so profound that their import cannot be assessed at this time.

Consideration of the impact upon current society of the streams of power, as identified by Counts, reveals the evolutionary nature of American society.

Perhaps no force of greater intensity exists in American society today than that which Counts calls science and scientific method. It is this force, of course, which largely accounts for the present age of technology. Science has so increased the productivity of the individual that he no longer need be a slave to his job; he has more time which he may use as he sees fit, time to think, time to play, and time to grow. Advances in medical science during this century alone have extended man's life expectancy by more than twenty years. Science has brought him comforts and conveniences undreamed of until recent years. He may view important affairs of the world from his own living room and he can know what people everywhere are thinking.

Science is, however, subject to controls. Philosophically, the Hebraic-Christian Ethic expresses one criterion toward which control is directed: preservation of the belief in the supreme worth and dignity of the individual. Science cannot be permitted to add twenty years to a man's life and at the same time chain him to a machine merely to increase his productivity. Another kind of control rests in the Rule of Law, which guarantees opportunity for the individual citizen to exercise the freedoms that the concept of human dignity and worth warrants. The Humanistic Spirit, expressing as it does confidence in man's capacity to chart his own course, is another kind of control. These forces together seek to ensure the wise use of science and the scientific method in achieving the state of welfare for man which his values dictate. Consequently, the maladjustments created as science progresses at varying rates in the diverse fields of human endeavor are less pronounced than they would have been had controls been nonexistent. These constant sources of power are interdependent and together they provide a relatively consistent and dynamic drive for the improvement of society, although the rate of improvement is uneven.

A society's growth can be conceived as ever-expanding, if its values are expressed as the controls of power. In such a society each force becomes a perennial goal, each value a fresh challenge to succeeding generations, a challenge to utilize and yet transcend the achievements of the past. This means, for example, that human behavior which manifests the concept of the dignity and worth of the individual will be redefined from time to time. The kinds of understandings concerning what is meant by man's capacity to make his own choices and to use his own powers for his best development likewise undergo redefinition from time to time.

On occasion, the re-evaluation of meanings of values may come from the force of the Rule of Law, expressed either in new legislation or in judicial interpretation.

VALUE COMMITMENTS EXPRESSED
THROUGH CHANGES IN SOCIETY

It is inevitable that what men believe and the things to which they are dedicated will be mirrored in how they behave and in the general pattern of change in their society. The American society has been described as one which may be expected to be in a state of change at all times because its value commitments are dynamic in quality and express ideals its members are always in the process of seeking to achieve. It is reasonable, therefore, to expect that the various social and economic developments of any given age will be an active expression of prevailing values.

It is pertinent to this undertaking to review briefly some of the currents of change which have characterized the first half of the present century. Some indication of the nature of these changes has already been suggested. For example, our century's two great wars, to which reference was made earlier, show that the nature and extent of our social action may be influenced profoundly by forces outside the American value pattern. Such forces, in posing a threat, may stimulate counter-actions unthinkable in terms of the national value-pattern alone.

Aside from such direct influence, the prosecution itself of these wars required that millions of American soldiers serve on battlefields in many foreign countries, contributing immeasurably to the creation of a feeling of world unity and responsibility in place of the narrow, national provincialism of earlier days. American soldiers caught something of a vision of the interrelatedness of all mankind as they came to sense the lofty idealism of world citizenship. These young Americans began to think of man in terms of what he stands for and what he is rather than in terms of race or creed. Perhaps these experiences were of greatest significance to the young men of the South, both white and Negro, since theirs is a region where cultural dichotomies are more overt than in other regions of the nation. More and more people everywhere, soldiers included, became aware of the great social and economic forces back of these wars and of the continuing impact of these forces upon the destinies of mankind. The influence of American soldiers on local, state, and national affairs cannot be measured; but it seems certain that, at least to some degree, these soldiers account for the trend toward certain types of liberalism in the United States.

The Great Depression of the thirties was also a powerful force in hastening profound socio-economic changes in America. Breadlines in a land of plenty seriously threatened the established social and economic order. There seemed to be no way to reconcile extremes of poverty and the surplus of goods except through the use of the power of government.

The ravages of the Depression could not be rectified by a *laissez-faire* theory of government. As a result, for the first time in American history a national policy was adopted which made of government an instrument for aggressive social and economic reforms. To be sure, there had been many examples of deliberate government influence on the economy, such as tariff legislation and some controls of big business, but this was the first large-scale effort to make government policy a means of achieving certain long-held values of American democracy. The majority of basic improvements in the American social order within the past half century may be attributed at least in part to governmental action. This precipitated a bitter struggle between the group which profited most from the existing system and those who wished to use the government for building a more balanced socio-economic order for all.

A tremendous body of legislation was aimed at bolstering and making more secure the economic life of the nation. Many governmental agencies were created and given power over the economy to an extent hitherto undreamed of. Among such agencies were the Reconstruction Finance Corporation, which provided government funds to support sagging business firms, the Federal Deposit Insurance Corporation to guarantee the safety of bank deposits, the Federal Housing Authority, the Home Owners Loan Corporation to stimulate housing construction, and the Securities Exchange Commission for the regulation of the issuance and sale of stocks and bonds. Such widespread and extensive use of government agencies in the business world was new to America.

Agricultural production controls were also invoked by the government as a means of strengthening the economy. Elaborate machinery was set up to determine the amount of agricultural production which the economy could wisely absorb, and quotas were issued to farmers which defined their production allotments. Thus, it became necessary for the farmers to give up their traditional freedom to produce as much as they saw fit in the interest of their own and the general welfare. It became accepted practice for the government to tell the cotton farmer how many bales of cotton he could produce, the wheat farmer how many bushels of wheat he could grow, and so on.

A further effort to build a healthy economy was the use of the government's power to set prices. Parity became a common word. In order to guarantee what was defined as a fair price for agricultural commodities, the government agreed to buy them at parity prices when the market fell below those levels. Price controls were also instituted in the industrial world.

It was possible for the Federal government to assume the various powers enumerated only because the people were willing to give up a measure of their individual freedom for their own and the common good. Many of the provisions instituted in the emergency found favor with enough people to be continued after the emergency was over; numerous innovations of the thirties have apparently become permanent fixtures of the American social order.

A second major area of Federal legislation to ensure the common welfare has been concerned with social reform. Efforts to protect the health and well-being of the individual have gone far beyond the regulations of working conditions and the number of hours in a work week. Social Security legislation designed to protect the worker against unemployment, poverty due to illness, and old age has been extended to the majority of American workers. Minimum wage laws have become an accepted way to protect the lower income groups against undue exploitation. The rising level of minimum wage provisions has been instrumental in heightening substantially the living standard of millions of Americans who heretofore could command only substandard wages. The strength commanded by those who espoused compulsory health insurance to provide for adequate medical care irrespective of income shows the vitality of the movement for social legislation which pushes ever closer to achieving the four freedoms enunciated by Roosevelt.

The growth in power of organized labor during recent years has undoubtedly helped bring about a better balanced distribution of profits between the worker and the owner of business. That the growing strength of labor has been promoted by favorable legislation is but one further evidence of the shift during this century in the use of governmental powers.

The most controversial phase of government control over the economy involves the Tennessee Valley Authority. Although an earlier venture—construction of Boulder Dam by the Hoover Administration —put the government into large scale business, the regional effort to control floods, provide cheap electric power, and improve agriculture by means of the TVA precipitated bitter struggles which have not yet been resolved. Opposition to this type of government control and influence has been so great that, despite determined efforts, the Tennessee Valley Authority concept has not been extended to other regions.

The extent to which the various governmental measures inaugurated to strengthen the economy were responsible for the continued high level of prosperity would be difficult to assess. The concept of the rights and responsibilities of business and industry have undoubtedly been substantially modified by efforts of the government to ensure a reasonable standard of living for all. The interdependence of the various phases of our economy were so vividly illustrated during the Depression years that it hardly seems likely that we shall dispense with the various services now rendered by the government in the interest of a continuing healthy economic order.

Special reference to certain patterns of change in the South is in order at this point. The Southern region has for some years been developing a broader social orientation and its values are becoming less provincial. It is no longer a region holding diffident attitudes toward itself; rather, it is a confident region which looks to the future with hope and pride. Its wealth is increasing more rapidly than that of any other region of the nation. The urbanization of the region, as shown by the very rapid growth in the number and size of metropolitan areas, is of great significance. The out-migration of Negroes and the concentration of Negroes in metropolitan centers is likewise of extreme importance. Rural life is vastly different from what it was a generation ago, and the average farm has greatly increased its productivity. Regional growth in wealth has produced a generally higher standard of living, a decrease in poverty, and greater freedom from the ravages of disease and malnutrition.

Organized labor is rapidly making gains in the region, and the labor movement is no longer opposed so bitterly as it was a few years ago. Illiteracy is decreasing rapidly, and the general level of educational achievement of the total population is moving upward at a fast rate.

Recent changes in political alignments indicate that some inroads are being made on the one-party system. There has also been some increase in liberal political thought. Control by traditional conservative forces may be somewhat on the wane. Suffrage has been extended finally to the long-disfranchised Negro of the South, and he has begun to become a force to be reckoned with in politics. While the Negro may not himself hold important office, except rarely, the fact remains that those who aspire to such office are beginning to hear his voice. Efforts to further fair employment practices have also hastened the change in the status of the Negro race in relation to that of the white in the region. Not only have new fields of employment been opened to the Negro but minimum wage laws applied without discrimination as to color have improved his economic lot considerably.

A sufficient number of illustrations of social and economic change characteristic of the first half of the twentieth century have been given to show that in a very real sense the great streams of influence which characterize our culture have been reflected in very significant achievements in the realization of goals important to the American people. The pattern of change which has been briefly described is one of constant emphasis on improving the lot of all citizens; their well-being is defined by the ideals which give impetus and direction to existing currents of change. That we are still in the midst of a period of great transition cannot be denied.

The analysis of change thus far minimizes conflicting elements in the American culture. There are forces not only from without this society which may profoundly affect the course of action which must be adopted but there are also forces from within which do not always act in harmony. It has been implied that voluntary means for achieving social and economic goals have been either limited or unavailable; consequently, the government itself has been the only agency which could express the aspirations of a majority of the American people. The government's guides for improvement were in reality legislative controls, and the course of action embarked upon by the government in the thirties precipitated violent opposition from conservative forces. There are many inconsistencies in American society which defy reconciliation in terms of fundamental values and beliefs.

PUBLIC EDUCATION
AND CHANGES IN AMERICAN SOCIETY

It was stated earlier that there is an interrelatedness between education and the environment of which it is a part. Public education in America is always a force of significance in the complex dynamics of social change. The schools carry a double responsibility. They provide the means for future adult citizens to acquire and develop the knowledges, understandings, appreciations, and allegiances which the democratic way of life requires. They provide an education which enables individual and cultural goals to be pursued more effectively. Public education expresses to a considerable degree the nature of the American culture, its successes, its failures, its problems, and its hopes and dreams. The purposes of public education are solidly rooted in values that are basic and dear to the American people. In a more specific sense, the schools seek to make American youth adherents of the Democratic Faith, the Hebraic-Christian Ethic, the Humanistic Spirit, Science and the Scientific Method, and the Rule of Law.

The second part of the responsibility with which the public schools are charged places them in a more creative role. The schools are regarded as an agency for the development of higher and higher levels of expression of American values in the behavior of individuals and groups. This means, of course, that schools are also changing constantly in nature and quality.

In a very real sense, therefore, reliance upon education as a means of achieving the good life as defined by the values by which Americans live makes of the schools an instrument of national policy. This means that schools cannot be without concern for the trends and influences which shape the contemporary scene and which at least in some measure determine the events of the future. In any other sense, schools could scarcely play more than a passive role. On the other hand, education is subject to the same forces which are bringing about change in other institutions and in other phases of life. Schools in many ways reflect and are conditioned by characteristics of their social and economic environment, and they cannot be understood adequately without some knowledge of these backgrounds. But schools cannot be prisoners of their environment if they are to carry out the role to which they have been assigned.

It is a far cry, however, from the determination of educational purpose in the philosophical realm to its translation into the realm of general educational practice. There are many points of view with respect to what constitutes adequacy in public education and the factors in school programs which make for defensible quality levels. The greatest discrepancies in points of view lie in the specific purposes, objectives, methods, and means on both verbal and practical levels. Few, if any, will deny that equal educational opportunities should exist for all. But what this actually means in terms of educational practice is not the same for all. In the Southern region a classic example of this conflict is the dual school system which in theory is based upon the doctrine of separate but equal programs. The conflict which has been created by the caste system, so deeply entrenched as a social and economic practice during the days of slavery, and the principle of equal educational opportunity has thus far resulted in school systems that reflect the relative status of the two races rather than equality of educational programs.

In spite of such divergence in beliefs and practices, the fact remains that the traditional dedication of the American people to education as a means toward a better life has been expressed more fully in this generation than ever before. Fundamental effects of the great era of social and economic change on the schools are in the areas of purpose and methods. As has been implied, the aims of education are strongly influenced by the forces which bring about changes in society. During the last generation Americans have become more anxious than ever that schools produce graduates who understand American ideals and are loyal to them. Emphasis on education to prepare people to cope with the whole gamut of life's problems is now common. Other influences which are changing schools are new understandings of what constitutes good teaching and more modern materials of instruction.

These qualitative changes have been accompanied by quantitative changes of great moment. The percentage of school-age population actually enrolled in school has increased rapidly. The rate of attendance of those enrolled has likewise increased. The school year has been lengthened and the average number of years spent in public schools has increased substantially. Teachers have more professional training on the average and more adequate materials of instruction with which to work. Furthermore, the teaching load of the individual instructor has been reduced. In addition, the number and percentage of persons enrolled in colleges and universities have increased rapidly in recent years. The action of the government in providing opportunities for soldiers returning from World War II and the Korean War to continue their education has resulted in thousands of young men entering college who otherwise never would have had the opportunity. Thousands of others have been able to obtain vocational training which presumably will enable them to maintain a higher standard of living than would otherwise have been possible.

THE ISSUE OF SEGREGATION IN THE PUBLIC SCHOOLS

The review of the American value system, the interpretation of this system through an analysis of recent social and economic changes and the influence of these forces on schools bring into sharp relief the interrelation of society and education. No better example of the impact of social forces and change on the schools is available than the Supreme Court decision ruling compulsory segregation in the public schools unconstitutional.

Great decisions in the affairs of men do not just happen nor do they happen precipitately. The coming of such decisions is foreshadowed by events which frequently point with clarity to the emergence of great issues created by conflicting beliefs, customs, and practices that must be resolved eventually by some choice of alternatives. Therefore, if one seeks to understand the present he must interpret it in relation to the past. By the same token, some reasonable knowledge of what the future may be expected to bring may be derived from comprehension of the present and the past.

This thesis is supported by a long chain of events and decisions which pointed logically toward the Supreme Court decision of May, 1954, rendering unconstitutional racial segregation in the public schools as a deliberate policy. Perhaps no better illustration can be found than the segregation issue of serious inconsistencies in American society and, at the same time, of a consistent and continuing effort to resolve social inconsistencies.

Although historically the Southern region has exhibited more serious inconsistencies in its cultural pattern than any other part of the nation, the patterns of change which have come into being and which have been accelerated in recent years have reduced these inconsistencies in a variety of ways other than those already cited. Nevertheless, differences of opinion with reference to the proper status of the Negro race still create and foster conflicts, of which the segregation issue in the public schools is but one example. The basic problem is reflected, of course, by the relative positions of the white and Negro races in the Southern culture, a culture which claims allegiance to democratic values. The problem of reconciling different Southern definitions of values as they are applied to the Negro race, on the one hand, and to the white race, on the other, has simply been highlighted by the Supreme Court's dictum on public school segregation. It is in no sense a new problem.

The introduction of the Negro to American society as a mere chattel to be bought and sold as any other property was the beginning of a long and bitter struggle to achieve the status, rights, and privileges of citizenship in a country to which he was brought originally through no choice of his own. It took a long and cruel war which frequently pitted brother against brother to throw off the shackles of slavery. The Thirteenth, Fourteenth, and Fifteenth Amendments to the Constitution were necessary in order to define in theory the Negro's new-found freedom. These amendments gave the Negro a new legal status, but they did not ensure him the freedom to exercise the prerogatives of an American citizen. The struggle of the Negro to achieve his destiny was only in its infancy with the attainment of legal status.

Concern for educating the Negro as a free man was slow to develop in the South. Philanthropic interests were mainly responsible for earlier efforts to educate the Negro. Gradually, public funds were provided for Negro schools. It was but natural that in a region which viewed the Negro as being an inferior person that separate school systems would develop. The separate school doctrine was finally tested in the Federal courts, culminating in a decree issued in 1896 concerning the separation of the races on trains. The Supreme Court stated that separation did not necessarily imply inferiority of either race to the other and observed that such separation was a matter of common practice, the most obvious example being the maintenance of separate public schools.[5]

The separate but equal doctrine was accepted as a principle throughout the region, apparently by both races, by the beginning of the twentieth century. The widespread practice of separate rather than equal facilities was not successfully challenged until the mid-thirties. A series of court cases resulted in the admission of Negroes to hitherto white graduate schools in all but five Southern states. In these court tests, case after case was decided on the grounds that equal facilities must be provided both races. The way was thus prepared for a direct challenge to the principle of segregation itself. It was argued by many that separate but equal schools are in fact impossible and that segregation itself is discriminatory. These arguments culminated in the historic May, 1954, decision of the Supreme Court which for the first time ruled directly on the issue of segregation and decided that compulsory separation of the races in the schools was a denial of constitutional rights. It is an important fact that this decision came at a time when Negroes had already been accorded more closely than ever before the same treatment as whites with respect to voting, serving on juries, eligibility for employment, and

---

[5] Plessy vs. Ferguson, 163 United States 537 (1896).

equivalent wages for equivalent work. Nevertheless, the decision is of profound significance for, in spite of many changes in segregation practices in recent years, this decision comes to grips with one area of Southern life—the public schools—where complete and absolute separation of the races has been inflexibly maintained.

It is of paramount importance to understand that the decision is not revolutionary in the sense that it defines new values or new aspects of the American spirit. It defines only a new way of achieving values long accepted as basic to this nation's ideals. Although but another manifestation of change in patterns of racial relationships, the decision is more fundamental than any others discussed; indeed, it opens up a new avenue for integration of more profound significance than all others put together.

It would be difficult to find a better example of the complex interrelatedness of the various factors of social change than the one afforded by the dual school system of the South in the segregation crisis. The real problem of integrating white and Negro children in the public schools cannot be understood except as the whole range of complexities in the dual society of the South is analyzed. Integration is not possible in isolation from the total social environment of both races, for it is by no means a problem of the schools alone. The dictum of the Supreme Court runs contrary to many of the traditions, customs, and beliefs upon which the Southern culture is based and which affect all avenues of living. The decree imposes upon the region a dilemma of only two alternatives, defiance of the highest law of the land or the violation of deep-seated mores which rest upon traditional assumptions that the white race is superior to the Negro race. Either choice can only bring a period of painful upheaval which will be reflected ultimately in the entire social scene of the region.

The public schools of the South for the first time in history find themselves the central agency in bringing about sweeping social change invoked by legal mandate. There is no other example in the history of the nation of a legal prescription that schools should perform a function so broad in remaking a social order. In the long run this precedent may become an historic landmark, for it unequivocally makes the public schools instruments of social revolution by order of the judiciary, whether or not such was the purpose of the Court. In effect, the decision seeks to raise the schools above the level of their environment insofar as racial segregation is concerned.

Obviously, critical decisions affecting the future of public education and, in turn, affecting all areas of living in the South are in the making and they cannot be avoided. Such decisions will be made either by positive action or by default. Coming at a time when the region is already geared to fast moving and momentous changes in its social, economic, psychological, and philosophical fabrics, the public-school issue places squarely upon the shoulders of responsible leadership the obligation of redefining the American spirit as it applies to the minority racial group.

THE NEED FOR PERSPECTIVE

Perhaps the foregoing discussion has served to indicate the need for a fairly comprehensive study of white and Negro schools in the South as a prelude to the great age of decision-making faced by the schools. Emphasis thus far has been not so much on the need for facts per se as on the need for understanding how our schools came to be what they are and what forces are changing them today. Actually, both a knowledge of facts and understanding are essential in the wise treatment of current educational problems.

It is difficult to arrive at wise public policy in such an atmosphere of emotionalism as has been created by the crisis in public education in the South. Perspective lends wisdom to decision-making. If the crisis can be viewed as a part of the long struggle for free public education for all children, and if it is clear that this issue is but one of many issues in an age of great transition, perspective may be achieved. Objectivity in the treatment of a problem which is so deeply imbedded in feeling rather than reason calls for a degree of knowledge and understanding of the public schools far beyond that which has been required in the resolution of previous issues. It is obvious that considerable attention will have to be given to the biracial aspects of Southern education.

The complexities of the problem cannot be understood through a mere examination of the actual facts concerning the differences in the dual school systems of the South, as important as this may be. In this chapter, basic value commitments of the American people have been reviewed. The nature of these commitments has been described in terms of the vast surge of social and economic change which is remaking the nation and the Southern region. Obviously, it was not within the province of the chapter to analyze critically or even to enumerate all of the factors involved in this greatest of all periods of change in world history. The intent has been simply to direct attention to the nature of American society and the great underlying forces which create its direction and which require that it always be in a state of change. Certain problems and conflicts in the Southern pattern of life have been pointed out briefly. The segregation issue in the public schools has been described as but one example of issues created by conflicting values, and its significance has been defined as being merely one of many factors in the complex picture of social evolution.

One of the distingishing features of a democracy is the manner in which it resolves issues and solves problems. In this respect, perspective is of paramount importance. Value commitments are nowhere reflected more clearly than in the way they are employed in the solution of problems. Thus, in times of decision, when judgments are passed and courses of action determined, it is all the more necessary to take into proper account American value commitments. This is the more compelling reason for reviewing them in connection with a presentation of factual information on white and Negro schools of the South.

In the next chapter, the historical origin and development of the biracial school systems of the South will be reviewed and analyzed as one means of searching for the perspective which seems so essential to a reasoned approach to the issue of desegregation.

TWO

The Historical Context
of Biracial Education
in the South

The struggle of the American people toward political, economic, and social maturity has been beset with certain paradoxes extremely difficult to resolve. The most fundamental of these paradoxes is suggested by Archibald MacLeish in a recent statement.

"The American dream may not have been everything American writers called it," said Mr. MacLeish, "but that it existed, down at least to the last generation, no one can fairly doubt. . . . *The dream of the brotherhood of men in freedom was as real as only the common dreams of a great people can be.* That dream we loved. That love made us a nation. . . ." [1]

Efforts of the American people to realize the dream of the brotherhood of men in freedom went forward through the years, while, at the same time, a considerable segment of the American population was subject to racial segregation, legally or socially instituted. Thus, a continuing dilemma was posed by the necessity of trying to reconcile conflicting social objectives. That the dilemma was more conspicuous in the South than elsewhere in the nation was the result of circumstances peculiar to the Southern region.

Within the framework of the paradox, it was perfectly consistent that segregation, particularly as it developed in the South, should entail separate public schools for whites and Negroes. But it was also consistent with values deeply engrained in the American culture that a most persistent effort to breach the pattern of segregation should be concentrated in the schools.

The values involved were ably reiterated several years ago by Gunnar Myrdal, who wrote:

As background for our discussion we shall have to remember the role

---

[1] Archibald MacLeish, "Love of This Land," as quoted in *ADL Southern Newsletter*, II, No. 2 (February, 1954), 1. (Italics added.)

of education in American democratic thought and life. Education has always been the great hope for both individual and society. In the American Creed it has been the main ground upon which "equality of opportunity for the individual" and "free outlet for ability" could be based. Education has also been considered as the best way — and the way most compatible with American individualistic ideals — to improve society.[2]

The remarkable faith of the American people in education, probably without parallel elsewhere in the world, was not peculiar to any level or segment of the social order. The respect for education was universal as the democratic objective was universal education. It was hardly surprising, then, that the population minority should object to state laws which maintained separate public schools according to race, even though the laws stated that the facilities should be equal.

The issue of segregation in the public schools was carried to its logical conclusion in the courts. On May 17, 1954, the Supreme Court of the United States declared that the principle of statutory provisions permitting or requiring racial segregation in the public schools, regardless of whether facilities were equal, was no longer an issue. The Court said: "We conclude that in the field of public education the doctrine of 'separate but equal' has no place. Separate educational facilities are inherently unequal." Segregation in the schools was declared to be "a denial of the equal protection of the laws" and was, therefore, a violation of the Constitution of the United States.[3]

The principle of segregation in public education has been legally rejected, but the issue of segregation has not yet been resolved. A legislative act or a court's interpretation of the Constitution may establish a law, but only the people can make the law effective. An issue which has such a long history and which so deeply involves the emotions of people as the segregation issue is not susceptible to an easy solution. The final decision on how best to implement the Court's decision depends upon the social and moral will of the American people.

Moral decisions which stand the test of time and circumstance must rest upon informed intelligence. In order to profit from the cumulative experiences of the past, the American people must have knowledge of the historical context within which segregation was established and within which it socially matured and legally withered. In order to make plans which are certain to cast a long shadow upon the lives of millions of American children, the people must clearly see the ramifications of segregation in a complex culture. In order to effect

---

[2] Gunnar Myrdal, *An American Dilemma,* II (3rd ed., New York: Harper and Brothers, 1944), 882.

[3] *Atlanta Constitution,* May 18, 1954, p. 10.

means for implementing the Supreme Court's decision with considered judgment and unimpassioned reason, the people must understand the social, economic, and educational implications of segregation. The will, the heart, the intelligence can best be brought to bear upon resolving the issue of segregation if all the facts are in hand.

The task of this chapter is to present the facts of biracial education, as it has existed in Southern communities. (The problem, in its total range, is by no means a limitedly regional one; but in certain legal senses, the South has experienced and exhibited the problem in a distinguishable form.) The exposition presented here is historically arranged. Experiences of the past and circumstances of the present are inseparable from decisions of the future.

Biracial education in the South, like other institutions of a people's culture, did not suddenly spring into existence at a fixed moment in history. It evolved from the whole complex of social, political, and economic development in the region. Tangible influences in education were, of course, a reflection of attitudes, and current attitudes toward education are as deeply rooted in the past as institutions are.

Edgar W. Knight predicated his life-long work in educational history upon this premise: "Every advance in education has been made on the background of the past, and present-day tasks in education can be understood only through a knowledge of conditions out of which they have evolved." [4]

The dual school system is just one of the numerous conditions which have affected education in the South. For instance, Knight, in writing about educational opportunity, stressed "the obvious inequality that exists between city children and rural children. . ." [5] Knight was writing more than a quarter of a century ago, but the struggle to correct the inequity cited still goes on.

In order to comprehend biracial aspects of education, then, it is necessary to be conversant with the chief factors which have shaped the kinds of schools and school programs found in the South. Many of the same factors which influenced the development of education, as such, contributed to the development of segregated schools.

This is not to say that each of the Southern states has had exactly the same educational history. The fact is that each has been in some respects unique. The states, nevertheless, have had such a generally similar history and culture that the more important influences on education were common to all of them. Common developments will constitute the central concern of this rather broad presentation of the

---

[4] Edgar W. Knight, *Public Education in the South* (Boston: Ginn and Company, 1922), p. 1.

[5] *Ibid.*, p. vi.

evolution of public education in the South; the biracial school system is one of these.

THE COLONIAL PERIOD (1607-1750)

Educational developments in the Southern colonies were few, scattered, and limited. They were not, however, without significance, for certain conceptions and ideas were woven into the fibre of the region and would exert strong influence far into the future.

The institution of education has throughout history reflected the social order of which it was a part. During the Colonial period, society was in a state of transition from the Old to the New World. The colonists transplanted European traditions and beliefs from Europe to America, which had its own indigenous characteristics. The resulting interaction ultimately produced economic, political, and social viewpoints which were distinctive to colonial America, although they were not necessarily identical in the several colonies; in other respects they were unique.

The unsettled social and economic conditions in England prior to the launching of the American settlements had led to a statutory foundation for relief of the poor. Laws were passed requiring contributions to aid the poor and unfortunate. The justices of the peace, under whose stewardship the funds were placed, provided relief to the poor, and they also had responsibility for apprenticing children of the poor to learn a trade. These measures did two things: they strengthened existent class distinctions, and they founded a tradition of social provisions for some vocational training for children of the poor. Both of these ideas were transplanted to the Southern colonies.

Protestant insistence upon universal literacy as a basis for religious instruction was less pronounced in the Southern colonies than in some other regions, for the influential early settlers of the South were moved more by interest in economic gain than by interest in religious freedom. Religious influences on education of another order were, however, to be found in the Southern colonies. The English Church was established by the charters of Virginia and South Carolina; it was established in Georgia after the royal assumption of government in that colony. Since Virginia and South Carolina exerted the strongest educational and political influence of any of the Southern colonies prior to the Revolution, the position of the Established Church was important.

While it was perfectly natural for the colonies in which the Established Church was dominant to adopt educational policies congenial to the English Church, some of the policies were deterrents to the furtherance of religious liberty and educational opportunity. Laws in some colonies requiring license of the Bishop of London as a prerequisite to offering instruction made it extremely difficult for dissenters to provide for any instruction. Prevailing policies supported higher education for only the more prosperous stratum of society, favored the tutorial system of instruction, and were committed to training of the poor through charity and to education as a function of the Church and not of the state.[6]

Scotch-Irish and German immigrants came to the Southern colonies in increasingly large numbers after 1700, bringing with them a strong tradition for education. Wherever they settled, churches and schools were soon built. The influence of these settlers did not begin to make itself felt, however, until after the middle of the eighteenth century.[7]

The fertile soil, mild climate, and plenitude of land led to the growth of the plantation system in the South. The population was, of course, widely dispersed. The plantations became economically independent, and cooperative endeavors in providing the necessities of life were exceedingly limited. The cleavage between small landowners and masters of vast plantations widened until class distinctions were firmly entrenched. With the growth of the plantations, the class system found its base at a level that reached far back into the English past; slaves and indentured laborers were imported by the shipload to work the plantations. In such a society, it was inevitable that the plantation owners should rise to the position of formulating policies which guided life in the colonies.[8]

Education in the South through this period was exceedingly limited, few children receiving even the rudiments of learning. For such education as was provided, aside from occasional home instruction by parents, four means were utilized.

Prosperous planters in all the Southern colonies, but especially in Virginia and South Carolina, often employed private tutors for their children. These were frequently Anglican ministers; but it was not unusual for educated indentured servants, who had escaped from intolerable conditions in Europe, to act as tutors.

A second means employed by the wealthy to educate their children was to send them to European schools. This was especially true for higher levels of education.

The third means for providing education was religious and chari-

[6] Ellwood P. Cubberly, *Public Education in the United States* (Boston: Houghton Mifflin Company, 1919), pp. 21–22.

[7] Knight, *op. cit.*, pp. 13–16.

[8] *Ibid.*, pp. 21–23.

table in motive. The Society for the Propagation of the Gospel in Foreign Parts, an auxiliary of the Established Church, founded charity schools in all the Southern colonies except Virginia. The curriculum was predominantly religious in character, but reading, writing, and arithmetic were taught. The educational work of the Society constituted probably the closest approach to a public school organization found in the region before the Revolution.[9]

The Moravians in Georgia and the South Carolina Society of Charleston also established charity schools. Some schools were supported by endowments and private donations; and families in a few communities contributed to the maintenance of the "old field schools" —private or community schools housed in old buildings on abandoned land and usually presided over by clergymen or lay readers of the Church.

These church and charity schools undeniably extended the rudiments of education to children who otherwise would have had no education at all, and the supporting agencies created or reinforced the idea of charitable support for education.

The fourth means by which education was provided entailed governmental action. The colonial governments passed legislation which provided apprenticeship training for orphans and children of the poor in order that they might become self-supporting. The training program, which usually included provisions for instruction in reading and writing, was carried out under the direction of a church until after the Revolution. Crude though the system was, it was the earliest form of compulsory education in America.[10] The system was so widely accepted that it was continued throughout the nineteenth century in all the Southern states. Like religious and endowed schools, however, this type of training served to delay the development of adequate public school systems and preserved the idea of charity in common school education.

Slaves were first brought to America in 1619, and thereafter the Negro population increased rapidly. By the middle of the eighteenth century, half of the population of Virginia was composed of African slaves, and they accounted for two-thirds of the population of South Carolina at the time of the Revolution. Negroes made up a smaller proportion of the population in Georgia and North Carolina, but they were numerous.[11]

The position of the Negro in the social order precluded practically all educational efforts in his behalf and none was considered necessary

9 *Ibid.*, p. 26.
10 *Ibid.*, pp. 47–70.
11 *Ibid.*, pp. 22–32.

by most people. A few Negroes were taught to read the Scriptures by missionaries of the Church of England sent out as early as 1695 by the Society for the Propagation of the Gospel in Foreign Parts.[12] The Quakers did a little of the same kind of work,[13] and Negroes who were apprenticed were sometimes taught to read and write.[14] None of these efforts were extensive.

In summary, educational efforts in the Southern colonies were quite restricted. The scatteredness of population, class distinctions, the absence of a strong religious motivation for the instruction of all children, and traditions of charity instruction for the poor all contributed to a conviction that education was the concern of the individual and of the church. Such education as was obtainable was dominated by religious and aristocratic conceptions. The only function of government in education was in legislating regulations for apprentice training, and this was in keeping with the idea of the charity school. With education beyond the reach of most white children, it was hardly surprising that the barest crumbs of instruction fell to the lot of Negro slaves.

The ideas and convictions given expression in the colonial South were to reverberate down through the years and were to raise echoes in the legislative halls of all the Southern states.

THE REVOLUTIONARY PERIOD (1750-1835)

In the years preceding the War for Independence, the extreme religious conservatism of earlier days gradually began to give ground. The shift was to have far-reaching effects on many aspects of American life, which directly or indirectly would be reflected in education after the war.

Ellwood P. Cubberley has written:

By 1750 the change in religious thinking had become quite marked. Especially was the change evidenced in the dying out of the old religious fervor and intolerance, and the breaking up of the old religious solidarity. While most of the colonies continued to maintain an "established church," other sects had to be admitted to the colony and given freedom of worship, and, once admitted, they were found not to be so bad after all.[15]

The change in religious attitudes was so pronounced by the time the Constitution was framed that the free exercise of religious belief

---

[12] Carter G. Woodson, *The Education of the Negro Prior to 1861* (New York: G. P. Putnam's Sons, 1915), p. 26.

[13] *Ibid.,* pp. 45–47.

[14] Knight, *op. cit.,* p. 66.

[15] *Op. cit.,* pp. 39–40.

was guaranteed to all in that instrument, Congress was forbidden to establish a state religion, and religious tests or oaths were prohibited as a prerequisite for holding any office under control of the Federal government. The original states which had state religions, religious tests for public office, and public taxation for the support of religion soon abandoned such things, and they were prohibited in new states from the beginning.[16]

One of the earliest educational effects of the shift in the place of religion in the Southern colonies was evident in the transfer of responsibility for training the poor from church to state and county authorities. Laws making the education of poor children a state function had been passed in all of the Southern colonies by the time of the Revolution. While the laws were a step forward in defining the social obligations of the state, they revealed a point of view that was to prove troublesome. The idea of charity education was not new, but these laws expressed a conception of *public* education as charity schooling. The idea persisted for decades and was a decided hindrance to the launching of public school systems in the South.[17]

For several years after the American Revolution education was at low ebb. The war had left the newly formed Union impoverished, and the states had such pressing internal problems that for some time little effort was directed toward improving education. The Society for the Propagation of the Gospel in Foreign Parts withdrew from educational work at the end of the war. A few charity schools continued to be supported by various churches; but, by and large, the times were not conducive to an extension of educational opportunity.

In the realm of ideas, however, a vast fermentation was stirring men's minds. Social theories projected during this period were to have a profound effect on the development of an awareness of the need for public education. Men of such stature as Washington, Jefferson, Madison, Jay, Hancock, and DeWitt Clinton spoke and wrote directly in behalf of universal education to prepare the people for civic responsibilities. Jefferson's plan for a public school system in Virginia, however questionable from a modern viewpoint in its selective process, was a provocative proposal at the time it was advanced.

The awakening social consciousness did not bear fruit over night. Many years passed before the political theory of equality was even nominally accompanied in practice by the related principle of equal educational opportunity. During the period under consideration, the belief persisted that education was a private matter. The conviction

---

[16] *Ibid.*, p. 55.
[17] Knight, *op. cit.*, p. 60.

found expression in private schools that only the wealthy could afford. Both wealthy and nonwealthy alike had contempt for free education because it carried the stigma of charity and pauperism.

The theory that representative government must rest upon an educated electorate gained acceptance slowly in the South. The earliest significant evidence of approval of the theory was in constitutional provisions for education and the means of education. Five of the nine Southern states which were created before 1835 made specific reference to education in their constitutions. The others and all new states subsequently provided for education in their constitutions.

Educational legislation before 1835 was exceedingly general and often vague; constitutional authorization itself might be nothing more than a statement that education should be encouraged. Despite limited results for the furtherance of public education during these years, the fact remains that seeds of an idea had been planted, the idea was gradually taking hold, and the climate was being conditioned for the later unfolding of the idea in definite and specific terms.

Meantime, private education was undergoing an important change. This was the period in which the academy got its start and underwent rapid growth. Soon after the Philadelphia Academy, proposed by Benjamin Franklin, opened its doors in 1751, academies began to spring up in the South. Some closely resembled the "old field schools," others were outgrowths of tutorial instruction common to the homes of prosperous citizens, still others had denominational support. In general, the academies were privately controlled, and they charged tuition. Incorporation by legislative enactment was usual, and in a few instances the poor were taught free in return for aid or privileges provided by the state. Most academies were non-sectarian, though they were religious in spirit.[18]

The aim of the academy movement was education designed to heighten individual development. The rapid growth and spread of the movement indicated increasing national interest in education, and the academy, in turn, stimulated educational progress. It was Franklin's idea that the curriculum of the academy should extend considerably beyond the classical curriculum of the Latin Grammar School to include practical subjects. The academy in the South, however, was primarily a college preparatory school; it took over from the Latin Grammar School such traditional college preparatory subjects as Latin, Greek, and elementary mathematics. In the first half of the nineteenth century, the classical curriculum was extended to include geography, English grammar, algebra, geometry, and ancient history. In time other subjects, presumed to provide practical training, were

---

[18] *Ibid.*, pp. 72–109.

added to the curricula of some academies; among the subjects intro-
duced were English literature, modern foreign languages, the natural
sciences, ethics, natural and moral philosophy, surveying and navigation, commercial subjects, especially bookkeeping, and oral reading and declamation.[19]

The academy movement was exceedingly popular in the South. In
1850, the year the movement reached its peak, there were 2,640
academies in the Southern states.[20]

The social doctrine of the period which proclaimed the equality of
men was not without its effect upon the Negroes. Frequent acts of
manumission were indicative of concessions on the part of not a few
individuals that Negroes were entitled at least to freedom of person.
In 1790, when the first census was taken, there were 757,181
Negroes in the United States and 59,557, or 7.9 per cent, of these
were free. In 1830 the Negro population was 2,328,642, of which
319,599, or 13.7 per cent, were free.[21] The opponents of slavery
espoused the education of the Negro for citizenship; others, who did
not believe in equal intellectual capacity of whites and Negroes,
thought that Negroes should be given vocational education. The scattered efforts on behalf of Negro education mentioned earlier were
extended by several church groups, and there are accounts of slave-
holders providing instruction to Negroes by informal means.[22] Such
efforts reached only a tiny fraction of the Negro population, however,
and circumstances soon arose which resulted in laws making any and
all education for Negroes illegal.

The invention of the cotton gin and other industrial developments
resulted in a tremendously increased demand for cotton and made its
production exceedingly profitable. The greater demand for cotton
created a greater demand for slaves and increased their value. The
slave population in the Southern states more than doubled from
1790 to 1830.[23]

Those forty years were marked by many slave revolts ranging from
the rebellion of one or two slaves on various plantations to well-
planned insurrections, such as those led by Gabriel in Virginia in
1800 and by Vesey in South Carolina in 1822.[24] The frequency of
these incidents reinforced the conviction of many Southern leaders

---

[19] *Loc. cit.,* pp. 72–109.

[20] Cubberley, *op. cit.,* p. 185.

[21] Maurice R. Davie, *Negroes in American Society* (New York: McGraw-Hill Book
Company, Inc., 1949), p. 34.

[22] Woodson, *op. cit.,* pp. 109–121.

[23] Davie, *op. cit.,* p. 21.

[24] E. Franklin Frazier, *The Negro in the United States* (New York: The Macmillan
Company, 1949), pp. 87–90. With the permission of the publisher.

that education made slaves unfit for their positions. Legislation regulating the assembly and movement of Negroes, both slaves and freed men, was passed in all Southern states. In several states legislation expressly prohibited the instruction of Negroes, and public sentiment enforced the prohibition in states where instruction was not legally forbidden.[25]

Thus, by the mid-thirties of the nineteenth century, when public education began to make some progress in the South, the Negro was effectively barred from instruction of any kind.

A PERIOD OF PROGRESS (1835-1861)

To call the years 1835-1861 a period of progress could be misleading. The designation is appropriate only in a relative sense and is possible only in the context of history. The progress made was chiefly in the fairly rapid furtherance of the public-school idea, an idea long hedged in by attitudes of indifference and contemptuous animosity. Both the growth of the idea and opposition to it left a lasting mark on the schools.

A fundamental principle upon which programs of public education are built is that education is a function of the state and the state has the right to levy taxes for the support of education.[26] There was a pronounced sentiment in the South by 1835 favoring education, but the principle cited was much too radical for wide acceptance. Education of the poor as a function of the state was acceptable but free, tax-supported, universal education was contrary to the traditions of the region.

A limited approach to state support for public education slipped in, nevertheless, through the back door during this period. The device utilized was the establishment of permanent public school endowments, the income from which was earmarked for the support of public elementary schools. Once public school endowments had become commonplace, the first slow, groping steps toward taxation for support of the schools were taken. The gradual stimulation of local initiative contributed in time to initial acceptance of the principle of public education as a function of the state and to the beginnings of public school systems. These developments were of such significance to Southern education that they are worthy of delineation.

Two factors were of prime importance in the establishment of permanent endowments for public schools. In most communities there were some public-spirited citizens so devoted to the cause of public

---

25 Woodson, *op. cit.,* pp. 151–169.
26 Knight, *op. cit.,* p. 161.

education as a necessity to democracy that they never relented in
their efforts to found state-supported school systems. It was difficult
enough for these leaders to promote the public-school idea, but it was
impossible to obtain state financial support through taxation. The
people were almost unanimously opposed to taxes except for minimum essentials of government.[27]

Advocates of public education turned to permanent endowments
as the solution of financial difficulties. These funds were derived from
such sources as escheats, confiscations, fines, penalties and forfeitures,
and, in one case, state lands.

The second factor which made the establishment of school funds
possible was aid of the Federal government. Before the turn of the
century, Congress had passed a law setting aside the 16th section of
every township in states subsequently admitted to the Union for the
support of education. Other land grants were made to the states for
educational purposes, and all or a part of treasury surpluses distributed to the states went into the permanent school funds.

All of the Southern states except South Carolina established permanent school funds before the Civil War. The major source of the
funds was the Federal government, but in some instances legislative
appropriation added to school revenues. Thus, the permanent endowments were a form of indirect taxation for school support and
they helped pave the way for later direct taxation.

The rather impressive list of revenue sources might suggest that
adequate funds were available to support public schools. Such was
not the case. Income from permanent endowments was never sufficient, at best, to build adequate public school systems. Unfortunately,
the schools failed by a very considerable margin to get even the money
they were supposed to get. The handling of permanent endowments
constitutes one of the most wretched episodes in educational history.
Knight says of the administration of the funds:

Few if any of the States entirely escaped from the evils of mismanagement
and the exploitation of public-school funds. The tendency toward careless
management appeared early and continued for many years, more rigid
control by additional legislation proving but little insurance against loss.
Among the recorded causes of loss may be seen almost every species of
violation of public trust. In some cases the school funds were grossly and
shamefully diverted from their original purposes; in other cases their
management was indifferently intrusted to incompetent officials, and the
result was unwise investments; in still other cases loans were insufficiently
secured and interest was often defaulted; and dishonest management and

embezzlement by officers intrusted with the care of school funds caused other losses.[28]

The chief benefits from permanent endowments in the *ante-bellum* South were that they helped extend favorable attitudes toward education, and they led to some progress in overcoming opposition to taxation for support of the schools. Adequate provision of schools on the meager permanent funds became so obviously impossible that the states began gradually to grant permissive local taxation with which to supplement the funds. By the time of the Civil War, over half of the Southern states had enacted such legislation, and, though very few rural areas had put the law into effect, not a few cities had instituted direct taxation for the schools. Local tax support for education, however limited, was indicative of progress.

Not all educational advances during these years were attributable to permanent funds. Social and political influences were at work. A slowly developing impatience with the assumed superiority of any one class, a correspondingly gradual development of faith in the power of the people, and extension of the suffrage were evidences of growth of the democratic spirit. The growth of cities and increase of industry in the South, while in no way comparable to developments in the East, made some impact upon the rural conservatism of the region. All these forces contributed to some educational reforms; if they were fewer in the older states where English traditions were strongest, they were felt in some measure in all the Southern states.

Beginning about the first quarter of the nineteenth century, constitutional and legislative provisions for education in each state became more specific. In general, these first enactments provided only for the distribution of revenues of permanent funds and legislative appropriations. In many states provisions were specified for education of the poor and for distribution of funds to already established schools, especially academies. Local commissioners or trustees were appointed to be custodians of the funds and to be responsible for their disbursement.

One of the important milestones in the evolution of public school systems was the development of some form of administrative controls both at the local and state levels. In the South before the Civil War, local control was exercised by commissioners, usually public-spirited citizens but untrained in school affairs. Only two states had made any legislative provision for the office of local or county superintendent.

Legislative enactments for an administrative officer at the state level were more numerous. By 1860, four Southern states—Ala-

---

[28] *Ibid.,* p. 164.

bama, Kentucky, Louisiana, and North Carolina—had provided for the office of state superintendent, and another, Tennessee, had had the office for a few years and abolished it. Four other states, Arkansas, Florida, Mississippi, and Texas, had recognized the need for such an office by giving authority to some state official, usually the secretary of state, to act, ex officio, as state superintendent.[29]

The messages of governors, statements of leaders in the educational movement, and reports by educational societies and legislative committees of the period indicate a widespread interest in education, but they suggest more progress than was actually made. Even constitutional provisions and legislative enactments were far better at stating aims than in obtaining results. The public-school idea was, nevertheless, being more firmly planted in the grass roots.

Emphasis on progress during the 1835-1861 period is not intended to distort the total picture. Powerful forces, most of them embedded in well-nigh unassailable tradition, were aligned against any educational revolution. The development of these forces has been discussed previously; a simple enumeration of them will underscore the fact that they were still potently operative.

The evolution of the public schools continued to be seriously hampered by the institution of slavery with its inherent class distinctions, by persistent aristocratic conceptions favoring private or religious schools, and by the tenacious conviction that state-supported education should be provided only to the poor. The general conservatism of a predominantly rural population blocked the provision of adequate financial support for public schools. Taxes were generally unpalatable; school taxes were intolerable to the plutocracy. The ruling clique, furthermore, was perfectly capable of appropriating scant public school funds to private and denominational schools. A final deterrent to establishing public school systems was the placing of educational authority in small, local units which, in the pursuit of selfish and provincial interests, often chose to thwart community cooperation.[30]

The main stream of the struggle in the South for free, universal education meandered among white groups; Negroes were not even touched by the backwash. At the time, there was no question of discrimination—the Negro simply was not considered. Laws and public opinion forbade that even the most elementary education be provided Negroes, and the position was considered just because of the prevalent belief honestly entertained by entrenched white classes that Negroes belonged to an inherently inferior race.

[29] *Ibid.*, pp. 195–267.
[30] *Ibid.*, pp. 264–5.

Despite legal restraints and misconceptions, a few slave owners or members of their families continued to consider it a Christian duty to give slaves some instruction. By 1860 approximately 5 per cent of the slaves and a larger proportion of free Negroes could read and write. A small proportion of the slaves also received excellent training as artisans and handicraftsmen.[31]

It was during this period that segregation in the public schools of the United States was first challenged and put to a test in the courts. The issue could not have been drawn in the South; the lawsuit was, in fact, filed in Boston, and the Massachusetts Supreme Court handed down its decision on the case, *Roberts v. City of Boston,* in 1849. Both the arguments against segregation and the decision were to resound at the bar of state and Federal courts for decades.

Boston had a local ordinance which provided for separate schools for whites and Negroes. When a Negro girl sought and was denied permission to enroll in a white school, Charles Sumner, ardent abolitionist and, later, protagonist of Reconstruction measures against the defeated Confederate States, brought suit on her behalf.

Sumner argued before the court that the bill of rights in the Massachusetts constitution ruled out legal distinctions based on race by proclaiming all citizens to be born equal. He maintained further that segregated schools tended "to deepen and to perpetuate the odious distinction of caste, founded in a deep-rooted prejudice in public opinion." Sumner produced a final argument, as many were to do afterward, that the separate schools of the city were not in fact equal.

The Massachusetts Supreme Court found against Sumner's client in terms which also were to be heard repeated down through the years. The court stated that racial segregation did not in itself constitute discrimination, and that, in the provision of substantially equal schools for Negroes, the Boston School Committee had exercised local powers not specifically denied it by higher authority. And, finally, said the court, any caste distinction intensified by segregated schools, "if it exists, is not created by law and probably cannot be changed by law."[32]

The issue of segregation was settled in Massachusetts in 1855 when the legislature passed a law specifically prohibiting segregation in the public schools. But the legal doctrine propounded by the Massachusetts Supreme Court was not throttled so quickly, and it served as a precedent for decisions handed down by the courts of other states outside the South. In the years after the Civil War state-enforced segregation was upheld in Ohio, Indiana, California, New York, West Virginia, and Missouri. These decisions may very well have served

---

[31] Myrdal, *op. cit.,* p. 887.
[32] 59 Mass. (5 Cush.) 198 (1849).

as conditioners for the first case involving segregation to be carried to the Supreme Court of the United States in 1896. The famous case of *Plessy v. Ferguson* will be discussed in due course.

So it is that the years 1835-1861, designated as a period of educational progress in the South, must be evaluated in relative terms and must be considered in their historical context. Despite the obstacles of retarding social, political, and economic factors, public education made greater progress during this period than ever before. Public school education was only elementary education, it was only for white children, it was meager and crude; but the public-school idea had sparked the imaginations of enough minds to survive an incredibly bloody war, an oppressive military occupation, and an era of cruelest poverty. A solid foundation for a tax-supported system of public schools had been laid throughout the South before the shadows cast by crumbling battle lines deepened into a twilight of extreme destitution. When the public-school idea again struggled up through the ruins, it had to encompass a new element in the social order, the Negro —free, lost, hungry for learning.

THE CIVIL WAR AND RECONSTRUCTION (1861-1877)

John S. Brubacher has written:

On the whole, education has made its greatest progress when it has ridden the crest of economic prosperity. It has been most retarded in the trough of economic depression. The conditions of war and peace are similar elemental forces conditioning the advance and retreat of education. On the whole, war is a great deterrent to educational progress. . . . Education thrives on peace and quiet, law and order.[33]

Seldom have those words been given meaning to the extent that they were in the South during and after the Civil War. Insofar as education is concerned, the period of the war itself can very nearly be dismissed. The energies and resources of the entire region were devoted to the prosecution of war; the school was a complete victim of the conflict in some states, in others it barely survived.

The end of the war found the South defeated, impoverished, and dispirited. A way of life had been destroyed, and there was no new way immediately to take its place. Social, economic, and political changes had as their counterparts conflict, hardship, and insecurity. No part of life was untouched, and education reflected the stress of the times.

[33] John S. Brubacher, *A History of the Problems of Education* (New York: McGraw-Hill Book Company, Inc., 1947), p. 641.

As Southerners recovered from the bitterness of Appomattox and sought to determine what kind of social order could be built upon the ruins of the old system that was gone forever, three groups of native whites emerged. One group was composed of members of the old planter class whom even war and defeat could not change. These extreme conservatives set out to build a postwar society as nearly as possible like that which existed before the cataclysm. Members of this group had wielded great power before the war, and it was natural that they should occupy a place of considerable eminence in the days immediately following the conflict. The clock could not be turned back, however, and from the first this group faced stern opposition.

Opposition came first from their own kind. Quite a large number of plantation owners realized that times had changed irrevocably and they sought to adjust to the new situation. These moderates, who in the total political scene constituted a wing of the conservative group, accepted the fact that the Negro was emancipated and enfranchised and that a place would have to be made for him in the new social order. That entailed ways and means of preparing the Negro race for the duties and responsibilities that went with the Negro's newly acquired citizenship.

The third, and by far the largest, group of native white Southerners was composed of small farmers and persons who owned no property. Even before the war, this group had begun to grow restless under the dominance of the aristocratic minority. Their resentment at having to compete with the slave system found expression during the war when many aligned themselves with the cause of the Union. In a continued effort to throw off the yoke of the oligarchy, great numbers of these poorer whites became Republicans, or "radicals," after the war. In this capacity they at first cooperated with Negroes in an effort to build a better social system for both. The time would come when the poorer white would turn against the Negro as a competitor, but immediately after the war they cooperated to bring about reforms which would lift them from the deprivation and hardship which had always been their lot.[34]

A fourth group with which the new social order would have to contend was composed of thousands of black men but recently slaves. A presidential proclamation had given the slaves their freedom, but they were by no means free in any but a legal sense. They were without status, they lacked means with which to earn an independent livelihood, and they were unlettered. To the newly emancipated Negro, education seemed to be the surest and quickest road to progress.

---

[34] Horace Mann Bond, *The Education of the Negro in the American Social Order* (New York: Prentice-Hall, Inc., 1934), pp. 15–19.

Learning was identified with wealth and leisure and status. Many Negroes were moved by an almost tragic faith that education could accomplish miracles, and accordingly sought learning with a hungry zeal.

Negroes were not alone in their tenacious faith in education. Citizens of New England had long held a passionate belief that the common school was the means to civic virtues. Thus it was that Northerners brought in schools for the Negroes hard on the heels of invading Union armies. Missionary societies and individual churches poured money and teachers into the South throughout the war as fast as territory was conquered and secured. Colonel John Eaton set up something of a system for Negro education in the Union Department of the West. By 1864 Louisiana was under control of an army of occupation and, in that year, Union General Banks established a regular system of free public schools for Negroes which was supported by taxes levied upon property.

The first state system in the South which provided separate schools for whites and Negroes was instituted during the war. In 1863 West Virginia became a separate political unit and its people adopted a constitution which provided for a state public school system. According to the constitution, Negroes were to be educated in schools which were separate but in every way equal to the schools for whites. Missouri included separate schools for Negroes in its public school system in 1865, when the state government was dominated by Unionists. These early efforts at Negro education did not reflect the sentiments of the Southern white population. Rather, they were an imposition initiated and supported by the bayonet.

The years 1865-1867 constituted the period of "Presidential Reconstruction," during which the policies of Presidents Lincoln and Johnson were in force. During these uneasy and impoverished times, most of the states looked to the conservatives, who had been in power before and during the war, for leadership. As part of the effort to reconstitute civilian life, some attempts were made to revive the schools. Once again the plea began to be heard that public schools were the best means to develop an enlightened electorate so necessary for the successful functioning of government. In general, the states which had made legal provisions for education prior to the Civil War revived the school laws previously enacted. In every state moderates took the position that provisions had to be made for the education of both white and Negro children, and several states passed legislation to that end.

The passage of legislation did not, however, guarantee schools. Most of the permanent school funds had been lost one way or another during the war, the people were too poverty stricken to contribute to education, legality of the acts passed by the legislatures was subject to considerable question, the times were uncertain and confused. Thus, very little was actually accomplished by the Southern states to further education, either white or Negro. Knight insists that conditions eventually would have been better for all concerned had the South been permitted to work out its own destiny. He writes:

> In the main . . . the leaders of the period recognized the changes which the result of the war had produced and courageously set themselves to the task of readjustment; and but for the inauguration of the congressional plan of restoring the South, the educational needs of both white and colored children would have been more properly cared for during the years following the war. The obstacles to peace and good order could have been more easily removed, and the public schools — which later became so unpopular because of the circumstances which surrounded their establishment — could have grown in popular favor and could have become more readily . . . the principal means of solving the great problem which the war left for solution to the white people of the South.[35]

Meantime, efforts outside the South to establish schools for Negroes received renewed impetus. The Federal government joined the various church societies in looking to the educational needs of the ex-slaves. In 1865 Congress created the Freedmen's Bureau, a powerful agency which exerted strong influence on many aspects of life in the South during the five years of its existence. The Bureau joined hands with the benevolent societies and effected a broad system of education for the Negro. By and large, the Freedmen's Bureau directed its efforts and moneys to the construction of school buildings, while the benevolent societies furnished teachers.

The Bureau, particularly in its personnel, rubbed salt into the wounds of the South. Most of the officials of the Freedmen's Bureau were recruited from the ranks of the Union army and were thoroughly hated by Southerners. Yankee school teachers, many of whom undoubtedly were animated by a genuinely benevolent enthusiasm, brought to their work a missionary zeal that not infrequently had the earmarks of fanaticism. The mistrust and hostility directed toward these "interlopers" were added to the belief still prevalent among the majority of Southerners that the education of the Negro was an unnatural phenomenon, anyway. The result was widespread and deep-seated opposition on the part of most Southerners to Negro schools. There were, as has been pointed out, prominent white citizens in every state who advocated education for the Negro as a necessary part

---

[35] *Op. cit.,* p. 317.

of the new social order. But the prevailing attitude was so antagonistic both to the Freedmen's Bureau and to the idea of education for Negroes that in many sections Negro schoolhouses were burned and the teachers of Negro children were beaten and driven away.

Despite external opposition and internal graft and theft of not inconsiderable proportions, the Freedmen's Bureau accomplished a good deal for Negro education. In five years of operation, the Bureau established 4,239 schools, employed 9,307 teachers, and instructed 247,333 pupils.[36] In order to carry on its work, the Bureau established a fairly well organized system of free schools throughout the South.

As the period of Presidential Reconstruction drew to a close, little had been done to promote schools for white children, except to pass laws that it was impossible to enforce, and efforts in behalf of Negro education had created a burning resentment on the part of white Southerners that was to leave deep scars on the region. Bond summarizes the attitudes that prevailed as follows:

Indeed, it would be contrary to all knowledge of human nature to assume that the once dominant social caste would accept such a transformation of the role of the Negro as was implied by his education within less than a decade after emancipation without harboring and exhibiting a violent feeling of outrage. It has been pointed out that the education of Negroes did do just this kind of violent outrage to the susceptibilities of persons steeped in a tradition that was founded upon the Negro as a chattel slave.[37]

In 1867 the period of comparatively mild Presidential Reconstruction came to an end with the passage of the Reconstruction Acts by the Congress of the United States. For ten years the South or some parts of it were to be subject to the severe measures of "Congressional Reconstruction." This tragic era was ostensibly brought about by refusal of the legislatures of the Southern states to accept the Fourteenth Amendment to the Constitution, which guaranteed privileges of citizenship to the Negro. But the amendment also disfranchised a considerable segment of the white population. All of the Southern states except Tennessee, which had already been readmitted to the Union, and Kentucky, which had not seceded, were placed under martial law. The region was divided into five military districts, and Federal armies of occupation moved in to enforce with military power the Fourteenth Amendment and the statutes relating to Negro suffrage.

Overnight the old leadership of the South was thrown out of and barred from office; new state governments were quickly established,

---

[36] Davie, *op. cit.*, p. 144.
[37] Bond, *op. cit.*, p. 31.

and soon new constitutions were written. The new radical state governments were formed by a coalition of "carpetbaggers," "scalawags," and newly enfranchised Negroes. The "carpetbaggers" were Yankees recently come to the South. Undoubtedly, many of these were men of integrity and capability, but many also were adventurers or outright rascals seeking to enrich themselves by every unscrupulous means. The "scalawags" were poorer white Southerners who had aligned themselves with the Republican Party to carry on the age-long fight against the vested power of the old Southern leadership. The Negroes, for the most part bewildered, anxious, and untutored, were seeking to find a secure place in the new system.

The constitutional conventions of the Reconstruction governments gave high priority to the establishment of systems of public education. Previous provisions for public schools were broadened and made more specific. Three important changes were made in the constitutions or found expression in statutes enacted by the legislatures. First, schools in all the states were opened to Negro children. Second, an attempt was made to provide greater centralization of authority and closer supervision by state officials. The office of state superintendent was created in all the states, and provisions were made for local administration. The third important change was in the financing of the public schools. The permanent school funds were reestablished, and additional funds were made available through heavy taxes levied directly upon the land. Small property owners were exempted and the taxes levied against the plantation owners were very nearly confiscatory.[38]

The traditional attitude of the Southern conservative toward public education and the crushing tax load caused him bitterly to resist each of these reforms, but in the legislatures he was represented by a meager and helpless minority. It is likely that systems of public education for white children, which had been slowly developing for years, would eventually have been effected. Be that as it may, the Reconstruction legislatures of carpetbaggers, scalawags, and Negroes, backed by Federal armies, immediately brought into existence systems of universal free education for all children.

During this period, Kentucky, which was not subject to the Reconstruction Acts, set a precedent in regard to taxes for the support of education which was to have lasting repercussions. This was the principle of earmarking for support of Negro schools only those taxes collected from Negroes. This precedent had actually been set by the Congress of the United States in 1862, a time when there was no representation from the Southern states. Congress decreed that the

---

[38] *Ibid.*, pp. 50, 58–59.

white and Negro schools in the public school system of the District of Columbia be supported by a pro rata distribution of school funds according to race. The principle of the allocation of school funds on the basis of taxes paid by the race to be educated was finally voided by the courts but not before it had created considerable confusion and turmoil.

With the advent of systems of universal free education for all children came the issue of mixed schools. The issue was brought to the fore by white idealists who believed that separate schools were undemocratic and that only through unsegregated schools could equal educational opportunity be provided all children.[39] The issues stirred passions so deeply bedded in the mores of the South that the controversy assumed proportions far beyond actual efforts made to integrate the schools.

Either by action of the constitutional conventions or by later legislative enactment, only five states—South Carolina, Mississippi, Louisiana, Florida, and Alabama—made mixed schools legal, and the Alabama law was farcical in that mixed schools were permitted only upon the unanimous consent of the parents of children in attendance.

Actually, mixed schools were tried in only a few places in three states. Mississippi had a few mixed schools for a brief period; then they withered away. Integrated schools were set up in Columbia and Charleston, South Carolina, but they survived for only a short time and amounted to no more than white and Negro children attending separate classes in the same school building. The records reveal only one instance in Louisiana in which Negroes sought admittance to a white school, and the incident was quickly closed when the Negro children were driven from the school by white pupils.

The first of the philanthropic organizations to lend support to Southern education became involved in the mixed school issue. The Peabody Fund, created in 1867, did a great deal for both white and Negro education by encouraging local initiative, by keeping schools operating, and by encouraging the training of teachers.

The Fund took the position that separate schools for the races were desirable in the Southern states and that Negroes had nothing to fear in the matter of inequitable distribution of state school funds. The Fund believed that the South was irrevocably committed to the provision of equal educational advantages for both races.[40]

Negroes, for the most part, were more interested in equal educational oportunity than in pressing for mixed schools. For this and other reasons, the Reconstruction governments made no real effort

---

[39] *Ibid.,* p. 56.
[40] *Ibid.,* pp. 54–55.

to integrate the new public schools. Bond, in his summary of the whole issue, says:

Those who argued against mixed schools were right in believing that such a system was impossible in the South, but they were wrong in believing that the South could, or would, maintain equal schools for both races. Those who argued for mixed schools were right in believing that separate schools meant discrimination against Negroes, but they were opposed to the logic of history and the reality of human nature and racial prejudices.[41]

Thus it was that the pattern of separate schools became operative as soon as the Negro was admitted to the public schools.

Ashmore sums up the Reconstruction era in the following passage:

Reconstruction, with its high-riding Negro hopes and its white despair, its occupation troops and its missionaries, its political chaos and its economic privation, lasted for varying periods in the Southern states, but it was over in all of them by 1877 when the last Federal troops were withdrawn. Out of that unsettled era emerged the rudiments of the public education system which still serves the South, and the traditions that have kept it segregated through the years. The principle of universal education written into the Reconstruction constitutions survived when the Southern whites returned to power, but everywhere the laws were changed to provide that the two races were to be educated separately.[42]

One of the by-products of efforts by non-local agencies to educate the Negro during this period was the genesis of an attitude on the part of Southern whites that Negro education was more a function of the Federal government and of private philanthropy than it was a local responsibility.

When Southerners again resumed control of their own affairs, they did so in the face of woeful poverty made worse by burdensome taxes on land which was barely producing, of a vivid memory of graft and theft and misappropriation in government, of grievous resentment and prejudice toward both Northerners and Negroes. The traditions and mores of the South being what they were, it is, perhaps, remarkable that Negro education survived at all. On this point, Myrdal writes:

The great wonder is that the principle of the Negroes' right to public education was not renounced altogether. But it did not happen. One explanation is the persistency and magnanimity of Northern philanthropy. But this activity was pursued under the indulgence of the Southern state and municipal authorities. And, though their own contributions to Negro education in many regions were not much more than facesaving, *the*

---

[41] *Ibid.*, p. 57.

[42] Harry S. Ashmore, *The Negro and the Schools* (Chapel Hill: The University of North Carolina Press, 1954), p. 9.

important thing is that facesaving was deemed necessary and that the Negroes' statutory right to public education remained unassailable in the South. The American Creed, backed by the Constitution, showed itself strong enough not to allow the sacred principle of public education to succumb. Even in the South — as it came out of the Civil War and Reconstruction — the caste interest could never be pursued wholeheartedly.[43]

In another passage Myrdal says:

There is petty pressure on Negro education in the South, but the truth is that the *Southern whites have never had the nerve to make of Negro education an accomplished instrument to keep the Negroes in their caste status.* It would have been possible, but it has not been done. The Southern whites' caste policy has been half-hearted all through, but particularly so in education. The explanation is again that they are also good Americans with all the standardized American ideals about education. The interest of educating the Negroes to become faithful helots has been obvious, but the Southern whites have not even attempted to make it effective in practice. Instead, they have merely kept Negro education poor and bad. And even on that point they have been gradually giving up resistance to the command of the Creed. This is the deeper dynamics of Negro education.[44]

At the end of Reconstruction the South had not yet fully accepted the standardized American ideals about education, which the ruined Southern states could not have afforded in any event. Circumstances that led to keeping Negro education "poor and bad" crystallized within the next few years.

FROM RECONSTRUCTION TO THE END OF THE CENTURY (1877-1900)

The electoral campaigns of 1874-1876 returned the Southern states to the control of the Democratic Party. The leadership of this party was the same that had been in power prior to the Civil War and for two years following the end of hostilities. They were members of the old Whig class, which had never been sympathetic to public education, but they still retained enormous prestige in the region. The weight of public opinion had, however, become so pronounced in favor of public schools that, in order to wrest power from the Republican Party of carpetbaggers, scalawags, and Negroes, the conservatives had to include the maintenance of public schools in their political platforms. Furthermore, the conservative party made a strong appeal to the Negro vote in order to assure victory, and they pledged

[43] Myrdal, *op. cit.*, p. 888.
[44] *Ibid.*, p. 896.

that schools for Negroes would be maintained on a basis of equality with those for white children. With the help of votes of dissident members of the poorer white class and of the Negroes, the conservative whites returned to political office and for some years successfully withstood the challenge of opposing factions.

For a quarter of a century education made little progress, however, and toward the end of the period discrimination became marked between white schools in some regions and white schools in other regions, and between white and Negro schools everywhere. Figures provide the bare facts in regard to educational progress. In 1876, about one-half of the school population—children of school age—in the South was enrolled in school; the length of the school term ranged from fifty days in North Carolina to 113 days in Virginia; and, among the states for which figures are available, expenditure per pupil enrolled in public schools ranged from $0.89 in Alabama to $8.93 in Louisiana.[45] In 1899-1900, nearly two-thirds of the school population was enrolled; the average school term was less than 100 days, with a range of from 71 days in North Carolina to 120 days in Louisiana; and the expenditure per pupil in average daily attendance in the public schools ranged from $3.10 in Alabama to $11.35 in Texas.[46] For the real story of what happened during these years it is necessary to look beyond the mere citation of figures.

The conservatives had included in their party platforms promises to retrench all along the line in governmental expenditures and to lighten the tax load upon the people. It was obviously impossible to maintain adequate school systems for both Negro and white children and at the same time reduce taxes. Adequate schools for both races would have necessitated a continuation of or an increase in the Reconstruction tax rate, but without tax reduction election pledges would have been violated. Had most of the available school funds been spent upon the education of white children at the expense of Negro children, pre-election promises also would have been broken. The only course remaining was to retrench in the operation of all schools, for both races, and to maintain an equality of expenditures between white and Negro schools. Be it said that the political leadership of the South kept faith with promises made to the Negroes and, upon resuming office, pursued the last course of action.[47]

The South was too poor, perhaps, to maintain anything approach-

---

[45] U. S. Bureau of Education, *Report of the Commissioner of Education for the Year 1876* (Washington: Government Printing Office, 1878), pp. xxi–xxix.

[46] U. S. Bureau of Education, *Report of the Commissioner of Education for the Year 1899–1900* (Washington: Government Printing Office, 1901), I, lxiii–lxxx.

[47] Bond, *op. cit.*, p. 86.

ing an adequate school system, but the post-Reconstruction legislatures made it difficult even to improve education. They refused to permit local taxation for the schools, and limitations were placed upon the legislatures with regard to the rate of taxation which they could levy at the state level for educational purposes and the amount of money which could be appropriated for the support of public schools. Approximately equal amounts of money were spent on white and Negro schools, but the sums were so limited that the whole educational enterprise was in a sad plight.

The small farmers, who composed the majority of the white population in the South, had long fought for an extension of the public school system to all white people. As the years passed, the small farmers organized a political movement in opposition to the conservatives. The political efforts of the small farmers, which culminated in the Populist movement, had pronounced effects on education. In the various legislatures this group began to argue against the system of distributing state funds according to the per capita enrollment of the school population. One reason for wanting a change was that, from year to year, funds were being increasingly diverted from Negro to white schools in those counties which had large Negro populations. The small farmers also wanted an increase in the state school funds and they favored local taxation. The small farmers were opposed in all these aims by the powerful Black Belt [48] conservatives who controlled the legislatures. Since reforms could not be instituted, the small farmers and inhabitants of "white" counties—those counties in which the Negro population was small— soon became openly hostile to Negro education because they wanted the funds appropriated for Negro schools to be used to support schools for their own children. Furthermore, the diversion of funds soon resulted in better schools for white children in "black" counties than for those in "white" counties. When job competition inevitably entered the picture, the doom of equalitarian ideals was sealed. The Negroes were helpless by themselves and even expediency no longer provided a champion.

One other factor of considerable import impinged upon education during these years. At the very time that financial support for the schools was proving so inadequate, the school population was increasing rapidly. In twenty years, from 1875 to 1895, school enrollment in ten Southern states increased by about two million pupils, or more than 150 per cent. It is interesting to note that the per-

[48] Black Belt is used interchangeably with "black" counties but the derivation of the terms is not the same. The Black Belt was so designated because of its dark, rich soil. Here vast plantations were located with a corresponding concentration of slaves. The preponderance of Negroes, who out-numbered the white population, gave rise to the term "black" counties.

centage increase of white students exceeded that of Negro students. From 1880 to 1895 the enrollment of white pupils in the ten states more than doubled, while Negro enrollment increased but one-half as fast. The crippling of Negro schools through diversion of funds was undoubtedly being reflected in the number of Negro children enrolled, but the fact remains that more white children than ever before were seeking education in the public schools.[49]

The way chosen to deal with the situation is described by Bond as follows:

Despite the pledges of conservative chiefs to Negroes that their educational rights should not be violated by the restored regime, it was inevitable that the divestiture of the Negro of any real political power should soon be followed by a diversion of school funds from Negro to white children. There were more children to be educated but less money available for their education; and if a choice had to be made between providing a wretched system for both races and providing a fairly good system for the white children as compared to a wretched system for Negro children, the student of human nature can understand what was actually done.[50]

Before the turn of the century, sentiment had reached a point that permitted the passage of "Jim Crow" laws in the Southern states and the Negro had been effectively disfranchised. Meantime, legislation affecting the dual school system had been passed in every Southern state; two or three examples, taken from Bond, will show the pattern that was followed.[51]

The situation in Mississippi at the time the Democrats regained control of the state government was not atypical. Under Reconstruction the large land owners had taxes levied against their property for the support of the schools. These men lived in counties in which the Negro school population far outnumbered the white school population; thus, the plantation owners, who had never been sympathetic to public education, were being taxed to support many more Negro than white schools. The radical legislatures had exempted most of the small farmers from property taxation. When the Democrats got back into power, educational revenues through property taxes were sharply curtailed and, as has been pointed out, the reduction in school revenues was concurrent with a rapid increase in school population. State school funds were the primary source by which the public schools were supported and the funds were distributed on a per capita basis. A per capita distribution of funds

---

[49] *Ibid.,* pp. 89–91.
[50] *Ibid.,* p. 92.
[51] *Ibid.,* pp. 93–114.

meant that considerably more money was spent on Negro schools in "black" counties than on white schools, while in "white" counties schools for white children received the greater apportionment of moneys. Such a situation was intolerable to the old planter class.

In the 1886 session of the state legislature, Black Belt represent-atives sponsored a law which set up a system of examinations for teachers with salaries based upon the kind of certificate granted, and with a wide range of salaries possible for the same type of certificate. There were two ways by which this law could be used to divert funds from Negro to white schools. Examining officers could give Negro teachers lower certificates with correspondingly lower salaries, or local boards of education could pay Negro teachers lower salaries than were paid to white teachers with the same certificate.

"Black" counties, with small enrollments of white children, found it possible to have quite adequate schools for white children from state funds alone. The constitutional requirement that Negro and white schools have terms equal in length created no problem; a Negro teacher could very well have as many as one hundred pupils, while an equal number of white children would have several teach-ers, and the schools would be in session the same length of time.

Since the per capita distribution sent large sums of state funds into "black" counties, a very considerable amount of money could be diverted to the few white schools and they could be maintained at a fairly high degree of efficiency. This situation created bitter antagonism on the part of the "white" counties. In those counties the Negro population was so small that the diversion of funds bene-fited white schools very little. The result was antagonism toward Negro education of any sort.

Equal appropriation of state funds to Negro children in "black" counties, if spent for Negro schools, meant that more money was being spent on the education of Negro children than on white chil-dren, and when funds were diverted from Negro to white children there was no need for additional revenue with which to support the white schools. Black Belt legislators, therefore, successfully fought off all efforts to permit the levying of local taxes. Citizens of "white" counties had schools hardly better than those afforded Negro chil-dren, and their schools were vastly inferior to the schools for white children in "black" counties. These citizens continuously fought for local taxation, but were unsuccessful in the face of the powerful oppo-sition of the Black Belt representatives. Even though complete diver-sion of funds from Negro to white schools in the "white" counties would have made the white schools but little better, the white citizens of those counties blamed Negro education for the inferiority of their schools.

The differential in expenditures for white and Negro education became more marked as the years passed. Discrimination against the Negro in the expenditure of funds was given further sanction in the Mississippi constitutional convention in 1890. The new constitution changed the method of distributing state school funds, leaving a great amount of discretionary power in the hands of local school boards. Consequently, the discriminations were no longer an evasion of the spirit of the old constitution which had required equal school opportunities for the two races. Local boards could apportion funds very nearly as they pleased.

At the constitutional convention the proposal was again heard that school funds be divided on the basis of taxes paid by the two races. Since the "black" counties could no longer have supported their schools so handsomely at the expense of Negro schools, Black Belt legislators defeated the measure. From 1885 to 1900 this proposal was vigorously fought over in each of the Southern states and was unfailingly defeated by citizens of "black" counties.

The rise of the small farmer to a place of political effectiveness came later in Mississippi than in most other Southern states, but when the small farmer achieved power just after the turn of the century he openly expressed his antagonism toward Negro education. He maintained that the moral stature of the Negro had not been improved as a result of education, and that, therefore, all money spent on education for the Negro was a waste. Discrimination in the expenditure of funds continued unabated but, as long as state funds provided the chief revenue for public schools, inequalities in the education of white children in "white" and "black" counties were as pronounced as inequalities in the education of white and Negro children within "black" counties. A comparison of two counties shows the extremes to which discrimination in school expenditures was carried. In 1907 a "white" county had a per capita expenditure for the education of white children of $5.65 as compared to $3.50 for Negro pupils. In the same year, a "black" county spent $80.00 per white child and $2.50 per Negro pupil.

In general, the pattern established in Mississippi was common to all the Southern states.

Circumstances in Alabama during the post-Reconstruction period were very similar to those in Mississippi. The school population increased while school revenues decreased, local taxation for education was prohibited, there was dissatisfaction with the distribution of state school funds, and the situation led finally to discrimination against Negro schools. The constitution provided for equal educational opportunities for both races, but in 1890 the constitution was circumvented. The legislature passed a law which gave county boards of education the power to use their share of state funds within the counties "as they should deem desirable in maintaining a system of schools equal for all children as nearly as practicable." "As nearly as practicable" could mean anything.

The state superintendent of education had given assurances that the law would not work any injustice upon Negro education. His assurances had no substantial basis. In 1891, the year the law took effect, the salaries of Negro teachers throughout the state showed a sharp decrease and the length of the school term for Negro children was shortened. It is not without significance that the annual report on education stopped carrying expenditures according to race after 1891 and the practice was not resumed until 1909. In that year, the records show that the percentage excess of per capita white expenditures over Negro expenditures was 514.8 per cent.

A constitutional convention was held in 1901 and the words of the 1890 law were incorporated in the new constitution. Local boards of education were directed to maintain school systems, not necessarily equal, but "equal as nearly as practicable." As was the case in Mississippi, the "black" counties profited greatly from the distribution of funds, "white" counties gained very little, and efforts of the latter to pass permissive legislation for local taxation were beaten down for many years.

In an effort to solve its educational problems, South Carolina had recourse to measures comparable to those employed in Mississippi and Alabama. In the constitution of 1895 local school boards were given discretionary powers to apportion school funds, and it was inevitable that discrimination against schools for Negro children should result. According to Bond:

The year 1895 may be taken as a general conclusion for the period in which Southern states struggled with the possibility of providing equal education for both races. Discrimination against Negroes had been adopted in every Southern state by this date.[52]

Emphasis on the biracial aspects of education should not obscure several other factors important to the development of public schools in the South. The tremendous increase in school enrollment was indicative of the ever-growing interest and faith in public education. This period was also marked by the acceptance of the public high school. The first public high school had been established in Boston in 1821, but the high school movement developed very slowly in the South. In 1876 only a few pupils were enrolled in the widely scattered high schools of the Southern states. By the school year 1899-1900,

---

[52] *Ibid.,* p. 204.

however, there were 1,013 public high schools operating in the South,[53] of which 65 were for Negroes.[54] Most of the high schools were located in cities, but there was a growing demand for secondary schools in rural areas.

Establishment of the first public high schools in cities points up the difference between urban and rural education, a difference which became more pronounced during this period. Toward the end of the nineteenth century, industry began to appear in some measure, cities increased in size, and in the last decade of the century, wealth increased by nearly 50 per cent.[55] Public education began to make faster progress in the cities and industrial areas than in rural sections with their scattered population and ingrained conservatism. Differences in rural and urban schools became more pronounced as the years passed, and subsequent sections of this work will show that a wide gap still exists.

Growth of the Populist movement has already indicated a shift in the political scene, and another group which was to exert marked influence on public schools began to emerge. Concurrent with improved economic conditions, a prosperous and influential middle class of business men began to develop.

Toward the end of this period, the United States Supreme Court handed down a decision which for more than fifty years would serve as the legal authority for segregated public schools. A decision in the case of *Plessy v. Ferguson* was rendered in 1896, with only one justice dissenting. The case at issue was an attempt to invalidate a Louisiana statute which required separation of the races on trains traveling within the state. Plessy, a man of one-eighth Negro descent, brought suit to invalidate the Louisiana law as being violative of his personal rights under the Thirteenth and Fourteenth Amendments to the Constitution. The adverse decision of the Court stated:

Laws permitting, and even requiring [separation of the races] in places where they are liable to be brought into contact do not necessarily imply the inferiority of either race to the other, and have been generally, if not universally, recognized as within the competency of the state legislatures in the exercise of their police power. The most common instance of this is connected with the establishment of separate schools for white and colored children, which has been held a valid exercise of the legislative power even by courts of states where the political rights of the colored race have been longest and most earnestly enforced.[56]

---

[53] U. S. Bureau of Education, *Report of the Commissioner of Education for the Year 1899–1900* (Washington: Government Printing Office, 1901) II, 2129.

[54] *Ibid.,* p. 2504.

[55] Knight, *op. cit.,* p. 425.

[56] 163 U. S. 537 (1896).

Ashmore says:

Thus the "separate but equal" doctrine in education was given the sanction of federal law by virtue of a *dictum,* or side remark of the Court. Actually, this circumstance may have given the precedent even greater strength, for here the Court went out of its way to recognize that segregation in education was a general American practice, not a uniquely Southern one. In any event, the Court had firmly imbedded the durable doctrine which has been the determinant in all subsequent litigation involving the dual school system.[57]

The South entered the twentieth century with public school systems which were inferior to those in the rest of the United States, with powerful forces agitating for better schools, with a still poor but greatly improved economy, and with the question of segregated Negro public schools settled by a "separate but equal" doctrine which in reality meant only "separate." Public education as a function of the state still had strong opposition, but the forces favoring the principle of public education supported by taxes on all the people were rapidly increasing in influence.

SOUTHERN EDUCATION IN THE TWENTIETH CENTURY
(1900-1952)

The first half of the twentieth century has witnessed many swiftly moving changes that have deeply affected life in the United States. Political reform and social legislation designed to improve the general welfare of the people have been widely instituted; business and industry have expanded amazingly, and so has the role of government; two world wars and a depression of gigantic proportions have sown destruction and accelerated change; democracy as a way of life has been threatened from without and challenged from within; the educational enterprise has grown enormously in size and complexity, and the role of the school has been the subject of vigorous controversies.

Perhaps no region of the nation has changed as much in the twentieth century as the South; but, in the beginning of the period, change came slowly, for the heritage of the Southern region did not encourage change.

Until the twentieth century, the Industrial Revolution, which had swept across other parts of the nation, had made very little real impact on the South. The South remained an agricultural region and a poor one. But in the early years of the twentieth century a portent of what was to come was evident. The Industrial Revolution

---

[57] Ashmore, *op. cit.,* p. 12.

with its mills and factories and industries, its improved communications and transportation, its concentrations of population, began to make inroads on the region. The beginnings were scattered and slow, but eventually the entire economy of the region would be changed.

The political revolt, highlighted by the Populist movement, continued to gain strength at the expense of the old "Bourbons." Among other changes, the drive for permissive local taxation with which to support public education was finally achieved. At the turn of the century more than 50 per cent of the revenues for school support came from state funds. Within ten years, local taxes had become the chief source of school revenues and the percentage of local support went steadily upward until the depression.

With increased local support, educational progress was rapid. Expenditures for public schools increased tremendously.[58] As a result, the school term was lengthened, teachers' salaries were increased, physical equipment improved and became more generally available. Better schools and teachers brought improvement in enrollment and attendance. The number of public high schools in twelve Southern states more than doubled from 1899-1900 to 1915-1916. In the latter year public high schools in the twelve states numbered 2,669.[59] At the beginning of the century, only one state, Kentucky, had a compulsory attendance law, but by 1918 all the Southern states required children between specified ages to attend school for all or part of the school term.[60]

The rapid educational advances made in the early part of the century left public schools in the South still lagging far behind those in other regions. The upward trend had started relatively late, the region was still predominantly agricultural and poor. In 1915-1916 few Southern states were spending one-half as much per pupil as the average for the United States. The disparity between urban and rural schools became even more accentuated as general progress was being made. The one-room school was the landmark of the rural areas with their widely scattered population. Taxation for the support of rural schools produced revenues decidedly less than the amounts available in urban centers. The inequality in educational opportunity between rural and urban schools began to be somewhat ameliorated in later years with the consolidation of schools and state minimum foundation programs, but the gap has never been closed.

Disparity of any sort among white schools was inconsiderable when

---

[58] See Chapter 6.
[59] Bureau of Education, *Report of the Commissioner of Education for the Year Ended June 30, 1917* (Washington: Government Printing Office, 1917) II, 513.
[60] Knight, *op. cit.,* p. 444.

compared to the disparity between white and Negro education during these years. Indeed, the stirrings and fermentation that were beginning to affect the whole social scene in the South very nearly passed the Negro by. He was a voiceless spectator at events which shaped his destiny but over which he had no control; he was no longer a slave, but he was no more than a disfranchised servant, sharecropper, tenant farmer, laborer. In rural areas, Negro schools, often housed in churches, lodges, or abandoned shacks, received such share of school revenues as white administrators cared to give them. That amounted to little more than enough to survive, and survival would have been more difficult had not outside help been made available.

In the early years of the century, Negro schools became the recipients of considerable help from philanthropic foundations. Myrdal sums up the assistance provided by the foundations as follows:

In the first two decades of the twentieth century, Negro education received a great boost when the Northern philanthropic foundations stepped into the picture on a much larger scale. Before then the George Peabody Fund (established in 1867) gave money to both white and Negro common schools and teacher-training schools in the South. The John F. Slater Fund (established in 1882) supported industrial and teacher-training schools. . . . In 1908 a Quaker lady of Philadelphia, Miss Anna T. Jeanes, established a Fund to give impetus to the small rural Southern Negro school. . . . [The Jeanes] plan calls for a rural industrial supervisor who goes from school to school in a county and helps the teachers organize their domestic science, their gardening and their simple carpentry work. At first the Fund paid the salaries of these "Jeanes' teachers," but gradually many of the county school boards took over the function. The remnants of the Peabody, Slater, and Jeanes Funds have been recently integrated into the Southern Education Foundation, which still helps to pay part of the salaries of the Jeanes teachers.

Another step was taken by the General Education Board, with money provided by John D. Rockefeller. . . . This foundation paid for state supervisors of Negro education who were to be under the state superintendents. The supervisors, who were white Southerners, had no official authority whatever, but they have been most important in raising the standards of the Negro public schools of the South. . . .

The General Education Board has also given much money for fellowships, colleges, libraries, and other educational facilities for Southern Negroes and has made it possible for the Slater and Jeanes Funds to continue with their work. In 1911, Mr. Julius Rosenwald began the successful activity of giving one-third of the funds required for the erection of a rural school building, provided the school authorities, with the aid of white friends and the Negro people themselves, would furnish the other two-thirds.[61]

[61] Myrdal, *op. cit.,* pp. 890–891.

The Rosenwald Fund contributed to the building of 5,358 rural Negro school buildings. Further help was provided to Negro education by the Phelps-Stokes Fund, the Carnegie Corporation, and many private contributions from both whites and Negroes.

There is no doubt that the philanthropic organizations were a great boon to Negro education. At the same time, the old charity-school idea was perpetuated and the lack of local responsibility for the education of Negroes, evident in the years after the Civil War, continued. On this point, Myrdal writes:

> In the author's judgment, *Northern philanthropy in its grand-scale charity toward the South, incidental to its positive accomplishments, has also had a demoralizing influence on the South.* The South has become accustomed to taking it for granted that not only rich people in the North, but also poor church boards, should send money South, thus eternally repaying "the responsibility of the North for Reconstruction." [62]

Even with outside help, Negro schools lagged far behind white schools. When the Rosenwald building program came to an end, the per pupil value of Negro school property was less than one-fifth that of white school property. Between 1900 and 1930, the average salary for white teachers increased from slightly less than $200 to $900, while the average salary for Negro teachers rose from about $100 to $400. The holding power of the Negro schools was about what might be expected in the circumstances. As late as 1920, 85 per cent of all Negro pupils in the South were in the first four grades of the elementary school. In 1916, there were fewer than 20,000 Negro high school students in all the Southern states and there were only 67 Negro public high schools. [63]

An important factor in the holding power of Negro schools was undoubtedly the type of curriculum which the schools had. A controversy, vigorously entered into by Southern whites, developed in the early years of the century in regard to what kind of education the Negro should have. Some argued that Negroes should have the same kind of "classical" education that white children had. Others contended that, the Negro's place in the social order being what it was, he should have an "industrial" education. The prevailing opinion seemed to be that, since Negroes were laborers, farm hands, and servants, they should simply be taught to do their jobs better.

Even though the majority of white people seemed to favor industrial education for Negroes, two telling factors resolved the issue. As the Industrial Revolution gained headway in the South, it was accompa-

---

[62] *Ibid.*, p. 905.
[63] Ashmore, *op. cit.*, pp. 17–19.

nied by an accelerated demand for skilled workers. A vocational program in the schools that would be anything but a travesty would of necessity have to help develop skilled workers. This would have brought the Negro into competition with white workers and that the latter would not have. Furthermore, a vocational program was exceedingly expensive and was simply beyond the budget allotted to Negro schools.

Thus, the controversy over whether Negroes should have a classical or an industrial education was carried on in a vacuum. Except for a little training in cooking and other menial tasks, Negroes were given the same kind of schooling as white children, the chief difference being in quantity and quality.

Despite the disparity between white and Negro schools, the latter did make some progress during these years. The slow, painful broadening of the educational base represented progress, for the memory of Reconstruction was still vivid in the minds of Southern whites and their attitude toward Negroes as being of a different and lower order of human being had changed very little.

It was during the early years of the century that a great Negro leader, Booker T. Washington, rose to prominence and, through the power of his intellect and the force of his personality, began to attack the citadels of prejudice and intolerance. Washington never made a direct attack on segregation, but he reminded the Southern white that he could not keep the Negro in the ditch without staying down with him. He said that, "In all things that are purely social," the two races could go forward together while remaining as separate as the spread fingers of his hand. In the institution which he founded, Washington went considerably beyond providing the bare elements of an industrial education for Negroes.

The objectives which Washington envisioned for Tuskegee Institute as an educational institution may be summarized as follows: (1) the development of attitudes and habits of industry and honesty in and the disciplining of raw, country youth through institutionalized activities; (2) the development of specific skills in definite crafts and occupations; and (3) the preparation of teachers for the public and private schools of the South who might, through spreading the gospel of thrift, industry, and racial conciliation, aid in constructing a firm economic foundation upon which the future aspiration of the race might stand.[64]

Myrdal evaluates Washington's contributions in the following words:

There is no doubt that . . . his message was extremely timely in the actual power situation of the Restoration. It reconciled many Southern

---

[64] Bond, *op. cit.*, p. 119.

white men to the idea of Negro education, and Washington has probably no small share in the salvaging of Negro education from the great danger of its being entirely destroyed.[65]

The first three decades of the twentieth century were marked by steady educational progress throughout the Southern region. As the economy improved, so did the quantity and quality of education. Even with a disproportionate share of school revenues, Negro education moved steadily forward. Ashmore says that "The South entered the 1930's with Negro school attendance proportionately as great as that of the whites for the first time; the 2.4 million Negro pupils comprised about one-fourth of the total enrollment. Negroes were, however, attending shorter terms for the most part and they were still leaving school earlier, although the number of Negro high schools had risen from 67 in 1916 to 1,860 in 1928." [66] Free public education supported by tax moneys was no longer an issue; public schools were generally accepted as comprising an institution that was basic to democracy. Even tax-supported Negro education of some kind and in some amount was no longer seriously challenged.

Then the South, together with the rest of the nation, ran head on into the Great Depression of the thirties. The still dominant agrarian economy broke down under the impact of plunging farm prices, and the new factories soon cast still shadows across the homes of unemployed thousands where actual hunger was not unknown. Problems were not essentially different from those faced in other regions of the nation, but, because the Southern region had developed relatively late and was still the poorest part of the country, it suffered most. The national administration identified the South as the nation's number one economic problem.

Brubacher's observation that education "has been most retarded in the trough of economic depression" seems a vast understatement. Survival was the paramount problem faced by thousands and the need for education could not compete with the need for bread. Many schools closed down. The school terms of those remaining open were generally shortened and many hundreds of teachers were paid in scrip which was, in turn, heavily discounted. For the first time since the turn of the century, school expenditures began to decrease from year to year; in many sections, tax revenues simply dried up.

A situation developed in the South during the depression years that was strikingly similar to one which existed in the post-Reconstruction period: as school revenues declined, the school population went up. School attendance showed an increase of 700,000 during the thirties,

[65] Myrdal, *op. cit.*, p. 889.
[66] Ashmore, *op. cit.*, p. 26.

reaching an all-time high in 1934. School attendance in the South reflected a birth rate that was higher than the national average, and the out-migration of the population that had seen 1.3 million Southerners, mostly Negroes, leave the South during the decade following the end of World War I was sharply curtailed. Since Southern youth, both Negro and white, could find very little else to do during the bleak years of the Depression, more attended school and stayed longer. The South was faced with the formidable task of trying to educate one-third of the nation's children on only one-sixth of the nation's school revenue. Current operating expenditure per pupil was $45 during the depression years, less than one-half the national average. Building and maintenance funds were in even worse shape. At the end of the depression the average capital expenditure for the South was $6 per year per pupil, while the average for the rest of the nation was $14.[67]

The Depression accelerated two changes in education which were to have lasting effect. Rural schools were hit harder than urban schools because the sources of local taxation were in worse plight in rural sections. The extension of minimum foundation programs supported by state equalization funds was undertaken by most Southern states during these years. Since the programs followed the procedure of providing state aid to those school systems least able to help themselves, rural schools were greatly benefited. The period also brought about an acceleration in the effort, started earlier, to consolidate schools. The objective of the consolidation movement was to provide better schools at lower cost.

The Federal government also helped to meet the crisis in the rural schools of the South; between 1933 and 1935, 80 per cent of the $21,000,000 spent by the Federal government on rural schools was spent in the South. Rural schools also received the largest share of the $200,000,000 spent on school construction in the South by the Public Works Administration. PWA funds for school construction had to be matched by equal funds within the states, and the disparity between white and Negro education was again emphasized by the fact that only 8 per cent of government funds spent on school construction went for Negro schools.

In absolute rather than relative terms, Negro education made progress even in the depression years. It has been pointed out that Negro attendance went steadily upward during this period. In 1939-40 the length of the term in Negro schools was, on the average, above that of 1929-30. The salaries of Negro teachers were higher at the end of the Depression than at the beginning, and the holding power of Negro schools was greater.

---

[67] *Ibid.,* pp. 25–27.

Perhaps the greatest progress lay in another direction altogether. After citing evidence of progress in Negro education, Ashmore adds:

But by far the most important of the gains in Negro education in the thirties was the white leadership's increasing recognition of its responsibility for maintaining it. There was a significant change in prevailing Southern attitudes between the beginning and the end of the decade. After the shock of the depression had worn off and the process of federal-stimulated recovery had begun, Americans everywhere tended to subject their democratic institutions to serious re-examination. It was an era of liberalism in politics and the federal government was paying more attention to the status of the Negro than it had since Reconstruction. It was a time, too, when improving communications were breaking down the South's traditional isolation. . . . Ideals which had heretofore reached the South only through the filter of its own leadership now arrived intact and left their mark.

There were no revolutionary changes to be sure. The double standard around which the bi-racial school system had been shaped survived the thirties, but it was being considered now in a new light. White leaders of standing began to question openly the validity of a system which operated on the theory that Negroes were entitled to only a limited education, presumably tailored to a permanently truncated opportunity for economic advancement. If it were not yet to be followed in practice the "separate but equal" doctrine began to gain acceptance in its literal meaning as a policy. And there arose a school of "gradualism" whose adherents argued that, while the time for basic changes in racial relationships may not have arrived, all public policies in regard to the Negro should be shaped to the end that he would ultimately be equipped for and admitted to full citizenship.[68]

In the midst of the shifting social scene, the Negro population developed an able leadership of its own that was no longer satisfied with passive acquiescence in decisions made exclusively by white members of society. The Negro turned to the courts for a re-examination and interpretation of his rights as a citizen. In the field of education, the Negro directed his initial efforts for equal educational opportunity at state-supported graduate and professional schools.

In 1935 a Negro applied for admission to the law school of the University of Maryland, was refused, and carried his case to court. The Maryland Court of Appeals handed down a decision in which it was stated that existing arrangements were discriminatory and that the only way in which the plaintiff could obtain equal treatment was by admission to the University. Comparable suits were subsequently filed in Missouri, Oklahoma, and Texas, and in each instance the case was carried to the Supreme Court of the United States. The Court consistently ruled that equal educational opportunity had to be provided

---

[68] *Ibid.*, pp. 29–30.

Negroes, although the decisions varied from case to case on what was meant by equal opportuntiy. In some instances the separate but equal doctrine was enforced; in others, state universities were directed to admit Negroes on an unsegregated basis. Prior to 1954, the Court dealt with individual cases on their merits and without exception ruled that facilities had to be equalized, but the Supreme Court took no position on the matter of segregation *per se*.

The Court's decisions, nevertheless, had far-reaching effects. In 1947 the University of Arkansas voluntarily agreed to admit any qualified Negro applicant to courses which were not offered at the state-supported Negro college. Since 1949 twenty public institutions of higher learning in the South have admitted Negroes to their previously segregated student bodies. By 1953 only five state universities—the Universities of Mississippi, Alabama, Georgia, Florida, and South Carolina—still barred Negroes from admission. In no instance has the admission of Negroes to Southern institutions of higher learning created undue racial tension.

The South recovered from the Great Depression and entered the 1940's on a ground swell of change of unprecedented proportions and velocity. H. C. Brearley, noted Southern sociologist, gives this version of a popular description of changes occurring in the South: "Cotton's going west, cattle's coming east, Negro's going North, and Yankee's coming South—everybody's going to town."

Education in the South since 1940 has made tremendous progress while having to meet new problems that unfailingly accompany periods of vital change. The rapid industrialization of the region, the change in farm patterns, and the great increases in per capita income—from 1940 to 1952, per capita income in the Southern states increased 237 per cent—are dealt with in detail in this volume. The vast population changes which are transforming what was an agrarian region into an urban one are also described in subsequent chapters. The impact of a second world war on education will become evident as the educational enterprise is analyzed over a period of years. One striking evidence of educational progress in the South in recent years is the tremendous advance in the professionalization of teaching as reflected in improved certification requirements, tenure and retirement provisions, and in-service education programs.

The long struggle to lift schools in the South to a level comparable to that of schools in other parts of the nation continues. The specifics of progress, the examination of problems, analyses of trends, and the projection of needs and the capacity to meet them constitute the bulk of this volume. A further brief word on the dual school system in the South is in order.

The Negro has been inextricably involved in the deep running changes which have occurred in the nation and in the South in recent years. He has to a considerable extent regained the franchise so long denied him in Southern states; by 1950 there were more than a million eligible Negro voters in the South. In the Korean War the Negro soldier finally achieved equal status with the white soldier. In 1953 the Defense Department of the government either terminated or set a terminal date for segregated schools operated at military installations in the Southern states. Numerous cases were brought before the courts involving inequality in the primary and secondary schools of the region. The courts consistently held that if separate schools were to be maintained they would have to be equal in fact. In the face of these decisions, most Southern states increased appropriations for Negro schools in an effort to equalize educational opportunity. Finally, the issue of segregation in the public schools reached its climax in the Supreme Court. Segregation as such was directly challenged in five cases, originating in South Carolina, Virginia, Kansas, Delaware, and the District of Columbia. On May 17, 1954, the Supreme Court handed down its historic decision stating that separate educational facilities were inherently unequal and that segregation in the public question of how best to implement the Court's decision remains yet schools was a violation of the Constitution of the United States. The to be resolved.

This brief resumé of the development of education in the South has included several references to the attitude on the part of whites in regard to the educability of Negroes. The distinction between myth and fact concerning the physical and mental characteristics of the Negro could conceivably have some bearing upon the implementation of the Court's decision. Gunnar Myrdal and associates have done a notable piece of work in exploring this matter.[69] Myrdal writes:

In trying to understand how ordinary white people came to believe in the Negro's biological inferiority, we must observe that there was a shift from theological to biological thinking after the eighteenth century. As soon as the idea was spread that man belongs to the biological universe, the conclusion that the Negro was *biologically* inferior was natural to the unsophisticated white man. It is obvious to the ordinary unsophisticated white man, from his everyday experience, that the Negro is inferior. *And inferior the Negro really is;* so he shows up even under scientific study. He is, on the average, poorer; his body is more often deformed; his health is more precarious and his mortality rate higher; his intelligence performance, manners, and morals are lower. The *correct* observation that the Negro is inferior was tied up to the *correct* belief that man belongs to the biological universe,

---

[69] *Op. cit.,* chapters 4, 5, 6.

and, by twisting logic, the *incorrect* deduction was made that the inferiority is biological in nature.

. . . It is difficult for the ordinary man to envisage clearly how such factors as malnutrition, bad housing, and lack of schooling actually deform the body and the soul of people. The ordinary white man cannot be expected to be aware of such subtle influences as the denial of certain outlets for ambitions, social disparagement, cultural isolation, and the early conditioning of the Negro child's mind by the caste situation, as factors molding the Negro's personality and behavior. The white man is, therefore, speaking in good faith when he says that he sincerely believes that the Negro is racially inferior, not merely because he has an interest in this belief, but simply because he has seen it.[70]

Myrdal continues:

In adhering to this biological rationalization, . . . the white man meets certain difficulties. A factual difficulty to begin with is that individual Negroes and even larger groups of Negroes often, in spite of the handicaps they encounter, show themselves to be better than they ought to be according to the popular theory. A whole defense system serves to minimize this disturbance of the racial dogma, which insists that *all* Negroes are inferior.[71]

Myrdal recommends efforts

. . . to rectify the ordinary white man's observations of Negro characteristics and inform him of the specific mistakes he is making in ascribing them wholesale to inborn racial traits. We may assume that, until the Negro people were studied scientifically—which in a strict sense of the term means not until recent decades—the raw material for beliefs which the average white man had at his disposal in the form of transmitted knowledge and personal observations placed only the most flexible limits to his opportunistic imagination. When, however, scientific knowledge is being spread among people and becomes absorbed by them through popular literature, press, radio, school, and church, this means that the beliefs are gradually placed under firmer control of reality. *People want to be rational, to be honest and well informed.* This want, if it is properly nourished, acts as a competing force among the opportunistic interests. To a degree the desire to be rational slowly overcomes the resistance of the desire to build false rationalizations.

. . . It is principally through encouraging research and through exposing the masses of people to its results that society can correct the false popular beliefs—by objectivizing the material out of which beliefs are fabricated. Seen in long-range perspective, a cautious optimism as to the results of gathering and spreading true information among the American people in racial matters seems warranted. The impression of the author is that the younger, and better educated, generation has, on the whole, somewhat

[70] *Ibid.*, pp. 97–98.
[71] *Ibid.*, p. 104.

fewer superstitious beliefs, and that, during the last decade at least, the racial beliefs have begun to be slowly rectified in the whole nation.[72]

In regard to psychic traits, Myrdal writes:

Most of this work has concerned intelligence, as measured by the Intelligence Quotient. The inferences to be drawn are, on the whole, negative as far as hereditary differences are concerned: it has not been possible to prove beyond doubt the existence of any differences at all in innate intelligence between American Negroes and whites; neither has it been possible to prove, on the other hand, that no differences exist. In regard to environmental factors the inferences are, however, positive: it has been proved that environmental differences account for large differences in the measured intelligence performances. Present evidence seems, therefore, to make it highly improbable that innate differences exist which are as large as is popularly assumed and as was assumed even by scholars a few decades ago.[73]

Myrdal says that the spread of the findings of modern research has been much slower among whites than among Negroes; this was natural since the conclusions of science

. . . do not coincide with their [the whites'] interests in defending the caste order, and in any case, do not have the same relevance to their own personal problems of adjustment. One most important result is, however, that *it is now becoming difficult for even popular writers to express other views than the ones of racial equalitarianism and still retain intellectual respect.* . . . The final result of this change might, in time, be considerable. Research and education are bolstering the American Creed in its influence toward greater equalitarianism.[74]

Whatever the decisions of the future may be, racial prejudice can obtain no sanction from science.

Education in the South, throughout its history, has reflected the prevailing attitudes of the Southern people. Value patterns are no less subject to change than other aspects of a people's culture are. Brearley says: "The people of the South are . . . changing their attitudes on many matters. No longer do they 'look back to glory'—they face toward the future with considerable hope and confidence."[75]

The alternatives that are enmeshed in the web of the future of the South and the nation are presented by Myrdal in the closing chapter of his monumental work:

---

[72] Ibid., p. 109.
[73] *Ibid.*, p. 147.
[74] *Ibid.*, pp. 96–97.
[75] H. C. Brearley, "Three Revolutions in the South," *The Baptist Program*, January, 1954, p. 5.

America feels itself to be humanity in miniature. When in this crucial time the international leadership passes to America, the great reason for hope is that this country has a national experience of uniting racial and cultural diversities and a national theory, if not a consistent practice, of freedom and equality for all. What America is constantly reaching for is democracy at home and abroad. The main trend in its history is the gradual realization of the American Creed.

. . . Mankind is sick of fear and disbelief, of pessimism and cynicism. It needs the youthful moralistic optimism of America. But empty declarations only deepen cynicism. Deeds are called for. If America in actual practice could show the world a progressive trend by which the Negro became finally integrated into modern democracy, all mankind would be given faith again—it would have reason to believe that peace, progress and order are feasible. And America would have a spiritual power many times stronger than all her financial and military resources—the power of the trust and support of all good people on earth. *America is free to choose whether the Negro shall remain her liability or become her opportunity.*[76]

---

[76] *Op. cit.,* pp. 1021–1022.

THREE

The Organization
and Administration of
Biracial Education

In the previous chapter the development of biracial education in the Southern states was traced and analyzed in order to provide some of the information deemed necessary for an adequate understanding of the segregation issue and other problems of public education in the region today. The content of this chapter bears more specifically upon how public education is organized and administered in the South, and draws upon historical perspective for interpretative purposes. The critical importance of the structure through which schools are provided, the allocation of power to educational agencies and officials, and the necessary interrelationships of the numerous factors that impinge upon public education are focal points in this treatment. The control of education and the way in which control is exercised are factors which must be seriously considered in taking into account the Supreme Court decision on segregation.

Allegiance in the United States to the principle that education is a function of the states rather than of the Federal government means that each of the forty-eight states in the Union has been free to create its own school system. Although certain elements, such as the state department of education, the state board of education, the chief state school officer, local school districts, local boards of education, and the superintendency, may be common throughout the United States, their functions differ widely from state to state. In view of such variations, it is impossible to understand adequately the educational system and problems of a particular state without some understanding of how it has exercised its prerogatives with respect to public education in terms of structure and administration.

Provisions a state may choose to make for its schools are not determined independently of decisions made on other matters of public policy. The way a state is organized to transact its business and the philosophy of public administration underlying the creation of local units of civil government inevitably influence the structure and administration of public education.

Such interrelatedness is a manifestation of the fact that public policy generally reflects a people's beliefs. Beliefs may be fashioned or conditioned by many factors, such as tradition, class distinction, density of population, distribution of wealth, and the necessity for interdependence.

The relationship of the beliefs held by the class that was dominant in the *ante-bellum* South to the organization of public education was quite simple and direct. The plantation system profoundly affected early attitudes toward local government, and the system was a strong influence in the creation and development of the county system of government in the region. The slave economy and its influence on political democracy helped to create an upper class, which assumed to a large extent control over both local and state governments. The plutocracy could most easily maintain its control and administer the affairs of government through the large county units. It was but natural that school systems in the South would develop under the impact of these and other forces which were indigenous to the region. In contrast, New England, with its population developing around town centers and without the inflexible class differences of the South, produced in the town meeting an instrument scarcely equaled as an example of democratic local government.

As was pointed out in the previous chapter, the development of public education in the South was long hampered by the existence of a large segment of the population for whom no formal education was considered necessary, by the reliance of well-to-do parents upon the tutorial system and private schools for the education of their children, and by little or no concern for whether or not children of poorer whites received any education. The academy movement, which resulted in the establishment of hundreds of private schools for those who could afford to pay tuition charges, made little contribution to the development of an educational system. Few legal provisions for either the organization or administration of the academies were considered necessary.

The struggle to achieve a free public school system has been prominently accompanied by a struggle to achieve an adequate structure for public schools and effective patterns of administration for them. Indeed, one is a part of the other, and a clear grasp of today's issues and problems calls for a brief consideration of the steps which brought about the present structure and administration of the schools and necessitates some appraisal of their adequacy. In reviewing the development of school administration in the South, it will be evident that state variations referred to earlier will be lessened by regional influences, some of which have been identified already. A vital influence which has produced some uniformity in educational organization and administration in the South has been the necessity for maintaining separate schools for the white and Negro races.

THE STATE AND PUBLIC EDUCATION

Assumption by the state of responsibility for public education neither assures an adequate educational system nor indicates how the state will discharge its obligation. These are matters which follow and they require unremitting effort. State constitutions define responsibility for publc education, and, generally in the South, they also specify that separate schools must be provided for Negro and white pupils. Uniformity of provisions ceases at this point. Specific provisions are limited in number and differ widely from state to state. The substance of constitutional provisions is simply that the state has power over public education.

How this power is to be exercised is left to the discretion of each state legislature, unless otherwise provided for in the state constitution. Thus, under compulsion of its own definition of responsibility for public education, each state has created and maintains a public school system; and much of the responsibility for the schools is in the hands of the state legislature. Within limitations imposed by the constitution, the legislature may choose to exercise its power in its own right or to delegate it to other agencies or bodies. In practice it does some of both. Delegation of power may be revoked or transferred. Therefore, continuous controls are exercised.

Powers which the legislatures cannot conveniently exercise themselves, or which they do not choose to exercise are delegated to agencies of their own creation or to constitutionally established bodies, such as state departments of education, state boards of education, and boards of local school districts. Each of these agencies, in turn, functions within a grant of power specified in the enabling act which created the agency. These bodies are so important in the organization and administration of education in the South that each will be given brief special attention.

State legislatures exercise wide control over the financing of schools through their power to provide or withhold revenues. Parts of the educational program to be supported by state revenues may be defined by the state legislature. Among the powers which may be exercised by legislative bodies are the approval of salary schedules, the passage of compulsory attendance laws, the investigation of textbooks, the teaching of special subjects, the observance of special days, and the length of the school term. Controls may be exercised in a negative as well as positive sense. The law passed by the Tennessee legislature prohibiting the teaching of evolution in the public schools, which brought on the famous Scopes trial in 1925, is an example of negative control.

Enabling acts for the creation of local school districts carry with them not only the description of choices of districts which may be created but a statement of method whereby a school district may come into existence. Legislation also covers the functions of local district officials, specifying the powers of the local board of education, which it authorizes; and the duties and responsibilities attendant to the position of superintendent of schools, which it also authorizes. The salary of the superintendent and his qualifications may be prescribed by law. In some cases, such specifics have been included in constitutional provisions. For example, at one time constitutional salary limitations for superintendents of schools (along with other state officials) were prescribed by one or two state constitutions. In time, these states were handicapped by the salary limitations, which had become absurd in the face of changes in the economy.

State courts exercise important controls over education, which may influence in important respects the structure and administration of schools. Such power is inherent in the courts' authority to pass on the constitutionality of law when test cases are brought before them. One example of this power was a decision of the Tennessee Supreme Court which ruled invalid the Minimum Program Act, passed in 1952 by the legislature, because of a technicality. Courts also exert controls in other kinds of litigation which may affect education; for instance, they are empowered to determine a teacher's rights under tenure laws. It should be pointed out that decisions of state courts in regard to educational matters are, like decisions on any kinds of litigation, not necessarily final. The principle at stake may be tested in higher courts or become the subject of subsequent legislation.

The attorney general of the state, through rulings and interpretations of legislation affecting schools and of the acts and regulations of the state board of education and of the state department of education, may exert considerable influence on the organization and administration of schools. These rulings, to be sure, may be subject to subsequent tests in the courts.

The political nature of the state's methods of carrying out its mandate with regard to education is obvious from what has been said. In the final analysis, educational policy on the state level is determined in the arena of politics. The instability this might connote is, in reality, mitigated by the public's unfailing belief that public education is important and is worthy of continuing support.

Educational controls at the state level which have been delineated here are not necessarily peculiar to the South. Distinctions appear, however, as laws, rulings, and interpertations reflect the mores of the region.

Each state in the Southern region has a state board of education, created either by constitutional provision or legislative enactment, which has extensive influence on educational policy on both state and local levels. It has been said that state boards of education have more influence in some states on educational policy in the local school districts than the local school boards do. The duties and responsibilities of state boards are defined in the acts which create them. The boards' powers may be subsequently modified or redefined by the state legislatures or by constitutional revisions.

The powers of state boards go beyond those specifically set forth, however. As a rule, state boards of education have attained such prestige that their pronouncements carry weight irrespective of whether or not they are carrying out some mandate as to function. This means that their leadership in educational affairs is not narrowly limited by prescriptions of the scope of their responsibility. A state board may or may not take action with regard to an issue in education as it develops. A choice not to take action may be quite influential.

In a very real sense, the state board is the policy body for the state department of education, except as policy may have been prescribed specifically by the legislature. Much of the direction for the work of the state department of education is derived from acts of the state board. Unless the legislature itself chooses to exercise specific powers involved, the board may determine courses of study for the public schools, qualifications for teachers, choices of textbooks, standards of certification, salary schedules, and other important matters pertaining to the operation of the public school system. In some cases, the state board of education has control over public institutions of higher learning. In other states, this power may be limited to control over state colleges, with the state university having its own board of trustees.

It is evident that the control of state boards of education is an important matter, in view of the power they exercise over public schools. In Louisiana and Texas state board members are elected by popular vote and are, therefore, directly responsible to the people. In Florida and Mississippi state boards are entirely ex officio. In all the other states of the region members of state boards of education are appointed by the governor; the governor himself frequently serves as an ex officio member, as does the state superintendent of public instruction. As a rule, terms of office are staggered, so that at no one time can the state board of education be composed of entirely new membership. Boards in the Southern states vary in size from three to twenty-one members. Each board has a certain number of stated meetings per year, but special meetings may be called if they are thought to be necessary. State board members serve without salary, but they are given a per diem allowance for days in session. It may be of interest to note that 130 of the 408 state board members in the United States, or 32 per cent, are in the Southern states.

In assessing the place of state boards of education in the administration of public education, it should be borne in mind that the preponderant practice is for board members to be appointed by governors, although few have the opportunity to appoint entire new boards. Infrequent cases have come to public attention of a governor seeking to control the state board of education. The fact remains, however, that the prevailing method of selecting state board members makes them subject to exploitation for political purposes, should a governor desire to engage in exploitation.

As has been implied, state departments of education are agencies created by the states for the purpose of carrying out educational policies determined by state governments. They are, therefore, subject to the control of the state legislatures and the direction of the state boards of education. Their functions are defined by legislative enactments and board regulations, except as certain functions may be provided for in the state constitutions.

The establishment of the position of state superintendent of public schools preceded the creation of state departments of education. Various factors combined to bring state education agencies and their chief officers into existence. The rapid growth of public schools was, of course, a major factor. Even before the period of expansion that made public education a gigantic enterprise, the establishment of permanent school funds and the management of public school lands created administrative problems; there was the necessity to delegate to someone supervisory responsibilities for the funds and lands. Sometimes this individual, who was eventually to be called the state superintendent of public schools, was responsible for other functions of state government.

Tennessee was the first state in the South to establish the office of state superintendent of public schools. The law establishing this position was passed in 1836. The law created an ex officio state board of education to be composed of the state treasurer, the comptroller of the treasury, and the superintendent of public instruction. By joint vote of both branches of the Tennessee General Assembly, the superintendent was selected for a two-year term of office at an annual salary of $1,500. The law said that his responsibilities in regard to "that branch of his duties which relates to the common schools shall be, amongst other things, to prepare and submit an annual report to the legislature, containing a full and comprehensive statement of the amount and condition, together with plans for the improvement and management of the common school fund, and such a plan for the organization of the system of common schools as he may think advisable, and such other matters relating to his office and to common schools as he shall deem expedient to communicate." [1] It will be noted that in this case at least, the superintendent was given specific leadership functions.

By 1860 most of the Southern states had either established the position of state superintendent of schools or had designated some state official to carry out the duties of the office. Stability was lacking, however, as the position was often shifted from one state official to another, who simply had the additional duties of the new office added to those he already performed. In some states the office was abolished for a period of years, then re-established. Only Kentucky, Louisiana, and North Carolina have had continuing offices of state superintendent of public instruction since before the Civil War. In the other Southern states, organization of a permanent state educational office dates from the Reconstruction period.

The position of chief state school officer has by now assumed such professional stature that it requires men of superior ability and professional insight. Ten of the states in the region choose their chief state school officer by popular vote. In Virginia and Tennessee the superintendent is appointed by the governor, and the Arkansas chief state school officer is appointed by the state board of education. It is frequently assumed that the necessity of gaining office by popular election deters many able persons from aspiring to the state superintendency. Appointment by the governor has likewise been frowned upon because of the possibility of inviting political pressure upon the schools. In spite of the uncertainty of tenure indicated by these two methods of selecting a chief state school officer, the records show that these public officials frequently succeed themselves and a tenure of many years is not out of the ordinary. Alabama and Kentucky present exceptions, for the chief state school officers of those states are prohibited by law from succeeding themselves.

---

[1] *Public Acts Passed at the First Session of the Twenty-First General Assembly of the State of Tennessee, 1835–36*, pp. 110–114, as quoted by Edgar W. Knight, *Readings in Educational Administration* (New York: Henry Holt and Company, Inc., 1953), p. 72.

Whether or not tenure is synonymous with aggressive and forward looking leadership is another matter. The operational situation in which the chief state school officer must function is such that a premium is placed on men of political sagacity who understand people well and who are sensitive to issues as they develop and to alignments thus engendered. The resolution of these issues often falls to other state officials and the chief state school officer's influence in such cases is dependent upon his skill in gaining consideration by them of his professional knowledge. Fortunately, the Southern states have usually selected chief state school officers of high calibre, men who were sincerely devoted to public education and dedicated to its improvement. The gradual and continuous professionalization of the position has been one of the reasons that state departments of education have assumed increasing importance in the region.

As public school systems have grown and as functions of educational administration exercised from the level of state government have increased, it has been necessary to provide in each state a staff to assist the chief state school officer in the discharge of his responsibility. The number of professional personnel in departments of the Southern states in 1950 was 1,400. This number constitutes more than one-third of the professional personnel of state departments of education in the entire United States. Staffs of the various state departments in the South range in size from a low of approximately 25 to a high of slightly more than 200. Approximately 40 per cent of the total of 1,400 employed in 1950 were engaged in vocational rehabilitation and vocational education services, leaving only 60 per cent to carry on all other educational services from the state level.

A trend accompanying the growth in size of staffs has been the improvement of the professional qualifications required of department personnel. Higher standards have posed additional problems. Salary schedules, which are frequently lower than those for many administrative positions in local school systems, make it increasingly difficult to attract and retain persons with the level of competency required of state department personnel in the effective exercise of their leadership role. Primarily due to the general political atmosphere which surrounds state departments of education, it has never been possible to achieve the security with respect to tenure in state departments that exists in many local school systems, although the records show that many competent persons have spent almost a professional lifetime in a state department of education. They have frequently done so without more than temporary assurance of security in their positions.

The marked expansion in the function of state departments of education has accompanied the growth of a broader concept of what constitutes an adequate educational program. The addition of new services to public school programs has added new functions to state departments. The lunchroom movement has added both to the organizational structure of state departments and to the number of personnel. The provision of textbooks and other instructional materials by the state has affected departments in a similar manner. The increased portion of school revenues coming from state sources has likewise created new duties and positions in the departments.

In general, much of the work of departments with respect to these and other functions, too widely known to need listing here, has tended to be regulatory in nature. Exercise of state responsibility for education has expressed itself in the definition of minimum standards designed to ensure a reasonable amount of educational opportunity for all children. The administration of this principle has resulted in a heavy emphasis upon rather detailed and specific regulations and requirements for the purpose of protecting any school system from falling below the minimum standards. This has led state departments to exercise a somewhat static function which has served to standardize schools and further uniformity among the systems within a state. Control over equalization programs, where expenditures are contingent upon meeting prescriptions intended to ensure justice and prudence in the expenditure of funds, has been of particular significance in developing patterns of uniformity in educational practices within a state.

The prevailing practice of the state department of education is to discharge its functions through a staff organized into separate divisions, each charged with the specific responsibility for a given area of the school program. This makes it exceedingly difficult for the state department to exercise the kind of leadership that would reverse the emphasis on conformity and uniformity. Isolation of divisions within a department has been such that the entire staff often has not had opportunity to work together in a coordinated development of state department policies and programs. In practice, this has served to encourage non-coordination, overlapping, and the inevitable competition within departments which has sometimes resulted in the development of little kingdoms, or, expressed another way, departments of education within the department.

An original function of state departments, that of gathering, organizing, and presenting essential information on the states' school systems, still remains an important part of the work of state departments of education. According to a bulletin of the Southern States Work-Conference, "In a dynamic, democratic society, the people must be provided with adequate data before they can intelligently evaluate existing school programs and make or support sound decisions on educational policies. It is in this larger sense that state school reporting assumes its greatest significance." [2] This statement suggests that the information function may be even more important than was formerly assumed.

In recent years, most of the state departments of education in the South have made serious efforts to achieve a leadership role in education which goes beyond that implied in the general functions heretofore described. In this broadened conception of role, regulation becomes less important. The real role of the department staff becomes an educative one, in which staff members make themselves available as resource persons to local school systems in the development of improved programs of education. The basic concept involved in this transition seems to be that the state department of education staff can be most useful when it provides such assistance as it can to local school people in working out their own professional problems. It is clear that achievement of this role will place state departments of education in an even more strategic position in the future than they have enjoyed in the past.

THE LOCAL SCHOOL DISTRICT

Effective assurance that the state will not exercise its power over education in an arbitrary and authoritarian fashion has been provided through the establishment of local school systems, each with a grant of power from the state which gives to people in the district considerable freedom in the development of their school system. While this freedom has not always been utilized as widely as it might have been, it has, nevertheless, been a preventive of absolute domination from the state level. The major function of a local district is the carrying out of state policy with respect to education within the district. State policy has always left considerable leeway for the exercise of a great deal of local initiative in school affairs.

The predominant school district in the South is the county unit. Thus, its boundaries are coterminous with the boundaries of the major unit of civil government. The second most prevalent school unit in the South is the city school district. Its boundaries coincide with those of the city. This means of setting boundaries, characteristic of Southern school districts, limits their number; only 10.7 per cent of the school districts in the nation are found in the South, and more than

---

[2] Southern States Work-Conference on School Administrative Problems, "State Responsibility for the Organization and Administration of Education," Bulletin No. 1, 1942, p. 96.

three-fourths of these are in the states of Mississippi, Oklahoma, and Texas. The other ten states in the region contain less than 3 per cent of the nation's school districts.

The pattern of keeping the number of districts to a minimum has been characteristic of some of the Southern states for many years, and other states have been moving in that direction. The total number of districts in the region was reduced from 20,700 in 1940 to 6,958 by 1953, a decrease of two-thirds. The greatest changes occurred in four states: Arkansas, which reduced its districts from 2,920 to 421; South Carolina, where the reduction was from 1,738 to 103; Texas, where 2,000 districts supplanted 6,540; and Oklahoma, which reduced its districts from 4,644 to 1,888. In contrast to these states, Florida has only 67 school districts, Louisiana 67, and Alabama 107.

The county unit has been vigorously supported and defended in some of the Southern states for decades. Alabama, after a brief and unsuccessful effort to establish school systems along township lines, established a county system with county superintendents in 1866. The first state superintendent of schools in Alabama said in his annual report: "The creation of the office of County Superintendent was a change of vital importance, . . .

"To systematize and facilitate the work of the County Superintendents, an account book was prepared, . . . so arranged and spaced, that if properly kept, it would contain a complete history, statistical and financial, of the county schools running through a series of years.

"The County Superintendents entered into their duties with energy and enthusiasm." [3]

In 1896, the superintendent of the Richmond County, Georgia, schools presented a forceful argument in defense of the county unit. He said, "If one system of schools can be made to extend over a whole county, including city and villages, the organization will be upon the basis of territory. By this means the entire country can after a while be brought under uniform organization. . . . A proper policy is to induce the people hereafter to organize by area, rather than by spots. The effect of this will be to give to the rural child the same school advantage as to the city child, and there is every reason in equity and good sense why these advantages should be the same." [4]

The structure of local school districts is the same for all states. Each has a board of education and a superintendent of schools. Powers granted the board and the superintendent vary from state to state but,

---

[3] William F. Perry, "The Genesis of Public Education in Alabama," in *Transactions of the Alabama Historical Society*, II, as quoted by Knight, *op. cit.*, 102–103.

[4] *Proceedings*, The National Educational Association, 1896, as quoted by Knight, *ibid.*, p. 114.

in any case, they are spelled out in legislative provisions which sometimes supplement more general constitutional stipulations. Although these powers can be changed and are from time to time, a reasonable degree of stability has been provided in all states for local school districts and their administration.

Within limits set by the state, the local board of education sets policies for the local school system, approves the school budget, the selection of teachers, the appointment of bus drivers and other school personnel, and in general represents the public in school matters. The superintendent's job is to carry out the policies of the board and to serve a general management function in the administration, organization, coordination, and supervision of local schools. It is evident that the superintendent is a very important individual and his opportunities for leadership are extensive. His influence is due in large measure to his initiative, energy, and vision rather than official status. In like manner, the board of education is an extremely important group on the local educational scene. Its success depends on the quality of individual board members, their patterns of operation, and the assistance provided them by the superintendent of schools.

Methods of selecting members of local boards of education vary from state to state and even within states. In Alabama they are chosen by popular vote in county-wide elections. They are appointed by the county grand jury in Georgia. The state legislature appoints them in North Carolina after they have been nominated in party primaries, while in South Carolina they are appointed by the governor in some counties and elected by popular vote in others. In Tennessee they are appointed by the county court or elected by popular vote, depending upon the county law. Virginia has the most indirect method of any state: its local school board members are appointed by a school trustee electoral board which in turn is appointed by the judge of the circuit court. Except for the method of popular election, the provisions for selecting members of local boards of education would seem to be fairly consistent with the earlier patterns of local government in the South, which clearly reflected the class system of the region.

More uniformity is to be found in the methods of selecting board members of city school systems; selection by popular vote or appointment by the city council are the predominant methods.

Methods of selecting the county superintendent are as varied as those employed in selecting members of county boards. The selection of county or district suprintendents by popular vote in party primaries and general elections is the most general method used in Florida, Georgia, Mississippi, Oklahoma, South Carolina, Texas, Alabama, and Tennessee. Exceptions exist, however, within almost every state. For example, in Tennessee almost half of the county superintendents are appointed by the county court, while the rest obtain office by popular election. In Louisiana and West Virginia, superintendents of county school systems are appointed by the county boards of education. As a general rule, city superintendents are appointed by city school boards in all the states.

Divided authority, which often results when the superintendent is elected independently of the board, has been a handicap to the development of unified administrative programs. Election of the county superintendent by popular vote has frequently plunged the office into a type of politics not altogether wholesome to the best interests of public education. The office of the county superintendent is frequently located in the center of the political life of the county, the county seat and county courthouse, and the superintendent is at times unfortunately subjected to political pressures in dealing with administrative problems such as those related to school construction and maintenance, school personnel, and the purchase of supplies. It has been difficult in states where such conditions exist to make of the county superintendency a stable position of leadership for good schools, regardless of the fact that many able county superintendents are doing splendid work despite these conditions. The county superintendency in such a situation is, perhaps, the most political of all administrative positions in public education.

Schools within large districts are organized into attendance areas or centers. Each center is under the direct administration of a principal, who, in a real sense, represents the superintendent. His general functions are to administer the affairs of the local school in accordance with the policies of the school district. He may or may not have a voice in the selection of teachers, depending upon how his superintendent exercises this particular function. Making the school budget is generally not a part of the principal's responsibility, although some superintendents enlist the cooperation of principals in preparing the county-wide budget. In his duties as general administrative and supervisory leader of the local school system, the principal comes in contact with the teachers on a day-to-day basis. His effectiveness is determined in large measure by how well he can encourage and stimulate teachers to put forth their best efforts.

The foregoing delineation of duties suggests that, in spite of considerable responsibility for education residing in the local school district, the citizen may be somewhat removed from his schools. As a matter of fact, the trend in recent years has been in the direction of a widening gap between the schools and the public. A result is that the public has seemed to look more and more to the state for the solution of local educational problems, while leaving relationships and planning in the hands of local school authorities. This divergence has been encouraged by the way many superintendents have regarded the public and by the behavior of many teachers whose attitudes toward laymen have not been such as to encourage growth of common interests and understanding. Fortunately, there are some signs that this trend is being reversed, and there are more and more instances in which an important place is found for the layman in the study of educational problems and in the development of more adequate educational offerings for the local community.

Attitudes of local boards of education vary greatly in respect to relations between schools and the public. The patterns of operation which sometime seem to have been given considerable emphasis have made boards of education appear overly possessive of the schools, instead of reflecting the principle that board members represent the public and act for it in school affairs. Such attitudes appear to be waning markedly at present.

THE ORGANIZATION AND ADMINISTRATION
OF EDUCATION FOR NEGROES

Mandatory constitutional provisions for separate schools for Negroes in the Southern states have posed difficult and complex problems of organization and administration. Such provisions have operated to deny Negroes school systems comparable to those provided for white children. This was hardly surprising, as the previous chapter pointed out, in a region where the prevailing opinion was that Negroes were entitled to little or no education and when it was difficult to obtain sufficient funds to operate schools for white children.

The development of separate school systems for Negroes in the several states led to some awkward and unusual arrangements in organizing and administering public schools. One method used in some states to keep the schools entirely separate has already been described; the method was to provide money for white schools from taxes paid by white persons, and money for Negro schools from taxes paid by Negroes. Another method was to draw district lines so as to include only white or Negro residents. This was successful in those states where school districts were small and little county or state supervision was available. By 1952 the only state in which such districts still existed was Mississippi. In Oklahoma a unique plan of majority and minority districts was developed. Under this system, a separate school of the race which had a majority of the population in a local district within the county secured its money from and was controlled by the local district, while the minority race received its school support from county funds. The purpose of such districting was to give white children the advantage of tax funds in local districts where financial resources were more substantial than they were for the county as a whole.

Negro school districts, with the single exception noted, have passed out of the picture. The same district, the same board of education, and the same superintendent serve both Negro and white schools. This arrangement has ruled out the participation of the Negro in school administration and supervision on the district level with the exception of the Jeanes' teacher. With administrative controls firmly in the hands of white persons, white and Negro schools have inevitably reflected the relative status of the two races in the Southern social structure.

Under prevailing class distinctions, it is to be expected that Negro attendance centers would be administered by Negro principals. Their functions are the same as those of principals of white schools. It also follows that segregated schools have ruled out mixed faculties; Negro schools are staffed by Negro teachers just as white schools have all-white faculties. Due to limitations in vocational opportunities available to Negroes, Negro principals and teachers are accorded higher status in the Negro community than white principals and teachers are in their community.

As was pointed out in the chapter developing the historical perspective of public education in the region, the general apathy toward Negro education has been such that, almost without exception, advances have come about through the influence of forces from outside the South. As Negro schools were established and grew in number and size, and as it became increasingly evident that the general administrative procedure was to pay little attention to Negro schools and their problems, various Northern philanthropies came to the assistance of Negro schools. The Jeanes' supervisors, made possible by philanthropic support, became the first administrative assistants for Negro schools on a general basis in the Southern states.

The concept of responsibility of state departments of education for the organization and administration of Negro schools has been such that departments of Negro education have been developed; these departments have sole responsibility for Negro education in the total state programs. The genesis and development of this phase of administration were similar to other efforts to assist Negroes with their educational needs; that is, support initially and for some time came from outside the South. Establishment of the office of state agent for Negro education through the use of funds provided by philanthropic foundations has been described.

The earlier duties of state agents dealt primarily with the problems of meeting the building and equipment needs of Negro schools. Their work soon expanded into general supervisory services to Negro education. In some states the state agent had almost complete responsibility for all aspects of Negro education which were of concern to the state department of education. This responsibility extended to higher education as well.

At first, the agents encountered indifference and even some hostility toward the expansion of Negro schools, but they worked zealously and effectively. Through long tenure and the excellent quality of their work, they became respected and important members of their state education agency staffs.

Without exception, state agents in charge of Negro education have been white men. This may be due in part to recognition of the possibility that a Negro in this position would not be able to exert as much influence as a white person. Negroes have served, however, as assistant state agents in a number of states. By 1952, there were some Negro professional educators employed in all except one of the state departments of education in the region. The work of state agents and the divisions of Negro education are now supported from tax funds. It goes without saying that, in the long struggle to give Negroes better educational opportunities in the South, divisions of Negro education have played an important role.

Negro education in the South has suffered because the Negro himself has lacked political power and could not represent his cause on educational policy-making bodies. This situation is gradually improving because the Negro is increasingly gaining freedom to exercise his vote. As late as 1940 there were no Negroes on school boards in any of the thirteen Southern states except Oklahoma. By 1953, there were Negroes on local school boards in at least seven of the Southern states. This representation was generally to be found in urban rather than rural areas, particularly in the larger cities, among them Atlanta, Nashville, and Richmond. In 1953, Kentucky and North Carolina each had a Negro member of the state board of education.

The effects of these changes are yet to be assessed. It seems reasonable to assume that such spokesmen for the minority race will be able to represent its cause with a little more freedom than would have been possible in the past; heretofore, Negroes in positions of responsibility in public education have been under greater compulsion to conform to prevailing beliefs and attitudes of the majority race because the positions they held were controlled by this group.

SUMMARY

The purpose of this chapter was to present and analyze such information on the organization, administration, and control of education in the Southern region as was deemed relevant to an adequate understanding of the crisis in education which was brought on by the Supreme Court decision on segregation.

More control of public education in the Southern region rests at the level of state government than is true in other regions of the United States. State departments of education tend to be larger and have more power in the South than is generally the case elsewhere in the nation. The resolution of issues through the use of state authority is, therefore, facilitated by existing patterns of organization and administration. Public administration policies of the region, traditionally under control of social and economic groups not overly favorable to public education, have profoundly influenced educational policy in the South. This control is now gradually shifting to a more universal base.

The local school district in the South is larger than it is in other regions. The county and city units which predominate are conveniently structured administratively in that they conform to the boundaries of existing units of civil government. The trend toward larger districts continues. Fewer districts foster closer relations with state agencies and are effective in promoting and carrying out unified state policy. Larger districts also make possible more effective administration and supervision because they usually have larger and more competent staffs than are possible in a multitude of small districts.

Convenience and ease in the administration of a state school system inherent in this arrangement has not been without its disadvantages. Removal of much control of education from the local community to the county and state has been accompanied by strong reliance on these larger governmental units to settle educational issues and problems without responsibility being assumed by the local community. This trend seems to have reached its maximum, and signs that it is breaking down are in evidence. Although the division of power between local districts and the state has been clear-cut, the way in which the state has performed its educational functions has tended to minimize emphasis on local initiative. Regulations from the state have played a dominant role and have resulted in some disposition to accept minimum requirements as being the maximum to be achieved.

Strong emphasis on a new leadership role for state departments of education is in evidence. The essence of this concept is that the state is a helping agency and not a directing one. Assistance is thus directed toward helping appropriate persons within the school district to achieve greater capacity for effective performance rather than toward solving their educational problems for them. Exponents of this belief insist that growth on the part of those responsible for local school systems can be assured through no other role of a state department of education. This concept, while nowhere completely expressed in practice, is intriguing and challenging to both state department staffs and local administrative officials. The present crisis in education offers a good test of the new leadership role.

Purely political influences, which have traditionally impinged upon schools from state, county, and city levels, still exist; but the professionalization of school administration and the emphasis on the new role of leadership appear to offer effective counterforces to the undesirable aspects of such influences.

Larger attendance centers continue to be developed. The decrease in the number of schools simplifies and streamlines administration and supervision. The current emphasis on twelve-grade centers is an additional factor of importance. Current administrative concerns for a unified twelve-year program is perhaps a normal development of larger twelve-grade attendance centers. These developments present challenging problems for creative leadership on the part of both state and local school officials.

The organization and administration of education have progressed much more slowly for Negro than for white schools. Credit for impetus leading to progress in Negro schools must be given largely to philanthropic agencies. The separate school doctrine has not resulted in the development of dual school districts except on an experimental basis. They have been abandoned in all states except Mississippi. In general, the Negro has had little or no part in either the determination or execution of educational policy, except as permitted by the system of separate Negro schools administered by Negro principals. The systems of organization and administration have truly reflected the traditional place of the Negro in the South. He has been able to speak for himself only through the courts.

Creation of the Jeanes' teaching positions was the first region-wide effort to provide supervisory leadership to Negro teachers. The subsidization of state agents, who were responsible for promoting Negro education, led to the development of divisions or departments of Negro education in the state departments. Under able and dedicated leadership, these divisions have worked patiently and tirelessly for a better educational system for Negroes.

The general design of public school structure and administration is firmly established in the various states of the region and it is supported by experience and tradition. Even so, frequent modifications in specifics occur from time to time, including basic changes in local district organization. The adaptability of existing structures and administrative practices to various conditions and aims has been demonstrated over and over. Subsequent chapters will show that substantial improvement in Negro schools has been made within recent years through the present systems of organization, administration, and control. Whether even more far-reaching and fundamental revisions are to be made in the face of present challenges remains to be seen.

The Public Schools—
Problems and Progress

FOUR

School-Age Population, Public School Enrollment, and Attendance

The concept that public education is an instrument of public policy has been generally accepted by the American people for many years now. It has long been expressed in common adherence to the principle that all children should receive an education and that it is the responsibility of the separate states to provide necessary school systems to assure achievement of this objective.

The formidable task of providing a satisfactory education for all children and youth requires a very considerable amount of information about the population which is to be educated in the public schools. It is not only necessary to know how many should be in school and where they are located but at what grade levels they fall. Since it has never been possible to enroll every eligible child in school, the total school enrollment, the distribution of those enrolled in the grades, and the relationships of these factors to the total school population are subject to serious inquiry. Similarly, in view of the fact that a variety of reasons other than health factors make perfect attendance at school of all who are enrolled an impossibility, comparisons of attendance and enrollment figures raise questions that cannot be lightly set aside.

In this chapter data which bear on these factors are presented and analyzed. Problems posed are complicated tremendously by the dual school systems of the region which necessitate comparisons by races. The integration problem now faced by the region because of the Supreme Court decision on segregation further complicates educational planning and makes even more important a consideration of the population that has a right to an education in the public schools of the South.

Statistics on elements basic to the school program are of primary importance in the determination of educational policy and the formation of plans for its execution. Forward-looking policy requires the collection and analysis of such data as will make possible proper school financing. Financial planning that fails to take into account trends in population, enrollment, and attendance in such a way that the orderly development and progress of school systems is assured is of limited value. A state cannot afford to wait until children are ready to go to school to make provisions for housing needs, the employment of teachers, and the purchase and distribution of materials of instruction.

Table 1 presents gross statistics for the Southern region on school population, enrollment, and attendance by decades from 1900 through 1940. In 1940 the total school-age population had increased 41.3

TABLE 1

SCHOOL-AGE POPULATION, AND PUBLIC SCHOOL ENROLLMENT AND
ATTENDANCE IN THE SOUTH (THIRTEEN STATES)

	1900	1910	Years 1920	1930	1940	Per Cent Change 1900–1940
School Population						
White	4,069,175	4,992,161	5,944,488	6,677,836	6,614,734	62.6
Negro	2,349,968	2,513,751	2,529,455	2,538,475	2,454,198	4.4
Total	6,419,143	7,505,912	8,473,943	9,216,311	9,068,932	41.3
6–13						
White	2,856,497	3,423,713	4,151,588	4,563,015	4,351,514	52.3
Negro	1,648,095	1,734,471	1,747,834	1,710,528	1,639,926	− 0.5
Total	4,504,592	5,158,184	5,899,422	6,273,543	5,991,440	33.0
14–17						
White	1,212,678	1,568,448	1,792,900	2,114,821	2,263,220	86.6
Negro	701,873	779,280	781,621	827,947	814,272	16.0
Total	1,914,551	2,347,728	2,574,521	2,942,768	3,077,492	60.7
School Enrollment						
White	3,108,700	4,149,148	5,184,380	6,109,860	6,234,508	100.6
Negro	1,436,663	1,651,652	1,915,258	2,133,600	2,251,169	56.7
Total	4,545,363	5,800,800	7,099,638	8,243,460	8,485,677	86.7
Elementary						
White	3,055,981	4,028,404	4,901,284	5,145,340	4,788,186	56.7
Negro	1,433,251	1,646,938	1,903,545	2,038,438	2,023,092	41.2
Total	4,489,232	5,675,342	6,804,829	7,183,778	6,811,278	51.7
Secondary						
White	52,719	120,744	283,096	964,520	1,446,322	2643.5
Negro	3,412	4,714	11,713	95,162	228,077	6584.6
Total	56,131	125,458	294,809	1,059,682	1,674,399	2883.0
Attendance						
White	2,096,123	2,716,031	3,653,991	4,771,417	5,221,782	149.1
Negro	895,301	1,037,043	1,284,207	1,556,735	1,800,351	101.1
Total	2,991,424	3,753,074	4,938,198	6,328,152	7,022,133	134.7

per cent over that of 1900.[1] The 1930 school-age population was slightly larger than that of 1940. During the same decade there was a gain of 9.6 per cent in total population for the region. The over-all gain in school-age population in the forty-year period was 62.6 per cent in the number of white children but only 4.4 per cent in the number of Negro children. Reasons for this tremendous difference will be analyzed in due course.

The distribution of school-age population according to the ages which correspond most closely to elementary and secondary school groupings shows important variations. An increase of 33 per cent in the 6-13 age group compared to the 60.7 per cent increase in the 14-17 age group suggests an important rearrangement in the age patterns of the total population. For example, the 1940 statistics reveal the severe decline in the birth rate during the depression of the thirties which was not to be felt in the secondary schools until later, while the figures for the 14-17 age group reflect birth rates of the twenties. Of the increase in the 6-13 age group, 52.3 per cent was among white children; there was a decrease of 0.5 per cent in the number of Negro children. Relatively little change occurred in the Negro group during the entire four decades, the peak coming in 1920 when there were approximately 100,000 more in the group than in 1900 and slightly more than 100,000 in excess of the number in 1940. The peak in the number of white children in this age group was reached in 1930. In the 14 to 17 age group there was a gain of 86.6 per cent in the number of white children compared to a gain of 16 per cent of Negro children.

The tremendous task of merely keeping abreast of school enrollment in terms of providing minimum school facilities and offerings, to say nothing of efforts to develop better educational programs, is dramatically reflected by the school enrollment section of Table 1. Nearly 4,000,000 more children were enrolled in the public schools of the South in 1940 than in 1900. This increase occurred at the rate of more than 1,000,000 each decade until 1940. The increase in enrollment of white children was slightly in excess of 100 per cent, while the increase in enrollment of Negro children was 56.7 per cent. Broken into the two grade groups,[2] the increase in enrollment of white children in elementary grades was 56.7 per cent, while the comparable figure for Negroes was 41.2 per cent, making a total gain of 51.7 per

---

[1] The definition of school-age population used here is all children between ages 6 and 17, inclusive. This definition rests upon an assumption most common in twelve-year school programs, that is, children will enter the first grade at age 6 and, progressing a grade each year, graduate at 17.

[2] Two methods are commonly used in analyses of grade distribution. One method is to divide public school enrollment into elementary and secondary, while another is to make a grade division such as grades 1–8 and grades 9–12. Neither method is

cent. The figures on the secondary grades showed an increase of 2643.5 per cent for white children compared to a gain of 6584.6 per cent for Negro children; the percentage gain for both groups combined was 2883.0. The enormous increase in this grade group clearly reflects the trend toward universal secondary education; the trend toward universal elementary education was well-advanced at the beginning of the twentieth century.

While society's potential educational load is defined by the school population, the actual load from the point of view of the school program is reflected more accurately by attendance figures, as measured by the average number of students present each day of school, than by either school enrollment or school population. As would be expected during an era of economic expansion and continued emphasis on the importance of public education, attendance gains have outstripped both population and enrollment increases. The extent of the gains is nonetheless striking. By 1940 attendance was 134.7 per cent greater than it was in 1900. The gain in attendance of white children was almost 150 per cent, while for Negro children it was 101.1 per cent. Compared to the negligible gain in Negro school population of 4.4 per

---

entirely satisfactory because of changes in the number of grades in the public schools and differing definitions of elementary and secondary grades among the states.

In this study a combination of both methods is used. The upper four grades, regardless of definition of elementary and secondary grades prevailing in the state, are counted as secondary and the grades below these are counted as elementary. This gives groupings which are more commonly accepted than any others. However, this method will give an additional grade in elementary schools for the latter years in those states which have changed from an eleven-grade to a twelve-grade system. Georgia, Louisiana, North Carolina, South Carolina, Texas, and Virginia have since 1940 made this transition. Thus, in these states elementary enrollment would normally show increases after the addition of the extra elementary grade. On this basis a case might be made for the grade division method for analytic purposes, but more serious objections could be raised. The addition of a grade to grades 9–12 in those states which have changed to a twelve–grade program would produce proportionately larger distortions of the increases in grades 9–12 than the addition of a grade to the elementary school by the former method. Since neither method is perfect, the one which produced the least distortion was used — elementary and secondary division.

The addition of a grade to the public schools in any state represents an increased educational load for that state. The fact that all Southern states had a twelve year program by 1952 and some were beginning to add another grade, kindergarten, is in itself an indication of the increased acceptance of public education in the South.

Another measure used in this study, while very useful, has certain limitations and should be explained. This is the percentage of school-age population groupings enrolled in elementary and secondary school. On the assumptions of an entrance age of six years and normal progress, elementary enrollment would come from the age group 6–13, while secondary enrollment would come from the age group 14–17. Retardation, nonenrollment of school-age children, enrollment of under- and overschool-age children, and changes in the number of grades in the public schools discussed above are distorting factors. Despite these shortcomings, it is a useful method of showing relationships of elementary and secondary enrollment to school-age population.

cent during the forty years, the increase in attendance is an extremely important figure: it reflects, among other things, the South's effort to include the Negro in its definition of educational responsibilities.

Regional figures, while important, are not used as the basis for determining policy. Educational policy is the concern of each individual state. Certainly, general regional trends should be taken into account in planning within a state for they help account for whatever is happening in the state. It is nonetheless necessary to engage in a more specific analysis of the regional data in terms of state figures in order to further understanding of this body of information; at the same time, breakdowns within states are necessary because state figures obscure variations which have to be taken into account in the determination of educational policy by a particular state. A more intensive analysis of data, beginning with 1940, follows.

THE SCHOOL-AGE POPULATION

A ten-year period of relative stability in the number of children of school age was coming to an end in 1950, when the increase in birth rates during the last years of World War II was beginning to be felt. Stability in region-wide figures for this decade, however, fails to show the pronounced shifts among states and within states. Alabama, Arkansas, Georgia, Kentucky, Mississippi, North Carolina, and Oklahoma lost in total school population, the range being from 0.7 per cent in North Carolina and Georgia to 17.3 per cent in Oklahoma. The

TABLE 2

SCHOOL-AGE POPULATION IN THE SOUTHERN STATES

State	*1939–40*	*1949–50*	*Per Cent Change 1940–1950*
Alabama	737,036	716,083	− 2.9
Arkansas	489,436	440,733	−10.0
Florida	393,720	490,561	24.6
Georgia	771,880	766,775	− 0.7
Kentucky	697,298	653,576	− 6.3
Louisiana	569,278	579,697	1.8
Mississippi	567,942	525,479	− 7.5
North Carolina	947,041	940,065	− 0.7
Oklahoma	562,218	465,248	−17.3
South Carolina	517,331	524,129	1.3
Tennessee	697,680	704,638	1.0
Texas	1,480,208	1,538,442	3.9
Virginia	637,864	667,563	4.7
TOTAL	9,068,932	9,012,989	− 0.6

remaining states, Florida, Louisiana, South Carolina, Tennessee, Texas, and Virginia, had increases in their total school population ranging from 1 per cent in Tennesssee to 24.6 per cent in Florida. The over-all change in the region was a decline of 0.6 per cent.

The breakdown by states is shown in Table 2. It is evident that the potential educational load of each state was shifting, the extremes being illustrated by Florida, which had 96,841 more children to educate in 1950 than in 1940, and Oklahoma, which had 96,870 fewer children. Fluctuations in birth rates, such as occurred during the Depression and the years following World War II, produced shifts in high and low numbers of children in different age groupings who were to be educated at certain future dates. This is illustrated by the fact that late war and post-war birth increases were felt in the lower grades of the elementary schools beginning with the early fifties. These peak numbers are moving through the grades one year at a time, each group to be in school for a period of twelve years.

Reflecting the birth rate of the war years, the 6-13 age group increased from 5,991,440 in 1940 to 6,260,757 in 1950, a gain of 4.5 per cent. This age group, which normally attends elementary school, represented 66.1 per cent of the total school population in 1940 and 69.5 per cent in 1950. The 14-17 age group, which was born during the low birth rate period of depression days and would normally not reach the secondary grades until the forties, decreased from 3,077,492 to 2,752,232, a reduction of 10.6 per cent. Such shifts in age groups present different kinds of educational problems, an increase in potential load for the lower grades and a decrease for secondary grades. The direction and extent of change in each of the Southern states and in each age group are presented in Table 3.

Only Arkansas, Kentucky, Mississippi, and Oklahoma, each of which had a large decrease in total school population, showed losses during the ten-year span in the 6-13 age group. The other nine states showed gains ranging from 0.4 per cent in Alabama to 33.7 per cent in Florida. On the other hand, every state, with the exception of Florida, had a decrease in the age group 14 through 17, ranging from 7.8 per cent in Texas to 24.8 per cent in Oklahoma. Florida showed an increase of 7.1 per cent.

Statistics for state totals do not show regional and state population shifts among rural, rural-urban, and metropolitan areas.[3] These shifts are of great magnitude and significance. Rural and rural-urban counties suffered a considerable decline in total school-age population. The decrease included both age groups, although the largest decrease was in the 14-17 age group. Counties in the metropolitan classification

---

[3] See Appendix A.

TABLE 3

SCHOOL-AGE POPULATION BY AGE GROUPS IN THE SOUTHERN STATES

State	1939–40	1949–50	Per Cent Change 1940–1950
Alabama			
6–13	493,959	495,885	0.4
14–17	243,077	220,198	− 9.4
Arkansas			
6–13	323,167	305,045	− 5.6
14–17	166,269	135,688	−18.4
Florida			
6–13	259,069	346,327	33.7
14–17	134,651	144,234	7.1
Georgia			
6–13	513,309	532,343	3.7
14–17	258,571	234,432	− 9.3
Kentucky			
6–13	461,141	451,070	− 2.2
14–17	236,157	202,506	−14.3
Louisiana			
6–13	376,701	409,173	8.6
14–17	192,577	170,524	−11.5
Mississippi			
6–13	381,019	365,537	− 4.1
14–17	186,923	159,942	−14.4
North Carolina			
6–13	624,010	646,805	3.7
14–17	323,031	293,260	− 9.2
Oklahoma			
6–13	367,146	318,543	−13.2
14–17	195,072	146,705	−24.8
South Carolina			
6–13	341,595	365,440	7.0
14–17	175,736	158,689	− 9.7
Tennessee			
6–13	460,603	487,322	5.8
14–17	237,077	217,316	− 8.3
Texas			
6–13	972,412	1,070,329	10.1
14–17	507,796	468,113	− 7.8
Virginia			
6–13	417,309	466,938	11.9
14–17	220,555	200,625	− 9.0
TOTAL			
6–13	5,991,440	6,260,757	4.5
14–17	3,077,492	2,752,232	−10.6

TABLE 4

WHITE AND NEGRO SCHOOL–AGE POPULATION IN THE SOUTHERN STATES

State	1939–40	1949–50	Per Cent Change 1940–1950
Alabama			
White	469,085	462,471	− 1.4
Negro	267,951	253,612	− 5.4
Arkansas			
White	367,756	334,827	− 9.0
Negro	121,680	105,906	−13.0
Florida			
White	279,941	366,428	30.9
Negro	113,779	124,133	9.1
Georgia			
White	484,432	497,463	2.7
Negro	287,448	269,312	− 6.3
Kentucky			
White	652,254	614,615	− 5.8
Negro	45,044	38,961	−13.5
Louisiana			
White	354,419	363,122	2.5
Negro	214,859	216,575	0.8
Mississippi			
White	275,419	258,888	− 6.0
Negro	292,523	266,591	− 8.9
North Carolina			
White	659,336	653,635	− 0.9
Negro	287,705	286,430	− 0.5
Oklahoma			
White	501,394	416,950	−16.9
Negro	60,824	48,298	−20.6
South Carolina			
White	272,781	284,735	4.4
Negro	244,550	239,394	− 2.1
Tennessee			
White	582,029	592,414	1.8
Negro	115,651	112,224	− 3.0
Texas			
White	1,252,850	1,325,316	5.8
Negro	227,358	213,126	− 6.3
Virginia			
White	463,038	496,373	7.2
Negro	174,826	171,190	− 2.1
TOTAL			
White	6,614,734	6,667,237	0.8
Negro	2,454,198	2,345,752	− 4.4

had such large increases in the 6-13 age group (27.7 per cent) that a decrease in the 14-17 age group was more than offset; the total school-age population showed a gain of 17.7 per cent.

During the decade, regional decreases occurred in the 14-17 age group for both whites and Negroes, but Negroes showed the largest percentage decrease. Increases in the white 6-13 age group were large enough to offset the decreases in the 14-17 age group and produce a gain in the total white school-age population of 0.8 per cent. Both Negro age groups decreased, the total decline being 4.4 per cent for the ten-year period.

Trends in white and Negro school-age population totals by states are reported in Table 4. As would be expected, the states show considerable variations in rates of change. The six states which had gains in total school-age population—Florida, Louisiana, South Carolina, Tennessee, Texas, and Virginia—showed increases in white school-age population. Georgia also had an increase in white school-age population, although it had a slight decrease in total school-age population. The other six states had decreases. Only Florida and Louisiana showed increases in Negro school-age population, all other states evidencing declines. The range was from a loss of 0.5 per cent in North Carolina to a loss of 20.6 per cent in Oklahoma. In the states where school-age population decreased for both races, the Negro decreases were by larger percentages than the white.

A breakdown of the totals into age groups is revealing. The white age group 6 through 13 decreased in four states—Arkansas, Kentucky, Mississippi, and Oklahoma—which were losing total school-age population. This age group increased in the nine other states. Negro population in this age group gained in Florida, Louisiana, South Carolina, Tennessee, Virginia, and North Carolina, and lost in the other seven states. All of the Southern states except Florida showed a loss in the white age group 14 through 17, and all thirteen lost in Negro population of this age group. Exact figures for each state and for each age group are shown in Table 5.

Changes in the three county population classifications were in the same direction for both white and Negro children. Thus, white and Negro school-age population decreased in rural and rural-urban counties and increased in metropolitan counties. The greatest decline was for rural white children, and the largest increase was for metropolitan white children. Both age groupings for each of the races decreased in rural and rural-urban counties; small decreases for whites and Negroes in the 14-17 age group in metropolitan counties were offset by large gains in the 6-13 age group. The complete analysis is shown in Table 6.

TABLE 5

WHITE AND NEGRO SCHOOL-AGE POPULATION BY AGE GROUPS
IN THE SOUTHERN STATES

State	Ages 6–13			Ages 14–17		
	1939–40	1949–50	Per Cent Change 1940–50	1939–40	1949–50	Per Cent Change 1940–50
Alabama						
White	311,957	320,179	2.6	157,128	142,292	− 9.5
Negro	182,002	175,706	− 3.5	85,949	77,906	− 9.4
Arkansas						
White	241,688	231,362	− 4.3	126,068	103,465	−17.9
Negro	81,479	73,683	− 9.6	40,201	32,223	−19.9
Florida						
White	183,688	259,502	41.3	96,253	106,926	11.1
Negro	75,381	86,825	15.2	38,398	37,308	− 2.8
Georgia						
White	319,695	345,216	8.0	164,737	152,247	− 7.6
Negro	193,614	187,127	− 3.4	93,834	82,185	−12.4
Kentucky						
White	432,064	424,659	− 1.7	220,190	189,956	−13.7
Negro	29,077	26,411	− 9.2	15,967	12,550	−21.4
Louisiana						
White	232,422	256,215	10.2	121,997	106,907	−12.4
Negro	144,279	152,958	6.0	70,580	63,617	− 9.9
Mississippi						
White	182,801	178,391	− 2.4	92,618	80,497	−13.1
Negro	198,218	187,146	− 5.6	94,305	79,445	−15.8
North Carolina						
White	433,133	447,788	3.4	226,203	205,847	− 9.0
Negro	190,877	199,017	4.3	96,828	87,413	− 9.7
Oklahoma						
White	327,087	285,510	−12.7	174,307	131,440	−24.6
Negro	40,059	33,033	−17.5	20,765	15,265	−26.5
South Carolina						
White	178,060	196,594	10.4	94,721	88,141	− 7.0
Negro	163,535	168,846	3.2	81,015	70,548	−12.9
Tennessee						
White	384,787	410,078	6.6	197,242	182,336	− 7.6
Negro	75,816	77,244	1.9	39,835	34,980	−12.2
Texas						
White	821,839	923,775	12.4	431,011	401,541	− 6.8
Negro	150,573	146,554	− 2.7	76,785	66,572	−13.3
Virginia						
White	302,293	348,226	15.2	160,745	148,147	− 7.8
Negro	115,016	118,712	3.2	59,810	52,478	−12.3
TOTAL						
White	4,351,514	4,627,495	6.3	2,263,220	2,039,742	− 9.9
Negro	1,639,926	1,633,262	− 0.4	814,272	712,490	−12.5

TABLE 6

CHANGES IN WHITE AND NEGRO SCHOOL-AGE POPULATION IN SAMPLE RURAL
AND RURAL-URBAN COUNTIES, AND IN METROPOLITAN COUNTIES
OF THIRTEEN SOUTHERN STATES

County Classification		Per Cent Change in Age Groups 1940 to 1950		
		6–17	6–13	14–17
Rural	White	−10.8	− 7.5	−17.3
	Negro	− 5.5	− 2.0	−13.0
Rural-Urban	White	− 7.5	− 3.4	−15.3
	Negro	− 9.6	− 5.2	−18.4
Metropolitan	White	20.9	32.3	− 0.1
	Negro	9.5	16.1	− 3.2

PUBLIC SCHOOL ENROLLMENT

Differences in the phenomena of school population gain and school enrollment gain are shown by the fact that *between 1900 and 1940 there was an increase of 2,649,789 in the school-age population while at the same time there was a gain of 3,945,314 in school enrollment.* The excess in enrollment gain over population gain of 1,290,525 is an extremely important figure in understanding the extent of achievement toward the goal of universal public education.

The trend toward a larger proportion of school-age population being enrolled in school is further emphasized by the fact that in 1900 public school enrollment was 70.8 per cent of the school-age population, while in 1940 actual enrollment was 93.6 per cent. While very substantial gains were made in total public school enrollment from the beginning of the twentieth century, there were also important shifts in the distribution of pupils among the grades. The development and acceptance of public secondary schools during this period is well illustrated by enrollment statistics. Elementary school enrollment increased from 1900 to 1940 by one-half, but during the same period *secondary school enrollment increased nearly thirty times.* In each of the first three decades of the century enrollment in secondary grades more than doubled, and the increase continued from 1930 to 1940, although at a reduced rate. It had amounted to only 1.2 per cent of the total school enrollment in 1900, but by 1940 it constituted 19.7 per cent. This extension of enrollment toward the upper grades of the public schools becomes more impressive with further analysis.

It should be noted that certain distortions are inevitable in the data presented in Table 7. For example, all children enrolled in the first grade are not six years of age. Children who have not yet reached their sixth birthday are frequently enrolled. Failures are more com-

TABLE 7

ENROLLMENT AS A PERCENTAGE OF SCHOOL-AGE POPULATION IN
THE PUBLIC SCHOOLS OF THIRTEEN SOUTHERN STATES

	1900	1910	1920	1930	1940	1950
Enrollment in Grades 1–12 as a Percentage of School-Age Population Ages 6–17	70.8	77.3	83.8	89.4	93.6	92.9
Enrollment in Elementary Grades as a Percentage of School-Age Population Ages 6–13	99.7	110.0	115.3	114.5	113.7	107.5
Enrollment in Secondary Grades as a Percentage of School-Age Population Ages 14–17	2.9	5.3	11.5	36.0	54.4	59.8

mon in the first grade than in any other; consequently, retentions are
included in the figures which inflate substantially the number enrolled
in relation to population age six. These factors account for the percentages of enrollment which are in excess of 100 and they are, to a
lesser degree, operative in all other grades since there is some retention at all levels.

The percentage of school-age children 6 through 13 enrolled in
public schools in 1900 was 99.7. This percentage rose to 115.3 in
1920 and declined to 113.7 in 1940. The increased percentages resulted from a larger proportion of this age group being enrolled, plus
a considerable number of children over 13 years of age being enrolled
in elementary grades and a certain number who were enrolled before
reaching their sixth birthday. The latter two factors, as was previously
explained, are the reasons more than 100 per cent of an age group

TABLE 8

WHITE AND NEGRO ENROLLMENT AS A PERCENTAGE OF WHITE AND NEGRO
SCHOOL-AGE POPULATION IN THE PUBLIC SCHOOLS OF THIRTEEN
SOUTHERN STATES

		1900	1910	1920	1930	1940	1950
Enrollment in Grades 1–12 as a Percentage of School-Age Population Ages 6–17	W	76.4	83.1	87.2	91.5	94.3	92.8
	N	61.1	65.7	75.7	84.1	91.7	93.4
Enrollment in Elementary Grades as a Percentage of School-Age Population Ages 6–13	W	107.0	117.7	118.1	112.8	110.0	105.0
	N	87.0	95.0	108.9	119.2	123.4	114.7
Enrollment in Secondary Grades as a Percentage of School-Age Population Ages 14–17	W	4.3	7.7	15.8	45.6	63.9	65.1
	N	0.5	0.6	1.5	11.5	28.0	44.6

may be reported as being enrolled in school. As retardation was reduced after 1920, the percentages declined.

In 1900 only 2.9 per cent of the 14 through 17 school population was enrolled in secondary schools. Consistent increases resulted in 54.4 per cent being enrolled in 1940. The increase in the 14-17 age group enrolled in secondary grades indicates the steady movement in the South toward universal secondary education.

Enrollment statistics for white children reflect the large increases in the number of white children of school-age, and the increased popularity of the policy that Negroes should be included in the movement toward universal public education is vividly reflected in statistics of Negro school enrollment. Table 8 illustrates these trends. The percentage of the white school-age population enrolled was only 76.4 in 1900 but reached 94.3 in 1940, while the percentage of Negro school-age population enrolled moved from 61.1 to 91.7 in the forty-year period.

Trends in the percentages of school-age children 6-13 enrolled in elementary schools were somewhat similar for Negroes and whites, with higher percentages of white children enrolled. A decline in the percentage of white children enrolled occurred between 1920 and 1930, reflecting, perhaps, a shift in educational philosophy with reference to retardation in white schools, while the percentage continued to rise for Negroes through 1940. Thus, the concentration of children in the lower levels of the public school grades continued longer for Negroes than for whites.

Dramatic increases in secondary enrollments for both races in the South during the first forty years of the twentieth century have been noted. While 4.3 per cent of the white 14-17 school-age population was enrolled in secondary schools in 1900, the comparable percentage for Negroes was only 0.5. By 1940 the percentages were 63.9 for whites and 28.0 for Negroes.

From 1940 to 1950 public school enrollments decreased by 1.3 per cent, the first decline in a ten-year period since the beginning of the century. This drop in enrollment was caused by a slight decrease in the total school-age population, and a reduction in the percentage of school-age population enrolled in public schools, the latter dropping from 93.6 in 1940 to 92.9 in 1950. The enrollment trend was reversed between 1950 and 1952 to such an extent that for the twelve-year period, 1940 to 1952, an increase of 2.2 per cent in public school enrollment was achieved. The pronounced acceleration in enrollment after 1950 foreshadowed tremendous increases to come in future years as a result of the high birth rate following World War II. On the whole, however, the period from 1940 to 1952, the period for which figures are available for detailed analyses, was one of stability in enrollment from the standpoint of the region as a whole.

Region-wide statistics, however, again fail to delineate important facts; as was the case with school-age population, enrollment changes show significant differences among the states. Table 9 cites state figures and percentages.

TABLE 9

PUBLIC SCHOOL ENROLLMENT IN THE SOUTHERN STATES

	1939–40	*1949–50*	*1951–52*	*Per Cent Change 1940–1952*
Alabama	686,767	686,908	679,274	− 1.1
Arkansas	472,014	425,173	416,314	−11.8
Florida	387,161	476,268	535,756	38.4
Georgia	734,414	713,733	744,113	1.3
Kentucky	608,621	563,540	561,321	− 7.8
Louisiana	469,496	477,996	508,121	8.2
Mississippi	598,612	533,925	535,473	−10.6
North Carolina	890,729	893,745	909,777	2.1
Oklahoma	605,322	499,311	499,955	−17.4
South Carolina	481,750	494,185	512,199	6.3
Tennessee	643,120	659,785	676,671	5.2
Texas	1,336,136	1,349,794	1,455,736	9.0
Virginia	571,535	602,031	633,018	10.8
TOTAL	8,485,677	8,376,394	8,667,728	2.2

The thirteen states may be grouped into three divisions according to the change among them. One group consists of states which show considerable increases in enrollment and is composed of Florida, Louisiana, South Carolina, Tennessee, Texas, and Virginia. In these states enrollments increased from 1940 to 1950 and continued to increase at accelerated rates from 1950 to 1952. Rate of change among these states varies considerably for the twelve-year period, from 5.2 per cent in Tennessee to 38.4 per cent in Florida. The six states in this group were shown earlier to have gained in total school population.

A second grouping of states includes those in which slight change took place in school enrollment. Alabama, Georgia, and North Carolina make up this group. Alabama had a small decrease and Georgia and North Carolina a slight increase. It will be noted that these figures correspond closely to over-all changes in school population in the three states.

TABLE 10

PUBLIC SCHOOL ENROLLMENT BY GRADE GROUPS
IN THE SOUTHERN STATES

State and Grade Group	1939–40	1949–50	1951–52	Per Cent Change 1940–52
Alabama				
Elementary	586,477	559,850	547,307	− 6.7
Secondary	100,290	127,058	131,967	31.6
Arkansas				
Elementary	398,246	343,782	334,095	−16.1
Secondary	73,768	81,391	82,219	11.5
Florida				
Elementary	306,448	375,664	424,109	38.4
Secondary	80,713	100,604	111,647	38.3
Georgia				
Elementary	602,305	559,319	570,309	− 5.3
Secondary	132,109	154,414	173,804	31.6
Kentucky				
Elementary	510,514	468,363	461,899	− 9.5
Secondary	98,107	95,177	99,422	1.3
Louisiana				
Elementary	368,001	394,340	413,410	12.3
Secondary	101,495	83,656	94,711	− 6.7
Mississippi				
Elementary	524,414	452,510	449,326	−14.3
Secondary	74,198	81,415	86,147	16.1
North Carolina				
Elementary	687,690	711,804	719,855	4.7
Secondary	203,039	181,941	189,922	− 6.5
Oklahoma				
Elementary	466,597	382,327	380,314	−18.5
Secondary	138,725	116,984	119,641	−13.8
South Carolina				
Elementary	394,950	415,146	426,476	8.0
Secondary	86,800	79,039	85,723	− 1.3
Tennessee				
Elementary	535,060	539,445	546,995	2.2
Secondary	108,060	120,340	129,676	20.0
Texas				
Elementary	989,547	1,074,083	1,158,107	17.0
Secondary	346,589	275,711	297,629	−14.1
Virginia				
Elementary	441,029	453,541	476,252	8.0
Secondary	130,506	148,490	156,766	20.1
TOTAL				
Elementary	6,811,278	6,730,174	6,908,454	1.4
Secondary	1,674,399	1,646,220	1,759,274	5.1

The third group of states is composed of those which had marked reductions in school enrollment for the period. It is composed of Arkansas, Kentucky, Mississippi, and Oklahoma. Kentucky showed the smallest decrease of any of these states, 7.8 per cent, and Oklahoma the largest, 17.4 per cent. While all four states had decreases for the period, Mississippi and Oklahoma had slight increases from 1950 to 1952. Thus, trends in enrollment are consistent with trends in over-all school-age population.

Direction of regional trends in enrollment by elementary and secondary school divisions paralleled the regional trends in total enrollment, that is, a small decrease from 1940 to 1950 and an increase in the ensuing two years. This increase toward the end of the period was of sufficient size for both divisions to overcome decreases in the decade beginning with 1940; a slight over-all increase was shown for the entire twelve-year period. The gain was proportionately larger in secondary than in elementary schools. The percentage of school-age population, 6 through 13, enrolled in elementary school continued the decline begun between 1920 and 1930, dropping from 113.7 per cent to 107.5 per cent between 1940 and 1950. The gain of earlier years in the percentage of 14 through 17 aged pupils enrolled in secondary schools continued during the years between 1940 and 1950, moving from 54.4 to 59.8. Changes in elementary and secondary school enrollment in the individual states, with regional totals, are shown in Table 10.

The significance of the small loss of 1.7 per cent in secondary school enrollment between 1940 and 1950 becomes more meaningful in view of the fact that the total number of children of secondary school age decreased during this period by 10.6 per cent. The increase in the proportion of 14 through 17 age children actually enrolled in the secondary school is explained by an extension of the average number of years children remain in the public schools, and it may to some extent reflect a decline of retardation in the elementary school. Implications for financing public education inhere in the gradual shifting upward of enrollment for the secondary schools; according to present standards, secondary education is more expensive than that for the elementary grades. Thus, more is involved in creating educational policy than a mere consideration of numbers.

Understanding the nature of the changes which have taken place requires consideration of what has been happening within the states. The most important demographic trend in the Southern region since 1940 has been the huge population migration from rural to urban areas. Table 11 clearly shows the vast changes that have taken place in school enrollments according to types of counties. The trend of

TABLE 11

County Classification	*Per Cent Changes*	
	1940 to 1950	*1940 to 1952*
Rural	− 7.5	− 7.5
Rural–Urban	− 5.5	− 4.8
Metropolitan	15.7	26.8

reduction in enrollment in rural and rural-urban counties was checked in the latter part of the twelve-year period, while the increasing enrollment trend in metropolitan counties was further accelerated. Metropolitan counties have long enrolled a larger proportion of the secondary age group than rural counties have. A recent change has been for the proportion enrolled in secondary schools in rural counties more nearly to approach the proportion enrolled in metropolitan counties. This represents an important extension of educational opportunity and is a significant aspect of the general movement toward universal secondary education in the South. Even with a decline in school-age population, these changes mean that rural counties now have almost as large an educational load as formerly. Metropolitan counties have a greatly increased load.

What the population shift means for financing education has not been fully probed. As a matter of fact, the foregoing generalization on educational load fails to take into account the fact that changes among rural counties, themselves, follow quite a varied pattern, with some suffering very substantial declines in school enrollment, while others made appreciable gains. It is, however, safe to conclude that the gigantic population shifts which have taken place and are continuing within the region have created greatly increased educational needs and, therefore, educational burdens in some counties, while in other counties adequate school facilities are no longer used to maximum capacity. The seriousness of these problems is attested to by the fact that population migration continues apparently at an undiminished rate, and, at the same time, tens of thousands of children reach school age every year and enter school systems in which the general trend is for them to stay a greater number of years.

A further aspect of enrollment in which considerable change has taken place has important implications for public education programs, irrespective of policy changes which may be brought about as a result of recent judicial decisions. Reference is made to changes in biracial school enrollment.

TABLE 12

WHITE AND NEGRO PUBLIC SCHOOL ENROLLMENT IN THE SOUTHERN STATES

State	1939–40	1949–50	1951–52	Per Cent Change 1940–52
Alabama				
White	447,109	444,183	439,901	− 1.6
Negro	239,658	242,725	239,373	− 0.1
Arkansas				
White	356,998	322,214	316,213	−11.4
Negro	115,016	102,959	100,101	−13.0
Florida				
White	282,977	357,857	408,370	44.3
Negro	104,184	118,411	127,386	22.3
Georgia				
White	468,903	463,066	489,723	4.4
Negro	265,511	250,667	254,390	− 4.2
Kentucky				
White	564,488	527,016	525,831	− 6.9
Negro	44,133	36,524	35,490	−19.6
Louisiana				
White	294,847	295,627	311,590	5.7
Negro	174,649	182,369	196,531	12.5
Mississippi				
White	305,767	268,859	267,565	−12.5
Negro	292,845	265,066	267,908	− 8.5
North Carolina				
White	619,767	625,167	636,505	2.7
Negro	270,962	268,578	273,272	0.9
Oklahoma				
White	558,221	461,618	463,860	−16.9
Negro	47,101	37,693	36,095	−23.4
South Carolina				
White	265,845	272,305	284,541	7.0
Negro	215,905	221,880	227,658	5.4
Tennessee				
White	535,006	552,858	565,892	5.8
Negro	108,114	106,927	110,779	2.5
Texas				
White	1,113,623	1,148,691	1,249,144	12.2
Negro	222,513	201,103	206,592	− 7.2
Virginia				
White	420,957	445,796	472,725	12.3
Negro	150,578	156,235	160,293	6.5
TOTAL				
White	6,234,508	6,185,257	6,431,860	3.2
Negro	2,251,169	2,191,137	2,235,868	− 0.7

TABLE 13

WHITE AND NEGRO PUBLIC SCHOOL ENROLLMENT IN THE ELEMENTARY
GRADES IN THE SOUTHERN STATES

State	1939–40	1949–50	1951–52	Per Cent Change 1940–52
Alabama				
White	364,000	352,487	346,493	− 4.8
Negro	222,477	207,363	200,814	− 9.7
Arkansas				
White	290,602	253,717	247,586	−14.8
Negro	107,644	90,065	86,509	−19.6
Florida				
White	213,702	276,312	318,017	48.8
Negro	92,746	99,352	106,092	14.4
Georgia				
White	357,553	347,557	360,305	0.8
Negro	244,752	211,762	210,004	−14.2
Kentucky				
White	473,128	439,024	433,216	− 8.4
Negro	37,386	29,339	28,683	−23.3
Louisiana				
White	210,792	233,024	243,451	15.5
Negro	157,209	161,316	169,959	8.1
Mississippi				
White	242,406	207,573	205,662	−15.2
Negro	282,008	244,937	243,664	−13.6
North Carolina				
White	456,331	487,666	494,258	8.3
Negro	231,359	224,138	225,597	− 2.5
Oklahoma				
White	427,220	352,652	352,342	−17.5
Negro	39,377	29,675	27,972	−29.0
South Carolina				
White	196,308	218,286	228,032	16.2
Negro	198,642	196,860	198,444	− 0.1
Tennessee				
White	439,841	450,639	456,213	3.7
Negro	95,219	88,806	90,782	− 4.7
Texas				
White	804,081	908,352	989,513	23.1
Negro	185,466	165,731	168,594	− 9.1
Virginia				
White	312,222	329,408	350,348	12.2
Negro	128,807	124,133	125,904	− 2.3
TOTAL				
White	4,788,186	4,856,697	5,025,436	5.0
Negro	2,023,092	1,873,477	1,883,018	− 6.9

TABLE 14

WHITE AND NEGRO PUBLIC SCHOOL ENROLLMENT IN THE SECONDARY
GRADES IN THE SOUTHERN STATES

State	1939–40	1949–50	1951–52	Per Cent Change 1940–52
Alabama				
White	83,109	91,696	93,408	12.4
Negro	17,181	35,362	38,559	124.4
Arkansas				
White	66,396	68,497	68,627	3.4
Negro	7,372	12,894	13,592	84.4
Florida				
White	69,275	81,545	90,353	30.4
Negro	11,438	19,059	21,294	86.2
Georgia				
White	111,350	115,509	129,418	16.2
Negro	20,759	38,905	44,386	113.8
Kentucky				
White	91,360	87,992	92,615	1.4
Negro	6,747	7,185	6,807	0.9
Louisiana				
White	84,055	62,603	68,139	−18.9
Negro	17,440	21,053	26,572	52.4
Mississippi				
White	63,361	61,286	61,903	− 2.3
Negro	10,837	20,129	24,244	123.7
North Carolina				
White	163,436	137,501	142,247	−13.0
Negro	39,603	44,440	47,675	20.4
Oklahoma				
White	131,001	108,966	111,518	−14.9
Negro	7,724	8,018	8,123	5.2
South Carolina				
White	69,537	54,019	56,509	−18.7
Negro	17,263	25,020	29,214	69.2
Tennessee				
White	95,165	102,219	109,679	15.3
Negro	12,895	18,121	19,997	55.1
Texas				
White	309,542	240,339	259,631	−16.1
Negro	37,047	35,372	37,998	2.6
Virginia				
White	108,735	116,388	122,377	12.5
Negro	21,771	32,102	34,389	58.0
TOTAL				
White	1,446,322	1,328,560	1,406,124	− 2.8
Negro	228,077	317,660	352,850	54.7

TABLE 15

WHITE AND NEGRO PUBLIC SCHOOL ENROLLMENT AS A PERCENTAGE OF WHITE
AND NEGRO SCHOOL-AGE POPULATION IN THE SOUTHERN STATES

State	1939–40	1949–50
Alabama		
White	95.3	96.0
Negro	89.4	95.7
Arkansas		
White	97.1	96.2
Negro	94.5	97.2
Florida		
White	101.1	97.7
Negro	91.6	95.4
Georgia		
White	96.8	93.1
Negro	92.4	93.1
Kentucky		
White	86.5	85.7
Negro	98.0	93.7
Louisiana		
White	83.2	81.4
Negro	81.3	84.2
Mississippi		
White	110.0	103.9
Negro	100.1	99.4
North Carolina		
White	94.0	95.6
Negro	94.2	93.8
Oklahoma		
White	111.3	110.7
Negro	77.4	78.0
South Carolina		
White	97.5	95.6
Negro	88.3	92.7
Tennessee		
White	91.9	93.3
Negro	93.5	95.3
Texas		
White	88.9	86.7
Negro	97.9	94.4
Virginia		
White	90.9	89.8
Negro	86.1	91.3
TOTAL		
White	94.3	92.8
Negro	91.7	93.4

Enrollment of white children decreased 0.8 per cent from 1940 to 1950 and increased sufficiently during the next two years to make an over-all gain in the twelve-year period of 3.2 per cent. The over-all percentage of school-age population actually enrolled declined slightly from 1940 to 1950. During this decade the number of Negro children enrolled decreased proportionately more than the enrollment of white children. Slight increases from 1950 to 1952 were not enough to offset the loss; consequently, Negro enrollment for the twelve-year period declined 0.7 per cent. Increases in Negro school-age population actually enrolled were such toward the end of the period that in 1950 the percentage of Negro children enrolled was for the first time higher than the percentage of white children.

In general, it may be said that trends in white and Negro enrollments are quite similar to total enrollment trends in the states, that is, those states which were gaining in enrollment were gaining in both white and Negro enrollment and those that were decreasing in enrollment were decreasing in both white and Negro enrollment. Table 12 shows that the only exceptions were Texas and Georgia. Such enrollment changes as have occurred are obviously closely related to changes in school-age population.

While the over-all changes in both white and Negro enrollment were small from 1940 to 1952, there were important shifts in elementary and secondary grades for the two races. The general increase in white enrollment was accounted for entirely by growth in elementary enrollment, as white secondary enrollment declined.

Negro enrollments showed quite opposite trends. The Negro elementary enrollment decreased slightly, while the secondary enrollment increased by over one-half. The gain occurred despite a much larger decrease in the secondary school population than in the elementary population. The percentage of Negro elementary population enrolled decreased from 123.4 per cent in 1940 to 114.7 per cent in 1950. At the same time the percentage of secondary population enrolled increased from 28.0 to 44.6. This very large shift in enrollment of Negroes toward the upper grades of the public schools corresponds to a trend in white school enrollments which began many years earlier.

Changes in elementary and secondary enrollments for white and Negro children in the separate states are shown in Tables 13 and 14. Wide variations in the direction and rate of change occur among them. The significance of the changes in Negro secondary enrollment is emphasized by the fact that every state had an increase for the period under consideration.

A further analysis of white and Negro enrollment is shown in

Table 15, which reports enrollment by each race as a percentage of school-age population for the race. Rather marked variations will be observed from state to state. Although the regional percentage for Negroes is 93.4 as compared to 92.8 for whites, reflecting a gain in the ten-year period for Negroes and a decline for whites, the breakdown by states shows that in Alabama, Florida, Mississippi, Oklahoma, and South Carolina the percentage of Negro enrollment is less than the percentage of white enrollment.

Trends in enrollment by county classifications followed the same direction for both races, although the extent of change was less for the Negro group. This means that enrollments declined for both races in rural and rural-urban counties, while enrollments increased for both races in metropolitan counties. The percentages of change are shown in Table 16. In general, rural and rural-urban counties showed

TABLE 16

CHANGES IN WHITE AND NEGRO ENROLLMENT IN SAMPLE RURAL AND
RURAL–URBAN COUNTIES, AND IN METROPOLITAN COUNTIES
OF THIRTEEN SOUTHERN STATES

County	Per Cent Change			
	1940 to 1950		1940 to 1952	
Classification	White	Negro	White	Negro
Rural	−10.2	− 2.0	−10.6	− 1.3
Rural–Urban	− 5.9	− 4.6	− 5.2	− 4.0
Metropolitan	17.7	10.5	30.5	17.3

losses in elementary school enrollment for both races, slight losses in white secondary enrollment, and gains in Negro secondary enrollment; the metropolitan counties showed gains in both elementary and secondary enrollment for each race.

PUBLIC SCHOOL ATTENDANCE

The third phase of educational load as defined by children to be educated deals with school attendance. It is related to school enrollment much as enrollment is related to school population; population denotes numbers of school age, enrollment applies to those actually on school attendance rosters, and attendance consists of the average number of students present each day of school.

It was shown in the previous section that increases in enrollment since 1900 were due, in part, to increases in the total school population and, in part, to a higher percentage of the population actually enrolling in school. In like manner, gains in attendance since the beginning of the century have been due, in part, to gains in enrollment and, in part, to a higher percentage of enrollment actually in average daily attendance at school. These relationships are clearly shown in the following percentages of increase from 1900 to 1940: school age population increased 41.3 per cent, public school enrollment increased 86.7 per cent, and public school attendance increased 134.7 per cent.

TABLE 17

AVERAGE DAILY ATTENDANCE AS A PERCENTAGE OF ENROLLMENT IN
THE PUBLIC SCHOOLS OF THIRTEEN SOUTHERN STATES

1900	1910	1920	1930	1940	1950	1952
65.8	64.7	69.6	76.8	82.8	86.4	86.3

The first four decades of the twentieth century saw an increase of slightly more than 4,000,000 in average daily attendance. Tables 17 and 18 present an analysis of trends in the relationship of attendance

TABLE 18

WHITE AND NEGRO AVERAGE DAILY ATTENDANCE AS A PERCENTAGE OF WHITE
AND NEGRO ENROLLMENT IN THE PUBLIC SCHOOLS OF THIRTEEN
SOUTHERN STATES

Race	1900	1910	1920	1930	1940	1950	1952
White	67.4	65.5	70.5	78.1	83.8	87.0	86.8
Negro	62.3	62.8	67.1	73.0	80.0	84.9	85.1

to enrollment. The percentage ratio of attendance to enrollment increased for both races, from 67.4 in 1900 to 83.8 in 1940 for the white race, and from 62.3 to 80.0 for the Negro race. These figures are a further measure of educational progress in the South during the first part of the twentieth century, for they show that, in keeping with a larger proportion of children enrolled in school, the children actually enrolled were attending school more regularly.

In spite of a slight decline in enrollment in the South from 1940 to 1950, there was an increase of 3.1 per cent in attendance, the number increasing from 7,022,133 to 7,240,521. The percentage, derived as the proportion that attendance was of enrollment, was based on 82.8 per cent in attendance in 1940 and 86.4 per cent in 1950. During the two years following the end of the decade the increase in attendance continued, paralleling the gains in enrollment. The percentage ratio of attendance to enrollment leveled off during this time and is apparently stabilizing at 86 or 87 per cent.

Improvement in attendance as measured by gains in percentages of enrollment took place in all thirteen states. Table 19 presents these

TABLE 19

<small>Average Daily Attendance in the Public Schools of Southern States</small>

State	1939–40	1949–50	1951–52	Per Cent Change 1940–52
Alabama	566,673	594,632	587,395	3.7
Arkansas	373,356	355,031	350,852	− 6.0
Florida	325,991	412,778	456,843	40.1
Georgia	583,875	619,846	637,529	9.2
Kentucky	493,210	480,256	477,605	− 3.2
Louisiana	398,114	420,740	445,710	12.0
Mississippi	474,020	472,149	471,469	− 0.5
North Carolina	790,003	797,691	816,036	3.3
Oklahoma	484,896	401,931	404,767	−16.5
South Carolina	384,995	413,551	427,326	11.0
Tennessee	536,715	583,126	594,520	10.8
Texas	1,116,263	1,151,959	1,255,597	12.5
Virginia	494,022	536,831	556,802	12.7
Total	7,022,133	7,240,521	7,482,451	6.6

statistics. Only those states which had considerable declines in enrollment—Arkansas, Kentucky, Mississippi, and Oklahoma—showed losses in attendance, and in each of these states the losses were smaller in attendance than in enrollment. The other nine states showed increases in attendance from 1940 to 1952.

Table 20 shows changes in attendance by states for white and Negro children during the twelve years subject to analysis. From 1940 to 1952 white attendance increased by 6.9 per cent. Since this increase is greater than the increase in enrollment, it reflects improvement in daily attendance of white pupils. This improvement is shown in the increase of percentage that attendance was of enrollment from 83.8 in 1940 to 86.8 in 1952.

During the same time, Negro attendance increased 5.6 per cent, even though there was a decline in enrollment for Negroes. This upward trend is well illustrated by the change in the percentage that attendance was of enrollment, the increase being from 80.0 in 1940 to 85.1 in 1952. It is evident that during this time the disparity between white and Negro attendance was almost eliminated at the state level and that the Negro child attended school about as regularly as the white child.

Reflecting the changes in population and enrollment in the county classifications, attendance decreased in rural and rural-urban counties and increased in metropolitan counties during the twelve-year period

TABLE 20

AVERAGE DAILY ATTENDANCE IN THE WHITE AND NEGRO PUBLIC
SCHOOLS OF SOUTHERN STATES

State	1939–40	1949–50	1951–52	Per Cent Change 1940–52
Alabama				
White	370,033	387,938	383,679	3.7
Negro	196,640	206,694	203,716	3.6
Arkansas				
White	284,274	271,577	268,235	− 5.7
Negro	89,082	83,454	82,617	− 7.3
Florida				
White	238,960	307,573	344,319	44.1
Negro	87,031	105,205	112,524	29.3
Georgia				
White	381,295	413,473	429,951	12.8
Negro	202,580	206,373	207,578	2.5
Kentucky				
White	457,793	448,753	446,909	− 2.4
Negro	35,417	31,503	30,696	−13.3
Louisiana				
White	253,722	263,390	276,662	9.0
Negro	144,392	157,350	169,048	17.1
Mississippi				
White	247,251	246,285	244,605	− 1.1
Negro	226,769	225,864	226,864	0.0
North Carolina				
White	559,779	564,612	576,117	2.9
Negro	230,224	233,079	239,919	4.2
Oklahoma				
White	447,434	370,704	373,083	−16.6
Negro	37,462	31,227	31,684	−15.4
South Carolina				
White	222,800	235,379	244,889	9.9
Negro	162,195	178,172	182,437	12.5
Tennessee				
White	446,766	488,832	496,574	11.1
Negro	89,949	94,294	97,946	8.9
Texas				
White	943,419	983,354	1,079,063	14.4
Negro	172,844	168,605	176,534	2.1
Virginia				
White	368,256	399,086	416,364	13.1
Negro	125,766	137,745	140,438	11.7
TOTAL				
White	5,221,782	5,380,956	5,580,450	6.9
Negro	1,800,351	1,859,565	1,902,001	5.6

TABLE 21

ATTENDANCE AS A PERCENTAGE OF ENROLLMENT IN THE PUBLIC SCHOOLS IN
SAMPLE RURAL AND RURAL–URBAN COUNTIES, AND IN METROPOLITAN
COUNTIES OF THIRTEEN SOUTHERN STATES

County Classification	1940	1950	1952
Rural	81.2	85.3	85.3
Rural–Urban	81.9	85.7	84.9
Metropolitan	84.7	87.4	86.2

from 1940 to 1952. The improvements in attendance, however, as
shown in Table 21, resulted in smaller decreases in rural and rural-
urban counties and larger increases in metropolitan counties for attendance than had occurred in those counties for enrollment. Attendance has long been at a higher rate in metropolitan counties than in
rural counties, but the difference was almost eliminated by 1952,
when for the first time the rural child was attending school about as
regularly as the urban child.

The movement during this period toward equalization of attendance between races as well as among county classifications is shown
in Table 22. The percentage of attendance in rural schools for Negroes
increased from 78.6 per cent to 84.1 per cent, compared to an increase from 82.5 per cent to 87.7 per cent in metropolitan counties.
It will be observed that during this time attendance as measured by
percentage of enrollment was very nearly equalized for the two races.
If, as has been suggested previously, the attendance rate has about
reached its maximum for the present, further gains in attendance will
come from the increases in school-age population, plus a further increase in the percentage of this population actually enrolled in the
public schools. It appears that this percentage may be rapidly approaching the leveling off point, also. This suggests the possibility
that the region can concentrate more of its resources on improving
the existing educational program.

TABLE 22

ATTENDANCE AS A PERCENTAGE OF ENROLLMENT IN WHITE AND NEGRO PUBLIC
SCHOOLS OF SAMPLE RURAL AND RURAL-URBAN COUNTIES AND IN
METROPOLITAN COUNTIES IN THIRTEEN SOUTHERN STATES

County Classification	1940		1950		1952	
	White	Negro	White	Negro	White	Negro
Rural	82.5	78.6	86.2	83.8	86.0	84.1
Rural–Urban	83.1	79.3	86.6	84.0	86.2	82.0
Metropolitan	85.5	82.5	87.2	88.1	85.6	87.7

SUMMARY

During the forty years which began in 1900, school-age population in the Southern region increased from 6,419,143 to 9,068,932, a gain of 2,649,789 or 41 per cent. Declining birth rates during the depression years of the thirties checked the steady upward trend in school-age population and brought a slight decline during the decade between 1940 and 1950. Changes within states for this decade were small, except for a large gain in Florida and a large loss in Oklahoma. Increases occurred in six states and decreases in seven. When broken down by age groups, opposite trends occurred during the forties; the increase in birth rate following the Depression was reflected in an increase in school population of the 6 through 13 age group, while the 14 through 17 age group decreased. Since 1950 the sharp increases in birth rates during the late war and post-war years, which still continue, have been reflected in a resumption of the rapid growth in school population that was checked by the Depression. As yet, this growth obviously falls only in the 6-13 age group.

Perhaps the enormous in-region and out-of-the-region population migrations are of equivalent importance. While such trends tend to be characteristic of American population patterns, the war and post-war years brought a substantial shifting of people in the South which is affecting profoundly the social and economic life of the region. Brought on primarily by urbanization, the trends are reflected in a declining rural and rural-urban population and a rapid increase in the population of metropolitan counties. Shifts in the distribution of school-age population are, of course, a part of this general trend, as shown by the fact that during the decade beginning in 1940 metropolitan counties showed a large increase in the 6-13 age group. The overall decline in the 14-17 age group reflects directly the reduced birth rate of the depression years; even in metropolitan counties, where large population increases occurred, this age group declined slightly in numbers.

The major aspects of out-migration between 1940 and 1950 was the exodus of more than 1,500,000 Negroes from the region. In addition to this movement out of the region, there was a rather heavy migration of Negroes from rural to metropolitan areas within the region. The net effect of these changes on Negro school-age population was a decline in both age groupings, 0.4 per cent for the 6-13 group, 12.5 per cent for the 14-17 group, making an over-all decrease of 4.4 per cent. Following the pattern of change in white school-age population, there was a decline in rural and rural-urban counties of Negro school-age children and an increase in metropolitan counties, although the increase was smaller than that for white children.

The number of children actually enrolled in the public schools of the region increased 86.7 per cent during the first forty years of the century. The gain in numbers was 3,940,314, making a total of 8,485,677 in 1940 as compared to 4,545,363 in 1900. The rate of gain in school enrollment in excess of the gain in school population is one measure of the extent to which universal public education was achieved in the South during this time. From 1900 there was a gain of 22.8 per cent in the proportion of school-age population actually enrolled in school, the figures being 70.8 per cent in 1900 and 93.6 per cent in 1940.

By 1940 elementary enrollment had increased by one-half. The growth in secondary enrollment showed a phenomenal increase of nearly 3000 per cent.

Paralleling trends in over-all school population, enrollment in the Southern region was relatively stable during the 1940-to-1952 period. Slight declines in the first ten years were offset by increases in the last two years, resulting in a small gain for the period. Changes within states corresponded roughly to changes in total school population.

Enrollments in both grade groups increased slightly during the period beginning in 1940 and ending in 1952, with a larger percentage of increase in secondary enrollment due to the continued efforts in the region to achieve universal secondary education.

Trends in rural, rural-urban, and metropolitan counties followed fairly closely changes in school-age population distribution and age groupings. Increases in enrollment in metropolitan counties offset rural and rural-urban losses so that a slight over-all gain in enrollment by 1952 resulted.

Again paralleling school-age trends, total enrollment in white schools increased; the gains occurred in the elementary grades, while secondary enrollment decreased. On the other hand, Negro enrollment decreased, but racial trends were reversed; decreases occurred in Negro elementary enrollment and increases in secondary enrollment. Growth in Negro secondary enrollment is dramatically illustrated by reference to the actual gain and percentage gain since 1900. In that year, 3,412 Negroes were enrolled. By 1940 there were 228,077, an increase of 6584.6 per cent. Even so, in 1940 only 28.0 per cent of the Negro secondary school-age group was actually enrolled in secondary school. The comparable figure for the white group was 63.9 per cent.

Public school attendance between 1900 and 1940 followed a pattern of rapid over-all increase, the actual gain for the period being 134.7 per cent. The total gain was 4,120,709, the difference between average daily attendance in 1940 of 7,022,133 and 2,991,424 in 1900. The increase in attendance made necessary the addition of almost 135,000 teachers to school personnel and comparable increases in facilities. The upward trend has continued since 1940 and, even though slight declines in enrollment occurred by 1950, attendance continued to gain slightly. When enrollment once more began to increase after 1950, it was accompanied by a comparable increase in attendance.

By and large, attendance trends followed rather closely enrollment trends; although, as has been shown, in the later years of the half century, the percentage ratio of attendance to enrollment had so increased that a small decline in enrollment was not reflected in a similar decline in attendance.

Two major attendance trends merit special emphasis. The first is the noticeable improvement in rural attendance for both white and Negro students. By 1952 the discrepancy in attendance between metropolitan and rural counties, which formerly favored metropolitan counties, had been for all practical purposes equalized. The second trend is the general improvement in Negro attendance, particularly in the upper age group.

A comparison of the 41 per cent gain in school population between 1900 and 1940, the 86.7 per cent gain in school enrollment, and the 134.7 per cent gain in school attendance indicates clearly the nature of the over-all problem of educational need in the region and indicates to some extent how it has been met during the past half-century. The South, starting later than other regions of the country in seriously setting about to develop a public school system, has made great strides in providing universal public education for its children. It appears that ratios of enrollment and attendance may be relatively stabilized at present levels for the immediate future. This means that increased educational need in the region will center upon the growing school population and efforts to raise the levels of minimum educational opportunity provided for all. Continued heavy migrations of population within the South and from it to other regions of the nation make this problem far from simple.

Improvements in Negro education, while very substantial during recent years according to enrollment and attendance figures, are far from complete; it is clear that pronounced gaps remain to be closed. The May, 1954, decision of the United States Supreme Court ruling out segregation of the races in public schools as a national policy creates an entirely new situation, the impact of which cannot be assessed at this time. That it will accelerate the marked trend toward improving educational opportunities for Negroes can hardly be gainsaid.

FIVE

Public School Revenues
and Related Factors

The purpose of this chapter is to describe the public school revenue picture in the South and to characterize the major factors which have a bearing on this picture. The necessity of facing more realistically than ever before the problem of providing educational programs without discrimination as to race requires, among other things, a critical appraisal of the region's ability to finance schools which measure up to the level of quality that American values indicate are desirable.

The problem of adequate support for the schools is a continuing one and inevitably so because the functions and services of public education are constantly expanding in scope and depth. Availability of revenue is one part of the problem. Another part, which may be of equal importance, is willingness on the part of the public to provide and allocate wisely existing revenues. Both are subject to change by deliberate design of society.

Various studies have established beyond doubt the economic value of education, for high per capita income is found in areas where the educational level is high. Research has also established a cost-quality relationship in education which shows that better schools are usually found where expenditures are higher. A corollary of this relationship is that states most in need of better schools are likely to be low income states and hard put, therefore, to meet their educational needs. This dilemma is not necessarily inevitable for states, like individuals, spend their income for things which are most important to them. Changing degrees of allegiance to values may be reflected in public revenues and the way in which they are allocated.

Complexities of the school revenue problem need not be labored. Purely objective factors can be examined, and these must be appraised in any realistic analysis of public school revenues. Income varies from time to time, depending upon the state of the economy. Revenue sources and practices also vary from time to time, and competition for the tax dollar ebbs and flows.

During the last stages of the Great Depression the late President Franklin D. Roosevelt said:

It is my conviction that the South presents right now the Nation's No. 1 economic problem—the Nation's problem, not merely the South's. . . .

. . . suffice it for the immediate purpose to get a clear perspective of the task that is presented to us. That task embraces the wasted or neglected resources of land and water, the abuses suffered by the soil, . . . problems presented by the population itself . . . the problems presented by the South's capital resources and the absentee ownership of those resources, and problems growing out of the new industrial era and, again, of absentee ownership of the new industries. There is the problem of labor and employment in the South and the related problem of protecting women and children in this field. There is the problem of farm ownership, of which farm tenantry is a part, and of farm income. There are questions of taxation, of education, of housing, and of health.[1]

While this statement irked many Southerners, the study of economic conditions in the South which followed supported by and large the thesis. Even then, however, developments in the economy were underway and have continued at an accelerated pace since World War II, developments which hold promise of making the South the nation's number one economic asset. Some of the forces affecting the economy are of paramount importance to this inquiry.

At the time President Roosevelt issued his now famed characterization of the economic plight of the South, no one could have foreseen the rapid recovery of the nation from the ravages of the Depression and the unprecedented period of prosperity which followed. All parts of the country and all classes of people have been affected profoundly by the astonishing increase in per capita and national income.

Government itself has become a tremendous factor in the economy. Its annual expenditures now exceed by a considerable margin the total national income of the mid-thirties. It uses the power to tax to serve a variety of functions, including the provision of additional government services and the redistribution of wealth. Its control of credit affects the pulse of business. Various governmental policies are designed to preserve and improve a healthy economy. Vast expenditures for military preparedness are an important factor, if only one, in government influence on the economy.

The South has profited substantially from the healthy national economy. Government expenditures have greatly benefited the region; fiscal policies have been such that many of the economic ills of the region pointed out by the late President have been partially amel-

---

[1] National Emergency Council, "Report on Economic Conditions of the South" (Washington: Government Printing Office, 1938), pp. 1–2.

iorated by government funds. The farm support program serves as one example.

THE POPULATION OF THE SOUTH

An understanding of the economy of any area is dependent upon knowledge of its human resources, therefore, certain factors concerning the population of the South will be treated here for their contribution to understanding the public school revenue picture in the region.

According to the report on economic conditions of the South issued in 1938, "The population problems of the South—the disproportion of adult workers to dependents, the displacement of agricultural workers by machines, the substitution of white workers in traditionally Negro occupations, the emigration of skilled and educated productive workers—are the most pressing of any America must face." [2]

Since this statement was issued, important changes have occurred in the population of the region. One of these has been the increase in population, which amounted to nearly four and three-quarter million persons during the decade beginning in 1940. The pattern of change has been quite uneven, however; Arkansas, Mississippi, and Oklahoma lost population, while Florida, Virginia, and Texas gained substantially. Such uneven changes create important differences in economic requirements and problems from state to state.

The percentage of Negro population has decreased steadily in every state for each census year since 1920. In 1900, 34.3 per cent of the total population of the South was Negro. By 1950 it had dropped to 22.5 per cent. The greatest decline occurred between 1940 and 1950. By 1950 the white population of the South had increased 124.7 per cent above the figure in 1900, while the Negro population had increased only 24.9 per cent. Great variations exist among the states with respect to the Negro percentage of the total population. In 1950, 45.2 per cent of the population of Mississippi was Negro, in Oklahoma the percentage was 6.5. In that year, above 20 per cent of the total population in nine of the thirteen Southern states belonged to the Negro race.

From 1900 to 1940, when the population of the region increased by about 15,000,000 persons, approximately 4,000,000 emigrated to other sections of the nation. The rate of migration has increased since then.

---

[2] *Ibid.*, p. 20.

A much higher percentage of Negroes than whites has migrated. It has been estimated that 1,500,000 Negroes left the region between 1940 and 1950. The search for economic opportunity and cultural equality has increasingly caused the Negro to move to cities outside the South.

Effects of population movements out of the South and within the South have been interpreted in various ways. Migration from the South is normally heaviest among men and women falling in the 25-30 age group who seek economic betterment in other regions of the country. This leaves the South with an unusually large percentage of the very young and the old. The heavy out-migration of Negroes has changed the racial complexion of the population in both the South and the non-South, thus making the socio-economic problems associated with segregation and other interracial problems of national as well as Southern concern. One point of view is that out-migration enables the remaining population to capitalize more fully on the economic potentialities of the area. Another point of view is that out-migration has taken the best of the Southern population and has been a detriment to the region.

The Southern population is predominantly native born. Only 1.2 per cent of the total population in the region in 1940 was classified as foreign-born.[3] There has been little change in this characteristic within recent years. The only foreign-born group of importance in any of the Southern states is the new Spanish-speaking immigrants in Florida and Texas.

The median age of the Southern population has increased in every state during each decade since 1920, the over-all gains ranging from 0.7 years in Florida to 4.2 years in Mississippi. By 1950 median age ranges among the states were from a low of 23.6 in South Carolina to 30.9 in Florida. The difference in economic productivity between two populations whose median ages vary as much as five years is tremendous.

Analyses according to age distribution of the population reveal that the proportion of both the youngest and oldest age groups are increasing. Should such a trend continue, the economy will be affected by the continued presence of a large body of non-productive persons, which will reduce per capita income. The increasing proportion of the very young in the population creates a critical problem in relation to the question of school revenues.

The South has been noted for the fertility rate of its people, the highest rate in the nation. The excess of births over deaths in 1917

---

[3] Calvin B. Hoover and B. U. Ratchford, *Economic Resources and Policies of the South* (New York: The Macmillan Company, 1951), p. 27. With the permission of the publisher.

stood at 14.2 per thousand but reached a low point of 8.7 in 1936. It had climbed back to 11.0 by 1940.[4] The combination of low income and high fertility rate has posed severe burdens for school revenues.

Improvement in the educational level of the population during the past decade is one of the forces which is influencing the economy of the South. Median years of school completed by those nineteen years of age increased by a full year or more in almost every state in the region during this decade. Kentucky is the only state in which the median did not advance as much as one year for either boys or girls. The median for girls in every state was higher than for boys for both 1940 and 1950. The increase for boys was greater, however, than for girls during this period in all states except Alabama, Arkansas, and Kentucky. In 1940 half the nineteen-year-old boys had completed nine years of school or more in only four states, whereas ten years later the median grade achievement of this group was nine years or more in every state. Since a greater proportion of men than women are in the labor force in the adult population, the trend toward increased training for boys in relation to girls indicates that the additional training of productive workers entering the labor force in 1950 rose faster than that of the general population.

Population movements within the region have been characterized largely by decreasing rural population and increasing metropolitan population. The urbanization movement received impetus during World War II and during the years immediately following.

Some idea of the magnitude of urbanization is suggested by the fact that in 1920 the population was one-fourth urbanized, and in 1950 the proportion had increased to two-fifths. Texas was the most highly urbanized state in the region in 1950 with 59.8 per cent of its population urban, while Florida and Louisiana had over half their populations so classified that year. In 1950 all states in the region except Arkansas, Mississippi, and South Carolina were more than one-third urban. In 1900 the fifty-eight largest cities in the South had a combined population of 1,894,901; by 1950 the total was 8,890,921, an increase of 369 per cent in contrast to an over-all population increase of 90 per cent.

The phenomenon of urbanization has affected profoundly the industrialization of the South as well as its agriculture.

THE ECONOMY OF THE SOUTH

An excellent climate, heavy rainfall, a long growing season, extensive forests, fish, natural gas and petroleum, and quantities of medium-to-

---

[4] Rupert B. Vance, *All These People* (Chapel Hill: The University of North Carolina Press, 1935), p. 73.

low-grade iron ore and coal deposits make the South a region rich in natural resources. Poor soils, erratic distributions of annual rainfall, a limited supply of metallic minerals other than iron, and the low quality of iron ore and coal deposits are deficiencies in natural resources of the region.

Climate, rainfall, and soil form a combination which makes possible the production of a great variety of mild-climate and subtropical crops. The sloping topography and high annual rainfall combine to provide the region with potential water and hydroelectric power of enormous value. The abundant supply of water encourages the development of the new synthetic and chemical industries, including paper, all of which require tremendous amounts of relatively pure water.

The long growing season and extensive tracts of land unsuitable for cultivation or grazing make timber growing an ideal industry. More than two-fifths of the land area of the South is in forests. In 1945 the South produced more than a third of the nation's softwood lumber, almost two-thirds of the hardwood, and half of the pulp wood, in addition to almost the entire naval stores output of the United States.[5] The timber industry offers great promise for the development of both industry and agriculture in the South.

Mineral production in the South was 24.1 per cent of the total for the nation in 1928. By 1948 it had increased to 42.0 per cent of the nation's total. Available reserves of various minerals in the region are known to be considerable.

Certainly natural resources of the region exist in such abundance as to lend optimism to predictions that the South has just begun to assume its rightful economic importance.

As the region has shifted from an agricultural to a combined agricultural and industrial economy, occupational patterns of its people have also changed. The decade beginning in 1940 brought occupational changes of great significance to the South.

In 1940 Virginia was the only Southern state in which there were not more people engaged in agriculture, forestry, and fisheries than in any other major industry group of occupations. Ten years later there were more people engaged in manufacturing and construction than in agriculture, forestry, and fisheries in Alabama, Florida, Georgia, Louisiana, North Carolina, South Carolina, Tennessee, Texas, and Virginia. This left agricultural occupations dominant in only Arkansas, Kentucky, and Mississippi. If mining were added to manufacturing and construction, Kentucky would fall in the list of states in which agricultural pursuits are no longer dominant.

---

[5] Hoover and Ratchford, *op. cit.*, p. 16.

The actual number of agricultural workers decreased in every state except Florida. Every state except Florida and North Carolina had a decline of more than 10 per cent in the number of persons in the labor force following agricultural occupations. A decline in the relative importance of personal services as an occupation also occurred during the same decade. Substantial increases occurred in manufacturing and construction pursuits. Other groups which gained percentagewise are the wholesale and retail trades, professional and related services, and public utilities occupations. It will be noted that these occupational changes are all in harmony with the picture of increasing technical complexity and urbanization in the region and are a part of the new forces which are changing the whole economy of the region.

Agricultural practices and income must be considered in order to understand the changing economy of the region. Until recent years, farming was an extractive and exploitive enterprise with little or no thought given to the conservation or improvement of the soil. Row crops, draining the soil of its nutrients and returning little of value to it, were common. Row farming also increased destructive soil erosion.

Within recent years the row crop pattern has been greatly modified by the introduction of soil conserving crops, crop rotation, contour plowing, and other soil conservation practices. At the same time, there has been a movement away from the one cash crop practice to diversi- fied farming, including the raising of fruits and the production of live- stock and poultry. Although the number of farm workers was de- creasing rapidly, mechanization of Southern agriculture became so widespread that farm cash income of the region was a slightly greater percentage of the total farm cash income in the United States in 1952 than it was in 1940. Improved farming practices greatly increased pro- duction per acre during these years. The introduction of electricity to farm homes has improved the standard of living and brought to the farm family relief from many of the tasks which formerly consumed much time and energy.

It is clear that the urbanization of the South is not proceeding at the expense of farm income. Indeed, the lot of the farmer is much better now in all respects than it has ever been.

The manufacture of cotton textiles and tobacco products, long the dominant industrial enterprises of the South, reflects the natural and agricultural resources of the region. Recently, diversification of the industrial output of the region has occurred through the increase in food processing plants, synthetic fiber manufacturing, and furniture and paper industries. The fastest growing industries in the South are the chemical industries, including fissionable materials, synthetic fibers, synthetic rubber, plastics, and fertilizers.

Cotton and tobacco manufacturing industries require workers of little skill. Wages in these industries have been traditionally low. The newer industries, particularly the chemical industries, require more skill, and the value added to raw material by manufacturing per worker is much greater than in either cotton or tobacco manufacturing. The average annual wage per production worker in manufacturing in the South was $770 in 1931, $791 in 1939, and $1,968 in 1947.[6] The value added to raw material per production worker in manufacturing for the same years was $2,188, $2,314, and $5,311.[7]

The trend in the South is toward the more complex industrial processes which require workers of greater skill, pay higher wages, and add higher value per worker. Should this trend continue, the South will have a diversified and balanced industrial structure to match a balanced agricultural pattern. The only industry group in which the South is making slow progress is the heavy industry group, particularly steel and heavy machinery manufacturing.

The result of industrial developments is an economy which enjoys a far better balance than at any time in the past. It seems reasonable to expect the industrial development of the South to continue its remarkable pace of recent years, barring national or international catastrophe.

Trade and transportation in the region are facilitated by a number of excellent harbors along the Atlantic and Gulf Coasts and a number of navigable internal waterways. The region has an excellent railroad system of over 60,000 miles. There are also 146,000 miles of highways.

Historically, lack of capital wealth has been one of the deficiencies of Southern finance. Much of the investment in industrial and business enterprises has come from outside the region. This means, of course, that dividends trace the course of capital investment back to its sources outside the region. In 1937 dividends and interest payments were only $17.55 per capita in the region, as compared to $68.97 for the rest of the nation.[8] Total assets of banks in the region have increased from 9.7 per cent of the total for the country in 1929 to 15.9 per cent of the total in 1949.[9]

The foregoing discussion of demographic and economic developments in the recent history of the South serves as a backdrop for a consideration of the capacity of the region to support public education.

---

[6] No adjustments to allow for fluctuations in the value of the dollar have been made in these or subsequent figures.

[7] Hoover and Ratchford, *op. cit.*, p. 136.

[8] National Emergency Council, *op. cit.*, p. 22.

[9] Hoover and Ratchford, *op. cit.*, p. 168.

ABILITY TO SUPPORT PUBLIC EDUCATION

The aggregate influence of trends and forces influencing the economy are reflected in per capita income figures. The ability of a state or region to pay for public education is closely related to annual per capita income. Table 23 shows per capita income for each of the states and the county population classifications within states for 1940, 1950, and 1952.

TABLE 23

PER CAPITA INCOME IN THE SOUTH

State and Population Classification	1940	1950	1952
Alabama			
State	$241	$ 778	$ 941
Rural	96	406	450
Rural–Urban	141	528	821
Metropolitan	428	1,074	1,388
Arkansas			
State	259	768	941
Rural	154	551	597
Rural–Urban	179	570	641
Metropolitan	494	1,302	1,711
Florida			
State	475	1,146	1,297
Rural	241	794	727
Rural–Urban	363	984	915
Metropolitan	602	1,334	1,564
Georgia			
State	322	913	1,058
Rural	185	587	678
Rural–Urban	307	858	875
Metropolitan	511	1,214	1,552
Kentucky			
State	306	872	1,041
Rural	134	455	623
Rural-Urban	212	654	797
Metropolitan	665	1,480	1,674
Louisiana			
State	334	984	1,140
Rural	147	508	708
Rural-Urban	203	696	870
Metropolitan	559	1,414	1,625
Mississippi			
State	$187	$ 604	$ 799
Rural	128	405	603
Rural–Urban	219	657	784
Metropolitan	404	1,016	1,457

TABLE 23 (continued)

State and Population Classification	1940	1950	1952
North Carolina			
State	305	899	1,016
Rural	160	540	714
Rural–Urban	254	808	869
Metropolitan	520	1,379	1,415
Oklahoma			
State	405	1,038	1,189
Rural	185	413	597
Rural–Urban	361	790	989
Metropolitan	686	1,569	1,753
South Carolina			
State	279	771	1,021
Rural	161	475	610
Rural–Urban	265	739	918
Metropolitan	425	1,069	1,397
Tennessee			
State	312	977	1,001
Rural	120	509	460
Rural–Urban	192	820	746
Metropolitan	553	1,379	1,383
Texas			
State	446	1,258	1,392
Rural	239	887	1,400
Rural–Urban	270	926	889
Metropolitan	582	1,602	1,914
Virginia			
State	397	1,042	1,266
Rural	239	720	780
Rural–Urban	284	822	926
Metropolitan	613	1,316	1,822
TOTAL			
State	$339	$ 975	$1,143
Rural	157	508	652
Rural–Urban	246	751	853
Metropolitan	553	1,344	1,593

In keeping with the rising economy of the period, the percentage of increase in every state and in each population classification within every state was very substantial for the twelve-year period. It will be noted that the greatest percentage increase occurred in those states with the lowest per capita income in 1940; the four lowest states at the beginning of the period had the greatest percentage increase and the four highest the lowest percentage increase. Thus, the gap in the ratio of income between the highest and lowest income states was decreased. This comparison may be made clearer by the following example. In 1940, Florida, the state with the highest per capita income, had $2.54 income for each $1.00 income in Mississippi, the lowest state. By 1952, Texas, the highest state, had $1.74 per capita income for $1.00 of per capita income for the lowest state, Mississippi. But the dollar difference between the highest and lowest state of $288 in 1940 had increased to $593 in 1952. The relative rankings of these states were about the same at the beginning and end of the period.

The lowest per capita income in both 1940 and 1952 was in rural counties. Rural counties, however, increased faster than either rural-urban or metropolitan counties. For each $1.00 of per capita income in rural counties in 1940, there was $4.15 in 1952, the total increase being from $157 to $652 per capita.

Per capita income in rural-urban counties for the entire region increased from $246 to $853, a percentage gain of 247. The dollar difference between the highest and the lowest rural-urban county increased from $222 to $384. The percentage increase was greatest in those counties with the lowest income in 1940.

Per capita income for metropolitan counties increased from $553 to $1,593 during the twelve-year period. The rate of increase in per capita income for these counties was 188 per cent. Variations for metropolitan counties from state to state were less than variations for the other county classifications. In every state per capita income from metropolitan counties exceeded that for rural or rural-urban groupings. On the basis of per capita income in 1940, the highest metropolitan counties, those in Oklahoma, had 7.2 times as much ability to support schools as the lowest rural counties, those in Alabama. By 1952 the highest metropolitan counties, those in Texas, had only 4.3 times as much ability as the lowest rural counties, which were still found in Alabama.

Effective buying income in the South increased from $12,565,849,-000 in 1940 to $49,025,650,000 in 1952, a per capita increase of from $339 to $1,143 and a percentage change of 237. Stated in different terms, for every dollar of income per person in the South in 1940 there was $3.37 in 1952.

Over-all results of the increases in per capita income and changes in patterns of variation among states and within states were to make the region somewhat more homogeneous in per capita income on a ratio basis, and to decrease the differences in income ability among the states and the population classifications. It should not be overlooked, however, that the dollar differences in per capita income among the states and among the population classifications increased.

Two more measures of ability to support public schools, which are more refined than per capita income, are income per school-age child and income per pupil in average daily attendance. Table 24 reduces per capita income to these measures for the Southern region, for the states within the region, and for county population classifications by

TABLE 24

INCOME PER SCHOOL-AGE CHILD (6–17 YEARS) AND INCOME PER CHILD IN AVERAGE DAILY ATTENDANCE IN THE PUBLIC SCHOOLS IN THE SOUTH

State and Population Classification	Income Per School-Age Child		Income Per Child in Average Daily Attendance		
	1940	1950	1939–40	1949–50	1951–52
Alabama					
State	$ 926	$3,328	$1,204	$ 4,008	$ 4,987
Rural	338	1,463	485	1,822	2,093
Rural–Urban	516	2,120	701	2,504	3,988
Metropolitan	1,899	5,314	2,405	6,545	8,538
Arkansas					
State	1,033	3,329	1,354	4,133	5,113
Rural	578	2,128	711	2,643	3,070
Rural–Urban	688	2,371	967	3,011	3,465
Metropolitan	2,532	7,317	3,191	9,071	11,360
Florida					
State	2,288	6,474	2,764	7,694	8,311
Rural	1,003	3,397	1,280	4,080	3,523
Rural–Urban	1,559	5,181	1,888	5,965	5,503
Metropolitan	3,923	8,661	4,077	10,459	11,434
Georgia					
State	1,305	4,101	1,725	5,073	5,928
Rural	677	2,293	893	2,935	3,438
Rural–Urban	1,160	3,499	1,464	4,160	4,535
Metropolitan	2,494	6,709	3,272	8,275	10,480
Kentucky					
State	1,251	3,929	1,768	5,346	6,577
Rural	500	1,887	684	2,421	3,420
Rural–Urban	872	2,842	1,168	3,692	4,566
Metropolitan	3,452	8,580	5,416	13,836	15,489
Louisiana					
State	1,387	4,555	1,984	6,276	7,194
Rural	543	1,992	732	2,418	3,329
Rural–Urban	763	2,760	935	2,933	3,649
Metropolitan	2,750	8,150	4,237	13,493	14,390
Mississippi					
State	721	2,504	863	2,787	3,771
Rural	445	1,493	493	1,480	2,336
Rural–Urban	885	2,792	1,052	3,181	3,848
Metropolitan	1,807	5,293	2,420	6,741	9,647

TABLE 24 (continued)

State and Population Classification	Income Per School-Age Child		Income Per Child in Average Daily Attendance		
	1940	1950	1939–40	1949–50	1951–52
North Carolina					
State	1,151	3,885	1,380	4,578	5,268
Rural	578	1,929	667	2,275	3,117
Rural–Urban	941	3,226	1,117	3,800	4,072
Metropolitan	2,273	7,322	2,651	8,602	8,801
Oklahoma					
State	1,682	4,982	1,951	5,767	6,729
Rural	853	1,717	....	2,039	2,877
Rural–Urban	1,442	3,646	....	4,070	4,999
Metropolitan	3,462	9,025	....	10,731	11,144
South Carolina					
State	1,026	3,115	1,378	3,948	5,232
Rural	538	1,613	768	2,109	2,681
Rural–Urban	957	2,903	1,305	3,707	4,577
Metropolitan	1,785	5,179	2,348	6,345	8,059
Tennessee					
State	1,306	4,564	1,698	5,515	5,677
Rural	472	1,983	613	2,660	2,506
Rural–Urban	765	3,926	998	4,666	4,426
Metropolitan	2,670	7,706	3,408	9,524	9,320
Texas					
State	1,931	6,306	2,560	8,422	9,185
Rural	908	3,608	1,224	4,842	7,465
Rural–Urban	1,095	4,266	1,408	5,318	5,272
Metropolitan	2,908	8,866	4,137	12,150	13,913
Virginia					
State	1,667	5,178	2,152	6,439	7,958
Rural	956	2,994	1,228	3,415	3,723
Rural–Urban	1,021	3,494	1,443	4,305	4,894
Metropolitan	3,152	8,386	3,911	10,610	13,827
TOTAL					
State	1,386	4,513	1,789	5,617	6,552
Rural	573	1,931	735	2,334	3,045
Rural–Urban	1,074	3,537	1,389	4,226	4,844
Metropolitan	2,686	7,582	3,483	9,772	11,207

states. Comparisons by states and population groupings are more valid, since distortions due to variations in the proportion of the total population of school age and in average daily attendance are eliminated. Only 1940 and 1950 are used in comparing income per school-age child; school-age population data for 1952 are not available.

Income per school-age child on a regional level increased 226 per cent during the decade, growing from $1,386 to $4,513. At the same time, income per child in average daily attendance increased 214 percent, from $1,789 to $5,617. A comparison of these statistics with per capita income suggests a decreased percentage of the total population of school-age and a larger per cent of that population in average daily attendance in public schools at the end of the period than at the beginning. In 1950, there was $3.26 in support of each school-age child and $3.14 in support of each child in average daily attendance for every $1.00 respectively in 1940.

For each $1.00 of income per child of school age in rural counties in 1940, there was $4.69 in metropolitan counties in 1940 and $3.93 in 1950. For every $1.00 of income per child of school age in rural-urban counties, there was $2.50 in metropolitan counties in 1940 and $2.14 in 1950. For every rural-urban child of school age in 1940 there was $1.87 as compared to $1.00 for each rural child and $1.83 in 1950.

Stated as income per school-age child, differences in ability between metropolitan and rural counties were much greater in both 1940 and 1950 than the differences when stated in terms of per capita income. The ratio of high to low income states and ratios of high to low counties in the population classifications were greater also than when stated on the basis of per capita income. The greater educational burden of some states is shown by the fact that in 1940 the state most able to support public schools in terms of income per school-age child had $3.17 for each $1.00 of income of the state with the least ability; in 1950 the figures were $2.59 to $1.00.

Differences among states and counties decreased when measured on a ratio basis but dollar differences increased. As would be expected, states and counties with high per capita income had higher income per child. But the high percentage of school-age children in the total population of the lower income states and counties made the concentration of income in the higher states and counties more pronounced when measured as income per child than when measured as per capita income.

The highest ratio in favor of metropolitan counties shows up in computing income per child in attendance. The ratio of metropolitan to rural counties in income for each child in average daily attendance was $4.74 to $1.00 in 1940, and $4.19 to $1.00 in 1950; whereas, on an income per child of school-age basis, the figures were $4.69 to $1.00 in 1940, and $3.93 to $1.00 in 1950. The higher ratios on the basis of average daily attendance are due to the fact that a larger proportion of the children of school age were in average daily attendance in rural counties than in metropolitan counties.

In general, the rank orders of the states on income per school-age child and income per child in average daily attendance were the same. These rankings also tended to be the same as those for per capita income.

Examination of ability to support public schools, which utilizes the three kinds of income illustrated here, can at best yield only a very general picture of revenue potential. The serious competition for public revenues must be borne in mind, as the demand for governmental services always far exceeds available revenues. Judgments have to be made constantly as to the proper allocation of revenues to various fields of governmental endeavor. It is necessary to take these conditions into account in assessing possible school revenues.

Furthermore, ability has to be measured against the program of education designed. In the final analysis, measurement must be in terms of educational outcome rather than in dollars expended. Problems inherent in providing an adequate program vary from one population classification to another and from state to state. For example, rural areas have more complex problems of providing educational adequacy than other population classifications due to such factors as sparsity of population and lack of ability to compete successfully for a fair share of the better teachers.

LEVELS OF SUPPORT AS MEASURED BY SCHOOL REVENUES

The income previously discussed which actually found its way into channels of school support requires careful analysis. The revenues

TABLE 25

PER CAPITA PUBLIC SCHOOL REVENUES IN THE SOUTHERN STATES

State	1939–40	1949–50	1951–52
Alabama	$ 7.62	$22.69	$27.71
Arkansas	7.00	22.82	23.77
Florida	12.87	33.68	38.81
Georgia	8.39	22.89	30.63
Kentucky	8.90	20.77	25.40
Louisiana	11.41	34.49	38.70
Mississippi	6.58	17.16	19.72
North Carolina	11.35	31.12	36.83
Oklahoma	13.23	. . . .	44.30
South Carolina	9.16	23.63	27.87
Tennessee	7.87	25.38	26.29
Texas	. . . .	34.43	37.88
Virginia	10.28	24.53	35.09
TOTAL*	9.23	25.72	30.77

* Does not include Oklahoma and Texas.

set aside for school support will be translated into per capita school revenue, revenue per school-age child, and revenue per child in average daily attendance.

Per capita school revenues in the South increased 233 per cent in the twelve-year period beginning in 1940. The dollar increase was from $9.23 to $30.77. Thus, for each $1.00 in per capita school revenue available in 1940, there was $3.33 in 1952. Table 25 presents a breakdown by states. The greatest percentage increases occurred in Georgia and Alabama, and the smallest in Kentucky and Mississippi. The difference in ratio between the highest and lowest state increased from $1.96 for each $1.00 in 1940 to $2.07 for each

TABLE 26

PER CAPITA PUBLIC SCHOOL REVENUES FROM LOCAL SOURCES IN THE SOUTH

State and Population Classification	1939–40	1951–52	State and Population Classification	1939–40	1951–52
Alabama			*Mississippi*		
State	$3.08	$ 6.01	State	$3.63	$ 9.05
Rural	1.57	2.58	Rural	2.68	5.52
Rural–Urban	2.26	5.85	Rural–Urban	3.89	9.36
Metropolitan	5.14	9.78	Metropolitan	5.03	14.83
Arkansas			*North Carolina*		
State	3.84	10.58	State	3.63	8.18
Rural	2.71	7.31	Rural	2.47	5.35
Rural–Urban	2.28	8.48	Rural–Urban	2.62	8.13
Metropolitan	6.55	16.00	Metropolitan	5.44	12.19
Florida			*South Carolina*		
State	6.19	18.75	State	4.82	10.31
Rural	4.93	18.20	Rural	3.40	6.74
Rural–Urban	5.12	13.52	Rural–Urban	3.82	9.01
Metropolitan	7.37	21.74	Metropolitan	6.42	11.39
Georgia			*Tennessee*		
State	3.78	9.68	State	4.78	10.31
Rural	1.66	5.59	Rural	2.02	4.36
Rural–Urban	1.65	6.27	Rural–Urban	3.85	7.87
Metropolitan	7.85	15.06	Metropolitan	7.64	15.07
Kentucky			*Virginia*		
State	5.35	14.43	State	7.02	18.77
Rural	4.03	11.42	Rural	5.58	13.52
Rural–Urban	4.53	13.90	Rural–Urban	6.42	16.77
Metropolitan	8.84	21.54	Metropolitan	8.92	24.21
Louisiana			TOTAL		
State	4.77	11.42	State	4.57	11.60
Rural	3.98	8.09	Rural	3.20	6.94
Rural–Urban	5.38	8.89	Rural–Urban	3.71	8.61
Metropolitan	5.68	14.34	Metropolitan	7.03	14.05

$1.00 in 1952. The three highest states in 1939-40, Florida, Louisiana, and North Carolina, were still the three highest and in the same order in 1952. The general tendency of the lowest states to increase faster than the highest states in per capita income did not hold true for per capita revenue. The net effect of the variations in the rate of increase was to widen the differences in both dollar amounts and dollar ratios between the highest and lowest states.

Total per capita revenues would be meaningless for counties because of the large sums of non-local funds contributed to the school districts by the state governments. The amount of revenue per capita of funds raised locally indicates how much each person on the average is contributing to the support of his local school system. These statistics are presented in Table 26. Great differences existed among the states in the per capita amounts raised locally in 1951-1952. One of the reasons was the high per capita revenues from non-district sources in some states. For example, North Carolina and Alabama had smaller amounts than Kentucky and Mississippi in per capita revenues raised locally but higher total per capita school revenues. Of the four highest states in local per capita revenues, three were among the highest four in total revenues; the other state, however, was among the lowest in per capita revenues.

On the regional level, per capita revenues from local sources increased 117 per cent in rural counties, 132 per cent in rural-urban counties, and 143 per cent in metropolitan counties. These rates compared with per capita income increases of 315 per cent in rural counties, 247 per cent in rural-urban counties, and 188 per cent in metropolitan counties. Per capita income thus increased much more rapidly than per capita local school revenues in all three county classifications. Metropolitan counties exhibited the greatest increase in per capita revenues and the smallest increase in per capita income. Florida was the only state in which per capita revenues increased more rapidly in rural counties than in metropolitan counties.

Revenues per school-age child in the South, as shown in Table 27, increased from $37 to $117, or 214 per cent, during the twelve years for which the comparison was made. For every $1.00 of school revenue per school-age child in 1940, there was $3.14 in 1950, while the per capita revenues were $2.79 in 1950 for each $1.00 in 1940. Because of the decreasing proportion of the total population to the school-age population, each $1.00 in school revenue per capita in 1950 provided a larger amount for each school-age child than it did in 1940. Using regional figures, there was $2.91 in 1950 for every $1.00 in 1940 in per capita income. These comparisons show that, although the increase in school revenues per capita was not as great

TABLE 27

PUBLIC SCHOOL REVENUES PER SCHOOL AGE CHILD (6–17 YEARS) AND PER CHILD
IN AVERAGE DAILY ATTENDANCE IN THE SOUTH

State and Population Classification	Revenues Per Child (6–17 Years)		Revenues Per Child in Average Daily Attendance		
	1939–40	1949–50	1939–40	1949–50	1951–52
Alabama					
State	$29	$ 97	$38	$117	$147
Rural	26	89	37	111	139
Rural–Urban	28	96	38	113	150
Metropolitan	33	104	42	128	157
Arkansas					
State	28	99	37	123	131
Rural	25	95	31	118	133
Rural–Urban	21	87	30	110	120
Metropolitan	45	122	57	152	168
Florida					
State	62	190	75	226	249
Rural	58	195	74	234	248
Rural–Urban	57	185	69	213	234
Metropolitan	69	208	85	251	275
Georgia					
State	34	103	45	127	171
Rural	30	91	39	117	153
Rural–Urban	25	99	31	118	166
Metropolitan	50	115	66	142	192
Kentucky					
State	36	94	51	127	161
Rural	30	81	41	104	134
Rural–Urban	33	93	45	120	149
Metropolitan	60	140	94	226	265
Louisiana					
State	47	160	68	220	239
Rural	54	182	72	220	235
Rural–Urban	52	188	63	200	217
Metropolitan	48	150	74	248	275
Mississippi					
State	25	71	30	79	92
Rural	23	69	26	68	78
Rural–Urban	27	67	32	76	89
Metropolitan	28	81	38	103	128
North Carolina					
State	43	134	51	158	189
Rural	39	113	45	133	174
Rural–Urban	40	136	47	160	187
Metropolitan	55	166	64	195	216

TABLE 27 (continued)

State and Population Classification	Revenues Per Child (6–17 Years)		Revenues Per Child in Average Daily Attendance		
	1939–40	1949–50	1939–40	1949–50	1951–52
South Carolina					
State	34	95	45	121	142
Rural	24	82	35	107	118
Rural–Urban	30	87	41	112	136
Metropolitan	42	102	55	125	159
Tennessee					
State	33	119	43	143	149
Rural	26	111	34	149	154
Rural–Urban	29	122	38	145	147
Metropolitan	46	129	58	159	167
Virginia					
State	43	122	56	152	216
Rural	38	101	49	115	141
Rural–Urban	37	109	52	134	196
Metropolitan	58	149	71	188	284
TOTAL					
State	37	117	48	144	173
Rural	32	105	42	126	149
Rural–Urban	34	114	44	136	162
Metropolitan	50	140	65	179	216

as the increase in per capita income, a greater increase in revenues per child was made than in per capita income.

In 1940 metropolitan counties had $1.55 in revenues per child for each $1.00 in rural counties. In 1950 the ratio had decreased to $1.33 to $1.00. Metropolitan counties held a smaller advantage over rural-urban counties, the ratio in 1940 being $1.48 to $1.00, and $1.28 to $1.00 in 1950. Little difference existed between rural-urban and rural counties on this item.

Variations within the county classifications were great. Among rural counties, the highest group had $2.45 for each $1.00 in the lowest group in 1940, and $2.58 for each $1.00 in 1950. The ratio of high metropolitan to low metropolitan counties was $2.43 to each $1.00, and $2.67 to each $1.00 in 1950. In the rural-urban counties the highest group in 1940 had $2.65 to each $1.00 for the low group, and in 1950, $2.81 to each $1.00.

When measured by ratios the gap among the states and among the population classifications was reduced somewhat. Within the classifications of counties, however, the ratio of differences between high and low groups increased. On a dollar basis the gap increased among the states, among the population classifications, and among the groups of counties by states within each population classification.

Revenues per child in average daily attendance is the more exact ot
the three measures utilized in this analysis. Reference to Table 27
will show that there was an increase from $48 to $173 in revenues per
child in average daily attendance from 1940 to 1952. The percentage
increase was 260. Alabama, Georgia, North Carolina, and Virginia
increased faster than the region as a whole. Florida was the highest
state and Mississippi was the lowest at both the beginning and end of
the period.

The dollar difference between the highest and lowest states had increased from $45 to $157, or 249 per cent. Mississippi, with $3.07
in school revenues for each child in average daily attendance in 1952
for every $1.00 in 1940, was still at the bottom of the list and the
gap between it and the highest state was greater. It appears that the
differences in the level of support among the states for each child in
average daily attendance were widening. At the same time, the ratio
of difference in per capita ability between the highest and lowest states
had decreased from $2.54 to $1.00 in 1940 to $1.58 to $1.00 in 1952.

Differences within rural, rural-urban, and metropolitan county
groupings increased during the period, except in metropolitan counties where there was a slight narrowing of the ratio difference between
the highest and lowest counties. Variations in the percentages of state
and Federal funds going to the counties, and differences in school
income within counties are reasons for these conditions. Table 27
points up these differences by states in the amount of school revenue
per child in average daily attendance in the three types of counties.

TABLE 28

AMOUNT OF SCHOOL REVENUES PER CHILD IN AVERAGE DAILY ATTENDANCE IN
METROPOLITAN COUNTIES FOR EACH DOLLAR OF REVENUE PER CHILD IN
AVERAGE DAILY ATTENDANCE IN THE POPULATION CLASSIFICATION
OF COUNTIES HAVING THE LOWEST LEVEL OF SUPPORT FOR
CHILDREN IN ATTENDANCE IN THE SOUTHERN STATES

State	1939–40	1951–52
Alabama	$1.14	$1.13
Arkansas	1.90	1.40
Florida	1.23	1.18
Georgia	2.13	1.25
Kentucky	2.29	1.98
Louisiana	1.17	1.27
Mississippi	1.46	1.64
North Carolina	1.42	1.24
South Carolina	1.57	1.35
Tennessee	1.71	1.14
Virginia	1.45	2.01
TOTAL	1.55	1.45

TABLE 29

GAINS IN PER CAPITA SCHOOL REVENUES AND REVENUES PER CHILD IN AVERAGE DAILY ATTENDANCE COMPARED WITH GAIN IN PER CAPITA INCOME IN THE SOUTHERN STATES

State	Ratio I/P in 1952 to I/P in 1940 [a]	Ratio R/P in 1951–52 to R/P in 1939–40 [b]	Ratio of R/ADA in 1951–52 to R/ADA in 1939–40 [c]	Ratio Column 3 to Column 2	Ratio Column 4 to Column 2
Alabama	3.90	3.64	3.87	0.93	0.99
Arkansas	3.63	3.40	3.54	0.94	0.98
Florida	2.73	3.02	3.32	1.11	1.22
Georgia	3.29	3.65	3.81	1.11	1.16
Kentucky	3.40	2.85	3.16	0.84	0.93
Louisiana	3.41	3.39	3.51	0.99	1.03
Mississippi	4.27	3.00	3.07	0.70	0.72
North Carolina	3.33	3.24	3.71	0.97	1.12
South Carolina	3.66	3.04	3.16	0.83	0.86
Tennessee	3.21	3.34	3.47	1.04	1.08
Virginia	3.19	3.41	3.86	1.07	1.21
TOTAL	3.42	3.34	3.60	0.98	1.05

[a] I/P is per capita income.
[b] R/P is ratio of total public school revenues to total population.
[c] R/ADA is revenue per child in average daily attendance.

Ranges in level of support between metropolitan and other counties are shown more clearly in Table 28 by the ratio of revenue per child in average daily attendance in metropolitan counties of each state to revenue per child in average daily attendance in the classification of counties in that state having the lowest level of support. In all states except Louisiana, Mississippi, and Virginia the differences decreased. For the region the difference declined slightly. Thus, during this time there was a trend toward decreasing the differences in the level of support which existed at the beginning of the period between metropolitan counties and less urbanized counties.

The highest group of metropolitan counties had 3.6 times as much support for each child in attendance as the lowest rural group of counties at the beginning and at the end of the period. As measured by per capita income, the highest metropolitan counties for the same eleven states had 6.9 times as much ability as the lowest rural counties in 1940 and four times as much in 1952. The two groups of counties representing the extremes in the region between metropolitan and rural counties had decreased differences in per capita income but not in school revenues for each child in attendance.

Changes in relationships between income and the level of school support for each state are indicated by comparing increases in income to increases in school support. The ratio of per capita income in 1952 to that in 1940 divided into the ratio of per capita school revenues in 1952 to those in 1940 gives the relative increase in per capita revenues compared to per capita income. The ratio of increase in revenues per child in average daily attendance to the increase in per capita income is another measure of the comparative gain in income and school support. These comparisons are shown in Table 29. It will be noted that for the region as a whole the increases in per capita income and per capita school revenues were almost equal. In Florida and Georgia the gain in per capita revenues was considerably above the gain in per capita income. The gain in revenues in Mississippi and Kentucky was well below that in per capita income.

Only four states gained faster in per capita revenues than in per capita income; six states had gains in revenue per child in average daily attendance which exceeded their gains in the per capita income. For the whole region, the gain in revenues per child in average daily attendance was greater than the gain in per capita income. In Mississippi the gain in revenues per child in average daily attendance was only slightly greater in relation to per capita income than the gain in per capita revenues. It may be concluded from this table that the gain in the levels of school support was just about equal to the gain in per capita income from 1940 to 1952.

FACTORS RELATED TO THE LEVEL OF SCHOOL SUPPORT

Since the ultimate purpose of school revenue is the support of children in the public schools, it is of vital importance to determine what factors affect the level of school support per child. Certain characteristics of the population and economy were related to public school support per child in average daily attendance by the use of rank order correlation by states. No high degree of relationship between the high percentages of funds from nondistrict sources and level of support per child in attendance was found. Neither was there any significant relationship between the percentage of Negro population in a state and the level of support per school-age child.

The two factors which showed a high positive correlation with revenues per child in average daily attendance were per capita income and urbanization. Since high per capita income is usually associated with urbanization, this fact is not surprising. The rank order correlation of per capita income to revenues per child in average daily attendance among the Southern states was .86 in 1940 and .84 in 1952. The correlations for percentage of urbanization and revenues per child in average daily attendance were .77 in 1940 and .74 in 1950.

A negative relationship appeared between a high percentage of school-age children in the total population and the level of support of each child in average daily attendance. Among the states there was in 1940 a correlation between the rankings on the two items of −.56 and in 1950 of −.70. A high percentage of children in the population is usually associated with rural areas as low per capita income is; therefore, a negative correlation was not unexpected. Nevertheless, it has important implications for the financing of public schools. The fact that low per capita income and high percentages of school-age children in the total population tend to go hand in hand influences unfavorably the level of support which is available for public schools in those states where such conditions prevail.

The provision of large amounts of aid through the state government certainly increased educational effort of the state, and it also decreased the differences in the level of support among the counties in the three population classifications. Since such aid did not reach beyond state boundaries, however, it did not decrease the differences in the level of support among states. The only recourse for states with low per capita income and high percentages of children of school age during this period was additional taxation of their own resources in order to raise the level of support for each child in school. The states were either unable or unwilling to increase taxes, as is revealed by the high correlation of per capita income and revenues per child in average daily attendance in such states.

TABLE 30

EDUCATIONAL EFFORT IN THE SOUTHERN STATES

State	Per Cent School Revenue Is of Effective Buying Income			Ratio of Revenue Per School Age Child to Per Capita Income	
	1939–40	*1949–50*	*1951–52*	*1939–40*	*1949–50*
Alabama	3.16	2.91	2.96	.1215	.1247
Arkansas	2.69	2.97	2.56	.1077	.1286
Florida	2.70	2.93	2.99	.1304	.1651
Georgia	2.60	2.50	2.87	.1054	.1125
Kentucky	2.90	2.38	2.45	.1187	.1072
Louisiana	3.40	3.50	3.32	.1419	.1622
Mississippi	3.51	2.84	2.45	.1352	.1174
North Carolina	3.72	3.46	3.59	.1403	.1495
Oklahoma	3.27	—	3.66	.1358	—
South Carolina	3.28	3.06	2.72	.1206	.1238
Tennessee	2.51	2.59	2.63	.1053	.1212
Texas	—	2.74	2.61	—	.1372
Virginia	2.58	2.35	2.72	.1086	.1169
TOTAL [a]	2.98	2.85	2.89	.1091	.1200

[a] Oklahoma and Texas are not included in regional averages.

One further measure of educational effort in the South will be presented. By use of two measures of educational effort developed in this study, Table 30 has been prepared to show the per cent school revenue is of effective buying income and the ratio of revenue per school-age child to per capita income.[10]

For the eleven states for which data were available for each of the three years, the ratio of school revenue to income decreased from 2.98 per cent in 1940 to 2.85 per cent in 1950, and then increased

---

[10] Educational effort may be roughly defined as the amount of support achieved divided by the available means or ability. The most commonly used measure of educational effort is total amount of money devoted to education (support) divided by total or net income (ability). This measure fails to take into account population. Many educational finance authorities have felt the need for reducing both support and ability to a unit measurement of some kind.

In this study the traditional measurement of effort has been used and supplemented by another measure of effort. The first measurement used here was simply the amount of school revenue divided by net disposable income.

The second measurement of educational effort is the ratio of school revenue per school-age child to per capita income. In this measure both numerator and denominator have been reduced to a unit basis. Revenue has been computed for each school-age child rather than for each child in average daily attendance because of an assumption that all school-age children should receive schooling. Also implicit in this measure are two assumptions regarding the economy: (a) As the proportion of children in the population increases, an increasing proportion of per capita income ought to be spent on schools; (b) The cost of feeding, clothing, and housing a child is less than that for an adult.

to 2.89 per cent by 1952. According to this measure, seven of the eleven states decreased in effort from 1940 to 1950, four decreased from 1950 to 1952, while seven decreased from 1940 to 1952. The greatest decrease was shown by Mississippi which, according to this measure, was making the second greatest effort in the South in 1940. In 1952 it was tied with Kentucky for the lowest effort of any state in the region. North Carolina was making the greatest effort of the eleven states in both years. Declines in effort were shown by Kentucky and South Carolina, in addition to Mississippi. Florida and Georgia showed the greatest increases in effort, the increase in Georgia coming entirely from 1950 to 1952.

While some states had consistent downward trends in the ratio of school revenue to income and others had consistent upward trends, the movement could be described in a general way for the region as downward from 1940 to 1950 with a noticeable upturn from 1950 to 1952. The 1952 level was still generally below that for 1940.

By use of the second measure of educational effort, that of the ratio of revenue per school-age child to per capita income, trends for the period from 1940 to 1950 were calculated. According to this formula, there was an upward trend for the region from .1091 to .1200 in contrast to the downward trend reflected by the first formula. All states showed an increase in the ratio from 1940 to 1950 except Kentucky and Mississippi, and the greatest increases were evident in Florida, Louisiana, Tennessee, and Arkansas.

Despite the varying results of the use of the two methods of measuring educational effort, certain conclusions were confirmed by both. First, Kentucky and Mississippi decreased educational effort from 1940 to 1950. Second, North Carolina ranked near the top among Southern states in educational effort in all three years. Third, Arkansas, Florida, Louisiana, and Tennessee increased educational effort from 1940 to 1950, although by 1952 Arkansas and Louisiana had dropped below the 1940 level on the ratio of school revenues to income. Other conclusions were not supported by the use of both methods and the need for further research on a suitable measure of educational effort which will receive general acceptance is indicated.

Neither of the measures of educational effort applied to the Southern states should be considered a measure of absolute effort, but rather a method of determining relative effort for the same states in different years. In order to determine the extent to which the two methods would result in the same rankings of states, the states were arranged in rank order from high to low on each measure and the rank order correlation computed. In 1940 the rank order coefficient of correlation was .88 and in 1950 it was .80. The ranking of states obtained from the two measures, therefore, was highly consistent.

SCHOOL REVENUE AND PUBLIC FINANCE

The foundation of school finance is the tax system through which funds are collected. School revenues, then, are in a real sense a part of total government finance. Financially, public schools are the most important service of local governments and, together with highways and welfare, are one of the three most important services of state government.

School revenues in the South, exclusive of Texas and Oklahoma, totaled almost $261,000,000 in 1940. By 1952 the total for the same states had risen to slightly over $1,000,000,000, a percentage gain of 279. Variations among the states in the percentage of increase range from Florida, with 365, to Kentucky and Mississippi, with 203 per cent each. Total school revenues for Texas in 1951 exceeded that of all the other twelve states in the region for 1940. Revenues for Texas and Oklahoma in 1952 amounted to approximately $400,000,000.

Based on eleven states, school revenues increased in rural counties by 252 per cent, in rural-urban counties 280 per cent, and in metropolitan counties 315 per cent. Changes in average daily attendance for the three classifications during the period were: −1.2 per cent in rural counties, 2.7 per cent in rural-urban, and 25.9 per cent in metropolitan. School revenues in metropolitan counties were 28.9 per cent of all school revenues in 1939-40 and 31 per cent in 1951-52.

The amount of public school revenues raised from local sources in the eleven states in 1940 was about the same as that coming from state and Federal sources. Although in 1952 the amount from local sources, $380,000,000, was much greater than the total school revenues for 1940, it compared with a total from state and Federal sources of $625,000,000. On a percentage basis, local source revenues had increased 194 per cent, while revenues from state and Federal sources had increased 375 per cent.

The trend for a greater percentage of the revenues expended in local school districts to come from sources outside the district, as shown in Table 31, was reflected in every state of the South except Florida. The percentage of revenues coming from local sources declined from 49.5 in 1940 to 37.7 in 1952. References elsewhere in this volume to the effect that local interest and responsibility for schools seem to decline as the state assumes more and more responsibility for the financing of schools are supported by this trend. In some states, the shift was particularly noticeable. Tennessee, Alabama, South Carolina, Virginia, and Georgia reported considerably higher proportions of school district revenue coming from local sources in 1940 than in

TABLE 31

PER CENT OF SCHOOL REVENUES OBTAINED FROM LOCAL SOURCES IN THE SOUTH

State and Population Classification	1939–40	1949–50	1951–52
Alabama			
State	40.4	24.1	21.7
Rural	21.4	10.8	8.5
Rural-Urban	30.0	18.2	19.0
Metropolitan	68.5	42.2	38.4
Arkansas			
State	54.8	35.7	44.5
Rural	39.9	22.0	28.2
Rural-Urban	40.9	26.5	38.2
Metropolitan	73.2	57.0	63.4
Florida			
State	48.1	46.9	48.3
Rural	35.3	33.1	35.6
Rural-Urban	38.6	32.4	34.8
Metropolitan	58.8	55.9	57.7
Georgia			
State	45.1	35.3	31.6
Rural	20.6	22.4	18.5
Rural-Urban	25.3	25.2	19.6
Metropolitan	76.3	61.6	53.0
Kentucky			
State	60.1	60.8	56.8
Rural	51.0	48.8	46.7
Rural-Urban	55.7	56.8	53.4
Metropolitan	77.0	78.3	75.1
Louisiana			
State	41.8	28.1	29.5
Rural	27.4	16.3	16.2
Rural-Urban	39.1	18.7	17.2
Metropolitan	58.5	45.8	46.2
Mississippi			
State	55.1	45.2	45.9
Rural	40.0	30.9	27.5
Rural-Urban	58.7	50.1	51.4
Metropolitan	79.8	74.7	76.7
North Carolina			
State	32.0	25.2	22.2
Rural	23.0	14.7	13.4
Rural-Urban	24.5	23.6	20.4
Metropolitan	43.6	39.0	35.1
South Carolina			
State	52.6	36.7	37.0
Rural	46.4	34.0	25.0
Rural-Urban	46.3	32.1	33.0
Metropolitan	64.0	40.5	41.4

TABLE 31 (*continued*)

State and Population Classification	1939–40	1949–50	1951–52
Tennessee			
State	60.8	36.9	39.2
Rural	30.5	16.6	15.4
Rural-Urban	52.7	30.3	31.7
Metropolitan	80.5	59.0	60.7
Virginia			
State	68.3	60.4	53.5
Rural	58.4	47.7	45.6
Rural-Urban	62.2	52.1	45.3
Metropolitan	79.6	72.4	64.8
TOTAL			
State	49.5	38.4	37.7
Rural	36.1	24.3	23.0
Rural-Urban	41.8	30.4	30.2
Metropolitan	67.8	55.8	54.1

1952. More than 50 per cent of school revenues expended in local school districts in six states came from local sources in 1940. By 1952 there were only two such states, Kentucky and Virginia. In 1940 there were no states in which less than a fourth of school revenues were derived from local sources, but by 1952 Alabama and North Carolina both fell into this classification.

The trend for larger percentages of public school funds to come from nondistrict sources appears to have been slowed down and even to have been reversed in some states, although the regional average continued to show a slight decline in the per cent of revenue from local sources. Six states showed an upward trend in the per cent of total school district revenues coming from local sources during the two-year period from 1950 to 1952, while five showed a continuing decline. Arkansas had almost 10 per cent more of its total school revenues from district sources in 1952 than in 1950, but in the other states which showed increases the differences were negligible. On the other hand, the decreases in Kentucky and Virginia were as great as for the previous ten-year period.

A major function of state school finance programs is to enable school districts with little wealth to offer better educational programs than their own limited resources permit. This principle is often expressed as taxing wealth where it is found and spending it for the education of children where they are. Table 31 shows that in no state, either at the beginning of the period or at the end, were rural districts raising as great a percentage of their revenues from local sources as were metropolitan districts. This is due primarily to higher per capita wealth in metropolitan areas. In 1940 the rural counties on a regional level raised from their own resources a little over one-third of their school funds, while metropolitan counties raised a little over two-thirds of theirs. By 1952 the rural counties raised less than one-fourth of their own funds, while metropolitan counties raised slightly over half of their revenues from local sources. The actual percentage difference between the two classifications was almost the same for both years.

Both at the beginning and at the end of the period, there was no state in which rural-urban counties were raising a larger percentage of their school revenues than metropolitan counties were. Rural-urban usually fell closer to rural counties than to metropolitan in these percentages. In Florida, South Carolina, and Virginia rural-urban counties had smaller percentages in at least one of the three years than did rural counties.

Although the percentages in Table 31 indicate that the decreases in the percentage of total funds coming from local sources was about the same in the three population classifications, rural and rural-urban counties received a slightly higher amount per child in average daily attendance from the increase in funds from non-local sources than did metropolitan counties. Using regional averages in 1940, rural counties were receiving from state and Federal sources $27 per pupil in average daily attendance, rural-urban $26, and metropolitan counties $21. During the next twelve years the increase in non-local funds amounted to $88 in rural counties, $87 in rural-urban counties, and $78 in metropolitan counties for each child in average daily attendance. In 1952, rural counties received $115, rural-urban counties $113, and metropolitan counties $99 in state and Federal funds for each child in average daily attendance. Considering differences in per capita income by county classifications, it would seem that the function of equalization through state finance programs has been only partly realized.

A different analysis throws further light on the distribution of outside support to school districts. Reducing Federal and state aid to a per pupil basis reveals that for $1.00 per pupil in average daily attendance received by metropolitan counties in 1940, rural counties received $1.27. In 1952, however, for $1.00 received from outside sources per pupil in metropolitan counties, only $1.16 was received by rural counties. A similar comparison of metropolitan and rural-urban counties shows a ratio of $1.00 to $1.21 in 1940, and $1.00 to $1.14 in 1952, both years favoring rural-urban counties.

The reverse side of this picture shows that for every $1.00 raised for each pupil in average daily attendance from local sources in rural counties in 1940, $2.95 was raised in metropolitan counties for each child in average daily attendance. This ratio had increased to $3.37

to $1.00 by 1952. At the same time the ratio between rural-urban and metropolitan counties decreased slightly from $1.00 to $2.43 in 1940 to $1.00 to $2.39 in 1952.

These figures show that the advantage of rural over metropolitan counties in the ratio of revenues per child in average daily attendance received from outside the district was diminishing during this period. At the same time, the substantial advantage metropolitan counties held over rural counties in the ratio of revenues per child in average daily attendance from local sources was increasing.

In view of the fact that state and Federal government supplied more than three-fifths of the total revenues of school districts in the South in 1952 and the percentage from these sources had been increasing, it is important to examine the trends in public finance at these levels.

While the proportion of revenues for schools derived from the Federal government continues to be small, the over-all effects of Federal finance influence local communities in their revenue raising abilities. Federal receipts in 1940 were $5,264,663,000. Twelve years later they had risen to $62,128,607,000, an astronomical increase of 1080 per cent. In 1940 total Federal expenditures stood at $9,182,682,000. This figure had increased to $66,145,247,000 by 1952, an increase of 620 per cent.[11] The increases in Federal expenditures resulted primarily from problems of national security.

State government revenues in the South for the fiscal year ending June 30, 1940, were $780,692,000; by 1952 they had increased to $3,047,207,000. In the meantime, Federal internal revenue collections in the Southern states increased from $921,027,000 in 1940 to $6,933,391,000 in 1952. A comparison of Federal internal revenues with state government revenues in the region shows that $1.16 in 1940 and $2.28 in 1952 were going to the Federal government for each $1.00 collected by the states. Percentagewise, increases in revenues from 1940 to 1952 were 194 per cent for school purposes, 290 per cent for state government uses, and 660 per cent for Federal internal revenue collections.

Equitable tax systems are concerned with using the power to tax so that it does not unduly hamper or strain the economy. Sources of revenue have to be considered carefully in this connection. Table 94 of the appendix presents a breakdown by states of the percentage contribution that each major source of revenue made to state government funds in 1940, 1950, and 1952.

States in the Southern region have relied heavily in recent years on sales taxes as sources of revenue. The most popular tax of this kind

---

[11] U. S Department of Commerce, *Statistical Abstract of the United States, 1952* (Washington: Government Printing Office, 1953) pp. 270–272.

is the motor vehicle fuel tax. It existed in every state during all three years covered by this investigation. The next most popular sales tax is the gross receipt or general sales tax. All Southern states except Kentucky, Texas, and Virginia had such a tax in 1952. Florida, Georgia, South Carolina, and Tennessee initiated the general sales tax during the period, while no states already using it abandoned it. The general sales tax recently adopted in the four states mentioned was passed largely to obtain additional revenues for education. Alcoholic beverage taxes are levied by all Southern states and tobacco products taxes by all except North Carolina and Kentucky.

Sales taxes provided 35.7 per cent of all state government revenues in 1940 and 39.2 per cent in 1952. Federal grants-in-aids were the second most important source of revenue for state governments for each of the three years. The largest of these grants in each year was for public welfare and the second was for highways. Federal grants-in-aid increased from 14.1 per cent to 18.8 per cent of total state revenues. Individual and corporation income taxes were levied in eleven of the thirteen Southern states, Florida and Texas being the exceptions. For the region, the two taxes brought in only 4.8 per cent of the revenue of the states in 1940 and 8.2 per cent in 1952. Severance taxes were of considerable importance in only Louisiana, Oklahoma, and Texas.

Unemployment compensation taxes declined in relative importance, from 10.4 per cent of the total state revenue to 5.3 per cent. Motor vehicle and other license taxes declined in relative importance also. For the region as a whole, they supplied 12.9 per cent of state funds in 1940 and only 7.7 per cent in 1952. The property tax also suffered a general decline in relative importance, having by 1952 become largely the prerogative of local governments. Seven and five-tenths per cent of all state revenues in 1940 came from this source, but by 1952 the figure was only 2.4 per cent. Five states were getting less than 1 per cent of their revenues from property taxes in 1952.

As demands on the tax dollar increase, it becomes more and more important to consider the total picture of government expenditures. Table 95 of the appendix shows the per cent of state government expenditures for the chief functions of state governments in each of the Southern states for 1940, 1950, and 1952.

Education, highways, and public welfare accounted for 68.2 per cent of total state expenditures in 1940, 72.9 per cent in 1950, and 74.9 per cent in 1952. Thus, in 1952 only 25.1 cents out of each dollar was available for all other state functions and services. Highways received the largest portion of state funds in 1940, but by 1950 education ranked first. Education took nearly 7.0 per cent more of total state money in 1952 than 1940, welfare 5.7 per cent more, while highways received 5.8 per cent less. In 1940 education was the recipient of 27.9 per cent of all state revenues; in 1952 the percentage had increased to 34.7.

The debt burden of states is an important consideration in public finance. The gross indebtedness of the Southern states increased only 47.5 per cent from 1940 to 1952. Expressed in per capita terms, the increase of the median was from $25 to $30. Chart I shows the

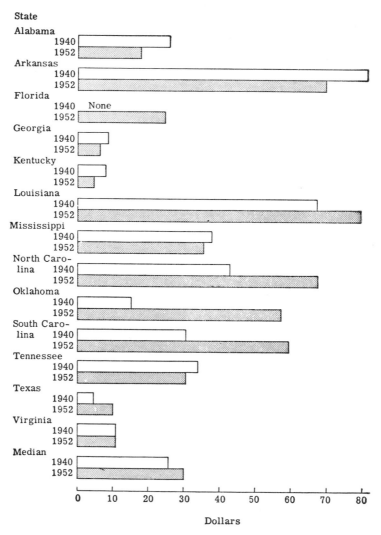

CHART 1. *Per capita debt of Southern state governments.*

per capita state government debts in the thirteen states for 1940 and 1952.

As has been indicated, the major source of local revenue is the property tax. Revenue problems of local units of government stem largely from weaknesses in the property tax as a source of revenue. Difficulty of equitable administration is the major weakness. Variations which occur in the tax rate on true value of property are enormous within the same political subdivision. Uniform assessment is an extremely difficult task. In spite of these limitations, however, the school districts in the South depend heavily on property taxes for local support. The extent of this dependence in 1949-50 is shown by Table 32. The median state was Virginia, which received 91.4 per cent of its school revenues raised locally from property taxes.

TABLE 32

ESTIMATED PER CENT OF COUNTY AND LOCAL SCHOOL REVENUE COMBINED
PRODUCED BY PROPERTY TAXES IN THE SOUTHERN STATES, 1949–50

State	Per Cent	State	Per Cent
Alabama	86.7	North Carolina	70.0
Arkansas	95.9	Oklahoma	58.2
Florida	93.4	South Carolina	86.6
Georgia	100.0	Tennessee	76.9
Kentucky	98.0	Texas	95.6
Louisiana	64.8	Virginia	91.4
Mississippi	95.7		

Source: National Education Association, Research Division, "Public School Revenues, 1949–50," *Research Bulletin*, XXX, No. 4 (1952), p. 117.

Unless additional taxing powers are granted to school districts by state legislatures, the property tax will continue to be the primary source of school revenues from the local school district. Some prospects for improvement in the property tax appear in efforts of local governments, sometimes under pressure from the state, to make equitable assessments and tax rates for all property. Another promising development is the use of economic indices rather than assessed valuation as a basis for determining local tax-paying ability.

POLICY AND PRACTICE IN PUBLIC FINANCE

The point has been made that school finance is a substantial part of public finance. Revenues for public education come from local, state, and Federal sources, with by far the greatest proportion coming from the state. The nature and control of public finance policy is, therefore, of great concern to educators at each level of government.

Certain conclusions with reference to this policy have been indicated already.

Reliance upon the property tax for support on the local level and the policy of state governments to withdraw more and more from this source of taxation has been mentioned. The prevalence of homestead exemption acts has seriously limited the amount of revenue available from this source. Election of tax assessors by popular suffrage seriously complicates the problem of arriving at equitable assessments on property. Constitutional tax provisions placing a ceiling on property tax rates is another limiting factor of policy. Neither practice nor policy is, therefore, conducive to the best system of school support.

State equalization programs designed to compensate partially for wide differences in the amount of taxable property per capita among school districts have been of great value. Nevertheless, financial policy still permits greater differences in levels of support than equality of educational opportunity dictates.

The continuing expansion of government services during the past twenty-five years has required a constant search for new sources of tax revenues as well as deficit spending. This is particularly true on the Federal level. The policy involved is one of increasing tax loads.

The seriousness of this problem is indicated by the general trend of states to depend more and more on regressive taxes such as the sales tax, although other factors help account for this trend. Such taxes are easy to levy and collect.

The inevitable competition for the tax dollar is unhealthy and calls into play the power of pressure politics in the allocation of revenues. Such practices rule out a unified long-range fiscal policy which would embody as equitable a balancing of revenue needs among government functions and services as is feasible. Instead, policies tend to be piecemeal and stopgap in nature, relying upon compromise where pressure fails. Pressure and competition as fiscal policy are unhealthy and wasteful. Integrated and coordinated programs of public finance would yield greater returns for the tax dollar.

SUMMARY

Revenues which governments make available for school support reflect both wealth and the value ascribed to education in relation to other values of concern to government. The power of education to increase wealth is well known. The need for wealth to produce good education is equally well known.

The economy of the South is in the midst of far-reaching changes. One of the forces at work which is profoundly influencing the econ-

omy is changes in the population. The heavy out-migration of Negroes, the continuing concentration of population in metropolitan
areas, and the attendant decline in rural population are major factors.
Other important changes are in the older median age of the population, the proportionate increase in the oldest and youngest age groups,
the substantial increase in median grade completed in school, and
changes in occupational patterns reflecting increasing numbers of
skilled and technical workers.

Industrial growth is going forward at a fast pace. Between 1940
and 1952 manufacturing and construction replaced agriculture,
forestry, and fisheries as the chief occupations in the region. The
region was in the midst of a transition from an agricultural economy
to an industrialized-agricultural economy.

The agricultural pattern of the South was changing from single
crop emphasis on cotton, tobacco, and corn to diversified, mechanized
farming. The production of livestock has become an important source
of income. Farm cash income of the South grew from $2,379,000,000
in 1940 to $8,951,000,000 in 1952, and Southern farmers produced
over half the value of home-consumed farm products in the United
States in 1952. Industry, like agriculture, was also becoming diversified. Chemical, paper products, and petroleum and coal industries
were growing more rapidly than the older textile and tobacco manufacturing industries. Industrial workers in the region were producing
an increasing percentage of the manufacturing output. This is due,
not to an increase in the proportion of industrial workers, but to an
improvement in the output per worker.

Public school revenues grew from $261,000,000 in 1940 to over
$1,000,000,000 in 1952. Revenues derived from local sources de-
creased from 49.5 per cent of the total to 37.7 per cent. Revenues
from local sources increased 194 per cent, while state and Federal
school revenues increased 375 per cent during the twelve years.

Southern states rely heavily on the sales taxes as a source of revenue, the most popular of which is the motor vehicle fuel tax, followed
by the general sales tax. The second most important source of revenue is Federal grants-in-aid, which have increased from 14.1 per
cent to 18.8 per cent of the total state revenues. Local governments
continued to rely almost entirely on the property tax for school
support.

By 1952 seventy-five cents out of every state dollar was being
spent on education, highways, and welfare. Education received a
larger percentage than any other function of state government, having
replaced highways. In 1940 education received 27.9 per cent of all
state revenues; in 1952, 34.7 per cent.

Per capita income in the region increased from $339 to $1,143, a percentage gain of 237. Revenues per school-age child increased from $37.00 to $117.00. The increase in revenue per child in average daily attendance was from $48.00 to $173.00. Wide differences existed with respect to each of these measures among states, among county classifications, and within these classifications.

Educational effort, as measured by the per cent school revenue is of effective buying income, declined from 2.98 to 2.85 from 1940 to 1950 and then increased to 2.89 by 1952. The ratio of revenue per school-age child to per capita income increased from .1091 to .1200 during the twelve years. Although the two measures of educational effort show somewhat varying results, they both support the conclusion that educational effort varies substantially among states, that some states increased effort during the twelve years, while others decreased it.

Policy with respect to public finance appears to depend largely on competition for the tax dollar and on political pressure. Long-range fiscal policy is needed to assure wisest use of the tax dollar.

The most important conclusion to be drawn with respect to the economy of the South in the appraisal of potential for solving the educational problems which confront the region is that substantial additional school revenues are available without placing an undue burden on income. Solution of the racial problem is possible without sacrificing the quality in education. Indeed, the healthy state of the economy suggests a continuation of efforts to improve quality.

SIX

Patterns of Public
School Expenditures

In the new look at Southern education required by the judicial mandate that racial segregation in public schools is untenable in a democracy, great emphasis will undoubtedly be placed upon the study of expenditures and, in particular, upon comparisons of expenditure levels between white and Negro schools. This chapter is concerned with a variety of cost analyses which are exceedingly relevant to the great issues in Southern education.

The upward spiral in public school expenditures has never been checked, except momentarily during depression periods, since the inception of public school finance. Friends of public education view this as evidence of the desire on the part of a maturing society to express in tangible form its historic belief in the power of education. The extent of this trend is shown by the following figures for the nation as a whole: in 1900 total public school expenditures were $214,965,000; in 1910, $426,250,000; in 1920, $1,036,151,000; in 1930, $2,316,790,000; 1940, $2,344,049,000; and by 1948, $4,311,176,000. Expenditure per pupil in average daily attendance for the same years was $20.21, $33.23, $64.16, $108.49, $105.74, $202.81.[1]

Various measurable factors account for these trends. The economy of the nation has consistently been an expanding one, except for brief interruptions caused by temporary business recessions. Economic expansion has been attended by an extension of services required by the public and willingness on the part of the people to underwrite the cost of the services they want. Public education has been one of the costliest public enterprises of any undertaken in the United States. The continually rising cost of education is attributable to two factors; the expansion of the educational program, and the extension of public education opportunities to a constantly growing body of children and youth.

---

[1] Paul R. Mort and Walter C. Reusser, *Public School Finance* (New York: McGraw-Hill Book Company, Inc., 1951), p. 7.

One of the most fascinating phases of the history of public schools is the constant redefinition of adequacy of the program itself. The value of a good teacher has always been recognized and has been objectified, in part, by raising qualifications, necessitating higher and higher levels of formal preparation. Better training has been recognized in salary schedules; consequently, it has been a part of the expanding school budget. The quantity and quality of teaching aids deemed necessary for satisfactory classroom performance have likewise undergone constant expansion. Assignment of additional services to the school, such as health, lunchroom, and transportation, constitutes a further explanation of modern school costs. Reductions in pupil-teacher ratio have brought about a substantial increase in the number of teachers. Other expansion factors increasing costs are insistence upon better housing for schools, an increase in the length of the school year, and a gradual extension of the average number of years children spend in the public schools.

The tremendous increase in birth rate has resulted in constant needs for new school facilities and additional teachers. At the same time, the rising trend in the percentage of school-age children actually enrolled in school has greatly increased school costs. A concurrent trend of improved average daily attendance of those actually enrolled is another important element in the cost picture. Reorganization plans extending the public school program upward and downward to include the twelfth grade and, in some cases, kindergarten add to the cost of education.

The gradual exercise of more and more control over school financing by state governments deserves special attention in a study of increased school costs. Many states, especially those in the South, have put into practice a doctrine of state financing based upon the proposition that minimum educational programs necessary to the welfare of the state must be provided. The general effect of minimum programs has been to add to the cost of education, since the floor of support has been set generally at a level to require substantial increases in expenditures within the districts in the lowest group, and to provide some increases to all districts.

Financial practices have been influenced in two ways by this development. The most important influence has been the great increase in the states' use of their power to tax; as minimum programs have come into existence, it has been necesary for states to exercise statewide taxation powers in order to obtain the funds necessary to support local school systems. The second influence has been on fiscal policies of local school districts. It is a general practice for state foundation or minimum programs to carry a proviso requiring the local unit to raise either a specified sum of money or to levy a minimum tax in order for the local district to have a share of state funds in financing its schools. There may be instances in which wealthy districts have spent less on their schools than they would have if the state had not siphoned off funds to support a state-wide program. There has also been some tendency for minimum programs to become maximum ones. The over-all effect of foundation programs, however, has been to provide better educational opportunities to more children.

Much public support, evidenced through increased taxes and additional taxes for schools, is undoubtedly due to the assumption that additional expenditures are reflected in better educational programs. Common sense and observation indicate that longer school terms, better teachers, more adequate buildings, and a wide range of materials of instruction are likely to produce better education; but they also cost more money. Success in objectifying the relationship between educational quality and cost was achieved by Paul Mort and his students in a series of studies which began in 1933.

. . . communities which spend more tend to be more adaptable, tend to utilize improved methods more quickly. In addition, higher expenditure schools get a different behavior pattern in the schools: The skills and knowledges are taught more in line with the best understanding of how human beings learn; more attention is given to the discovery and development of special aptitudes; more attention is given to the positive unfolding in individual boys and girls of stronger patterns of behavior—citizenship, personality, character.[2]

In a nation-wide analysis of patterns of public school expenditures by classroom units, Norton and Lawler recognize the relationship between expenditure and the quality of education in the following statement:

It is true that the amount spent to run a classroom does not wholly determine quality of schooling. Good education may be had in some classrooms financed at a poverty level, and poor education may go on in a magnificent building. These are exceptions, however. . . . In well-financed schools will generally be found the best teachers, excellent buildings and equipment, many fine books, and a well-rounded curriculum. . . . In poorly financed schools, one will generally find a very different situation—less competent teachers, miserable buildings and equipment, few books and a meager curriculum.[3]

While it is not within the province of this inquiry to probe extensively the interesting question of what kinds of education are being

---

[2] *Ibid.,* pp. 140–141.

[3] John K. Norton and Eugene S. Lawler, *Unfinished Business in American Education* (Washington: The American Council on Education, 1946), p. 5.

bought in the South at the various levels of expenditure, from an analysis of patterns of expenditure inferences may be drawn as to differences in the quality of education in various parts of the region.

EXPENDITURES FOR EDUCATION IN THE REGION

As shown earlier, expenditures for public education have had a phenomenal growth throughout the nation since the beginning of the twentieth century. Reflecting the national trend, current expense per pupil in average daily attendance in the Southern states increased more than seven times from 1900 to 1940. Expenditures more than doubled in the South in each decade up to 1930, and, despite the setback experienced during the Depression, a slight increase was made from 1930 to 1940. Even with these large gains, however, the South continued to spend one-half as much or less for public education as the national average.

Inequalities between racial groups and among geographical areas in the South became more pronounced as total expenditures mounted. Costs for white and Negro public schools had maintained nearly equal levels for several years following the Civil War. But as improvements were made, most of them came in the white schools, creating a gap between them and Negro schools. Concurrent with a change in the major sources of revenue from state to local sources, the pattern of development was such that the schools in urban areas made the most rapid progress. Rural schools reflected some of the general improvement but lagged farther and farther behind. Even though Negro schools developed more slowly than white schools, the general pattern was the same: better schools were available to Negroes in urban than in rural areas.

The inequality of expenditures for white and Negro schools perhaps reached its peak about the time of the first World War, with slight declines thereafter. Despite these declines, by 1930 expenditures per pupil were three times as much for white children as for Negro children in the Southern states. Since regional averages obscure differences among states, it should be pointed out that substantial deviations from this average were to be found; some states exceeded the average, others fell below it. Wide variations also occurred among school districts of a state, some counties spending twenty times as much per white child as per Negro child in 1930.

Costs of public schools fall largely into two budget items. One is capital outlay, which includes buildings and all items of fixed equipment; the other is current expense, which is made up of the day-to-day cost of operating the schools and includes such items as teachers' salaries, instructional materials, administration, custodial and maintenance expenses, special services of which health and lunch programs are examples, transportation, lights, water, and insurance. Teachers' salaries are the major item in these costs and, together with instructional materials, are given the special budgetary designation of "instruction" which usually accounts for from 70 to 75 per cent of all current expense.

Instruction is separated from current expense in this discussion, since it makes up the major part of current expense and is more uniformly budgeted from state to state, especially in white and Negro divisions. The reasons for this are obvious. Some expenditures are hard to keep separate. For example, one maintenance crew serves an entire school system, working on both white and Negro schools. In like manner, one administrative staff serves the entire school system. To keep separate records would entail considerable effort and expense. Therefore, some states make no attempt to keep separate expenditure records for the races in current expense, but they do keep very adequate separate records for the item of instruction.

The acceleration in recent years of total expenditure trends, which was set in motion about the turn of the century, is well illustrated by statistics for current expense and capital outlay. As shown in Table 33, current expense increased over three and one-half times in twelve years, rising from a gross expenditure of $329,891,103 in 1940 to $1,214,263,251 in 1952. While instruction costs increased rapidly, expenditures for the other items in current expense increased even more rapidly, indicating that the South was undertaking to provide more than just a teacher and minimum equipment in the public schools. Further indication of this change is evidenced by the fact that, while instruction accounted for 74.7 per cent of the total current expenditure in 1940, by 1952 this percentage had dropped to 73.2. It should be observed that these increases occurred during a period when enrollment and attendance were only slightly in excess of figures for 1940. The tremendous increase in capital outlay ex-

TABLE 33

TOTAL EXPENDITURES FOR CURRENT EXPENSE AND CAPITAL OUTLAY IN THE PUBLIC SCHOOLS OF THIRTEEN SOUTHERN STATES

Budget Item	*1939–40*	*1949–50*	*1951–52*	*Per Cent Increase 1940–1952*
Current Expense				
Instruction	$246,317,284	$ 738,738,497	$ 889,141,618	261
"Other"	83,573,819	280,961,705	325,121,633	289
Total	329,891,103	1,019,700,202	1,214,263,251	268
Capital Outlay	38,521,761	218,053,947	314,905,741	717

penditures is a reflection of such factors as internal shifts of population, capital deficits built up during the Depression and World War II days, and the consolidation movement. Capital outlay increased over eight times, from $38,521,761 in 1940 to $314,905,741 in 1952.

Statistics on gross expenditures show only the tremendous dollar increases in the South. The amount spent per pupil in average daily attendance is a more important measure of the quality of the educational effort. Subsequent analyses in this chapter will be concerned with this measure.

EXPENDITURES ON THE STATE LEVEL

It may be assumed that the cost of instruction is more closely related to the quality of the school program than any other item of cost, since it includes the salaries paid teachers and expenditures for instructional materials and supplies. Expenditures for instruction increased 239 per cent in the twelve-year period beginning with 1940, the dollar gain being from $35.08 to $118.83. Of the absolute increase of $83.75, $66.95 came in the 1940-50 decade, while the remainder, $16.80, was added in 1950-1952. This indicates that the trend was accelerated during the latter part of the period.

The great range in expenditures among the states of the South is shown in Table 34. Differences, which were considerable in 1940,

TABLE 34

EXPENDITURES PER PUPIL IN AVERAGE DAILY ATTENDANCE FOR INSTRUCTION
IN THE PUBLIC SCHOOLS OF SOUTHERN STATES

State	1939–40	1949–50	1951–52	Per Cent Increase 1940–1952
Alabama	$26.60	$ 81.20	$102.37	285
Arkansas	20.89	69.14	74.04	254
Florida	44.25	134.78	150.09	239
Georgia	31.28	82.73	116.07	271
Kentucky	34.52	79.73	101.17	193
Louisiana	38.41	121.34	131.87	243
Mississippi	19.52	52.46	61.89	217
North Carolina	31.42	100.88	111.39	255
Oklahoma	45.01	133.96	150.66	235
South Carolina	30.13	77.81	103.47	243
Tennessee	33.37	92.33	101.27	204
Texas	49.41	147.99	160.85	226
Virginia	36.18	100.18	117.62	225
TOTAL	35.08	102.03	118.83	239

increased throughout the period. In 1940, for each dollar spent on each child in Mississippi, the low state, $2.53 was being spent in Texas, the high state. These two states held their respective positions in the South in 1952, but for each dollar being spent on a child in Mississippi, $2.60 was being spent per child in Texas. The dollar difference per pupil between the high and the low states had increased from $29.89 in 1940 to $98.96 in 1952. Thus, the dollar difference in expenditures for instruction among the states had more than tripled. The range among states is shown by Chart 2.

It will be noted that the state with the greatest percentage increase in instructional expenditures for the period was Alabama, with 285 per cent, and the state with the least increase was Kentucky, with 193 per cent. The greatest dollar increase was $111.44 in Texas, and the least dollar increase was $42.37 in Mississippi.

Although changes since 1940 have not been corrected for trends in inflation, such wide variations among the states in cost of instruction indicate without doubt that some children had better teachers, more adequate supplies, and greater quantity and quality of other items which make up a good school program than did other children. Why these differences are increasing is not clear, but it is safe to assume that there is some relationship to such factors as the changing economy of the region, differences in willingness to support schools, and the quality of leadership at work.

The provision of a teacher in each classroom, the cost of which is covered in the budget item for instruction, is obviously a minimum essential. Additional sums for current expense may, then, be an indication of efforts to enrich this minimum provision, to insure maximum use of teacher competency. School services indicative of this effort, such as adequate maintenance of a clean, sanitary building, satisfactory lighting and heating, and so forth, may be of great

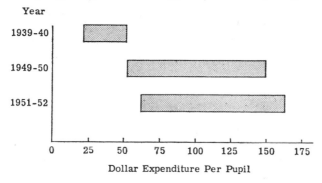

CHART 2. *Range in expenditure for instruction per pupil in thirteen Southern states.*

importance in determining whether or not a child's school experience is as rich and meaningful as parents expect it to be. More and more services are being required for modern educational programs. The addition of lunchrooms and health services are two recent examples. Acceptance of the concept that a wider range of services should be provided by the schools is indicated by a large increase in mean per pupil expenditures for these "other" services, from $11.90 in 1940 to $43.45 in 1952.

As mentioned earlier, this shift had reduced the percentage of current expense allocated to instruction by 1.5 per cent on a regional basis. This trend has been reflected in a widely varying regional pattern, as is vividly shown in Table 35.

TABLE 35

EXPENDITURE PER PUPIL IN AVERAGE DAILY ATTENDANCE FOR CURRENT EXPENSE
OTHER THAN INSTRUCTION IN THE PUBLIC SCHOOLS OF SOUTHERN STATES

State	*1939–40*	*1949–50*	*1951–52*	*Per Cent Increase 1940–1952*
Alabama	$ 7.98	$21.49	$26.24	229
Arkansas	8.06	29.01	31.77	294
Florida	13.31	37.93	43.12	224
Georgia	9.34	32.31	44.85	380
Kentucky	11.23	34.12	40.94	265
Louisiana	15.61	82.49	85.35	447
Mississippi	9.85	21.74	27.34	178
North Carolina	9.15	41.12	41.83	357
Oklahoma	17.94	—	53.49	198
South Carolina	8.58	25.47	33.23	287
Tennessee	10.18	32.45	36.45	258
Texas	17.31	45.60	52.52	203
Virginia	11.79	34.11	39.84	238
TOTAL	11.90	38.80	43.45	265

Reduction of the differences between states to a ratio shows that in 1940 for each dollar spent per child in average daily attendance in Alabama, the low state, $2.25 was being spent per child in Oklahoma, the high state. The increase in the differences among the states is shown by the fact that in 1952, for each dollar spent per child in Alabama, still the low state, $3.25 was being spent per child in Louisiana, the high state. A dollar difference between the high and low state of $9.96 per child in 1940 had increased about six times, to a difference of $59.11, in 1952. Louisiana had both the highest percentage increase and dollar increase, while Mississippi had both the lowest percentage increase and dollar increase.

Expenditures for capital outlay are much more unstable from year to year than either expenditures for instruction or for "other" current expense. The reasons are not difficult to determine. A building, once constructed, does not have to be replaced for many years, barring catastrophe. The amount spent per pupil for capital outlay in any particular year, therefore, loses some of its meaning as considerable construction may take place in one year and very little in the next. Another disadvantage in using the amount spent for each pupil, is that consideration cannot be given to need. A school system may have spent very little, if anything, on capital outlay in a particular year, or series of years, and yet have been adequately supplied with buildings and equipment. These disadvantages may be partially offset by considering expenditures for an entire state, as there is some consistency from year to year in a state's needs and, usually, in its provisions for meeting these needs, although it is a fact that school building progress commonly follows a pattern of peaks and valleys. Even on a per pupil basis, capital outlay is more responsive to increases in enrollment than other budget items. Increases in enrollment in one state, necessitating new buildings, raise the per pupil expenditure; while in another state, with a stable enrollment, per pupil expenditures may remain stable. Expenditure per pupil is used in this analysis, despite its limitations, because no better measure is available.

Mean expenditures per pupil for capital outlay increased in the South from $5.49 in 1940 to $42.09 in 1952, an increase of 667 per cent. The dollar increase was $36.60, of which $24.63 came from 1940 to 1950, and $11.97 from 1950 to 1952. This gain in the rate of increase in the latter years of the period is consistent with trends which occurred in expenditures for instruction and other current expense.

As would be expected, the differences among the states are proportionately greater in capital outlay than in the other budget items analyzed. Those states with rapidly increasing enrollments found it necessary to spend much more than the states with decreasing enrollments. In 1940, Louisiana, the state with the highest expenditure per pupil, was spending $14.63; while Georgia, the low state, was spending $1.48 per pupil. In 1952, Virginia, with a rapidly increasing school enrollment, was spending $92.39 per pupil; Kentucky, with a relatively stable enrollment, was spending $11.14 per pupil. Florida, with a rapidly growing school enrollment, increased expenditures per pupil during the period by 1437 per cent. Alabama, on the other hand, with an almost stationary school enrollment increased expenditures by only 167 per cent. Thus, dollar increases reflect enrollment trends, as is demonstrated by the fact that Virginia increased by $81.53 per pupil, and Kentucky by only $7.59 per pupil. Figures by states are shown in Table 36.

TABLE 36

EXPENDITURE PER PUPIL IN AVERAGE DAILY ATTENDANCE FOR CAPITAL
OUTLAY IN THE PUBLIC SCHOOLS OF SOUTHERN STATES

State	1939–40	1949–50	1951–52	Per Cent Increase 1940–1952
Alabama	$ 4.58	$14.36	$12.24	167
Arkansas	2.60	38.35	29.47	1034
Florida	4.90	42.50	75.29	1437
Georgia	1.48	17.11	22.72	1435
Kentucky	3.55	10.64	11.14	214
Louisiana	14.63	49.62	50.30	244
Mississippi	2.35	6.20	29.83	1184
North Carolina	4.82	35.10	57.86	1100
Oklahoma	1.67	11.51	11.43	584
South Carolina	3.89	17.58	19.04	390
Tennessee	8.02	46.05	38.80	384
Texas	7.19	43.96	57.25	696
Virginia	10.86	39.77	92.39	751
TOTAL	5.49	30.12	42.09	667

Effects of the tremendous acceleration in the long-term trend toward higher expenditures for public education since 1940 have not been properly assessed. Increases of nearly three and one-half times in expenditures for instruction, of more than three and one-half times on other items of current expense, and of more than seven times in capital outlay most certainly have been reflected in improvement in the educational program itself. For one thing, the qualifications of teachers have improved appreciably. It can hardly be denied that more adequate buildings, better maintenance, the provision of additional services, and so forth, have meant improved instruction. As great as these increases are, however, the South remains considerably behind the rest of the nation in public school expenditures. This lag is indicated by an expenditure per pupil in average daily attendance for current expense in the United States of $208.83 in 1950, the last year for which figures for the United States are available, and of $140.83 in the South. Despite the general national increase in expenditures, the South is nearer national cost averages than ever before.

It is clear that equalization among states in the region is far from a reality. Advances are made by fits and starts, and each state has its own tempo. This tempo is subject to change, for one state may lead the way for a while and then drop back, while another state comes to the forefront. But the relative positions of states change slowly.

EXPENDITURES BY COUNTY LEVELS

It has been emphasized that within recent years the South has been making vast improvements in its public education programs. State averages, however, which have been used up to this point, tend to obscure the similarities and differences among local school systems. The really significant measure of educational opportunity must be made at the local level. A question which deserves serious consideration is whether expenditure increases within states have promoted general educational opportunity or whether they have been made in such a way as to accentuate existing educational inequality.

As has been suggested, the item of instruction is the most closely related to the quality of the school program of any school cost. Hence, the budget item of instruction is used here as a basis for examining the changes among local school systems. There is reason to believe, however, that because most states in the South have uniform salary schedules that instruction is the most nearly equalized budget item among local school systems. Differences among population classifications which may be found in the cost of instruction would, therefore, undoubtedly be found to exist in an even greater degree in other budget items.

Wide differences in educational programs for country and city children, as reflected by expenditures, have long been known to exist in the South, and they were very evident in 1940. For example, $26.63 per pupil was being spent on the average on rural children, while children in metropolitan counties were recipients of an average expenditure of $46.51 per pupil. At the same time, children in rural-urban counties, the category into which a majority of Southern counties fall, received an average of $29.24 per pupil for instruction. Thus, it is evident that in 1940 where a child lived made a difference in what kind of educational opportunity he had.

The great increases in expenditures, looked at by one measure, seemed to favor rural children. Expenditures for instruction during the twelve-year period for children in rural counties increased by 253 per cent, in rural-urban counties by 250 per cent, and in metropolitan counties by 197 per cent. But, as is evident in Table 37, the greatest dollar increases did not favor the rural child, but rather the child who lived in a large metropolitan county. The absolute increase for rural children was $67.40, for rural-urban children $73.24, while the child in metropolitan counties had an expenditure increase

TABLE 37

EXPENDITURE PER PUPIL IN AVERAGE DAILY ATTENDANCE FOR INSTRUCTION IN
SAMPLE RURAL AND RURAL-URBAN COUNTIES AND IN METROPOLITAN
COUNTIES OF THIRTEEN SOUTHERN STATES

Type of County	1939–40	1949–50	1951–52	Per Cent Increase 1940–1952
Rural	$26.63	$ 80.31	$ 94.03	253
Rural-Urban	29.24	86.94	102.48	250
Metropolitan	46.51	118.05	138.08	197

of $91.57. It is clear that, if equalization of expenditures for rural
and metropolitan children were to be accomplished, it would cost
more money in 1952 than it would have in 1940. The actual dollar
difference in expenditures for children in rural and metropolitan
counties, which was $19.88 in 1940, had more than doubled in
1952, the difference being $44.05. Perhaps even more significant is
the fact that the dollar differences continued to increase from 1950
to 1952.

Whatever effects cost-of-living differentials between metropolitan
and rural counties may have on the cost-quality relationship in education have not been taken into account in these figures. The general
increase in the cost of living, accompanied as it has been by a leveling
off of differences between costs in rural and metropolitan areas, appears to make this a relatively unimportant consideration.

Another measure of the differences in educational opportunity is
the range within the population classifications themselves. This range
in expenditures for instruction in the rural counties in 1940 was from
$11.52 to $57.07. Expressed another way, a child in the highest
expenditure rural county had five times as much spent on his instruction during this year as a child in the lowest expenditure rural county.
The range in 1952 was from $29.30 to $247.17, which means that
over eight times as much was spent per child in the highest rural
county as was spent in the lowest rural county. The comparable
range in metropolitan counties in 1940 was from $12.60 to $74.35,
and in 1952 from $77.22 to $202.62. In metropolitan counties the
ratio between the high and low counties was reduced during the
period. Comparable differences were found in rural-urban counties,
with the ratio between the high and low counties being over three to
one in both 1940 and 1952.

While the ratio between the high and low counties was increasing
during the period in rural counties and decreasing in rural-urban and
metropolitan counties, the dollar differences between expenditures
per child in the high and low counties were increasing in all three
population classifications. In rural counties the dollar difference be-

tween high and low counties, which was $45.55 in 1940, increased to $207.87 in 1952; in rural-urban counties the dollar difference increased from $35.62 to $118.88; and in metropolitan counties the differences increased from $61.75 to $125.40.

Table 38 shows the ratio, perhaps the most significant measure, between rural and rural-urban counties, and between rural and metropolitan counties. While the large ratio between rural and metropolitan counties had been substantially reduced during the period, the fact was still evident at the end of the period that much more money would have to be spent to equalize opportunity.

TABLE 38

RATIO BETWEEN EXPENDITURE PER PUPIL IN AVERAGE DAILY ATTENDANCE FOR INSTRUCTION IN RURAL-URBAN AND RURAL COUNTIES AND METROPOLITAN AND RURAL COUNTIES IN THIRTEEN SOUTHERN STATES

County Classification	1939–40	1949–50	1951–52
Rural-Urban and Rural Ratio	1.10:1	1.08:1	1.09:1
Metropolitan and Rural Ratio	1.75:1	1.47:1	1.47:1

Ranges in the different county classifications are partially a result of the differences in expenditures among the states. Continued existence of such wide variations in expenditure levels among states will preserve great inequalities of educational opportunity for children on the basis of states in which they happen to reside.

The foregoing statistics demonstrate quite simply that expenditures for instruction in the region are highest in metropolitan counties and lowest in rural counties. While this is true for the region as a whole, the states show variation in the amounts of difference and in the trends in differences. The purpose of state minimum foundation programs is, of course, to reduce inequalities, and these analyses seem to show that some progress is being made; but much remains to be done. Shifts in population from rural to metropolitan areas also mean that the differences between these two areas will be significant for fewer children than formerly. The fact remains, however, that, as long as extreme differences exist, some children get instruction in well-equipped, modern buildings, with well-trained competent teachers who have adequate teaching materials; while other children attend schools in wretched buildings under the direction of poorly trained teachers who have little in the way of equipment with which to work.

There is one other important level in which inequalities of educational opportunity occur. In large school systems great differences in educational programs may be found from one attendance center to another. Such differences have not been included in this inquiry, but other research has shown them to be as substantial as those existing among school systems and among states. Further inequalities obviously occur within a given school because teaching competency may range there from poor to superior.

EXPENDITURES FOR WHITE AND NEGRO SCHOOLS

The relative positions of the white and Negro races in the South have made inevitable enormous inequalities in the expenditures for public education on a racial basis. The development of dual public school systems afforded a ready-made device for maintaining these differences. Social values, attitudes, and cultural practices were such that differences were accepted as a matter of course for many years. Perhaps this accounts for the general lack of comprehensive data on the extent and nature of the differences.

Within recent years, notably since World War II, an awakening public conscience, plus the impetus of a series of court decisions emphasizing without exception the discriminatory aspects of the dual school policy of the South, has brought about a strong movement toward the equalization of educational opportunity. An increase in publicity on actual conditions brought widespread attention to the problem. The May, 1954, verdict of the United States Supreme Court that segregation in public schools as public policy is unconstitutional has made the problem in the region of equalizing educational opportunity infinitely more complex. Whatever policies are now set in motion, it is assumed that they will be developed on the basis of a realistic study of actual conditions. An analysis of shifts in expenditure since 1940 with reference to the racial situation, therefore, seems pertinent.

In 1940, for each $1.00 spent for instruction in the South per pupil in average daily attendance in Negro schools, $2.58 was spent per pupil in average daily attendance in white schools. Both races benefited from the increases in expenditures during the following twelve years, with the largest proportionate increases coming to Negro schools. Expenditures for instruction in white schools increased 214 per cent, while expenditures in Negro schools increased 451 per cent. This pattern of increase was such that the ratio between the two races decreased during the period; in 1952 for each $1.00 spent in Negro schools on a per pupil basis, $1.47 was spent in white schools. These increases unquestionably brought to the Negro child better trained teachers and more adequate instructional materials.

As is evident in Table 39, however, the absolute increase was greater in white schools than in Negro schools. The reason for this lies in the greater dollar increase for whites than for Negroes between 1940 and 1950. This trend was reversed from 1950 to 1952, making

TABLE 39

EXPENDITURE PER PUPIL IN AVERAGE DAILY ATTENDANCE FOR INSTRUCTION
IN WHITE AND NEGRO PUBLIC SCHOOLS OF SOUTHERN STATES

| | 1939–40 | | 1949–50 | | 1951–52 | |
State	White	Negro	White	Negro	White	Negro
Alabama	$34.25	$12.20	$ 87.55	$ 69.28	$107.64	$ 92.45
Arkansas	23.93	11.17	75.88	47.21	80.15	54.21
Florida	51.96	23.09	142.79	111.24	156.04	131.79
Georgia	40.50	13.92	93.42	61.31	124.08	99.49
Louisiana	51.78	14.93	141.89	86.92	151.46	99.82
Mississippi	31.33	6.64	78.71	23.84	88.97	32.68
North Carolina	34.63	23.60	103.18	95.29	113.72	105.81
South Carolina	42.00	13.81	92.40	58.54	120.17	81.04
Texas	53.09	29.36	153.59	115.35	167.54	119.92
TOTAL	41.99	16.29	115.68	72.70	132.38	90.20

the dollar increases greater in Negro schools. The net result of the over-all increase did not further equalization dollarwise between 1940 and 1950; many more dollars would have had to be spent on Negro than on white schools, and the reverse was true. Between 1950 and 1952, however, the increase in dollar expenditures was greater for Negro than for white education, so that there was a trend toward equalization.

The over-all changes in the South — larger percentage gains in expenditures for Negroes than whites, a reduction in the ratio between expenditures for the two races, and a reduction of the dollar difference between expenditures from 1950 to 1952 — indicate that the South was moving rapidly toward racial equalization as measured by the dollar. General trends, however, hide the fact that a wide range of differences existed among the states in their efforts to achieve equalized expenditures. In 1940, of the states for which complete records are available, North Carolina had most nearly equalized expenditures between the races; it was spending $1.47 per white pupil for each dollar spent per Negro pupil in average daily attendance. This ratio may be compared to the ratio in Mississippi, where $4.72 was spent per white pupil for each dollar spent per Negro pupil in 1940.

While all states made progress during the twelve-year period toward equalization, these two held their relative positions. In 1952 North Carolina was spending $1.07 per white pupil for each dollar spent per Negro pupil in average daily attendance, while Mississippi was spending $2.72 per white pupil for each dollar spent per Negro pupil. Part of this difference is accounted for by the patterns of population distribution in the two states. For example, in Mississippi most of the Negroes live in rural areas where expenditures for both races are lowest; while in North Carolina, the Negro population is not so widely dispersed in the rural counties.

Differences in expenditures among the states is vividly illustrated by the range in Negro and white levels. In 1940, the range in expenditure per pupil in white schools for the nine states providing separate data was from $23.93 to $53.09, and in Negro schools it was from $6.64 to $29.36. The expenditure for Negroes of $29.36 in Texas, the highest in the South, was lower than the expenditure for whites in all the states except Arkansas. In 1952 the range in white schools was from $80.15 to $167.54, and in Negro schools it was from $32.68 to $131.79. Another measure of change is reflected in the figures for Florida, where the Negro average of $131.79 exceeded the average expenditure for white children in six of the states. Chart 3 shows the scope of these differences.

The range in the percentages of increase in expenditures per pupil in average daily attendance among the states for white and Negro schools is also considerable. The state with the highest increase for white schools, Arkansas, had a gain of 235 per cent, while the state with the highest percentage increase for Negro schools, Alabama, gained 658 per cent. The state with the lowest percentage increase for white schools was Mississippi with 184 per cent, and

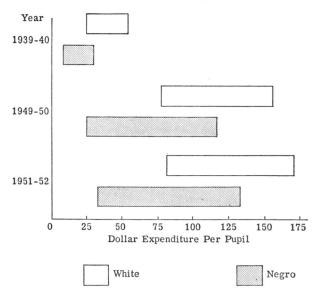

CHART 3. *Range in expenditure for instruction per pupil in average daily attendance in white and Negro schools of nine Southern states.*

the state with the lowest increase for Negro schools was Texas, with 308 per cent. Texas had the greatest dollar increase for both white and Negro schools, while Mississippi had the lowest dollar increase for both races. Interestingly enough, the dollar difference between expenditures per pupil for the two races increased in Arkansas, Louisiana, Mississippi, South Carolina, and Texas, while it decreased in Alabama, Florida, Georgia, and North Carolina.

These statistics indicate quite clearly that all states in the South in recent years have been moving toward equalization of expenditures for the two races. The patterns of movement are different from state to state, some states moving quite rapidly and others more slowly. Because of differences in the starting point in 1940 for the various states and the different rates of movement since, some states were in a position in the years from 1950 through 1952 to begin to reduce the dollar difference between the two races, while other states had not quite reached that point. It is obvious that if these trends should continue, equalization of public school expenditures between the races would be accomplished in time; however, it is equally obvious that progress would be uneven and that it would be a long time before equalization of expenditures would be a fact in some states.

Expenditures by races in different types of counties are, of course, closely related to the general pattern of state level expenditures and to the expenditure patterns found in the different types of counties. Changes in these expenditures are very similar to patterns of change in the state level and county level cost pictures. In general, the greatest percentage increase occurred for both races in the rural counties, and the least percentage increase for both races occurred in the metropolitan counties. The greatest dollar increases for both races occurred in metropolitan counties, and the smallest dollar increases for both races occurred in the rural counties. The largest percentage increases in expenditures in all three types of counties occurred in

TABLE 40

EXPENDITURE PER PUPIL IN AVERAGE DAILY ATTENDANCE FOR INSTRUCTION IN WHITE AND NEGRO PUBLIC SCHOOLS OF SAMPLE RURAL AND RURAL-URBAN COUNTIES AND OF METROPOLITAN COUNTIES IN NINE SOUTHERN STATES

County Classification	Race	1939–40	1949–50	1951–52	Per Cent Increase 1940–1952
Rural	White	$35.56	$ 98.54	$112.01	215
	Negro	11.86	59.80	74.96	532
Rural-Urban	White	37.96	101.78	117.68	210
	Negro	13.69	65.34	82.33	501
Metropolitan	White	52.06	124.32	143.07	175
	Negro	21.50	86.42	109.76	411

Negro schools, and the largest dollar increases were in white schools. The trend within county classifications was for the dollar gap to increase from 1940 to 1950 and to decrease from 1950 to 1952. Decreases, however, were insufficient to balance the larger gains of the previous ten years. Dollar differences between expenditures per pupil in white and Negro schools in rural counties were $23.70 in 1940 and $37.05 in 1952; in rural-urban counties the differences were $24.27 in 1940 and $35.35 in 1952; and in metropolitan counties they were $30.56 in 1940 and $33.31 in 1952. Table 40 shows these trends.

Complete separate expenditure records for white and Negro schools in budget items of current expense[4] other than instruction and for capital outlay were available in only six states. Consequently, no comparable statistics could be secured for these two items for use with the statistics on instruction for the two races. The six states which did keep separate records may be used, however, as illustrations of the relationship among instruction, other items of current expense, and capital outlay expenditures.

Expenditures for current expenses other than instruction increased at a faster rate than expenditures for instruction in both white and Negro schools. Consequently, as is shown in Table 41, the percentage

TABLE 41

INSTRUCTION AS A PERCENTAGE OF CURRENT EXPENSE IN WHITE AND NEGRO PUBLIC SCHOOLS OF SOUTHERN STATES

State	1939–40		1951–52	
	White	Negro	White	Negro
Alabama	75.2	87.2	77.0	85.7
Arkansas	71.6	75.7	69.8	70.6
Florida	76.0	82.6	76.4	83.0
Georgia	75.6	85.3	68.9	82.0
North Carolina	75.9	83.3	70.6	78.5
South Carolina	76.4	84.1	73.5	80.4

ratio of instruction to current expense decreased during the period for both races. The percentages shown in this table are higher in every state for Negroes than whites, indicating a larger proportional expenditure in white schools for the enrichment services such as health services, lunch programs, transportation and maintenance. With the exception of Florida, in which very slight increases were made in schools for both races, every state had a decline in the proportion that instruction was of current expense, indicating a more rapid increase

---

[4] The budget item of general control, which is part of current expense, has been prorated between the two races on the basis of average daily attendance.

in the other items of current expense than in instruction in the public schools.

Table 42 shows the ratio between white and Negro expenditures on a per pupil in average daily attendance basis for the budget items of

TABLE 42

RATIO BETWEEN EXPENDITURE PER PUPIL IN AVERAGE DAILY ATTENDANCE FOR WHITE AND NEGRO PUBLIC SCHOOLS IN SOUTHERN STATES FOR THREE BUDGET ITEMS

State		Instruction	Current Expense Other Than Instruction	Capital Outlay
Alabama	1940	2.81:1	6.30:1	10.77:1
	1950	1.26:1	2.34:1	2.67:1
	1952	1.16:1	2.08:1	1.66:1
Arkansas	1940	2.14:1	2.65:1	4.57:1
	1950	1.61:1	1.71:1	1.47:1
	1952	1.49:1	1.54:1	1.69:1
Florida	1940	2.25:1	3.38:1	7.99:1
	1950	1.28:1	2.16:1	2.18:1
	1952	1.18:1	1.78:1	0.93:1
Georgia	1940	2.91:1	5.45:1	9.30:1
	1950	1.52:1	3.24:1	2.69:1
	1952	1.25:1	2.57:1	1.88:1
North Carolina	1940	1.47:1	2.33:1	3.28:1
	1950	1.08:1	1.84:1	1.45:1
	1952	1.07:1	1.64:1	1.08:1
South Carolina	1940	3.04:1	4.95:1	9.47:1
	1950	1.58:1	2.81:1	2.93:1
	1952	1.48:1	2.19:1	2.16:1

instruction, current expense other than instruction, and capital outlay, and changes in these ratios from 1940 to 1952. They mean that, in Alabama for example, in 1940 for each dollar spent in Negro schools for each of the three budget items, the corresponding expenditure in white schools was $2.81 for instruction, $6.30 for current expense, and $10.77 for capital outlay. Reductions in these ratios by 1952 were such that for each dollar spent for each budget item in Negro schools in Alabama, the expenditure in white schools was $1.16 for instruction, $2.88 for "other" current expense, and $1.66 for capital outlay.

By using the ratios of Table 42 as a measure of equalization, it is evident that in 1940 instruction was the most nearly equalized and capital outlay the least equalized, with the "other" items of current expense falling between the two. Translated into its import for school programs, this means that Negro schools were provided the minimum essential of a teacher and little else. In 1940 this Negro teacher was paid about half as much as the white teacher, and he had 20 per cent more pupils. Advantages provided by "other" items of current expense which were given Negro schools were only about one-fourth of those provided for white schools, and those provided the latter were meager enough. Negro school buildings were on the average very poor, frequently not publicly owned, and about one-seventh as much was being spent to improve them as was being spent for white schools.

Changes in the ratio by 1952 mean that in this year a teacher was provided the Negro schools who was nearly as well trained and as well paid as his white colleague, and he had about the same number of pupils. Expenditures for buildings and equipment were only about one and one-half times as much for white pupils as for Negro pupils, and there were, by this time, many buildings for Negro children as good as could be found for white children in any part of the South. Services which enrich school programs and are paid for out of funds for current expenses other than instruction were being provided to Negro schools to some extent, but not in sufficient quantity to prevent a lag of this budget item in the movement toward equalization.

Trends in expenditures for the two races in two budget items, current expense other than instruction and capital outlay, are consistent with trends in the expenditures for instruction; that is, the ratio decreased, the percentage of increase was larger in Negro schools, and the dollar difference between white and Negro expenditures became greater. The latter fact means that more dollars were required to equalize expenditures between the races in 1952 than were required in 1940.

No analyses were made of racial expenditures for capital outlay and current expense at the county level. There seems to be no reason, however, why such an analysis would not reveal the same relative degrees of difference that were found in expenditures for these items for whites and Negroes at the state level.

FACTORS IN EQUALIZATION

Irrespective of the means by which educational opportunities for white and Negro children are to become of equal quality, certain factors exist which will have to be taken into account. For example, it has been recognized for a long time that an important relationship exists between the equalization of expenditures for the two races, and the ratio of Negro to white population. In general, where the percentage of Negro population was higher, the ratio between expenditures in white and Negro schools was higher. In the twelve-year period beginning in 1940 significant changes occurred in this relationship.

These changes were shown by the simple process of ranking the nine states, which keep separate records of white and Negro expenditures for instruction, according to percentage of Negro population and according to a ratio derived by dividing expenditure per pupil for instruction in white schools by a similar figure for Negro schools. A rank of one was assigned to the state with the lowest percentage of Negro population, with the other states following in rank order, the state with the highest percentage of Negro population being given a rank of nine. The state having the lowest ratio of expenditures of instruction between the two races was ranked one, followed by the others in similar order.

These ranks are shown in Table 96 of the appendix. The rank order correlation coefficient of this distribution was found to be .87 in 1940, .53 in 1950, and .47 in 1952. The correlation coefficient in 1940 indicates a significant positive relationship between percentage of Negro population and the Negro-to-white ratio of expenditures per pupil for instruction. The coefficients for 1950 and 1952, while still showing a positive relationship, were not statistically significant; and they indicate that it was no longer possible to predict with such certainty that the states with the higher percentages of Negro population would have the higher ratios of per pupil expenditures in favor of white students.

A further illustration of this change is shown by an analysis of counties. The county with the highest percentage of Negro population and the county with the lowest percentage of Negro population in each of the population samples in each state were compared according to degree of equalization. The results are shown in Table 43.

This table is to be read as follows: In the median rural county with a high percentage of Negro population in 1940, for each $1.00 spent per pupil in average daily attendance for Negro instruction, $4.00

TABLE 43

MEDIAN RATIO BETWEEN EXPENDITURE PER PUPIL IN AVERAGE DAILY ATTENDANCE FOR INSTRUCTION IN WHITE AND NEGRO PUBLIC SCHOOLS IN SAMPLE RURAL, RURAL-URBAN, AND METROPOLITAN COUNTIES WITH HIGH AND LOW PERCENTAGES OF NEGRO POPULATION IN NINE SOUTHERN STATES

County Classification	1939–40		1949–50		1951–52	
	High County	Low County	High County	Low County	High County	Low County
Rural	4.00:1	2.15:1	1.74:1	1.23:1	1.59:1	1.19:1
Rural-Urban	3.55:1	1.77:1	1.63:1	1.20:1	1.46:1	1.02:1
Metropolitan	2.79:1	1.96:1	1.39:1	1.22:1	1.13:1	0.94:1

was spent for white instruction per pupil. In the corresponding county with a low percentage of Negro population, for each $1.00 spent for Negro instruction, $2.15 was spent for white instruction. The equalization movement was such that by 1952, in the county with a higher percentage of Negro population, for each $1.00 spent for Negro instruction, $1.59 was spent for white instruction; and in the county with a low percentage of Negro population, for each $1.00 spent for Negro instruction, $1.19 was spent for white instruction. The ratios for rural-urban and metropolitan counties may be read similarly.

These statistics point up some interesting conditions. First, there was a rather general consistency in the ratios which were highest in rural counties and lowest in metropolitan counties. Some exceptions occurred among rural, rural-urban, and metropolitan counties, however, where there were low percentages of Negro population. Second, the ratios in counties with a high percentage of Negro population were always higher than the ratios in counties with a low percentage of Negro population, but the differences in the ratios between the two were vastly smaller in 1952 than in 1940. This is consistent with the findings in state statistics which show that the percentage of Negro population was still positively related to the degree of equalization in 1952, but not so significantly as formerly. These statistics were for the item of instruction. It should be remembered that instruction was the most nearly equalized of all items. Larger differences, therefore, in the ratios between expenditures for the two races could normally be expected in other budget items.

Another significant change in educational finance in the South during recent years has been the decided shift toward a smaller percentage of revenues coming from local sources. One of the persistent problems in equalization of educational opportunity has been to level off rural and urban differences. The influence of stronger state controls on educational finance, as it relates to this problem and as it may bear on subsequent efforts to equalize these differences, is worthy of note. The current shifts in Negro population from rural to metropolitan counties indicate that the same problem may be equally important in future programs designed to minimize racial differences in educational opportunity.

Eleven states for which data were available were ranked according to the degree of equalization between rural and metropolitan counties based on ratios between expenditures in these two types of counties, the state having the lowest ratio being ranked first, followed by the others in rank order. The same states were then ranked according to the percentage of school revenues coming from local sources, a rank of one being assigned to the state with the lowest percentage of revenue from local sources, the others following in order. The rank order correlation was then obtained. It was found to be .61 in 1940, .65 in 1950, and .75 in 1952. The ranks are shown in Table 97 of the appendix. The correlation coefficients indicate a significant positive relationship between the source of revenue and the degree of equalization of expenditures for instruction between rural and metropolitan counties. In general, the state with the lowest percentage of revenue from local sources had the lowest ratio between expenditures in rural and metropolitan counties.

Great variability in expenditure levels exists among states, among school districts within states, and among school attendance centers within large school districts. In the final analysis, equalization must be judged at the school attendance center within the district level. State and regional figures can give only indications of expenditures at the local level and are, at best, but measures of central tendency. Since state and regional figures are frequently cited and are used to support arguments over the extent to which equalization has been achieved, it may be profitable to seek an answer to the question: If equalization were achieved at the state level, would regional figures show equalization? The effects of variability among states on regional figures will now be analyzed, only expenditures for instruction being used.

An equalized expenditure for instruction between the two races was calculated from actual expenditures in each of the nine states by simply dividing the total cost of instruction by the total average daily attendance for the two races. This average expenditure per pupil was then multiplied by the average daily attendance of white students and the average daily attendance of Negro students. The products of this multiplication for whites in each of the nine states were summed, and the products of the multiplication for Negroes were similarly summed.

This process yielded a regional figure for whites and another for Negroes. The sum for whites was divided by the regional total of white average daily attendance. The same division was made for Negroes. The resultant average expenditure would have been $35.35 for whites and $31.69 for Negroes in 1940. Comparable results for 1952 would have been white expenditures of $123.26 and $110.64 for Negroes. Thus, a disparity between races on the basis of regional figures would be present, even though every state had absolutely equalized expenditures. This disparity results from the fact that, in general, states with higher percentages of Negro population had lower average per pupil expenditures.

A simple hypothetical example should clarify this concept. Assume that two states constitute a region. State A has 1,000 white and 1,000 Negro pupils in average daily attendance and an average expenditure of $50 per pupil for the two races. State B has 1,000 whites and 500 Negro pupils in average daily attendance and an average expenditure of $100 per pupil. Then State A expends $50,000 on white pupils and $50,000 on Negro pupils, while State B expends $100,000 on white students and $50,000 on Negroes. Summing the two state totals, there are 2,000 white pupils with expenditures of $150,000 and 1,500 Negro pupils with expenditures of $100,000. Dividing the $150,000 expenditure for whites by the 2,000 white pupils in average daily attendance, a cost of $75 per white pupil results. A similar computation for Negro totals gives a cost of $66.67 per Negro pupil. Although both states were absolutely equalized, the region composed of the two states would not show equalization.

Similar analyses could be made for each state by using the totals of the local school systems within the states. If the majority of Negro population lived in high expenditure areas, then the state averages would show expenditures higher for Negroes than for whites. This state average in favor of the Negroes could result, even though every local system had a higher expenditure level for white students than for Negro students.

This discussion of the effects of variability among the states points out the complexity of the problem of equalization of expenditures within states and in the region. The computations which have been presented make it possible to derive an index measure of equalization which can be applied to different years to measure movement toward complete equalization.

The ratio of expenditures for instruction between the two races on the equalized state level basis computed above were 1.12 to 1 in 1940, and 1.10 to 1 in 1952. The actual expenditure ratios for these two years were 2.58 to 1, and 1.47 to 1. By computing the part that the actual expenditure ratio was of the equalized expenditure ratio, the index of equalization was found to be .43 in 1940 and .75 in 1952. Said another way, expenditures for instruction in Negro schools of the South were 43 per cent equalized in 1940 and 75 per cent equalized in 1952. This seems to be an accurate indication of the movement toward equalization in expenditures for the item of instruction during the twelve-year period. Similar analyses for current expense and capital outlay would, no doubt, show somewhat smaller percentages of equalization.

A comparable index at the state level would require computations for all the local school systems within the state and will not be undertaken here. Some general observations can be made, however. The states of the South would show wide variability in such an analysis. Those states in which the Negro population is predominantly rural, as in Mississippi, would have considerable differences in racial expenditure in favor of the whites at the state level, even if expenditures at the local level were absolutely equalized. This is due, of course, to the fact that the per pupil expenditures in rural counties are lower than in any other type of county. Other states, having a small percentage of Negro population and a considerable part of it concentrated in metropolitan counties, as in Kentucky, would probably show differences in racial expenditures at the state level in favor of the Negroes, even if expenditures at the local level were absolutely equalized.

These conclusions point up an important factor which has been working toward racial equalization of expenditures at the state level. That factor is the migration of Negroes to metropolitan areas and away from rural areas. Since metropolitan county expenditures are consistently higher than rural county expenditures, this migration of Negroes would bring about considerable equalization of expenditures between the races in terms of state averages, even without a change in public policy toward financial expenditures.

A further factor of importance which has worked toward equalization of racial expenditures is the large increase in Negro high school enrollment. No investigation has been made for this study of the differences between elementary and secondary school costs, but they are considerable. In some states, despite a general trend toward equalized costs, the expenditures per pupil in elementary schools were half or less than half the expenditures in secondary schools on a per pupil basis. Arkansas reported expenditures per pupil of $72 in secondary and $31 in elementary schools in 1940; expenditures in 1952 were $208 in secondary and $113 in elementary schools. Louisiana spent $171 for elementary and $419 for secondary schools per pupil in 1952. Even though Negro secondary school expenditures were not as high as white secondary expenditures, they are consistently higher than Negro elementary costs. Thus, the increase in Negro secondary enrollment resulted in some increase in average Negro expenditures.

SUMMARY

Public school expenditures, one of the most valid measures of educational progress, have been expanded tremendously since the educational awakening in the South about the turn of the twentieth century. Even with the intervention of the Great Depression, which brought substantial reductions in expenditures for a time, the level achieved by 1930 was regained or slightly surpassed by 1940. On a per pupil basis, expenditures were about seven times higher in 1940 than in 1900. These gains were made despite a constantly increasing enrollment and percentage of pupils in average daily attendance. Even so, the region lagged behind averages for the rest of the nation; per pupil expenditures were scarcely more than one-third the national mean in 1900 and slightly less than one-half in 1930.

Concurrent with improvements in the economy, the period from 1940 through 1952 was one of even more rapid increases in public school expenditures, though enrollments were relatively constant. Children of the high post-war birth rate period were just beginning to reach school in 1952. In the twelve-year period expenditures more than quadrupled. The South, however, still remained considerably behind the national averages in public school expenditures.

Expenditures for current expense in the twelve-year period increased three and one-half times. Capital outlay was more than seven times as great per pupil in 1952 as in 1940. The item of instruction, which makes up about three-fourths of current expense, increased nearly three and one-half times and accounted for the major part of the increase in current expense. The differences, even though slight, in the rate of increase in total current expense and instruction indicated a growing emphasis on additional school services, such as lunch programs, health services, and transportation. This trend is reflected in a decrease in the percentage that instruction is of current expense, a decrease from 74.7 in 1940 to 73.2 in 1952. Teachers' salaries remained the largest single school cost and, although salaries showed large increases, the South's educational systems were now spending proportionately more for services designed to provide enriched educational programs.

Considerable variation existed among the states in 1940; and, in the following period of accelerated change, some states expanded school budgets more rapidly than others, resulting in even greater variations in educational opportunity than formerly.

A large gap has long existed in expenditures between rural and urban areas in the South. Expenditures in rural areas increased by larger percentages than in metropolitan areas from 1940 to 1952, and the ratio of expenditures between them decreased. At the same time, the dollar difference in expenditures increased in favor of the metropolitan counties, and the difference was continuing to increase at the end of the period. These differences in expenditures among counties, compounded by the variations existing among states, result in some pupils who live in metropolitan counties of high expenditure states having at least ten times as much spent on their education as children in rural counties of low expenditure states. Such differences can only mean that some children receive instruction in well-equipped buildings from well-trained, competent teachers who have adequate teaching materials, while other children attend school in wretched buildings under the direction of poorly trained teachers who have inadequate instructional materials with which to work. Some decreases in the extreme differences undoubtedly occurred during the past few years, but the condition was still a serious one in 1952.

Another large gap has long existed in expenditures between schools for white and Negro children. Expenditures for Negro schools increased from 1940 through 1952 by larger percentages than those for white schools, and the ratio of expenditures between them decreased appreciably. The dollar difference for the twelve-year period, however, actually increased in favor of white schools. The trend was reversed and the dollar difference decreased from 1950 to 1952. Throughout the twelve-year period, the largest difference in the ratio of racial expenditures was in rural counties and the least difference was in metropolitan counties.

Expenditures for instruction were the most nearly equalized of all budget items, largely because of the adoption by most states of single salary schedules for teachers. Capital outlay ratios between the races, which reached as high as ten-to-one in some states in 1940, were reduced by a greater percentage than any other budget item.

The pattern of movement toward equalization between the races in the various items of the budget has been to reduce the ratio of instruction expenditures first. Undoubtedly influenced to some extent by recent Supreme Court decisions, expenditures for capital outlay were next most nearly equalized. Last came the items of current expense other than instruction, such as transportation, maintenance, and operation of health services and lunchrooms.

Considerable variation among states exists in the extent and pattern of movement toward equalization of expenditures between the races. In at least three states, North Carolina, Tennessee, and Virginia, the average salary for Negroes was higher than for whites in 1952. Only one state, Florida, was spending more for capital outlay per pupil for Negro schools than for white schools. Some states, then, were moving rapidly toward equalization, while others lagged behind.

The percentage of Negro population was significantly related to the degree of equalization of expenditures in 1940. By 1952 the relationship was still positive but no longer significant. The shift of Negroes to metropolitan counties, where expenditures were higher, and the large increase in Negro secondary school enrollments were among the factors which contributed to the trend toward equalization. Instructional expenditures between the races were calculated to have been 43 per cent equalized in 1940 and 75 per cent in 1952. Current expense other than instruction and capital outlay would show somewhat smaller degrees of equalization.

A significant positive relationship between the sources of school revenue and the degree of equalization of expenditures between rural and metropolitan counties existed throughout the period. In general, the states in which a larger percentage of school revenue came from local sources had larger ratios between expenditures for rural and metropolitan counties.

The foregoing analysis clearly shows that large increases in expenditures are called for if equalization of educational opportunity in the region is to be achieved. The problem is so complex that the biracial issue cannot be approached except as a part of the entire equalization problem.

SEVEN

Public School Personnel

The central place of school personnel, the teacher in particular, is obvious in educational improvement. In considering the problems faced by the biracial schools of the region as the issue of segregation is met, what information concerning personnel is needed? What inequalities exist among schools in the distribution of able teachers? These are among the questions dealt with in this chapter.

One of the developments of critical importance in education during the past fifty years has been the emergence of the teacher as a professional person. While his status in the social order may rank low according to standards applied to other professions, the growth in public acceptance and appreciation of public education clearly identifies the importance attached to teaching. Any discrepancy between the heavy reliance society places upon education as a means of self-advancement and the tangible rewards it establishes for those who teach may be due to inadequate knowledge of the problems of teaching and the competence necessary for meeting them successfully.

Control by the state of admission to the teaching profession, which has come about in the South in the last half century, is one way public definition of the value of teaching has been expressed. Requirements for certification have mounted steadily as the relationship between teacher education and effective teaching has been better understood. Other devices designed to improve teaching, which have reached the level of legal sanction, are tenure laws, welfare provisions, including retirement benefits, and salary schedules.

As the purposes of education have been broadened and new functions have been taken on by the schools, specialized fields of teaching have grown up which require important extensions and modifications of the former general teacher preparation programs. Specialized fields, plus the emphasis on method in teacher education and the tremendous increases in public school enrollment, have been primarily responsible for the growth of a large number of institutions of higher learning

179

whose major reason for being is to supply the demand for well-trained teachers in the public schools.

Formalization of the structure of education, together with the various safeguards society has set up to assure some measure of effectiveness in teaching, has gone far toward making possible a stable profession. The itinerant teacher traveling from community to community and making his own contracts for employment and remuneration with an interested parent or group of parents, who paid him from their own funds, has been supplanted by legal contracts with responsible agencies of government. Nonetheless, stability to a degree which might be expected from the foregoing professionalization measures has not been achieved. Some of the reasons will be apparent from the discussions which follow.

NUMBERS OF SCHOOL PERSONNEL

Although those actually engaged in the processes of teaching make up the great body of professional school personnel in the region, about 93 per cent, other types of personnel are essential. These cannot be ignored, even though analyses of statistics on teaching personnel will receive chief attention.

It was pointed out in Chapter 3 that the number of professional persons in the thirteen state departments of education in the region total 1,200. To these key people must be added the administrators and supervisors of local school districts in order to obtain an adequate picture of leadership personnel in the South. Since the trend toward fewer districts developed, the number of school superintendents has been steadily decreasing. Excluding Mississippi, Arkansas, and Texas from this summation, there are only 1,650 school superintendents in the region. The three states named have 5,300 superintendents, which makes a total of 6,950 for the region, all of whom are white.

The number of school principals has been declining also, although the number of full-time principals has been increasing. As small schools have been eliminated and larger attendance centers have taken their place, competent, professionally trained principals have been in demand for administering these new schools. Accurate figures on the number of full time principals in the region are not available, but 12,000 appears to be a reasonable estimate.

Professionally trained teachers charged with the responsibility of working with teachers toward the improvement of instruction have become common in all the states. Generally called supervisors, they have been delegated much of the responsibility, formerly exercised by the superintendent, for working directly with teaching personnel. Approximately 2,100 supervisors are employed in the region. The vast majority are white.

The development of large school districts has brought about district administrative staffs, which, in addition to the superintendent and supervisor, are often composed of a person in charge of school attendance, a director of transportation, a supervisor of buildings and maintenance, and a director of business and finance. This pattern, of course, varies from school system to school system and state to state. Sometimes, several supervisors or other persons will be employed in leadership positions as research directors, personnel directors, and so forth.

The task of organizing, administering, and supervising school systems has called for specialized training of workers for the positions thus created. The administrative impact upon the teaching program is such that sound leadership from the district level and the school attendance center is essential to good educational programs. Indeed, the requirements on individuals holding these positions become more demanding year by year.

By 1940, 258,277 persons were employed as classroom teachers in the thirteen Southern states. Their aggregate income from teaching amounted to a quarter of a billion dollars. An additional 30,000 teaching positions had been created by 1952, and the 288,855 teachers then employed earned three-quarters of a billion dollars in salaries. In an economic sense, therefore, the teachers were a substantial part of the economy; on the one hand, they accounted for a major expenditure of public funds and, on the other, their contribution to the total income of the region was of some consequence.

There were only 97,980 teachers in the South in 1900, 23.2 per cent of the national figure. The quarter of a million in 1940 represents a gain of 163.6 per cent in the forty-year period. The South's proportion of the nation's teachers has increased steadily; in 1920 it accounted for 26.3 per cent and in 1950, 29.9 per cent.

The 30,000 new teachers added to the public schools of the South between 1940 and 1952 constituted an 11.6 per cent increase. Only two states, Oklahoma and Kentucky, had fewer teachers in 1952 than in 1940, the result of a decline in school enrollment and attendance. Extremes within the region are represented by Oklahoma and Florida. Oklahoma had a decrease of 21.4 per cent in teachers; Florida, in the midst of a rapid expansion, had an increase of 43.8 per cent. A breakdown of changes by states is shown in Table 44.

TABLE 44

NUMBERS OF PUBLIC SCHOOL TEACHERS IN SOUTHERN STATES

State	1939–40	1949–50	1951–52
Alabama	19,405	21,613	22,354
Arkansas	12,852	12,845	12,995
Florida	12,923	16,559	18,589
Georgia	22,779	23,380	25,642
Kentucky	18,417	17,793	18,188
Louisiana	14,830	16,675	18,038
Mississippi	13,985	15,627	16,016
North Carolina	24,530	27,491	28,397
Oklahoma	20,980	15,930	16,494
South Carolina	15,042	16,753	17,479
Tennessee	20,147	22,202	23,033
Texas	44,807	47,103	50,992
Virginia	17,580	19,056	20,638
TOTAL	258,277	273,027	288,855

Teachers in the secondary schools in 1940 numbered 40 per cent of those in the elementary schools. During the next twelve years twice as many teachers were added to secondary schools as to elementary schools. A part of this gain was accounted for by the addition of a twelfth grade in several states during this time. Perhaps a more significant explanation was the continued growth of the secondary education movement in the region, especially the expansion of Negro secondary schools. In Florida, Mississippi, and South Carolina there was an increase of more than 50 per cent in secondary teachers. A breakdown of regional figures shows a 5.5 per cent gain in the number of elementary teachers and a 26.4 per cent gain in secondary school teachers. Three states, Arkansas, Oklahoma, and Kentucky, had fewer elementary teachers in 1952 than in 1940, while the number of secondary school teachers increased in every state.

Changes in the distribution of teachers within states show some patterns which are inconsistent with regional totals. There was an over-all increase in the number of rural teachers between 1940 and 1952 in spite of declines in enrollment and attendance. The number of rural elementary teachers declined 7.7 per cent, while secondary school teachers increased 38.3 per cent. The latter figure indicates the marked extension of secondary education to rural children, although a part of the increase is attributable to the addition of twelfth grades to many rural schools which in 1940 had only eleven.

More than half of the increase in the total number of teachers in the region occurred in metropolitan counties; they showed a gain of 40.3 per cent. Since most metropolitan counties already had a twelfth grade in the secondary school in 1940, the increase was influenced more heavily by enrollment gains than was true of rural counties. Table 45 presents a breakdown by population classifications.

TABLE 45

CHANGE FROM 1940 TO 1952 IN NUMBERS OF PUBLIC SCHOOL TEACHERS I
SAMPLE RURAL AND RURAL-URBAN COUNTIES AND IN METROPOLITAN
COUNTIES OF SOUTHERN STATES

County Classification	Total [a]	Elementary [b]	Secondary [b]
Rural	3.8	— 7.8	43.8
Rural-Urban	8.8	2.9	27.4
Metropolitan	40.3	41.3	40.4

[a] Eleven states.
[b] Ten states.

In 1920, 20.7 per cent of all Southern teachers were Negroes. By 1950 this figure had increased to 24.8 per cent. Since the ratio of Negro to white population had declined, the increase represents a substantial gain in educational opportunity for the minority race. Between 1940 and 1952 there was an increase of 18.0 per cent in the number of Negro teachers as compared to a 10.1 per cent gain in white teachers, although average daily attendance in white schools increased slightly more rapidly than in Negro schools.

Roughly one-third of the total increase in teachers in the South during this time is accounted for by Negro schools. Some idea of the more equitable distribution of teachers by races which came about between 1940 and 1950 may be gained from these statistics: at the beginning of the decade there were only 29.8 per cent as many Negro as white teachers, while there were 38.8 per cent as many Negro as white children; when the decade came to an end, there were 32.2 per cent as many Negro teachers as white teachers, and 36.7 per cent as many Negro as white school-age children.

By reference to Table 46, comparisons by states may be made. The most significant change in the number of teachers occurred in Negro high schools. In 1952 there were nineteen Negro high school teachers for every ten in 1940, a 90 per cent increase. The gain in white high school teachers was from ten to twelve, or 20 per cent. A further indication of the strength of the Negro high school movement was in the increase in the percentage high school Negro teachers were of all Negro teachers, the increase having been from 14.6 in 1940 to 25.9 in 1952. On the elementary level the percentage of increase in white teachers was greater than the percentage of Negro increase.

TABLE 46

NUMBERS OF WHITE AND NEGRO PUBLIC SCHOOL TEACHERS IN SOUTHERN STATES

State	1939–40	1949–50	1951–52
Alabama			
White	13,786	14,428	14,863
Negro	5,619	7,185	7,491
Arkansas			
White	10,286	10,219	10,286
Negro	2,566	2,626	2,709
Florida			
White	9,705	12,514	14,097
Negro	3,218	4,045	4,492
Georgia			
White	15,979	16,204	17,781
Negro	6,800	7,176	7,861
Kentucky			
White	16,999	16,562	16,942
Negro	1,418	1,231	1,245
Louisiana			
White	10,711	11,420	12,268
Negro	4,119	5,255	5,770
Mississippi			
White	7,728	9,075	9,360
Negro	6,257	6,552	6,656
North Carolina			
White	17,534	19,924	20,561
Negro	6,996	7,567	7,836
Oklahoma			
White	19,236	14,579	15,168
Negro	1,744	1,351	1,326
South Carolina			
White	9,398	9,895	10,345
Negro	5,644	6,858	7,134
Tennessee			
White	17,207	18,894	19,507
Negro	2,940	3,308	3,526
Texas			
White	38,663	40,197	43,757
Negro	6,144	6,906	7,235
Virginia			
White	13,430	14,685	15,934
Negro	4,150	4,371	4,704
TOTAL			
White	200,662	208,596	220,869
Negro	57,615	64,431	67,985

Changes in the number of teachers according to county classifications afford some interesting contrasts. The greatest percentage gain in white teachers occurred in the elementary schools of metropolitan counties, while the greatest gain in Negro teachers took place in rural secondary schools. There was a decrease of 14.0 per cent in rural white elementary teachers as compared to a 44.3 per cent gain in metropolitan counties for white elementary teachers. In rural counties 27 high school Negro teachers were to be found in 1952 for every ten in 1940, an astounding increase of 270 per cent. Gains in rural-urban counties amounted to 100 per cent and in metropolitan counties to 90 per cent. Table 47 presents the percentage analysis for the county classifications.

TABLE 47

CHANGE FROM 1940 TO 1952 IN NUMBERS OF WHITE AND NEGRO PUBLIC SCHOOL
TEACHERS IN SAMPLE RURAL AND RURAL-URBAN COUNTIES, AND IN
METROPOLITAN COUNTIES OF SOUTHERN STATES

County Classification	Grades 1-12 [a]	Elementary [b]	Secondary [b]
Rural			
White	− 1.7	−14.0	15.5
Negro	20.1	2.9	174.2
Rural-Urban			
White	6.2	4.8	14.2
Negro	15.1	2.3	103.7
Metropolitan			
White	38.3	44.3	30.3
Negro	46.7	34.3	89.3

[a] Eleven states.
[b] Ten states.

TEACHER LOAD

A 184 per cent increase in the number of teachers as compared to an increase of 134.7 per cent in attendance between 1900 and 1940 indicates in some measure concern for work assignments consistent with maximum teaching performance. A great many factors, some of them intangible and therefore very difficult to isolate, enter into the determination of teacher load. Current practices which tend to lighten the burden of teaching include the following: assignment of a teacher to one grade in contrast to former responsibility for several grades; the development of a variety of instructional materials of high quality; availability of supervisory assistance and help of other specialists as needed; and a usual school day of six hours in contrast to a day seven and eight hours in years not too far past.

On the other hand, there are current practices, some of them relatively new, which require much more of the teacher than was once the case; certain practices, in fact, tend to subject the teacher to an arduous and rigorous series of demands which are a heavy drain on physical, intellectual, and emotional energy. Newer teaching methods require a knowledge of each child, highly individualized instruction, and comprehensive evaluation. There is the necessity for continuous study in order to keep abreast of current developments in education relevant to the teacher's work. He is often required to participate in in-service education programs which must, of necessity, fall outside school hours; while rewarding, these activities are an additional drain on teacher energy. The pressure to continue formal training in order to progress on the salary schedule frequently prevents teachers from taking needed vacations.

Community demands, which vary widely from community to community, also add to the teaching burden. Such demands may not be positive; they may consist simply of taboos which tend to narrow teachers' lives by limiting wholesome contacts with people outside the teaching profession and by restricting the means for needed recreation. Certain community demands are more teacher-imposed than community-imposed because stress is now placed on school programs which take into account community conditions. This trend impels teachers to understand their communities to a greater degree than was necessary in the traditional textbook-centered school program.

The difficulties of developing a comprehensive method of calculating teaching load have been such that no adequate measure has yet been devised which takes into valid account any of the elements of importance that do not readily lend themselves to objective measurement. For that and other reasons, the most acceptable measure of teacher load is pupil-teacher ratio, which means the average number of pupils in attendance for each day taught by the teacher. Many studies have been made which indicate an important relationship between the ratio of pupils to teacher in a classroom and the effectiveness of teaching. Teachers who have been assigned an excessive number of students may find it difficult to organize, plan, and conduct their work in a way which will provide maximum learning opportunities to all students. Pupil-teacher ratio is one convenient way of analyzing objectively the one factor which is by all odds the most important single aspect of teacher load.

On a region-wide basis, pupil-teacher ratio computed for grades one through twelve was 27.2 in 1940 and 25.9 in 1952, a decline of 1.3 pupils per teacher. Among the states in the region only Oklahoma was an exception to the trend toward reduction. In that

state pupil-teacher ratio increased by 1.4 pupils. The greatest decrease, 4.5 pupils per teacher, was in Mississippi. Mississippi had
the greatest pupil ratio in the region in 1940 with 33.9 and, despite
the decline, still had the highest ratio in 1952. The lowest ratio in
1940 was 23.1 in Oklahoma. These figures reveal a range of 10.8
in pupil-teacher ratio among the states at the beginning of the period.
The range had declined to a difference of five pupils by 1952, the
lowest being in South Carolina, which had 24.4 pupils per teacher.
Table 48 indicates that pupil-teacher ratio in 1952 was approaching

TABLE 48

NUMBER OF PUPILS IN AVERAGE DAILY ATTENDANCE PER CLASSROOM TEACHER
IN PUBLIC SCHOOLS OF SOUTHERN STATES

State	*1939–40*	*1949–50*	*1951–52*
Alabama	29.2	27.5	26.3
Arkansas	29.1	27.6	27.0
Florida	25.2	24.9	24.6
Georgia	25.6	26.5	24.9
Kentucky	26.8	27.0	26.3
Louisiana	26.8	25.2	24.7
Mississippi	33.9	30.2	29.4
North Carolina	32.2	29.0	28.7
Oklahoma	23.1	25.2	24.5
South Carolina	25.6	24.7	24.4
Tennessee	26.6	26.3	25.8
Texas	24.9	24.6	24.6
Virginia	28.1	28.2	27.0
TOTAL	27.2	26.5	25.9

relative stability around a figure of 26. In 1940 the national average
was 25.2 and in 1950 it was 24.4. Thus, Southern regional figures
are slightly higher than those for the nation; when expressed in percentages of difference, the gap is rather substantial.

Pupil-teacher ratio in elementary schools was consistently higher
than in secondary schools. The difference in 1940 was 7.4 pupils.
Ten years later, the difference had increased to 10.8 pupils. Justifi-
cation for this differential would be difficult indeed. The importance
of early school years in establishing good learning habits and attitudes toward school and the responsibility of one teacher for the
entire school day of the child are arguments frequently advanced
for pupil-teacher ratios in elementary school at least as small as
those in secondary school. Reasons for the difference in load appear
to be a fairly large number of small high schools in the region which
must maintain a low pupil-teacher ratio in order to offer programs

which meet the standards of accrediting agencies, pressures to keep enrollments in certain primarily vocational courses fairly small, and the traditional difference in status society ascribes to the secondary and the elementary school. Table 49 shows the differences between

TABLE 49

NUMBER OF PUPILS IN AVERAGE DAILY ATTENDANCE PER CLASSROOM TEACHER
IN PUBLIC ELEMENTARY AND SECONDARY SCHOOLS OF SOUTHERN STATES

State	1939–40		1949–50		1951–52	
	Elem.	*Sec.*	*Elem.*	*Sec.*	*Elem.*	*Sec.*
Alabama	31.2	25.1	29.9	23.8	28.4	23.1
Arkansas	30.0	25.2	30.0	21.0	29.0	22.0
Florida	25.1	25.4	26.8	22.2	26.0	22.4
Georgia	28.4	17.8	29.1	20.4	27.3	19.6
Kentucky	28.4	22.6	29.1	21.9	28.1	21.9
Louisiana	29.8	19.7	30.1	14.3	29.7	14.2
Mississippi	37.7	20.6	36.0	16.3	35.7	15.7
North Carolina	33.4	28.9	30.8	23.7	30.6	23.3
Oklahoma	24.9	18.9	30.6	16.5	31.0	14.6
South Carolina	26.9	21.4	26.1	21.2	26.1	20.5
Texas	26.7	21.4	28.3	16.2	28.6	16.1
Virginia	30.1	22.1	32.8	19.7	31.5	18.9
TOTAL	29.4	22.0	30.1	19.2	29.5	18.7

the two school levels for twelve of the thirteen states covered by this analysis.

Differences among rural, rural-urban, and metropolitan counties in pupil-teacher ratio are so small that they are almost negligible. It appears that low pupil-teacher ratios in many small rural high schools and in one- and two-teacher schools are offset by larger ratios in other rural schools. The pupil-teacher ratio differential between rural and metropolitan counties is becoming smaller. In 1940 there was an average of two pupils more per teacher in metropolitan counties than in rural counties. By 1952 the ratios were almost the same. In the three years for which averages were computed, 1940, 1950, and 1952, rural-urban counties averaged slightly higher than rural and lower than metropolitan counties.

Pupil-teacher ratio differences between elementary and secondary schools were somewhat more pronounced in rural than in metropolitan counties in both 1940 and 1952. The analysis by classifications of counties is shown in Table 50.

TABLE 50

County Classification	1939–40		1951–52	
	Elementary	*Secondary*	*Elementary*	*Secondary*
Rural	29.7	21.7	30.0	18.5
Rural-Urban	30.5	22.6	29.2	20.1
Metropolitan	31.4	25.3	29.1	21.1

As provisions were made for Negro schools in the early decades of this century, attendance increased rapidly and many classrooms were filled to overflowing. In 1920 pupil-teacher ratio in Negro schools of most of the Southern states averaged more than 35. The following decade brought a great increase in the number of Negro teachers and, while it was a period during which large numbers of Negroes migrated to the North, attendance in Negro schools continued to grow. By 1930 only one state had a Negro pupil-teacher ratio of more than 35. During this ten-year span the ratio in white schools of the South generally remained under thirty.

Region-wide statistics by races show a pupil-teacher ratio differential in favor of white schools continuing into 1940, 1950, and 1952. The gap was narrowed, however, over the period, as shown by a difference of 5.2 pupils in 1940 and a difference of 2.7 pupils in 1952. Expressed another way, in 1940 the average Negro teacher had 20 per cent more pupils than the average white teacher, in 1952 he had 10.7 per cent more. These ratios by states are shown in Table 51.

TABLE 51

State	1939–40	1949–50	1951–52
Alabama			
White	26.8	26.9	25.8
Negro	35.0	28.8	27.2
Arkansas			
White	27.6	26.7	26.1
Negro	34.7	31.8	30.5
Florida			
White	24.6	24.6	24.4
Negro	27.0	26.0	25.0

TABLE 51 — (*continued*)

State	1939–40	1949–50	1951–52
Georgia			
White	23.9	25.5	24.2
Negro	29.8	28.8	26.4
Kentucky			
White	26.9	27.1	26.4
Negro	25.0	25.6	24.6
Louisiana			
White	23.1	23.1	22.6
Negro	35.1	29.9	29.3
Mississippi			
White	32.0	27.1	25.9
Negro	36.2	34.5	34.1
North Carolina			
White	31.9	28.3	28.0
Negro	32.9	30.8	30.6
Oklahoma			
White	23.3	25.4	24.6
Negro	21.5	23.1	23.9
South Carolina			
White	23.7	23.8	23.7
Negro	28.7	26.0	25.6
Tennessee			
White	26.0	25.9	25.5
Negro	30.6	28.5	27.8
Texas			
White	24.4	24.5	24.7
Negro	28.1	24.4	24.4
Virginia			
White	27.4	27.2	26.1
Negro	30.3	31.5	29.9
TOTAL			
White	26.0	25.8	25.3
Negro	31.2	28.9	28.0

It should be pointed out that the states having the lowest Negro pupil-teacher ratio are those with the smallest percentage of Negro population. Table 52 shows the differences between white and Negro pupil-teacher ratios for 1940 and 1952, according to elementary and secondary schools.

TABLE 52

NUMBER OF PUPILS IN AVERAGE DAILY ATTENDANCE PER CLASSROOM TEACHER
IN WHITE AND NEGRO PUBLIC ELEMENTARY AND SECONDARY SCHOOLS
OF SOUTHERN STATES

State	1939–40		1951–52	
	Elementary	Secondary	Elementary	Secondary
Alabama				
White	28.3	24.4	28.2	22.7
Negro	36.8	28.2	28.9	24.1
Arkansas				
White	31.5	18.7	35.7	13.5
Negro	38.3	15.3	39.1	12.9
Florida				
White	24.1	25.4	25.8	22.5
Negro	27.6	25.6	26.6	22.2
Georgia				
White	26.7	17.7	26.6	19.5
Negro	31.6	17.8	28.5	19.7
Kentucky				
White	28.6	22.7	28.2	22.1
Negro	26.3	21.7	27.4	19.6
Louisiana				
White	26.4	18.9	27.7	13.5
Negro	36.3	25.7	33.3	16.4
Mississippi				
White	36.6	22.3	34.0	14.9
Negro	38.7	14.1	37.4	18.3
North Carolina				
White	33.5	28.3	30.1	22.5
Negro	33.2	31.6	31.8	26.0
Oklahoma				
White	25.2	18.8	31.1	14.6
Negro	22.0	19.2	29.1	14.7
South Carolina				
White	25.1	20.6	26.1	19.5
Negro	29.1	25.4	26.2	23.2
Texas				
White	26.2	21.1	28.9	15.8
Negro	29.2	24.0	26.5	17.9
Virginia				
White	30.2	21.9	30.6	18.5
Negro	32.0	23.3	34.2	20.3
TOTAL				
White	28.2	21.7	29.1	18.2
Negro	32.7	23.8	30.6	20.5

The state and regional pattern of lower pupil-teacher ratios for white than for Negro schools was found to prevail in each of the county classifications. The figures in 1940 were 7.1 for metropolitan counties, 5.4 for rural-urban counties, and 3.8 for rural counties, each figure representing the average number of pupils Negro teachers had above the average for white teachers in the respective county groupings. The figures for 1952 show that differences in all types of counties were approximately 3, about the average difference on a region-wide basis.

The shift in differential from elementary to secondary schools by 1952, pointed out previously as a regional trend, was found to prevail in the county groupings also. The greatest shift occurred in the rural counties. Totals for eight states for 1940 showed 5.5 more Negro pupils per teacher than white pupils per teacher in rural elementary schools, and 1.9 more Negro pupils per teacher in secondary schools than white pupils per teacher. By 1952, the difference in these states was only 0.8 in the elementary schools, but it had increased to 2.8 in the secondary schools. Table 53 shows a comparison of the county classifications in eight states.

TABLE 53

NUMBER OF PUPILS IN AVERAGE DAILY ATTENDANCE PER CLASSROOM TEACHER IN
WHITE AND NEGRO PUBLIC ELEMENTARY AND SECONDARY SCHOOLS IN
SAMPLE RURAL AND RURAL-URBAN COUNTIES, AND IN
METROPOLITAN COUNTIES OF EIGHT
SOUTHERN STATES

| County | 1939–40 | | 1951–52 | |
Classification	Elementary	Secondary	Elementary	Secondary
Rural				
White	27.4	21.4	29.7	17.8
Negro	32.9	23.3	30.5	20.6
Rural-Urban				
White	28.7	22.2	28.3	19.7
Negro	33.2	24.3	30.6	21.1
Metropolitan				
White	29.1	24.5	27.9	20.7
Negro	36.3	28.8	32.0	22.3

TEACHER TRAINING

Data on the number of years of training of teachers for the early decades of the century are quite limited, but there is sufficient evidence to indicate the meagre professional qualifications of teachers at a time when certification was in the hands of local school trustees and the school districts. As late as 1922, Knight said of the Southern states:

> Careful estimates show that more than 15 per cent of the rural and small-village teachers in these States have had only an elementary-school training. Ten per cent have had only one year, about 18 per cent have had two years, 19 per cent three years, and 40 per cent four years in high schools. *Less than 5 per cent have had college training. . . .*[1]

While it may be assumed that the teachers in urban schools were somewhat better prepared, it is not likely that their preparation approached the average for all teachers in the region in 1939-40, when 55.5 per cent had four years of college training.

McCuistion, in a study of the training of Negro teachers in 1930, including thirteen Southern states plus the border states of Maryland and Missouri, reports that only 12 per cent were college graduates, 32 per cent had two years of college training, 19 per cent had less than two years of college training, and 37 per cent had less than high school training.[2] The advance in the training of Negro teachers since that date has been tremendous.

Demands for better qualified, more competent teachers grew as the public schools reached larger and larger proportions of the school-age population. The expansion of local school systems influenced the licensing of teachers by placing the authority in school boards or superintendents rather than in trustees of local schools. Some certificates were issued on the basis of examinations, others on the basis of work in the local training school or in a normal school. The next forward step in teacher certification was the projection of uniform standards on a state-wide basis and the centralization of authority for issuance of certificates in the hands of state departments of education.

The history of state control of certification has been one of continuous upgrading of standards. Even in times of extreme teacher shortages, qualifications have not been waived except on a temporary basis. All states in the region define levels of qualification which are recognized in salary schedules. Thus, the salary schedule is commonly used as a device for encouraging teachers to improve their preparation.

One of the most perplexing and persistent problems in the field of teacher education is the measurement of teaching competence. Personality, initiative, motivation, and physical, mental and emotional

---

[1] Edgar W. Knight, *Public Education in the South* (Boston: Ginn and Company, 1922), p. 440. (Italics the authors'.)

[2] Fred W. McCuistion, "The South's Negro Teaching Force," *Journal of Negro Education,* Vol. I, No. 1 (Apr., 1932), p. 21.

health are obvious factors entering into the success of a teacher. Difficulties inherent in the objective measurement and evaluation of such factors have thus far made it impractical to take them into account in teacher certification. Qualitative measurements require a high degree of subjectivity, and authorities have not used them as a means of rating teachers for certification purposes.

Amount of training, however, can be measured in terms of quarter or semester hours of college work, or in the number of years of college work completed. It is generally assumed that there is a positive relationship between the amount of training a teacher possesses and the quality of his classroom instruction. More specificity is injected into this objective measure by the general practice of requiring for certification a designated number of hours of college work in particular fields of professional education. There is also a requirement that those who qualify to teach a particular subject must have taken a minimum number of college hours in the particular field. A second measure of teacher competence widely recognized is experience in teaching. Salary schedules take into account experience, up to a specified number of years, in the provision of increments.

The weaknesses of these two methods are obvious. They do not discriminate as to quality among the large groups of teachers who may fall into a given category of training and experience. The advantages of these two measures is that they are objective and easily administered. Requirements that teachers be able to secure certificates of good health are becoming more common, although they are prudential measures rather than measures designed to aid in defining teacher competence.

Maintaining and improving levels of teacher training are related to the general social and economic conditions of a country or region. The supply of teachers and their level of training may improve during periods of serious depression, when remunerative employment in other fields is hard to find. On the other hand, the supply of teachers may decline sharply in times of unusual prosperity because the business world offers strong financial inducements to teachers and prospective teachers. Serious crises occurred in teacher personnel during World War II, when many teachers left the classrooms to accept higher salaries in rapidly expanding defense industries. Thousands of young men were lost to the teaching profession during the war as they were called into the armed services, many failing to return after their military service ended. Many who left the profession during World War II continued in industry and business as the upward spiral in the economy continued after the war. In those periods, former teachers who had retired or married or had failed to meet more strenuous certification requirements returned to the classrooms.

During and after World War II, tens of thousands of teachers were in the classrooms who, for one reason or another, had at one time left the profession but returned with provisional or emergency certificates. The average level of training of teachers declined considerably during this time in many school systems. One effect of this situation was to create a very rapid turnover of teachers, especially in rural districts. The more highly trained teachers were drained off to the better school systems and their positions were filled in many cases with anyone who was willing to undertake the job.

Under these conditions it is a somewhat surprising fact that the average training of teachers in the Southern region actually increased slightly from 1940 to 1950. Chart 4 shows the extent of improve-

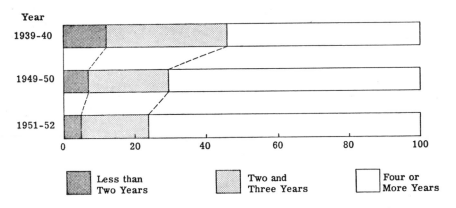

CHART 4. *Percentage of classroom teachers with specified amounts of college training in ten Southern states.*

ment. By 1950, 4.0 per cent fewer of all teachers had less than two years of college training than in 1940, and 15.4 per cent more of the total had as much as four years of college training. This was a general trend, as shown by the fact that, in each of the states for which statistics are available, the percentage of teachers with four years of college training was greater in 1950 than in 1940.

Differences among states were great. Chart 5 compares the states which fall at the extremes. It will be noted that in 1940 eight out of ten teachers in North Carolina had completed four or more years of college, whereas in Arkansas only three out of ten had done so. In 1950 nine out of ten teachers in North Carolina and Texas had received four or more years of college training; the low states are represented by Tennessee and Mississippi, and less than half the teachers in these two states had four or more years of college training.

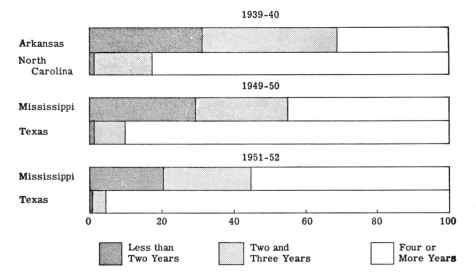

CHART 5. *Percentage of classroom teachers with specified amounts of college training in the high and low states of the South.*

The trend toward improved teacher qualifications as measured by college training continued at an accelerated rate. Figures for 1952 show that 20 per cent more of the total number of teachers in the ten states reporting had four or more years of college training than in 1940. At the same time, the proportion with less than two years of training was reduced from 11.6 per cent to 4.8 per cent. In Alabama, Georgia and Mississippi, 10 per cent more of the total classroom teaching force had four years of college training in 1952 than in 1950. By 1952 Florida, North Carolina, Oklahoma, and Texas each had as many as nine out of ten teachers with four or more years of college education. In these four states the percentage of teachers with less than two years of college training was almost negligible. Variations which existed among the states in 1940 and 1950 continued into 1952, as illustrated by Mississippi where only five and one-half out of ten teachers had completed as many as four years of college training, and two out of ten had completed less than two years of college training.

Historically, qualifications for secondary school teachers have been higher than those for elementary school teachers. This situation may be accounted for by several factors: the assumption that teaching in the secondary school is more difficult and requires a more adequate grasp of subject matter; standards of accrediting agencies; the influence of college entrance requirements on secondary schools; and the edge in status which has been generally accorded secondary school teachers. Forces that have been operating to reduce differences in levels of training are single salary schedules based on qualifications and experience, a lengthened elementary school term to correspond to that of the secondary school, and wider recognition of the importance of the early years in school.

Unfortunately, teacher training data by elementary and secondary divisions are available for only five states for the three years covered by this analysis. The validity of comparisons for the purpose of establishing trends is weakened by the fact that only two of the five states appear in each of the years for which comparisons are made. The data are nonetheless revealing. Of the secondary school teachers in Alabama, Arkansas, Tennessee, Texas, and Virginia, 88.4 per cent had four or more years of college work in 1940, while only 38.8 per cent of the elementary school teachers in these states had an equal amount of training. Only 1.4 per cent of the secondary school teachers had less than two years of college training compared to 13.9 per cent of the elementary teachers. The greatest percentage of elementary teachers was found to have two and three years of college training, which undoubtedly reflects the influence of earlier requirements of two years of college work for certification to teach in elementary schools.

In 1950 and 1952 the states reporting teacher training by elementary and secondary schools were Alabama, Oklahoma, South Carolina, Texas, and Virginia. Considerable differences in training between elementary and secondary school teachers prevailed in 1950; 92.6 per cent of the secondary school teachers had four or more years of college training compared to 66.2 per cent of the elementary school teachers. The percentage with two years or less of college was 1.4 for secondary school teachers and 8.6 per cent for elementary school teachers.

Training improved during the next two years, as 75.4 per cent of the elementary teachers had four or more years of college training and the percentage with only two years or less dropped to 5.6. Secondary school teachers had reached the point where 94.9 per cent of them had four or more years of college training. Chart 6 summarizes these comparisons.

It seems logical to conclude that the great differential between training of elementary and secondary school teachers which has long existed in the South was well on its way out by 1952. The trend toward requiring four years of training as a basis for issuing the initial teacher certificate supports this observation. The concentration of better prepared teachers in metropolitan areas continues to pose a problem, however.

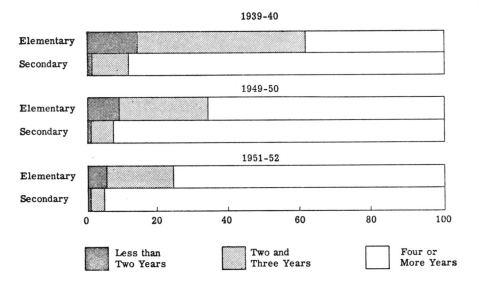

CHART 6. *Percentage of elementary and secondary teachers with specified amounts of college training in the high and low states of the South.*

An analysis of teacher training by county classifications is restricted by the fact that state records for only a limited number of states are kept in a way to provide the necessary information. The data are summarized in Chart 7, the five states reported being Alabama, Georgia, Louisiana, Oklahoma, and Tennessee.

Wide differences in levels of teacher training prevailed in county classifications in both 1940 and 1952, with the metropolitan teachers in each case having the highest level of training, the rural-urban group next, and the rural group having the lowest. In 1940, 62.9 per cent of all teachers in metropolitan counties had four or more years of college training, while 47.7 per cent of the rural-urban teachers and 35.3 per cent of the rural teachers achieved this level of training. By 1952, 81.2 per cent of the teachers in metropolitan counties, 70.5 per cent of rural-urban teachers, and 61.9 per cent of rural teachers had four or more years of college work. Substantial progress obviously was made in all the county groupings during the twelve-year period, with the most rapid progress coming in rural counties.

Nevertheless, the differential between metropolitan and rural counties remained considerable. As a matter of fact, by 1952 rural counties did not have quite the percentage of teachers with four years of training that metropolitan counties had twelve years earlier.

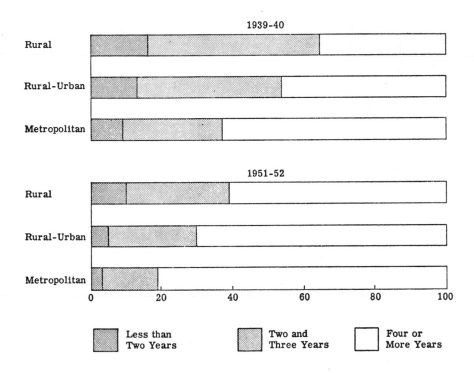

CHART 7. *Percentage of classroom teachers with specified amounts of college training in rural, rural-urban, and metropolitan counties of five Southern states.*

Teaching as a career is more important to Negroes than to white persons in the South because the dual culture of the region severely restricts Negroes in their choices of professions. Consequently, to be a teacher is a greater mark of distinction among Negroes than among whites and the Negro teacher enjoys higher status among Negroes than a white teacher does among whites. It was not surprising, therefore, to find that as opportunities in professional education became available Negroes were quick to take advantage of them, and they have exploited the opportunities of professional training to a greater degree than white teachers have. The story, then, of differentials in levels of training between the races is one of a constant narrowing of the gap. Indeed, in some states the level of teacher training for Negroes is higher than the level for whites. The gain in average years of training for Negroes was 0.8 of a year and for whites was 0.4 of a year. On a regional level in 1952 there was only 0.3 of a year's difference in the training of the two races.

In 1952, 37.3 per cent more of all the Negro teachers had four years of college training than in 1940, and 16.7 per cent more of all the white teachers had four years of college training than in 1940. In 1940 three out of ten Negro teachers had less than two years of college training, but by 1952 the figure had dropped to less than one out of ten. The percentages of teachers of both races with two and three years of college training decreased to about the same extent.

Variations among states in differences between races are considerable. In 1940 there was no state in which the average training of Negroes was higher than the average training of white teachers, but in 1952 average Negro training exceeded that of the majority race in six Southern states, namely, Georgia, North Carolina, Oklahoma, Tennessee, Texas, and Virginia. The greatest difference existed in Mississippi for both years, the percentage of white teachers with four years of college training being twice that of Negro teachers. Even in 1952, only a fourth of the Negro teachers in Mississippi had four or more years of college education, which represented the smallest gain made in any state. The percentage of Negro teachers in Georgia with four or more years of training more than tripled from 1940 to 1952. From 1940 to 1952, the percentage of Negro teachers with four years or more of college training in the ten states for which records are available, increased from 35.5 to 72.8.

There were practically no Negro teachers in Oklahoma with less than two years of college training in 1940, and none in 1952. Almost half of the Negro teachers in Georgia had less than two years training in 1940, but by 1952 only 1.2 per cent fell into this classification. Of the total number of teachers in the South with less than two years of training in 1940, more than half were Negroes. In both 1950 and 1952, however, there was a larger number of white than Negro teachers in this group. In 1940 a larger proportion of Negro teachers than white teachers had less than two years of college training in every state. By 1952, however, in the states of Georgia, North Carolina, Tennessee, Texas, and Virginia, a larger porportion of white teachers than Negro teachers had less than two years of college training. Chart 8 is a graphic representation of the comparisons.

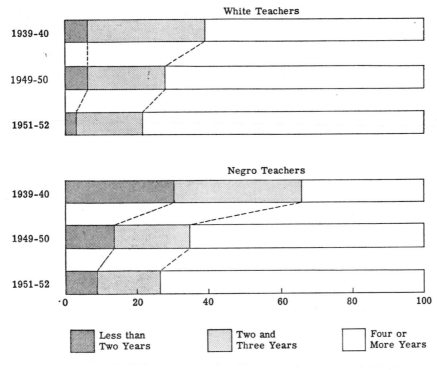

CHART 8. *Percentage of white and Negro classroom teachers with specified amounts of college training in ten Southern states.*

TEACHERS' SALARIES

The ancient adage that one gets what he pays for is applicable to teaching. The relationship between the salary paid and the quality of teaching has been established by research. The most casual observer knows that, other things being equal, teachers seek out school systems which have higher salary schedules, and that systems with higher schedules have them because they desire a higher quality of education than can be purchased for less money.

Unfortunately, services contracted for a public expense seldom command the financial remuneration which private business and industry pay for services requiring equivalent training and ability. Additional factors seem to have conspired to establish and maintain salaries for teachers below the level commanded for a similar level of competence in the business world. Some of these factors follow: teachers are employed only nine months of the year and, therefore, cannot expect to receive a full year's salary; the public seems to think that, since schools are actually in session only about six hours a day, five days a week, teachers do not work hours comparable in length to those of people engaged in other pursuits; length of service in the teaching profession is usually shorter than that of other professions, which means that fewer teachers attain maximum salaries; and teachers are not required to spend as many years in minimum formal preparation as doctors, lawyers, engineers, and other professional people. Many able people who would make excellent teachers choose more remunerative occupations.

Teachers' salaries have, nevertheless, risen slowly over the years. Chart 9 shows the generally upward trend in teachers' salaries in the

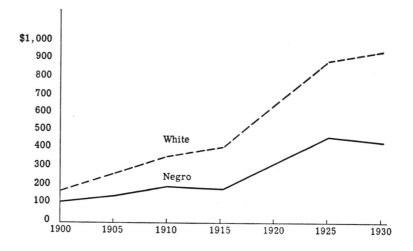

CHART 9. *Trends in teachers' average annual salaries in thirteen Southern states.*

South between 1900 and 1930. The depression period slowed the trend, but its upward march was resumed in the latter part of the thirties and has continued since. Attention is called to the fact that Negroes' salaries declined slightly between 1910 and 1915, and 1925 and 1930. The greatest dollar difference between salaries of white and Negro teachers shown on the chart occurred in 1930. Salaries of the two groups were closer together in 1900, when the salaries for white teachers averaged $162 per year and those for Negroes $106 per year. At this time the Negro teacher received 65 per cent as much as the white teacher. Although the salaries of both had materially increased by 1930—white teachers were receiving $901 and Negroes $423—the Negro teacher's salary was then only 47 per cent of that received by the white teacher.[3]

In 1940 the average annual teacher salary in the Southern states was $851. The range was from a low of $533 in Mississippi to a high of $1,059 in Texas. Ten years later salaries had increased 175 per cent to an annual figure of $2,341, and by 1952 the increase was 210 per cent over the 1940 figure, the average being $2,636 per year. In the latter year, Mississippi was again the low state with $1,587 and Texas continued in first place with $3,186. The rate of increase in the thirteen states ranged from 252 per cent in Georgia to 161 per cent in Tennessee. In terms of dollars, teachers were being paid three times as much in 1952 as in 1940, and in both years the teachers in the state with the highest salaries were receiving twice as much as those in the state with the lowest salaries. Table 54 shows the average salaries for teachers by states for 1940, 1950, and 1952.

TABLE 54

ANNUAL SALARIES OF TEACHERS IN THE PUBLIC SCHOOLS OF SOUTHERN STATES

State	1939–40	1949–50	1951–52
Alabama	$ 719	$2,061	$2,486
Arkansas	574	1,757	1,845
Florida	982	2,874	3,129
Georgia	722	1,997	2,541
Kentucky	820	1,917	2,371
Louisiana	864	2,815	2,958
Mississippi	533	1,390	1,587
North Carolina	911	2,602	2,880
Oklahoma	996	2,667	2,979
South Carolina	732	1,872	2,375
Tennessee	828	2,014	2,158
Texas	1,059	3,018	3,186
Virginia	885	2,236	2,527
TOTAL	851	2,341	2,636

These differences influence to a very considerable degree the distribution of teachers among the states according to levels of training. Trends in levels of qualification tend to parallel quite closely trends in average annual salaries. For example, there was a relatively small increase in the percentage of teachers with four or more years of college training in Mississippi, Virginia, and Tennessee, as compared

---

[3] Julius Rosenwald Fund, *School Money in Black and White*. (Chicago: The Fund, 1934), p. 14.

to larger increases in Texas, Florida, and Louisiana. In the three states named first, the percentage increase in average salaries from 1940 to 1952 was low. In the last three states named, very substantial increases in teachers' salaries had been made during the twelve-year period, thus encouraging well-trained teachers from other states to seek employment in those states with the better salary schedules. The increased mobility of the population has tended to encourage this shift of better-trained teachers to those states which have better salary schedules.

Differentials between elementary and secondary school teachers decreased during the twelve years for which intensive analyses were made. The elementary teacher in nine of the Southern states—data for Florida, Mississippi, Oklahoma, and Tennessee were unavailable—averaged $374 a year less than secondary school teachers in 1940, $401 less in 1950, and $347 less in 1952. Considering the substantial raises during the period, it will be seen that the relative stability of the dollar difference really amounts to a decline percentage-wise. This is, in part, attributable to the single salary schedule and, in part, to the increases in the levels of training of elementary school teachers. In no state did the average annual salary of elementary teachers equal that of secondary school teachers for either of the three years. Differences among states are considerable. In 1952 Mississippi secondary school teachers received $698 more annually than elementary teachers, but in North Carolina they received only $134 more.

In the face of the growth of state aid to school districts and the adoption of state-wide minimum salary schedules, the dollar difference between average annual earnings of teachers in rural and metropolitan counties actually increased. In 1940 the difference in favor of the metropolitan county teacher was $503, in 1950 it was $742, and in 1952 it was $800. The percentage increase in teacher salaries was, however, higher in rural than in metropolitan counties. Data by classifications are presented in Table 55.

TABLE 55

ANNUAL SALARIES OF TEACHERS IN THE PUBLIC SCHOOLS OF SAMPLE RURAL AND RURAL-URBAN COUNTIES, AND IN METROPOLITAN COUNTIES OF TEN SOUTHERN STATES

County Classification	1939–40	1949–50	1951–52
Rural	$ 686	$1,993	$2,285
Rural-Urban	731	2,148	2,473
Metropolitan	1,189	2,735	3,085

Data on salaries of elementary and secondary school teachers by county classifications for the three years could be computed for only eight of the Southern states. The dollar difference in salaries for elementary and secondary teachers was greatest in rural counties, both in 1940 and 1952. The gap increased during these years in both rural and rural-urban counties, but it decreased in metropolitan counties.

Differences between elementary teacher salaries in rural and metropolitan counties were greater than differences between secondary teacher salaries in the same types of counties. In 1940 rural elementary school teachers were receiving $489 per year less than metropolitan elementary teachers, and rural secondary teachers were receiving $420 a year less than metropolitan secondary teachers. By 1952 the differences in both groups between rural and metropolitan counties had increased dollar-wise, with rural elementary teachers receiving $825 less than metropolitan teachers, and rural secondary teachers $604 less. The largest differential was, of course, between the rural elementary teachers and metropolitan secondary teachers; the difference in 1940 was $836, and in 1952 it had reached $1,123.

Since salary schedules are pegged to levels of training and experience, it should be borne in mind that the differences are attributable in part to differences in training of teachers in the county classifications. Another important part of the difference is due to the fact that experience and tenure of teachers tend to be higher in metropolitan counties than in rural counties. Also, salary schedules tend to be higher in metropolitan counties. It was pointed out earlier that experience is an important factor in determining the position of a teacher on a salary schedule.

The gradual breakdown of cultural sanctions that permitted the payment of higher salaries to white teachers than to Negro teachers of equivalent training and experience is reflected in the dramatic rise in teacher salaries for Negroes since 1940. Salaries of Negro teachers in grades one through twelve increased 374 per cent in the twelve years, while salaries of white teachers increased 186 per cent. Expressed in dollars, this amounted to $1,885 for Negroes and $1,781 for white teachers. In 1940 white teachers averaged $456 a year more than Negro teachers, but in 1952 the average was $352 a year more. Differences between salaries of teachers of the two races in 1940 ranged from $657 in Louisiana to $27 in Oklahoma, both in favor of white teachers. In other words, in 1940 average salaries of Negro teachers were lower in every state than average salaries for white teachers. In 1952 the greatest difference was in Mississippi, where white teachers averaged $982 more per year than Negro teachers. On the other hand, in North Carolina, Oklahoma, Tennessee, and Virginia Negro teachers' salaries in 1952 averaged slightly higher than the salaries for white teachers. The single salary schedule was in general operation in each of these four states. The training of Negro teachers in these states was slightly higher than that of white teachers and the Negroes were paid accordingly. Another factor operative in these four states was the concentration of Negro population in urban areas, where salaries for both races were higher than in rural areas.

Complete figures for the states keeping separate records for the races are presented in Table 56. The range for white teachers' salaries in 1940 was from $1,120 in Texas to $626 in Arkansas; in 1952 the range was from $3,204 in Texas to $1,929 in Arkansas. Equivalent ranges among the states for Negro teachers was $971 in Oklahoma and $232 in Mississippi for 1940, and $3,078 in Texas to $1,019 in Mississippi in 1952. Oklahoma was paying Negro teachers on an average more than four times as much as Mississippi in 1940, and Texas was paying Negro teachers an average of three times as much as Mississippi in 1952. Thus, greater variations in the average salaries of Negro teachers existed than for white teachers in both of these years. A part of this may be explained by the fact that extremes in levels of training may also be represented in these variations.

White secondary school teachers in the South averaged $329 more than white elementray school teachers in 1940, and $307 more in 1952. For Negro teachers the averages were $249 more in the secondary school than the elementary school in 1940, and $267 more in 1952. The percentage increases in salaries for both white and Negro elementary teachers were greater than the equivalent increases in secondary teachers' salaries, another illustration of the effect of increases in training.

A consideration of differences according to types of counties reveals that the greatest percentage increase in teachers' salaries occurred among rural Negro teachers and the smallest percentage increase occurred among metropolitan white teachers. Even so, the dollar difference in the average salaries of these two groups in 1952 was $821. The difference between the same two groups in 1940 had been $914. The smallest percentage increase for teachers in both races was in metropolitan counties. The dollar difference between white teachers' salaries in metropolitan and rural counties increased from $520 in 1940 to $775 in 1952, notwithstanding the fact that the ratio decreased.

TABLE 56

ANNUAL SALARIES OF TEACHERS IN WHITE AND NEGRO PUBLIC SCHOOLS
IN SOUTHERN STATES

State	1939–40	1949–50	1951–52
Alabama			
White	$ 848	$2,157	$2,551
Negro	402	1,870	2,359
Arkansas			
White	626	1,852	1,929
Negro	368	1,384	1,524
Florida			
White	1,116	2,965	3,195
Negro	577	2,591	2,922
Georgia			
White	863	2,148	2,599
Negro	390	1,656	2,410
Louisiana			
White	1,047	2,991	3,095
Negro	390	2,432	2,666
Mississippi			
White	776	1,855	1,991
Negro	232	747	1,019
North Carolina			
White	988	2,582	2,859
Negro	717	2,653	2,935
Oklahoma			
White	998	2,668	2,978
Negro	971	2,660	2,985
South Carolina			
White	939	2,131	2,644
Negro	388	1,498	1,985
Tennessee			
White	858	2,001	2,142
Negro	651	2,089	2,244
Texas			
White	1,120	3,029	3,204
Negro	681	2,957	3,078
Virginia			
White	969	2,233	2,512
Negro	613	2,247	2,577
TOTAL			
White	960	2,482	2,741
Negro	504	2,028	2,389

Both the ratio and dollar differences between teachers' salaries of the two races in each county classification decreased from 1940 to 1952. The decrease was most marked in metropolitan counties, where the greatest dollar difference between white and Negro teachers' salaries prevailed in 1940 and the smallest dollar difference in 1952. By 1952 the greatest difference in the salaries of the two races was found in rural-urban counties. The complete comparison is presented in Table 57.

TABLE 57

ANNUAL SALARIES OF TEACHERS IN WHITE AND NEGRO PUBLIC SCHOOLS IN SAMPLE RURAL AND RURAL-URBAN COUNTIES, AND IN METROPOLITAN COUNTIES OF TEN SOUTHERN STATES

County Classification	1939–40	1949–50	1951–52
Rural			
White	$ 798	$2,094	$2,346
Negro	404	1,786	2,159
Rural-Urban			
White	835	2,245	2,552
Negro	461	1,917	2,288
Metropolitan			
White	1,318	2,787	3,121
Negro	784	2,580	2,980

The relative improvement in Negro teachers' salaries is shown further by comparing Negro salaries in metropolitan counties with salaries of white teachers in rural counties in 1940, and by making a similar comparison in 1950 and 1952. Whereas the Negro average salary in metropolitan counties was less than the salary of white teachers in rural counties in 1940, by 1950 it had passed the white average in rural counties by $486. Two years later the difference had increased to $634.

Dollar differences between salaries for white and Negro teachers were greater in elementary than in secondary schools for all three types of counties in 1940. The gap between both white and Negro elementary teachers' salaries in rural counties and between white and Negro elementary teachers' salaries in metropolitan counties was greater than the gap between salaries of white and Negro secondary school teachers in rural counties and white and Negro secondary school teachers in metropolitan counties. Differentials in levels of training are reflected in the salary differences. Table 58 gives a breakdown of the dollar difference between white and Negro teachers' salaries in the classifications of counties.

TABLE 58

DIFFERENCE BETWEEN ANNUAL SALARIES OF TEACHERS IN WHITE AND NEGRO PUBLIC SCHOOLS IN SAMPLE RURAL AND RURAL-URBAN COUNTIES, AND IN METROPOLITAN COUNTIES OF TEN SOUTHERN STATES

County Classification	*Dollar Difference Between White and Negro Teachers' Average Salaries*		
	1939–40	*1949–50*	*1951–52*
Rural	$394	$308	$187
Rural-Urban	374	328	264
Metropolitan	534	207	141

STATUS OF TEACHERS IN THE ECONOMY

Charting the rise of teacher income from 1940 to 1952 without giving attention to the relative position of the teacher in the economy is very misleading. Increases in average annual teachers' salaries already detailed do not represent absolute gains, for salaries of other occupational groups were increasing during the same time. It must be borne in mind that the period was also characterized by sharp increases in the cost of living.

Per capita income in the United States increased quite rapidly, and the gain in the South was more rapid than that in the nation as a whole. Per capita income in the South in 1939-40 was 59 per cent of the United States average, and in 1951-52 it was 72 per cent of the national average. The cost of living index also rose rapidly during this period, and the increase in the South was greater than that for the country as a whole. In 1950, when the national cost living index stood at 178.8, the index in Atlanta was 180.7 and in Memphis 182.7. The national cost of living index stood at 189.6 in 1952; at the same time it reached 196.0 in Atlanta and in New Orleans it was 191.4. The index was higher than the national average in 1950 and 1952 in all large Southern cities except Mobile. It would, therefore, be necessary to plot teacher salary increases in the South against the cost of living index for the region rather than against the national index in order to understand clearly the real changes in the status of the teacher in the region's economy. Since a regional index is not available, it is impossible to plot average teachers' salaries against cost of living.

A more convenient measure of the financial status of the teacher can be derived from the relationship of teachers' salaries and per capita income figures. Any change in the relative position of teachers' salaries to per capita income would be reflected in a ratio derived from dividing the average annual salaries of teachers by the per capita income of the region. If the ratio of the two remain constant, no change in the status of the teachers' financial position is indicated.

These ratios were computed for 1940, 1950, and 1952. Teachers were in a better position financially in 1940 than in either of the other two years for which computations were made. For the region as a whole, the 1940 ratio of average annual teachers' salaries, grades one to twelve, to the per capita income of the population was 2.6 (meaning that the teachers' annual salary was 2.6 times the average per capita income). Ten years later, the ratio had decreased to 2.4, and in 1952 it had declined further to 2.3. It may be concluded from these figures that teachers' salaries had not risen as rapidly as the income of the population generally in the South during this time. Since teachers' salaries were included in the per capita income of the region the figures also indicate that in some other occupations annual earnings must have increased more rapidly than teachers' salaries. Table 59 shows the ratios of teachers' salaries to per capita income by states in the South for 1940, 1950, and 1952.

TABLE 59

RATIO OF ANNUAL SALARIES OF PUBLIC SCHOOL TEACHERS TO PER CAPITA
INCOME IN SOUTHERN STATES

State	1939–40	1949–50	1951–52
Alabama	2.8:1	2.6:1	2.5:1
Arkansas	2.3:1	2.2:1	2.0:1
Florida	2.2:1	2.5:1	2.4:1
Georgia	2.4:1	2.2:1	2.3:1
Kentucky	2.7:1	2.2:1	2.2:1
Louisiana	2.4:1	2.7:1	2.5:1
Mississippi	2.6:1	2.1:1	2.0:1
North Carolina	2.9:1	2.9:1	2.7:1
Oklahoma	2.8:1	2.5:1	2.5:1
South Carolina	2.7:1	2.3:1	2.3:1
Tennessee	2.7:1	2.2:1	2.0:1
Texas	2.6:1	2.4:1	2.2:1
Virginia	2.1:1	2.3:1	1.9:1
TOTAL	2.6:1	2.4:1	2.3:1

The highest ratio between teachers' salaries and per capita income in each of the three years was in North Carolina, where it was 0.3 more than the regional average in both 1940 and 1952. The lowest ratios at the beginning and at the end of the period were in Virginia, where it was 0.5 lower than the regional average in 1940 and 0.4 lower in

1952. The greatest decline in the ratio occurred in Tennessee, where the decrease was from 2.7 in 1940 to 2.0 in 1952. Mississippi and Kentucky suffered declines of 0.6 and 0.5, respectively. Only two states, Florida and Louisiana, had a higher ratio in 1952 than in 1940. The decline in the index of the economic well-being of teachers came in the face of substantially improved levels of training.

SUMMARY

Public concern for improving public education and extending its opportunities to greater numbers of children and youth during the past forty years has been expressed through an increase of 163.6 per cent in the number of school teachers, while average daily attendance increased 134.7 per cent. Population shifts from rural to urban areas have been reflected in a corresponding growth in the number of urban teachers, although there has been a considerable increase in the number of rural teachers also.

As would be expected in a period when secondary schools were rapidly increasing, the gains in numbers of teachers have been greater in secondary schools than in elementary schools, particularly in Negro secondary schools. The increase in the number of rural teachers is accounted for by secondary teachers, as the number of elementary teachers actually decreased. Trends in the growth of numbers of teachers reflect considerable effort to improve educational opportunities for two groups, rural and Negro secondary school youth.

The most important factor in the work load of a teacher is the number of pupils in his charge. The fact that the number of teachers increased more rapidly than average daily attendance is expressed in a declining pupil-teacher ratio between 1940 and 1952. The figures for the region show a decline of 1.3 pupils per teacher. The number of pupils in average daily attendance per classroom teacher in elementary and secondary schools differs markedly, with the smaller ratios in the secondary school. The difference increased from 7.4 pupils to 10.8 pupils during the twelve-year period. Based on regional averages, the difference in pupil-teacher ratio between Negro and white schools dropped from 5.2 pupils in 1940 to 2.7 in 1952, pupil-teacher ratios for white teachers being the smaller in each case. Rather extreme differences among the states which existed in 1940 had been reduced by more than half in 1952. Teacher load as measured by pupil-teacher ratio does not vary significantly in rural, rural-urban, and metropolitan county classifications. The distribution of state aid on the basis of formulas which use pupil-teacher ratio as one factor may help account for this.

Further evidence of the general emphasis on improving public education is found in an analysis of teacher-training trends. Despite the instability of the 1940-52 period and the large scale depletion of the teaching profession because of larger salaries available in the business world, the teaching force in every state was better trained at the end of the period than at the beginning, as measured by the number of years of college work completed. Widespread differences which had existed in the level of training of teachers among states between elementary and secondary schools, among the three classifications of counties, and between white and Negro teachers decreased. Indeed, by 1952 Negro teachers in five states had achieved a higher level of professional training than the white teachers in those states. Averages for Negroes in the region as a whole were only slightly under those for white teachers.[4] Greater differences in training existed in both 1940 and 1952 between rural and metropolitan teachers than between Negro and white teachers. Considerable improvement took place in the training levels of elementary school teachers as compared to secondary school teachers, although a sizable difference still existed in favor of the secondary teacher.

Measured by dollars, teachers' salaries increased sharply in all classifications during this time. In fact, teachers in the South were being paid over three times as much in 1952 as they received in 1940, a percentage gain of 210. Salaries for Negro teachers increased much more rapidly than for whites, the over-all gain being 374 per cent as compared to 186 per cent for white teachers. The differential between secondary and elementary teachers' salaries lessened measurably. Differences in dollars of average salaries of metropolitan and rural school teachers continued to grow, although the ratio of the two salaries diminished. In four states the average Negro salary was higher than the salary for the average white teacher. The range in average teacher salaries among the states was greater for Negro than for white teachers in both 1940 and 1952. Salaries of the two races were closer together in metropolitan counties than in other counties. By 1950, salaries of Negro teachers in metropolitan counties exceeded those of white teachers in rural and rural-urban counties, a difference which continued to increase during the next two years. In spite of the very large dollar increase in teachers' salaries during the period, salaries did not keep pace with the rise in general income level. Consequently, teachers were relatively worse off financially in 1952 than in 1940.

---

[4] It would be a mistake to assume that Negro and white teachers of equivalent training, as measured by years of college training are equally competent. It is generally agreed that on the average Negro teacher-training institutions are below white training institutions in the quality of their programs.

Trends affecting the number of teachers, their levels of preparation, their work assignments, and salaries all moved in the general direction of the development of a more professional teaching group. In the main, differences in types of schools, in county classifications, and between races diminished. Notwithstanding the great progress of the period, many problems remain before the time is reached when adequately trained teachers are equitably distributed throughout the region in all types of schools and in all geographical areas.

EIGHT

Public School Facilities

The efficiency of school personnel is closely related to the quality, kinds, and quantity of educational facilities provided for their use and the use of children. Attention in this chapter is given to the provision and distribution of facilities and the problems posed thereby in the light of the segregation crisis.

The problem of providing adequate housing and equipment for the public schools has become increasingly serious in recent years. The Great Depression of the thirties so hampered the development of public education that, in many cases, it was barely possible to keep schools open. The backlog of building needs which developed during these years was heavily augmented during World War II, when the nation's greatly improved economy was geared to the most gigantic war effort in history. When this fifteen-year drought in school building construction came to an end, the great post-war increase in birth rates called for tremendous additions of new facilities over and beyond those which needed to be replaced or remodeled because of obsolescence and decay.

The problem in the South was seriously complicated because of the steeply accelerated migration of population within and among the various states. Frequently, existing facilities could not be used to capacity because people had moved away from the communities they served. In the 1940 decade, migration trends were such that 700 counties in the Southern states lost population, while 600 gained. The very rapid growth in urban areas brought about critical shortages of school facilities which could be met only by heavy expenditures for capital investment.

The long-range trend of increase in the proportion of school population actually enrolled and in attendance was a further factor which brought about additional needs for school buildings and equipment. At the same time, the average number of years children remained in the public schools had also increased, placing a further load on school facilities. These factors have been more pronounced in their impact on Negro than white schools, because both the proportion of school population enrolled and the number of years in public school have increased at a much more rapid rate for Negro than for white children. The increase in educational load, coupled with the fact that Negro

214

education traditionally has been poorly housed, indicates a problem of considerable magnitude.

Recent changes in the school program itself require more building space and equipment. Lunch programs are now considered an essential element of a good school. Their advent has called for additional floor space and extensive new equipment necessary in the preparation and serving of meals to the student body and faculty. The emphasis on sports, health, and physical education makes gymnasia and their paraphernalia almost mandatory in a satisfactory school. Special areas or rooms for libraries, audio-visual aids, and music are other examples of components of a good educational program which call for new facilities.

Increased interest in public schools and improved understanding of the nature of a satisfactory educational program on the part of the general public have been important factors in redefining adequacy of school facilities. Health and safety require buildings which are well constructed, properly maintained, well lighted, and adequately heated. The effects of environment on learning are well known. It is generally recognized that the quality and quantity of school buildings and equipment are strongly indicative of the quality of educational opportunity available to children. Over a period of time, the value a community ascribes to its schools and children may be inferred, in part, from the kinds of physical facilities it is willing to provide for purposes of public education.

One way in which community aspirations have affected school building programs and needs is in the pronounced trend to abandon small schools in favor of larger, more elaborate attendance centers, which almost invariably necessitates either completely new plants or substantial additions to existing plants. Large attendance centers have resulted in the provision of maintenance and operation services heretofore left to the local community, to the teacher and students, or not provided at all.

It is safe to say that school building and equipment needs have always outrun available facilities. Various conditions have operated, however, to bring about more emphasis on meeting such needs at some periods than at others. One of the periods in which interest in public education in the South was pronounced began about 1900. At that time school buildings, especially in rural areas, were frequently dilapidated, often had a minimum of equipment except for crude benches, were unsanitary and poorly heated. Many buildings used for school purposes were not even owned by the public, churches or old dwellings being utilized. As schools usually served only one neighborhood, transportation for pupils was nonexistent and unnecessary. The length of the school term averaged less than a hundred days as compared with the national average of 144 days.

Much improvement in public education was made in the South during the first quarter of the twentieth century, but the improvement was primarily in schools for white children. One part of the general improvement was in school plants and equipment, as increased school budgets made possible some expenditures for items other than salaries of teachers. The development and improvement of facilities for public schools always came first in white schools; in the initial stages of development, nothing or very little was done for Negro schools. Statistics for 1930 indicate that by that year considerable general progress in public education in the South had been made, but the disparity between provisions for white and Negro schools had increased since the beginning of the century.

In 1930, the length of the school term, which had been only 68 per cent of the national average in 1900, had increased to an average of 152 days, or 80 per cent of the national average. The average term for white schools was 162 days per year, and the average term for Negro schools was 132 days. The value of school property was $165.00 per white pupil enrolled and $32.00 per Negro pupil enrolled, a ratio of over 5 to 1. The consolidation movement was rapidly gaining momentum in 1930 and the number of one-room schools was being reduced, especially for white children. Nevertheless, the number of one-teacher schools was still 43 per cent of the total number of white schools and 63 per cent of the total number of Negro schools. By this time, the need for pupil transportation was increasing annually and school transportation systems were being developed. In 1930 about 17 per cent of the white enrollment was being transported, but the movement had barely touched the Negro enrollment, only 0.6 per cent being furnished this service.

Schools located in urban areas were leading the way in making improvements, resulting in steadily widening gaps between rural and urban schools. By any standard of measurement, children in urban counties were receiving better educational opportunities than children in rural counties.

VALUE OF PUBLIC SCHOOL
BUILDINGS AND EQUIPMENT

As has been suggested previously, any criterion of adequacy of school buildings and equipment involves complex value judgments which do not readily lend themselves to objective measurement. Value judgments of such nature are outside the purview of this inquiry. Nevertheless, any comprehensive study of public education requires that careful attention be given to this phase of school facilities. Perhaps the most satisfactory single available measure for purposes of analysis in the dollar value of buildings and equipment per child in average daily attendance. At best, it is a crude measure, for methods of calculating the value of school property vary widely from state to state and complete records are not available in all states. Furthermore, dollar values compared from period to period should be corrected for changes in the value of the dollar. Despite these defects, use of the measure is acknowledged to be of great importance in understanding the progress that has been made in recent years in providing better school facilities.

Expenditures for capital outlay in the Southern region have increased by leaps and bounds during the twelve years from 1940 through 1952. The amount spent in 1952 was more than eight times the amount spent in 1940. These increases indicate clearly how the public is responding to the conditions depicted in the introductory paragraphs to this chapter.

The average per pupil value of school buildings and equipment in the South increased from $148 in 1940 to $372 in 1952. Almost half of this increase of $224 per pupil came from 1950 to 1952, which reveals the extent of the vast building program then underway. The increases were due in large measure to the heavy capital outlay program authorized and begun in the years immediately following the end of World War II. Some part of the increase was due, however, to reassessment of the value of existing buildings and equipment. Alabama will serve as an extreme illustration. The value of buildings and equipment in this state in 1950 was $66,711,240; it increased to $188,926,759 by 1952. The increase of over $120,000,000 certainly was not all attributable to expenditures during the two-year period, but available records do not show how much of the increase resulted from a re-evaluation of facilities already constructed.

Table 60 shows that those states which had the lowest per pupil values in 1940 made the largest percentage increases during the period under consideration. Alabama and Arkansas are illustrations. The largest dollar gain was made in Virginia, which had a relatively high per pupil value in 1940. The $304 per pupil increase in Virginia during a period in which enrollments were rising in the state reflects something of the magnitude of the capital outlay expenditures involved.

Since the upsurge of effort to improve public schools, which began in the early part of the twentieth century, metroploitan counties have spent much more than rural counties for buildings and equipment. The cumulative effects of larger capital outlay expenditures in these counties is dramatically shown in Table 61. Differences in value per pupil in attendance of over 2 to 1 in favor of metropolitan counties in 1940 were widened by 1952 by a dollar increase of $153 in rural counties, $188 in rural-urban counties, and $328 in metropolitan counties. Even though the percentage increases were slightly larger in rural counties than in metropolitan counties, the ratio still remained more than 2 to 1 in 1952. Thus, in this period of general improvement in Southern education, no reductions were made in the large differences which existed between the facilities for children in rural areas and children in metropolitan areas. The differences take on added significance in view of the fact that metropolitan counties were faced with tremendous increases in enrollment during the period, while rural counties were losing enrollment.

TABLE 60

VALUE PER PUPIL IN AVERAGE DAILY ATTENDANCE OF PUBLIC SCHOOL
BUILDINGS AND EQUIPMENT IN SOUTHERN STATES

State	1939–40	1949–50	1951–52	Per Cent Increase 1940–1952
Alabama	$102	$112	$322	215.7
Arkansas	116	278	366	215.5
Florida	259	352	433	67.2
Georgia	128	247	324	153.1
Louisiana	182	332	480	163.7
North Carolina	148	283	340	129.7
South Carolina	137	218	278	102.9
Virginia	160	371	464	190.0
TOTAL	148	270	372	151.4

TABLE 61

VALUE PER PUPIL IN AVERAGE DAILY ATTENDANCE OF PUBLIC SCHOOL
BUILDINGS AND EQUIPMENT IN SAMPLE RURAL AND RURAL-URBAN
COUNTIES, AND IN METROPOLITAN COUNTIES OF EIGHT
SOUTHERN STATES

County Classification	1939–40	1949–50	1951–52	Per Cent Increase 1940–1952
Rural	$100	$206	$253	153.0
Rural-Urban	128	253	316	146.9
Metropolitan	218	413	546	150.5

Table 62 shows that the value of Negro public school property increased by 280 per cent per child, while the value of white public school property increased by 127 per cent per child. This distribution reduced the ratio from 4 to 1 in favor of white children in 1940 to 2.39 to 1 in 1952. What these ratios mean is that in 1940 for each dollar of Negro school property per Negro pupil, there were four dollars of white school property per white pupil. By 1952 for each dollar of Negro school property per Negro pupil, there were two dollars and thirty-nine cents of white school property. It would appear from this single measure that equalization of facilities was proceeding rapidly. It should be noted, however, that the dollar increase was much larger in white schools than in Negro schools, amounting to $254 per white pupil as compared to $140 per Negro pupil. Thus, absolute dollar equalization in 1952 would have required a heavier expenditure than would have been necessary in 1940.

TABLE 62

VALUE PER PUPIL IN AVERAGE DAILY ATTENDANCE OF WHITE AND NEGRO PUBLIC SCHOOL BUILDINGS AND EQUIPMENT IN SOUTHERN STATES

State	Race	1939–40	1949–50	1951–52	Per Cent Increase 1940–1952
Alabama	W	$140	$155	$412	194.3
	N	29	23	152	424.1
Arkansas	W	140	324	423	202.1
	N	40	128	180	350.0
Florida	W	329	435	502	52.6
	N	66	110	223	237.9
Georgia	W	172	319	405	135.5
	N	45	104	156	246.7
Louisiana	W	263	461	643	144.5
	N	41	118	213	419.5
North Carolina	W	182	341	402	120.9
	N	65	143	191	193.8
South Carolina	W	206	316	391	89.8
	N	44	89	126	186.4
Virginia	W	188	418	510	171.3
	N	77	234	329	327.3
TOTAL	W	200	341	454	127.0
	N	50	115	190	280.0

Variations in these trends among the states were considerable. For example, Arkansas increased the per pupil value of public school property in white schools by $283, or 202.1 per cent, while the value of school property for white children in Florida increased by $173, or 52.6 per cent. Similar variations occurred among the states in the increases for Negro schools. In Virginia the per pupil value increased $252, or 327.3 per cent, for Negro schools, while in South Carolina the increase was $82, or 186.4 per cent. The data show clearly that all states were moving toward equalization of value of facilities per child but at markedly different rates, with some having much farther

to go than others. Differences among states, the progress which they
have made, and gaps that still remain are shown in Table 63.

TABLE 63

RATIO BETWEEN VALUE PER PUPIL IN AVERAGE DAILY ATTENDANCE OF WHITE
AND NEGRO PUBLIC SCHOOL BUILDINGS AND EQUIPMENT
IN SOUTHERN STATES

State	1939–40	1949–50	1951–52
Alabama	4.83:1	4.84:1	2.71:1
Arkansas	3.50:1	2.53:1	2.35:1
Florida	4.98:1	3.95:1	2.25:1
Georgia	3.82:1	3.07:1	2.60:1
Louisiana	6.41:1	3.91:1	3.02:1
North Carolina	2.80:1	2.38:1	2.10:1
South Carolina	4.68:1	3.55:1	3.10:1
Virginia	2.44:1	1.79:1	1.55:1
TOTAL	4.00:1	2.97:1	2.39:1

The figures in this table represent the value per white pupil of
buildings and equipment for each dollar of value per Negro pupil
of buildings and equipment. Thus, for each dollar's worth of property
per Negro pupil in Alabama in 1940, the value of white property per
pupil was $4.83; but by 1952 the ratio had been reduced and for each
dollar of property per Negro pupil, the value of white property per
pupil was $2.71.

As public school property has increased in value per child, the
number of non-publicly owned buildings used for school houses has
been markedly reduced. Statistics from Alabama illustrate the extent
of this change. In 1940, over half of the buildings used for Negro
schools and 10 per cent used for white schools were privately owned.
By 1952, slightly over one-third of the Negro buildings and only 2
per cent of the white school buildings were privately owned. This
change may be interpreted to reflect a growing acceptance of
responsibility for Negro schools by state and local governments.

It has been shown that the dollar differences between rural and
metropolitan counties in the value of school property have grown
larger, and the ratios between the two have undergone little change
during a period of rapid improvement in public school property. Table
64 shows changes in the value of white and Negro public school buildings and equipment of the three classifications of counties used in this
analysis. Interestingly enough, the percentages of increase in white
schools in all three classes of counties were almost identical. The
percentage increases were larger in Negro schools than white schools

in each of the three groups of counties, with the largest Negro increases being made in rural counties. Consequently, the ratio of expenditures for the two races has declined steadily throughout the period in all three classifications of counties. The ratio between the value of white and Negro school property in rural counties was reduced from 5.26:1 in 1940 to 2.85:1 in 1952; in rural-urban counties from 4.33:1 to 2.98:1; and in metropolitan counties from 3.03:1 to 1.91:1. According to this measure, the value of school property was most nearly equalized between races in metropolitan counties and least equalized in rural counties for both the beginning year and the terminal year of the period under study.

TABLE 64

VALUE PER PUPIL IN AVERAGE DAILY ATTENDANCE OF WHITE AND NEGRO PUBLIC SCHOOL BUILDINGS AND EQUIPMENT IN SAMPLE RURAL AND RURAL-URBAN COUNTIES, AND IN METROPOLITAN COUNTIES OF EIGHT SOUTHERN STATES

County Classification	Race	1939–40	1949–50	1951–52	Per Cent Increase 1940–1952
Rural	W	$142	$289	$339	138.7
	N	27	71	119	340.7
Rural-Urban	W	173	336	414	139.3
	N	40	96	139	247.5
Metropolitan	W	273	487	639	134.1
	N	90	226	335	272.2

Contrary to the direction indicated by the reduced ratio, the dollar difference between the value of school property for the two races increased during the period in each of the three groups of counties. The difference by races was $115 per pupil in 1940 in rural counties and $220 in 1952; a difference of $133 in rural-urban counties in 1940 and $275 in 1952; a difference of $183 in metropolitan counties in 1940 and $304 in 1952. Although metropolitan counties appeared to have more nearly equalized school facilities as measured by the ratio between races, these counties would have required more money to achieve absolute dollar equalization both in 1940 and in 1952 than either of the other two classifications of counties.

No analysis from available data is possible which would show the extent to which these increases reflect the provision of such space and equipment as are deemed essential to a good school program. The newer buildings, however, tend to be larger than older buildings, and they usually contain relatively adequate provisions for educational services which have come to be desired by the public, such as gymnasia, lunchrooms, libraries, special purpose rooms, and so forth.

Substantial as capital expenditures in the Southern states have been during recent years, building and equipment needs remain acute. Overcrowded rooms and schedules requiring double sessions so that two classes can use the same facilities, frequently resulting in only a half-day session for each, are as common as ever in the South.

NUMBER AND SIZE OF PUBLIC SCHOOLS

The consolidation movement has been the most important single influence on the number and size of public schools in the Southern region. Shortly after World War I, interest in better schools began to take form in widespread efforts to combine conveniently located neighborhood schools into larger schools which could provide better educational programs at no greater per pupil cost. Since only small schools were involved in these consolidations, it was usually necessary to erect new buildings and purchase new equipment when consolidations were effected.

Consolidation was one of the factors involved in the increased value of school buildings described in the preceding section of this chapter. The consolidation movement gained momentum and the trend is still underway. The magnitude of the trend is revealed by Table 65, which shows that there was a decline of 32.5 per cent in the number of schools for the region as a whole between 1940 and 1952. The maximum impact of this trend apparently has not been reached, for nearly one-fourth of the total reduction in the twelve-year period came in the last two years. The consolidation movement almost amounted to a revolution in Southern education, and there can be little doubt that the educational effect on the children in these larger schools is more desirable than the schooling received in the small one- or two-teacher school of earlier years.

TABLE 65

NUMBERS OF PUBLIC SCHOOLS IN SOUTHERN STATES

State	1939–40	1949–50	1951–52	Per Cent Increase 1940–1952
Alabama	4,602	3,356	3,105	32.5
Arkansas	4,671	2,593	2,264	51.5
Florida	2,066	1,508	1,390	32.7
Georgia	5,554	3,906	3,290	40.8
North Carolina	4,831	3,810	3,654	24.4
South Carolina	3,483	3,328	2,911	16.4
Tennessee	5,627	4,632	4,076	27.6
Virginia	4,541	3,368	3,174	30.1
TOTAL	35,375	26,501	23,864	32.5

Table 66 tells a story of rapid increase in average number of pupils enrolled per school. For the region as a whole, the increase came to an average of 76 pupils, or 55 per cent. The extent of consolidation is reflected in these figures, although it does not account for all of the increase.

TABLE 66

AVERAGE NUMBER OF PUPILS ENROLLED PER SCHOOL IN SOUTHERN STATES

State	1939–40	1949–50	1951–52
Alabama	149	205	219
Arkansas	101	164	184
Florida	187	316	385
Georgia	132	183	226
North Carolina	184	235	249
South Carolina	138	148	176
Tennessee	114	142	166
Virginia	126	179	199
TOTAL	138	187	214

As shown by Tables 65 and 66, rates of consolidation have varied widely from state to state, but every state has had a considerable reduction in the number of schools. It will be noted that, from 1940 through 1952, South Carolina reduced the number of schools by 16.4 per cent, or 572 in number, while Arkansas reduced her schools by 51.5 per cent, or a total of 2,407 schools. The extent of consolidation in the states has been affected by several factors, including the extent to which consolidation has taken place prior to 1940, the interest of citizens in larger school attendance centers, and the degree of urbanization which prevailed in the states. Arkansas made the largest reductions in the number of public schools during the twelve-year period. Its average school, however, was still much smaller than North Carolina's, a state which had already undergone a considerable degree of consolidation by 1940, and Florida's, a state which had a much higher percentage of urban population. South Carolina serves as an illustration of the rapid acceleration in the consolidation trend toward the latter part of the period; more schools in that state were eliminated in the last two years than had been eliminated in the previous ten years.

Rapid consolidations have been accomplished to a considerable extent by eliminating one-teacher schools and replacing them with larger schools in strategically located centers. During this period, two out of every three one-teacher schools were abandoned. One-teacher schools had comprised 40.5 per cent of the total schools in the region in 1940, but they were reduced to 22.0 per cent in 1952. This reduction was felt in every state in the region. The extent of reduction ranges from Arkansas, which started the period with 2,581 one-teacher schools and reduced them to 468 in 1952, to Florida, which had only 691 such schools in 1940 and reduced them to 164 by 1952. Some one-teacher schools will remain, of course, because of isolated sections and bad roads. It seems evident, however, that within a few years the one-teacher school will be found only in those sections where it is absolutely essential. It will be observed from Table 67 that by 1952 North Carolina had already reduced one-teacher schools to 9.4 per cent of the total. Tennessee, at the other extreme, had 32.5 per cent of all of her schools in the one-teacher category.

TABLE 67

ONE-TEACHER SCHOOLS AS A PERCENTAGE OF TOTAL PUBLIC SCHOOLS
IN SOUTHERN STATES

State	*1939–40*	*1949–50*	*1951–52*
Alabama	38.5	24.3	21.1
Arkansas	55.3	27.1	20.7
Florida	33.4	18.2	11.8
Georgia	43.4	35.6	24.5
North Carolina	23.2	10.2	9.4
South Carolina	35.5	27.6	23.3
Tennessee	45.5	37.7	32.5
Virginia	43.2	29.9	25.8
TOTAL	40.5	27.3	22.0

Unfortunately, differences among the states in methods of reporting the sizes of schools make it impossible to present any regional picture of the increases in large schools. But Georgia and North Carolina may be cited as examples of the rapid change that is taking place. The number of fifteen- (or more) teacher schools increased from 324 in 1940 to 605 in 1952 in Georgia, while in North Carolina the increase was from 202 to 443. Thus, the large schools almost doubled in Georgia and more than doubled in North Carolina. The fifteen- (or more) teacher school is not used here to suggest an ideal size, but merely to illustrate the increases in the number of larger schools. It may be assumed that the educational program offered in such schools is different in many respects from that which is offered in the smaller one-, two-, and three-teacher schools.

State statistics tend to obscure changes which have occurred in various areas within a state and these may differ substantially from state-wide averages. Since small schools were to be found more frequently in rural counties, it is to be expected that the greatest reduction in the total number of schools occurred in such counties. The percentage reduction by classifications of counties was 38.0 per cent in rural counties, 32.7 per cent in rural-urban counties, and 9.0 per cent in metropolitan counties. Decreases came in metropolitan counties at the same time their schools were increasing in enrollment. The speed of reduction in numbers of schools was accelerated in all three groups of counties during the latter part of the twelve-year period. The consolidation movement, therefore, was going on in all types of counties, irrespective of what was happening to school enrollment.

In 1940, as shown by Table 68, about half of the schools in rural counties were of the one-teacher type, about one-third in rural-urban counties, and approximately one-sixth in metropolitan counties. The rates of reduction of these schools was about the same in each of the three types of counties so that by 1952 the ratio of one-teacher to total schools was about one in three in rural counties, approximately one in five in rural-urban counties, and about one in twenty in metropolitan counties.

TABLE 68

ONE-TEACHER SCHOOLS AS A PERCENTAGE OF TOTAL PUBLIC SCHOOLS IN SAMPLE RURAL AND RURAL-URBAN COUNTIES, AND IN METROPOLITAN COUNTIES IN NINE SOUTHERN STATES

County Classification	1939–40	1949–50	1951–52
Rural	49.9	38.4	31.5
Rural-Urban	35.0	24.6	22.1
Metropolitan	16.6	7.9	6.2

Oddly enough, the rate of reduction in the total number of schools for the whole period was the same for Negroes and whites. But during the first ten years of the period, the rate of consolidation was much more rapid in white schools than in Negro schools. A change occurred in this trend from 1950 to 1952, and the rate of consolidation of Negro schools became much more rapid. Table 69 compares the number of white and Negro schools by states, showing the percentage of decrease in each for the twelve-year period. The trend was the same in all states, although the rate varied considerably. South Carolina reduced the number of her Negro schools by only 4.7 per cent, while the reduction in Georgia was 46.8 per cent. The reduction in white schools ranged from 15.3 per cent in North Carolina to 54.8 per cent in Arkansas. These figures do not, of course, indicate the extent to which the consolidation movement had already been felt by 1940.

TABLE 69

NUMBERS OF WHITE AND NEGRO PUBLIC SCHOOLS IN SOUTHERN STATES

	Race	1939–40	1949–50	1951–52	Per Cent Decrease 1940–52
Alabama	W	2,210	1,497	1,438	35.0
	N	2,392	1,859	1,667	30.4
Arkansas	W	3,393	1,759	1,537	54.8
	N	1,278	834	727	43.2
Florida	W	1,098	875	862	21.5
	N	968	633	528	45.5
Georgia	W	2,258	1,596	1,535	32.1
	N	3,296	2,310	1,755	46.8
North Carolina	W	2,544	2,188	2,157	15.3
	N	2,287	1,622	1,497	34.6
South Carolina	W	1,520	1,253	1,039	31.7
	N	1,963	2,075	1,872	4.7
Tennessee	W	4,554	3,686	3,211	29.5
	N	1,073	946	865	19.4
Virginia	W	2,776	2,043	1,967	29.2
	N	1,765	1,325	1,207	31.7
TOTAL	W	20,353	14,897	13,746	32.5
	N	15,022	11,604	10,118	32.6

Even though the reduction in the total number of schools has been at the same rate for white and Negro children, population factors are such that the average number of Negro children enrolled per school has continued to be smaller than the number of white children enrolled per school. The average number of pupils enrolled per school increased for white children during the twelve-year period from 167 to 263 and for Negro children from 98 to 148.

In 1940 three of every ten white schools in the South were one-teacher schools, while five of every ten Negro schools were one-teacher schools. By 1952 about three in twenty white schools were still one-teacher and about six in twenty Negro schools. As is shown in Table 70, there were wide variations among the states.

No regional statistics are available on the large fifteen- (or more) teacher schools and the increase in their numbers. In Georgia and North Carolina the larger schools almost doubled for white children and more than tripled for Negro children from 1940 to 1952. In 1952 in these two states the proportion of schools of this large size to the total number of schools was about one in five for whites and about one in twenty for Negroes.

The percentage reduction in the total number of schools was slightly greater for whites than for Negroes in rural and rural-urban counties.

TABLE 70

ONE-TEACHER WHITE AND NEGRO SCHOOLS AS A PERCENTAGE OF TOTAL WHITE
AND NEGRO PUBLIC SCHOOLS IN SOUTHERN STATES

State	Race	1939–40	1949–50	1951–52
Alabama	W	20.2	7.9	6.9
	N	55.5	37.4	33.3
Arkansas	W	52.9	21.5	15.8
	N	61.4	38.8	30.9
Florida	W	18.3	6.9	3.8
	N	50.6	34.0	24.8
Georgia	W	15.0	8.5	5.9
	N	62.9	54.3	40.8
North Carolina	W	11.6	3.7	3.9
	N	36.0	19.0	17.2
South Carolina	W	17.2	12.5	8.1
	N	49.7	36.6	31.7
Tennessee	W	42.0	34.9	29.0
	N	60.5	48.7	45.3
Virginia	W	35.8	20.9	18.2
	N	54.7	43.8	38.2
TOTAL	W	30.7	17.7	14.0
	N	53.8	39.6	32.9

Just the opposite was true in metropolitan counties where most of the
decline in the total number of schools was accounted for by the
reduction in the number of Negro schools. The decline occurred
despite the fact that Negro enrollment was rapidly increasing in
metropolitan counties, indicating the development of large Negro
attendance centers in these counties.

The decline in the number of one-teacher schools in different types
of counties, mentioned earlier, greatly reduced these schools for both
races. In 1940, 4 of every 10 white schools and 6 of every 10 Negro
schools in rural counties were one-teacher, while in metropolitan
counties only 6 of 100 white schools and 33 of 100 Negro schools were
of this size. By 1952, 2 of 10 white and 4 of 10 Negro schools were
one-teacher in rural counties and 3 of 100 white and 14 of 100 Negro
schools in metropolitan counties were one-teacher. Thus, the white
one-teacher schools were rapidly disappearing except in isolated rural
areas, and Negro one-teacher schools, recently so important in the
Negro educational picture, were rapidly decreasing.

The phenomenon of thousands of local communities giving up their
schools to have them absorbed by large attendance centers, newly
created and frequently located without reference to natural communi-

ties, has not yet been properly assessed. New and modern buildings and equipment certainly provide cleaner, more pleasant, and more healthful surroundings. Facilities not available in the smaller schools clearly make possible a more valuable educational program. Larger faculties supply a greater diversity of teaching talent and make possible administrative and supervisory services which could not be provided to the smaller schools. Advantages made possible by improved and extended facilities can hardly be questioned. Whether or not this trend, which is a part of various forces changing the character of local community life, carries with it adequate substitutes for former neighborhood interests and attitudes toward the school is a matter which deserves attention.

PUPIL TRANSPORTATION

The interrelatedness of educational problems is nowhere better illustrated than by the trends in providing essential facilities, larger attendance centers, and pupil transportation. As has been shown, much of the large increase in enrollment per school is accounted for by the trend towards a given school serving a larger geographical area. As the school has been removed beyond convenient walking distance from the homes of many children, it has been necessary to provide pupils with transportation. This has come to be accepted as a responsibility of the school.

Pupil transportation has placed the school district in a new type of business. It has called for increasingly heavy expenditures for equipment as the trend toward ownership of busses by the schools has developed, and for large expenditures for the operation and maintenance of the equipment in those school districts where any considerable proportion of the enrollment is transported. A new group of school employees has also entered upon the educational scene; in addition to bus drivers, service and repairmen, supervisors of transportation have assumed responsibility for the administration and supervision of transportation systems.

Cooperation with other officials and agencies of government has increased. The relationship of school transportation officials to road construction and maintenance departments of the county are important, since the latter may be required to facilitate pupil transportation. Health requirements for bus drivers are frequently assured through examinations prescribed by some agency of government other than the school. Safety and health provisions for equipment may be similarly underwritten.

In many districts children have to spend long periods of time on a bus on their way to school in the morning and back home in the afternoon. This practice has been pointed to as a possible health hazard. Since frequently a single bus may be charged with two separate routes, some children have to leave home soon enough for the second trip to be completed before school opens, and, by the same token, one group has to remain at school in the afternoon until the first group has been returned home. The waiting periods may be as hazardous as overlong trips.

Absence of ways for children profitably to use such periods of time as are spent on school busses and in waiting constitutes a serious failure to utilize fully available educational opportunity. Such problems multiply the supervisory duties of teachers, who frequently are already overburdened with other school duties. Casting rural or semi-rural and urban children together in the same school environment has presented social and educational problems to school faculties which have sometimes been difficult to solve. Unfortunately, such problems may be ignored, leaving children to struggle to make their own adjustments.

As pupil transportation has increased in extent and as parents have sought larger, safer, and more comfortable busses for their children, costs have multiplied over and over again during the past thirty years. At present, a substantial part of the budget for education in each Southern state is earmarked to underwrite costs of transportation. The magnitude of this expenditure is shown in Table 71, which reports the annual cost of transportation by states.

TABLE 71

EXPENDITURES FOR TRANSPORTATION IN SOUTHERN STATES

State	1939–40	1949–50	1951–52
Alabama	$ 2,093,501	$ 4,905,850	$ 5,640,985
Arkansas	1,103,179	3,694,056	4,152,820
Florida	1,370,535	3,131,275	3,788,943
Georgia	1,910,350	5,889,452	7,801,949
Kentucky	1,443,196	4,012,228	4,955,369
Louisiana	2,431,313	6,280,577	7,762,687
Mississippi	2,478,407	4,536,854	5,290,008
North Carolina	2,417,660	6,110,739	6,486,084
Oklahoma	1,782,204	3,909,069	4,748,796
South Carolina	1,116,070	2,603,014	—
Tennessee	1,643,717	5,136,003	6,248,033
Texas	4,521,128	11,149,818	14,951,340
Virginia	1,978,641	4,503,634	5,441,745
TOTAL [a]	25,173,831	63,259,555	77,268,759

[a] Twelve states.

These figures are not adjusted for inflation, consequently a part of the increased costs can be accounted for by this factor rather than by increased services.

The number of children transported to public schools in the South increased during the twelve-year period by 45.7 per cent. The average yearly increase in number of children transported was greater at the end of the period than in its earlier years, a reflection of the accelerated rate of the consolidation movement. In 1940, 28.3 per cent of the total public school enrollment were transported; by 1952 the figure had reached 41.4 per cent.

The differences among the states in the percentage of increase in the number of children transported and in the percentage of total enrollment transported were, of course, due in part to the extent and distribution of consolidation which took place during the time. Consolidation and transportation obviously go hand in hand. Another factor which accentuated the differences is the time at which states began various programs of change. Just as some states began consolidation movements later than others, transportation systems were not developed extensively in some states until after 1940. Still another factor is the change which has occurred in the number of pupils enrolled.

The influence of these factors is shown in Table 72. South Carolina, a state which was not transporting a large percentage of its school enrollment in 1940, entered extensively into this field after that date; but after 1940 it also had increases in enrollment, which helped account for the number of children transported. North Carolina, on the other hand, was already transporting a large percentage of its enrollment in 1940; during the twelve-year period it had only slight changes in enrollment, so there was no startling increase in the percentage of the number of pupils transported.

TABLE 72

NUMBER OF PUPILS TRANSPORTED TO PUBLIC SCHOOLS IN SOUTHERN STATES

State	*1939–40*	*1949–50*	*1951–52*	*Per Cent Increase 1940–1952*
Alabama	217,897	291,595	301,507	38.3
Arkansas	114,326	166,284	174,306	52.5
Louisiana	146,100	203,460	239,416	63.9
North Carolina	334,362	396,783	410,692	22.8
Oklahoma	119,239	126,690	131,356	10.2
South Carolina	80,615	130,973	178,598	121.5
Virginia	168,956	251,065	285,695	69.1
TOTAL	1,181,495	1,566,850	1,721,470	45.7

The transportation problem is obviously more severe in rural counties than in metropolitan counties, for transportation is primarily necessitated by population sparsity. Even so, a surprisingly large percentage of enrollment in metropolitan counties is transported. Rural county enrollments were decreasing between 1940 and 1952 and, even if transportation services had not been extended to additional children, the percentage of enrollment transported would have increased. In metropolitan counties, where enrollments increased rapidly, a slight increase in the percentage of enrollment transported would mean a considerably larger number were extended this service than formerly. Table 73 shows that the number of children transported in relation to the total enrollment is closely related to the degree of urbanization.

TABLE 73

NUMBER OF PUPILS TRANSPORTED AS A PERCENTAGE OF ENROLLMENT IN
THE PUBLIC SCHOOLS IN SAMPLE RURAL AND RURAL-URBAN
COUNTIES, AND IN METROPOLITAN COUNTIES
IN SEVEN SOUTHERN STATES

County Classification	1939–40	1949–50	1951–52
Rural	34.8	53.4	58.2
Rural-Urban	29.6	39.6	45.6
Metropolitan	14.1	19.6	20.3

As late as 1940, transportation services were almost exclusively for white children. Since then the service has been extended rapidly to Negro children as well. Table 74 shows that between 1940 and 1952 there was an increase of 20.6 per cent in the number of white children transported, while the increase in the number of Negro children transported was 408.5 per cent. Interpretation of these percentages should be made in recognition of the fact that in 1940, 37.3 per cent of white enrollment was transported, while the percentage of Negro enrollment transported was only 6.3 per cent. In 1952, 45.5 per cent of white children enrolled and 31.6 per cent of Negro children enrolled were being transported.

Table 75 shows that states which had extremely meagre transportation facilities for Negroes in 1940 were providing considerable transportation services for Negroes in 1952. Variations by states in the matter of transportation provided for white children are considerable, but the trends were such that those states making the least provision in 1940 for transportation achieved the largest percentage gains, while the states which already had moved toward meeting transportation needs made smaller percentage gains. South Carolina

TABLE 74

NUMBER OF WHITE AND NEGRO PUPILS TRANSPORTED TO PUBLIC SCHOOLS
IN SOUTHERN STATES

State	Race	1939–40	1949–50	1951–52	Per Cent Increase 1940–1952
Alabama	W	209,923	234,105	229,114	9.1
	N	7,974	57,490	72,393	807.9
Arkansas	W	106,013	136,861	139,447	31.5
	N	8,313	29,423	34,859	319.3
Louisiana	W	143,104	164,103	174,667	22.1
	N	2,996	39,357	64,749	2061.2
North Carolina	W	299,428	313,747	317,972	6.2
	N	34,934	83,036	92,720	165.4
Oklahoma	W	113,799	119,923	124,174	9.1
	N	5,440	6,767	7,182	32.0
South Carolina	W	80,187	111,238	119,545	49.1
	N	428	19,735	59,053	13697.4
Virginia	W	152,441	200,881	227,125	49.0
	N	16,515	50,184	58,570	254.6
TOTAL	W	1,104,895	1,280,858	1,332,044	20.6
	N	76,600	285,992	389,526	408.5

TABLE 75

NUMBER OF WHITE AND NEGRO PUPILS TRANSPORTED AS A PERCENTAGE
OF WHITE AND NEGRO ENROLLMENT IN THE PUBLIC SCHOOLS OF
SOUTHERN STATES

State	Race	1939–40	1949–50	1951–52
Alabama	W	47.0	52.7	52.1
	N	3.3	23.7	30.2
Arkansas	W	29.7	42.5	44.1
	N	7.2	28.6	34.8
Louisiana	W	48.5	55.5	56.1
	N	1.7	21.6	32.9
North Carolina	W	48.3	50.2	50.0
	N	12.9	30.9	33.9
Oklahoma	W	20.4	26.0	26.8
	N	11.5	18.0	19.9
South Carolina	W	30.2	40.9	42.0
	N	0.2	8.9	25.9
Virginia	W	36.2	45.1	48.0
	N	11.0	32.1	36.5
TOTAL	W	37.3	44.7	45.5
	N	6.3	23.6	31.6

and Louisiana are examples of states that were making slight provisions for Negro transportation in 1940. As a result of a considerable increase in this service for Negro children in these states, astronomical percentage increases were achieved in the number of children transported in 1952. North Carolina, Louisiana, and Alabama are examples of states which were transporting a considerable portion of their white school enrollment in 1940, and their percentage of increase was small for the period.

Rural, rural-urban, and metropolitan county patterns of transportation trends for white and Negro children were similar to patterns revealed by the analysis of state totals. In all types of counties the service for Negro children increased at a much more rapid rate than for white children. Notwithstanding the difference in percentage of increase for the period, the percentage of Negro enrollment transported was smaller in all county classifications than was the case for white enrollment. The largest increases for Negroes occurred in rural and rural-urban counties, a development that may be explained, in part, by the patterns of population distribution. In rural areas, where the Negro population is generally dispersed, the rapid development of consolidated schools necessitated increased transportation services; whereas, in metropolitan areas, where segregated housing patterns prevail, larger Negro schools were developed without a corresponding increase in transportation facilities. Despite enormous increases in the number and percentage of school children transported, many factors make it evident that the maximum is yet to be reached in pupil transportation.

USE OF FACILITIES

Watchdogs of public expenditures with an eagle eye for economy have often called attention to the loss resulting from only partial use of school buildings and other educational facilities. Plants which stand idle three or four months in the year and during the rest of the year are normally used for only six hours per day provide leeway for many extensions of educational and community programs which could be of great value. As buildings have become more expensive and important additional kinds of equipment have been added, opportunities for wider community service have increased.

Today emphasis is toward wider utilization of these facilities. Both student and parent groups frequently carry on projects in the evenings and during summer vacations using school property and equipment. In many communities summer and even year-round recreational programs are in vogue. Adult education is increasing rapidly and is now an integral part of public education programs in some school systems.

Groups not directly connected with the schools sometimes utilize school facilities. Vocational education programs often serve the entire community and equipment is from time to time available for use by citizens. School busses have become useful in instructional programs for various trips and excursions.

The daily formal program of instruction for children continues, however, to constitute the major use to which school facilities are subjected. Consequently, a valid measure of use is the length of time children actually are engaged in educational pursuits which employ school buildings and equipment. The best way of computing this measure is the number of days per year which are used in the education of children. This is, of course, equally valid as a measure of the educational opportunity of children, assuming that a day in school is worthwhile.

Current practice seems to have established a nine-month term, or 175 to 180 days of actual teaching, as the desirable length of a public school year. During the period from 1940 to 1952, the South moved to this optimum length of school term. The average length of the school term in the Southern region increased from 163 days per year in 1940 to 177 days per year in 1952. The differences which existed among the states in 1940, illustrated by the range of from 144 to 180 days, were almost entirely eliminated by 1952 when the states were stabilizing the length of the school term between 175 and 180 days. In fact, Arkansas and Mississippi were the only two states which did not have a term in this range in 1952 and their terms were 172 and 163 days, respectively. Table 76 shows the increase in the length of school term by states in the region.

TABLE 76

AVERAGE LENGTH IN DAYS OF THE PUBLIC SCHOOL TERM IN SOUTHERN STATES

State	1939–40	1949–50	1951–52
Alabama	154	176	176
Arkansas	159	173	172
Florida	168	180	180
Georgia	159	178	180
Kentucky	164	179	179
Louisiana	165	177	177
Mississippi	144	151	163
North Carolina	164	180	180
South Carolina	163	177	179
Tennessee	163	176	176
Texas	170	176	176
Virginia	180	180	180
TOTAL	163	175	177

In 1940 the average length of the school term was 169 days for white children and 153 days for Negro children. The term in Negro schools was 90 per cent of that in white schools, and was, perhaps, the most nearly equalized of any aspect of the public school program. As is shown in Table 77, rapid gains toward complete equalization between the races was made, so that by 1952 the length of the school term was virtually completely equalized. The movement among the states is illustrated by the fact that in 1940 only two states, North Carolina and Virginia, had completely equalized the school term for the two races. In 1950 seven states had completely equalized, and by 1952 eight states had equal terms for both races. Of the four states that had not completely equalized in 1952, Arkansas and South

TABLE 77

AVERAGE LENGTH IN DAYS OF THE SCHOOL TERM IN WHITE AND NEGRO PUBLIC SCHOOLS IN SOUTHERN STATES

State	Race	1939–40	1949–50	1951–52
Alabama	W	157	176	176
	N	147	177	176
Arkansas	W	163	175	172
	N	144	169	171
Florida	W	169	180	180
	N	164	180	180
Georgia	W	170	180	180
	N	135	176	180
Kentucky	W	166	179	179
	N	159	177	179
Louisiana	W	180	180	179
	N	144	171	174
Mississippi	W	160	160	167
	N	124	141	158
North Carolina	W	164	180	180
	N	164	180	180
South Carolina	W	175	180	180
	N	147	174	178
Tennessee	W	164	176	176
	N	162	176	176
Texas	W	174	176	176
	N	162	176	176
Virginia	W	180	180	180
	N	180	180	180
TOTAL	W	169	177	177
	N	153	173	176

Carolina were within a day or two of equalization, and Louisiana and Mississippi had differences of five and nine days, respectively.

Disparities similar to those found in other factors among rural, rural-urban and metropolitan counties existed in the length of the school term. The term was longest in metropolitan counties and shortest in rural counties for both races. Considerable differences between the length of term for the two races in rural counties in 1940 were almost eliminated by 1952, but the slight racial differences which did exist were in rural counties. Metropolitan counties were completely equalized by 1950. Table 78 presents the complete analysis.

TABLE 78

AVERAGE LENGTH IN DAYS OF THE SCHOOL TERM IN WHITE AND NEGRO
PUBLIC SCHOOLS IN SAMPLE RURAL AND RURAL-URBAN
COUNTIES, AND IN METROPOLITAN COUNTIES
IN TWELVE SOUTHERN STATES

County Classification		1939–40	1949–50	1951–52
Rural	W	165	177	177
	N	147	172	175
Rural-Urban	W	169	177	177
	N	154	175	176
Metropolitan	W	175	179	179
	N	168	179	179

SUMMARY

Greatly increased expenditures for capital outlay and inflation of property values have resulted in a very substantial increase in the value of Southern public school buildings and equipment per child in average daily attendance. A tremendous backlog of need for facilities had accumulated, however, as a result of the curtailment of school buildings during the Depression and war years, the greatly accelerated birth rate since World War II, and public desires for better buildings and equipment for school children. This need has by no means been adequately met. Shortages are still critical in many areas, usually due to rapid population growth which has exceeded the capacity and willingness of school districts to provide adequate additional facilities.

Children in metropolitan areas continue to be better housed than children in rural areas. The increases of the past few years in expenditures for capital outlay and value of buildings and equipment have not reduced the disparity between these two groups.

The Southern states were moving toward racial equalization of facilities between 1940 and 1952, as shown by percentage increases in the value of school property in favor of Negro schools. The ratio of property values between the two races declined. However, while $150.00 per Negro pupil would have been necessary for absolute dollar equalization in 1940, $264.00 per Negro pupil would have been required in 1952.

Throughout the period under consideration, the most disproportionate ratios between the values of school properties for the two races were in rural counties and the least were in metropolitan counties. Yet, the absolute amounts necessary for equalization were greater in metropolitan counties than in rural counties.

The general aspiration toward better schools and the belief that larger attendance centers are one means of achieving this goal have resulted in an accelerating trend in recent years in the South in the reduction of the number of public schools. Many larger schools have been brought about by abolishing smaller schools and combining them into larger attendance areas. The one-teacher school has been the chief target for elimination.

The rate of consolidation among the states varied considerably from 1940 to 1952, depending upon such factors as sparsity of population, degree of consolidation attained before 1940, extent of urbanization, and public attitudes toward the consolidation movement.

Consolidation of schools has occurred in all types of counties, although the rate has been greater in rural counties. Negro and white school consolidations occurred at the same rate for the twelve-year period.

The trend toward the establishment of larger centers and the zeal for new or better facilities have been accompanied by an enormous increase in public school transportation. An important new responsibility has been created for the schools and the spread of its impact continues to accelerate.

Increases in transportation services varied from state to state in relation to the degree of consolidation and to population changes within the states. The number and percentage of those enrolled who were transported increased, however, in each of the three population classifications, rural, rural-urban, and metropolitan. Throughout the period, the largest percentage of enrollment transported was in rural counties and the smallest was in metropolitan counties.

The extent to which the public is able to secure adequate returns for its investment in school buildings, equipment, and transportation is dependent upon the extent to which there is maximum use of these facilities. Expansion of community uses of facilities and extended school uses comprise a very important trend during the period covered by this inquiry.

The length of the school year is the most important measure of adequacy of use of school facilities. Between 1940 and 1952 almost all the Southern states increased the length of their public school term to 175-180 days, which is generally considered the desirable length of a public school year. The length of term was nearly equalized between rural and metropolitan counties.

The length of the school year was almost completely equalized for white and Negro children. Slight differences remaining were found in the rural areas and, as has always been the case, favored white children.

The interdependence of developments within all these phases of public education is clear. Each and all together raise problems with respect to the financing of education, its administration and supervision, and the social aspects of larger schools and their impact on children and community life that are a continuing challenge to both lay and professional people.

NINE

The Educational Program

Information on revenues, costs, facilities, personnel, the school population, and other kinds of data of value in understanding a school system, while very important, can at best provide only a base for drawing inferences concerning the nature and adequacy of the educational program itself. These and other factors are means through which learning opportunities are provided and which make education possible. A satisfactory appraisal of educational opportunity requires a study of the program of instruction and of the degree to which it reaches those for whom it is intended. This chapter is concerned with the difficult task of throwing light on questions concerning the adequacy of the educational program and the extent to which variations in adequacy occur among schools and between Negro and white schools.

Some of the difficulties which are inherent in this task may be obvious. In the first place, educational adequacy can be defined only in terms of objectives. Since objectives are necessarily value oriented, adequacy of objectives is a philosophical question and can, therefore, only be subjectively evaluated. The second major aspect of adequacy is the means by which educational objectives are pursued. Means consist of the curriculum, the instructional supplies, the teacher and his methods, and, broadly defined, the physical plant of the school, and even the community. Both the scope and depth of the curriculum must be considered. In another sense, the criterion of adequacy must be weighed in terms of whether or not all educables receive the amount and quantity of education which society considers desirable.

It is obviously not within the province of this chapter to present a thorough coverage of these topics. Such efforts to achieve educational adequacy are presented, however, as may have some evaluative merit.

UTILIZATION OF THE AVAILABLE
EDUCATIONAL PROGRAM

Numerous data pertinent to the discussion at hand have already been presented; some are briefly repeated because they are a direct measure of one phase of educational adequacy.

239

Compulsory attendance laws, an expanding economy, child labor laws, and confidence in education as a way to a better life help account for the continuing growth in the percentage of children enrolled in public schools. In the chapter on school population, enrollment, and attendance, it was pointed out that in 1950 the percentage of children in Southern public schools had reached 92.9. Those attending private and parochial schools would, of course, swell this percentage. It seems reasonably clear that the schools now reach, at least in some measure, close to the maximum number who should be in attendance.

The number of years spent in school is another matter. The assumption that minimum educational needs require completion of a high school education sets up a criterion for a rough measure of the unfinished task of providing high school education for all. One research study has shown that of one hundred children entering the first grade, only twelve graduated from high school. A similar study conducted in another state showed that fourteen out of one hundred entering the first grade were graduated from high school twelve years later. Both of these studies were for white children. Statistics for the Southern region reveal that in 1940 there were 1,507,791 children in the first grade. In 1952 high school graduates in the region totaled approximately 283,000.

The relationship of education to economic well-being has been too well established to be questioned. The appalling loss resulting from failure to extend the education of all educable youth at least to high school graduation has great social consequence, and it has significance for the individuals who do not receive the amount of education which they have a right to expect.

As reported in Chapter 4, school attendance has improved to the point that it is no longer a problem in most school systems. The maximum percentage of attendance which may be expected will vary according to the prevalence of epidemics in a given year, weather conditions, especially in rural areas, and general health conditions of the community. The latter seems to be closely related to economic status. Some further improvement in attendance may be expected if the general health level continues to rise.

The percentage of eligible children enrolled in schools no longer varies to any important degree between metropolitan, rural, and rural-urban counties. Overcoming the discriminating effects of geographical location on school enrollment is an important achievement. Attendance, likewise, is little affected by geographical location. The rural child is likely to have an attendance record closely paralleling that of his metropolitan counterpart.

A factor in school enrollment and attendance more important than geographical location seems to be the economic level of the parents. The problem of getting all eligible children enrolled in school is greatest in blighted areas where the standard of living is subnormal. Attendance problems are also pronounced in these areas.

Until recent years, considerable difference existed between white and Negro children in both school enrollment and attendance. These differences are rapidly disappearing, although they still exist. The generally lower economic and health levels of Negro families account for the major part of this difference. Dropouts between the first and twelfth grades are still much higher for Negroes than for whites. In 1940 there were 670,009 Negroes enrolled in the first grade. In 1952 a few less than 48,000 Negroes were graduated from high school. These figures do not, of course, take into account the number in the first grade who have been in the same grade before or the number who may have moved out of the region or died. Great strides are being made in closing the gap between Negro and white enrollment and attendance.

If general practice is acceptable as a satisfactory measure of adequacy, the length of school terms is no longer a factor which discriminates against children in receiving an adequate education. Chapter 8 revealed that the school year in the Southern states is gradually settling at a figure of 175 to 180 days per year.

The above measures are wholly quantitative and are but gross measures of the first level of the problem of educational adequacy— the extent of exposure to the available school program. Other levels will approach more nearly the instructional program itself.

EDUCATIONAL OBJECTIVES AND MEANS

While free, universal education for all has long been a part of the American dream, the purposes of education have undergone important changes from time to time. Without exception these redefinitions of educational goals have steadily broadened demands on the schools. The expectation of what education should accomplish has increased under the impact of social and economic changes. Historic faith in the power of education to improve the lot of the individual has been supplemented by a new recognition of the social values education offers for an entire society.

A broad range of opinions is to be found on the objectives of the schools. Strong support for the traditional "classical" education continues. The wave of protest against what was called progressive education appears to have subsided markedly, however, as rather general agreement has been reached that education should equip people to lead productive lives, which include both self-satisfaction and social worth in harmony with American ideals. According to this definition, concern for good citizenship, good physical and emotional health, and the ability to be a harmonious member of society, in addition to mental development, are essential. The definition finds expression in college preparatory courses for some and vocational education programs for others, but both include elements believed to be essential to the all-round development of youth.

Agreements on educational objectives are easier to reach on the philosophic than on the operational level. It is when educational means are set up to achieve agreed-upon objectives that differences of opinion may become most pronounced. These differences occur among professional educators as well as laymen, and they are one indication of the gap between educational theory and practice. Worthy objectives set forth for an educational program do not necessarily indicate the existence of a program which is consistent with the objectives.

Nevertheless, improved curricula have accompanied the broadening of educational objectives. By *improved* is meant a larger variety of educational experiences, more varied instructional materials and practices, the provision of free textbooks and other supplies, and better quality of curricula materials, all within the scope of means consistent with objectives.

Newer aspirations for education are reflected in a variety of services which have been added to the school program. Among them are health services, including immunizations, physical examinations, dental care, and sight conservation. The school lunch movement is another evidence of concern for physical well-being, and it has also been justified as a basis for improving learning. Guidance services are now considered a part of any good school program. Education for a variety of vocational purposes is also commonplace. Special provisions for the physically and mentally handicapped are included in an adequate school program.

Among the most significant contributions to improved adequacy of the educational program is the progress in the field of teaching methods. During the past fifty years, great strides have been made in the accumulation of tremendously important knowledge concerning how children grow and develop and how learning takes place. A whole new body of teaching methods was called for when psychologists discovered that the mind is not developed as a muscle is developed. Disavowel of faculty psychology called for new teaching methods. Discoveries of the importance of the social orientation of the learner, his need for success, and the importance of his having a sense of belonging have helped bring about more effective teaching. There is now common recognition that teaching consists of helping the learner find his own way rather than charting an inflexible course for him.

It is not to be implied from this discussion that a majority of the classrooms in the region reflect a substantial part of the newer concept of method. Even teacher-training institutions by and large still do not fully reflect the influence of these developments. Furthermore, many teachers received their training before there was any general acceptance of the principles enumerated, and they have not kept up with developments. Indeed, one of the great barriers to the achievement of a reasonable level of educational adequacy for all is the great range of teacher effectiveness, of which method is a critical part. It is not unusual to find under the same roof teachers who run from one extreme to the other in effectiveness. But it goes without saying that the means toward more universal achievement of desirable educational objectives have been greatly strengthened by discoveries in the field of teaching method.

Improvements in educational administration and supervision have played an important part in bringing about better quality of school programs. The development of supervision in the Southern region has occurred within recent years and indicates concern of responsible officials for the improvement of instruction. Persons occupying administrative and supervisory positions have usually been given special training in fields which contribute to their effectiveness in improving teaching. Supervisors work with both individual teachers and groups of teachers. Frequently, the superintendent allocates responsibilities for the instructional program to the supervisor or director of instruction.

The rapid growth in the number of organized and continuing in-service education programs within school systems is another noteworthy factor in the improvement of the quality of education in the region. Recognition that teachers can always learn to be better teachers and that education changes with new conditions and with new discoveries affecting the learning process are important reasons for the current emphasis on in-service education. The large number of teachers with provisional certificates, who entered the profession during the war years and later, is another reason for this emphasis. Concern of administrators for teacher morale and growth of the concept that administration is a facilitating device for education rather than a means in itself are other factors which have contributed to better educational programs.

State departments of education are rapidly expanding services designed to function directly in the improvement of instruction. Staff members are emphasizing a role of leadership in the improvement of instruction, and they frequently assist administrative staffs of local school systems in developing and carrying on in-service education programs. Teacher-training institutions are also adopting a new role with respect to teachers and administrators in service. They now generally recognize a responsibility for helping in the professional upgrading of school personnel in the field. Staff members may carry on in-service education workshops in the field, assist local staffs in consultative capacities, or team up with state department of education personnel. These developments, which amount to trends, are being reflected in improved instructional practices.

Larger administrative units and larger attendance areas have resulted in improved instruction, although neither is a guarantee of improvement. The larger district permits a larger administrative staff, which is likely to have more specialized training, thereby providing a wider array of administrative and supervisory abilities. Larger attendance centers likewise lead to better trained principals and a greater wealth of teacher talent in a given school system.

The impact of the foregoing developments has not been the same for Negro and white schools. In general, white schools have come under the influence of the factors enumerated with Negro schools following at a later date. Educational objectives each race holds for itself have never been very different; differences have appeared in means available to achieve objectives. Objectives are products of the mind. They represent aspirations. Means are more tangible and are subject to greater control by the dominant group. Broader and more varied curricula are subject to control through the extent to which means of implementation are available. Measurement of these factors has never been undertaken for either race insofar as is known, but in order to make an evaluation of educational adequacy an analysis of at least some parts of the instructional program is necessary.

SELECTED AREAS OF THE SCHOOL PROGRAM

In order to shed more light on the instructional program of the public schools of the region, three special areas have been chosen for intensive study. These are lunch programs, library services, and vocational education. It will be noted that one—the lunch program—is concerned with the general physical and health conditions of children; another—library services—deals with a part of the curriculum which cuts across all levels of the public schools; and the third—vocational education—deals with an area of the instructional program itself. It may be inferred that conditions found to exist in these three areas may be found generally to exist in other areas of the instructional program.

SCHOOL LIBRARY SERVICE. The purposes of this section are to analyze school library services as a feature of the school curriculum, to present a very brief description of the background and development of the service, and to analyze some trends in quantitative measurements of school library services in the Southern region from 1940 to 1952.

Perhaps the earliest expansion of the simple textbook curriculum was the establishment of a school library where a collection of volumes considered to be of value to the students could be kept in the schools. The evolution of this service has, of course, been a part of increased expectation of the schools and has accompanied broadened curricula. The creation of the position of school librarian and the professionalization of her training indicate the stability and importance of the library movement.

Two related concepts of function have existed with reference to the role of the school library. Some educators have held to the point of view that the school library should supply material that is closely related to the work of the classroom, thereby performing an information function. Others have looked upon the library as a more general means to curriculum enrichment, that is, a reading service similar to that of public libraries. In carrying out the latter function, the library must of necessity maintain collections of books on a wide variety of subjects appealing to and developing personal interests of individual pupils. Fortunately, the two points of view have never been in serious conflict and the modern school library serves both functions.

The development of the library movement is of interest. The early colonial period has not been considered important in school library development because the nature and purposes of education of that time did not require the service. The first period in the growth and development of school library services began in 1835 and extended through 1876; they followed the establishment of educational and political patterns in this country. The provision of free public schools opened the door for public school library service. Horace Mann and other pioneers in the field of education saw the importance of the library function.

A brief middle period in library service history falls between 1876 and 1900. It is notable for the beginning of cooperation between public school libraries and public libraries. Public librarians and laymen furnished most of the leadership, which led to a great deal of progress toward making public libraries available to schools and school libraries available to communities. Important landmarks in this period were the Federal report of 1876 on the history, condition, and management of libraries, and, in the same year, the organization of the American Library Association and publication of the first issue of the *Library Journal*. In 1896 a library department was established in the National Education Association.

The modern library movement began early in the twentieth century. This period of rapid growth in school libraries is a part of the tremendous expansion of the public school system during the first half of the century. Important changes in the basic philosophy of education placed new emphasis on the need for school libraries.

National and regional library associations have concerned themselves with the study of conditions and needs in library service and in the formulation of standards and recommendations. A committee of the American Library Association, appointed to consider the future development of school library service, said in a report made in 1945:

> It appears that a full-time librarian with clerical assistance is needed in any school, elementary or secondary, with a school membership of 200 pupils or more and in which the full possibility of the library is realized in the school program. One trained, experienced, full-time school librarian can serve effectively a school enrollment of not more than 500 pupils.[1]

The committee recommended a book collection ranging from a minimum of 2,000 volumes in schools of 200 or fewer enrolled to a minimum of 15,000 in schools with as many as 5,000 pupils. Other recommendations of the committee, which together with those already mentioned have been incorporated in the American Library Association standards, had to do with personal traits, formal training, and remuneration considered desirable for librarians. An excellent treatment in the report was devoted to state library supervision.[2]

No review of the major points in the evolution of library services would be complete without reference to the interest and support of foundations. Andrew Carnegie and the Carnegie Corporation contributed many millions of dollars to communities and schools for erecting and equipping public and school libraries. They also provided endowments to the American Library Association, to library schools, to college libraries, college librarianships, and they sponsored a nation-wide study of rural school library services. The General Education Board promoted state supervision of school libraries in some Southern states by the subsidization of pilot programs. The Rockefeller Fund contributed to library buildings, library schools, and other general developments in the field. The Julius Rosenwald Fund made substantial grants

---

[1] *School Libraries for Today and Tomorrow*, A Report of the American Library Association Committee on Post-War Planning (Chicago: American Library Association, 1945), p. 17.

[2] *Ibid.*, pp. 16–35.

for establishing libraries for Negro elementary and secondary schools and for the purchase of new books for Negro colleges. It also sponsored demonstration library systems in counties of Southern states.

National interest in school library service has been evident in Federal government activities related to education. This interest was indicated in the first regular report of the U. S. Bureau of Education, issued in 1870. Continued interest was shown by publication of a comprehensive report on libraries by the United States Department of the Interior in 1876. In 1936 a library service division was created in the U. S. Office of Education, headed by a chief and assisted by two specialists, one each in the public and school library fields. This division collects and publishes records on school libraries. Perhaps more indicative of public interest in school libraries has been the consistent provision for library support in proposals for Federal aid to education.

As was to be expected in a region which was slow to establish the principle of universal free education, the provision of library services in the South lagged behind other parts of the country. The establishment of school libraries on a sound basis, especially in rural schools, was not undertaken on a wide scale until state aid was provided. A majority of the Southern states passed rural school laws between 1901 and 1909, which provided that the state and local school district would each match any amount up to $10.00 contributed by the local school for school libraries. Other kinds of state support for school library services have been provided by several Southern states and amounts of assistance have steadily increased, accounting for much progress in school library services in the Southern region.[3]

During the earlier years of the century progress was slow, and by 1915 the movement had passed little beyond simple collections of books, for all that they were called "school libraries." Standards of the Southern Assocation of Colleges and Secondary Schools as late as 1926 required only that a library be "adequate" and have 500 volumes. Adequacy apparently referred primarily to the number of volumes.

Progress in school libraries has been noteworthy since about 1925. Teachers and administrators began to understand and appreciate library services. Improved educational, social, economic, and political conditions made possible the supervision of library services on the state level. Emphasis on qualitative standards came into prominence during this time.

State library supervisors have made important contributions to the

---

[3] Frances Lander Spain, "High School Libraries in the South," in *Secondary Education in the South,* edited by W. Carson Ryan, J. Minor Gwynn, and Arnold K. King (Chapel Hill: University of North Carolina Press, 1946), pp. 96–97.

development of library services in the Southern region. Virginia first appointed a state director of school library services in 1923. Between 1929 and 1933, Alabama, Kentucky, Louisiana, North Carolina, and Tennessee began state library supervision with aid from the General Education Board for a five-year period. By 1952 all states included in this study with the exception of Oklahoma had a state supervisor of school library services. Their work has consisted of developing understandings of the value of school libraries, stimulating schools to develop adequate library services, interpreting regulations applying to school libraries, cooperating with other agencies and institutions concerned with libraries, conducting library research, and encouraging professional affiliation and participation of librarians in local, state, and national library organizations and activities.

Despite progress, the South continued to lag behind the rest of the nation. In 1935, 36.7 per cent of the people in the United States who did not have access to library service lived in the South, although only 21 per cent of the population was in the South. Negroes for the most part were without library services; 80.7 per cent of the Negroes in the South had no access to public library facilities.[4] As late as 1938, of eighteen million children under twenty years of age in the United States who were without public library service, seventeen million lived in rural areas. Rural children in the South accounted for at least one-half of the number. Louis R. Wilson found that, when the forty-eight states were ranked according to the number of volumes per inhabitant 5-17 years of age in libraries having 3,000 or more volumes, ten of the lowest thirteen states were in the Southern region. The highest ranking state, California, had 9.45 books per ten inhabitants, while the highest Southern state averaged 5.92 and the lowest 0.58. The same study applied an index of educational development and an index of public library development to the forty-eight states. Of the thirteen lowest states in each distribution, ten were in the Southern region.[5]

A study of libraries in 922 high schools belonging to the Southern Association of Colleges and Secondary Schools, made in 1930, reveals that not a single library met the combined standards of the Association. Most schools, 52.9 per cent, conformed to the requirements on expenditures for books, periodicals, etc., while only 39.4 per cent of the schools had the required number of volumes per pupil.[6]

---

[4] Louis R. Wilson and Edward A. Wight, *County Library Service in the South* (Chicago: The University of Chicago Press, 1935), pp. 16–18. Copyright 1935 by The University of Chicago.

[5] Louis R. Wilson, *The Geography of Reading* (Chicago: University of Chicago Press, 1938), pp. 156–267. Copyright 1938 by The University of Chicago.

[6] Doak S. Campbell, *Libraries in the Accredited High Schools of the Association of Colleges and Secondary Schools of the Southern States* (Nashville, Tennessee: Division of Surveys and Field Studies of George Peabody College for Teachers, 1930).

A survey of Southeastern public schools conducted in 1946 and 1947 covered library services for both white and Negro schools. Of the secondary schools reporting, 25.8 per cent were able to meet the combined quantitative standards of the Southern Association of Colleges and Secondary Schools. Almost 28 per cent of the white schools and 14 per cent of the Negro schools were able to meet the standards. Eighty-seven per cent of the white schools and 62 per cent of the Negro schools had the required number of books per pupil, while 62 per cent of the white schools and 32 per cent of the Negro schools met the standards on appropriation. When the same schools were measured by the combined standards of the American Library Association, only 5.5 per cent met them. Only 5.6 per cent of the white schools and 4.2 per cent of the Negro schools met the standards. Less than 25 per cent of the white schools and about 12 per cent of the Negro schools met the requirements for volumes per pupil. When the standards of the American Library Association were applied to elementary and junior high schools reporting in the survey, only one elementary school out of 231 and two junior high schools out of 107 were able to meet the combined standards. According to the reports from all schools, $1.17 per white pupil and $0.75 per Negro pupil were being spent for library services, excluding salaries of librarians. For all schools reporting, there were 6.5 and 4.4 volumes for white and Negro pupils, respectively.[7]

Library services, like most other services, have been provided through separate facilities for Negroes. A region which did not provide adequate facilities of any sort was hardly to be expected to provide adequate duplicate facilities in library services for a race which occupied an inferior position in the culture. A statistical treatment of quantitative measures of library services highlights the difference in the services provided the two races. Before proceeding to this analysis, a brief statement setting forth generally acceptable aims of the school library is presented.

The purpose of a school library is:

1. To enrich the school curriculum by providing adequate books, materials, and supporting services to meet the demand of the curriculum and the needs of pupils;

2. To develop pupils' skill and resourcefulness in the use of the library through guidance and assistance in its use as a medium of learning;

3. To share responsibility with other departments of the school for fruitful social training;

---

[7] *Libraries of the Southeast,* A Report of the Southeastern States Cooperative Library Survey, 1946–47, ed. by Louis R. Wilson and Marion A. Milczenski (Chapel Hill: The Southeastern Library Association, 1949), p. 79–114.

4. To foster informational reading as a means of lifelong education;

5. To help establish a wide range of significant interests sufficient to provide a continuing desire to read for pleasure.[8]

These objectives make it possible for anyone to appraise for himself certain aspects of the adequacy of library facilities in Southern schools.

Volumes per pupil in school libraries. Table 79 shows that the region stood very low in the number of books per pupil in school

TABLE 79

NUMBER OF BOOKS PER PUPIL IN PUBLIC SCHOOL LIBRARIES IN SOUTHERN STATES *

Population Classification	Library Volumes Per Pupil Enrolled			Change Per Pupil 1940–1952	
	1939–40	*1949–50*	*1951–52*	*Actual*	*Per Cent*
State Totals (7 states)	2.3	3.8	3.4	1.1	48
Rural County Sample (10 states)	2.1	3.6	3.4	1.3	62
Rural-Urban County Sample (10 states)	2.1	2.9	3.3	1.2	57
Metropolitan Counties (10 states)	2.1	3.5	3.5	1.4	67

* See Table 99, Appendix B, for states included.

libraries in 1940. Furthermore, a 48 per cent increase in the number per pupil by 1952 in the seven states for which data were available provided pupils with no more than half the number recommended by library standards. Data for a directed sample of rural and rural-urban counties and for metropolitan counties reveal that the three county classifications stood at the same level of 2.1 books per pupil in 1940: gains through 1952 were also rather uniform, with metropolitan counties showing only a slightly larger gain. Judged by purely quantitative standards, differences in educational adequacy among types of counties were not substantial.

Similar comparisons for Negro and white pupils are shown in Table 80. Libraries in Negro schools in 1940 contained less than one-fourth the number of volumes per pupil that libraries in white schools had. Increases during the next twelve years were almost the same quantitatively, an addition of 1.4 volumes per white child and 1.3 volumes per Negro child. Although this represented a gain of 48 per cent for

[8] These purposes reflect the broadening conception of the functions of library services.

white students and 186 per cent for Negro students, the actual difference in the number of volumes increased slightly.

TABLE 80

NUMBER OF BOOKS PER PUPIL IN PUBLIC SCHOOL LIBRARIES FOR WHITE AND
NEGRO PUPILS IN SOUTHERN STATES *

Population Classification	Library Volumes Per Pupil Enrolled			Change Per Pupil 1940–1952	
	1939–40	*1949–50*	*1951–52*	*Actual*	*Per Cent*
State Totals (7 states)					
White	2.9	4.6	4.3	1.4	48
Negro	0.7	1.7	2.0	1.3	186
Rural County Sample (10 states)					
White	2.8	4.9	4.5	1.7	61
Negro	0.6	1.4	1.6	1.0	167
Rural-Urban County Sample (10 states)					
White	2.7	4.4	4.2	1.5	56
Negro	0.8	1.5	2.0	1.2	150
Metropolitan Counties (10 states)					
White	2.5	3.9	4.0	1.5	60
Negro	0.8	2.2	2.4	1.6	200

* See Table 99, Appendix B, for states included.

Differentials between the races in 1940 varied considerably among the county classifications, being largest in rural counties, less in rural-urban, and smallest in metropolitan. By 1952 rural and rural-urban counties had made substantial increases in the number of books per white pupil but comparatively fewer gains for Negro pupils, while metropolitan counties had made notable gains for white pupils and similar gains for Negro pupils, the increase for Negro pupils even being slightly greater. This pattern evidences larger gaps being created in the more rural counties but a closing of the gaps in the more urban counties, with the highest degrees of equity being reached in metropolitan areas.

A concise picture of differentials in the number of volumes in school libraries for white and Negro pupils and changes in this relationship since 1940 are given in Chart 10. In each year and for each county classification books per white pupil are considered to equal 100 per cent. The number of books per Negro pupil is then shown as a percentage of the number for white pupils. For example, in 1940 the number of books per Negro pupil in the states reporting was only 24 per cent as large as the number per white pupil, but this percentage increased to 47 by 1952. An examination of the data in this

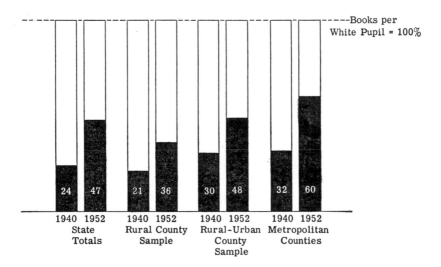

CHART 10. *Percentage ratio of books per Negro pupil to books per white pupil.*

chart according to county classifications reveals that books per Negro pupil measured as a percentage of those per white pupil was lowest in rural counties, slightly higher in rural-urban counties, and highest in metropolitan counties in both 1940 and 1952. Increases during the period were highest in metropolitan counties, next in rural-urban counties, and lowest in rural counties.

A further analysis of the differences in the number of books by races and trends in these differences is presented in Chart 11. It is readily seen that a difference of 2.2 in the region in 1940 was increased 5 per cent by 1952. This regional trend was influenced significantly, no doubt, by the trend in rural and rural-urban counties, which widened the gap by 32 and 16 per cent, respectively. The stabilizing force apparently came from metropolitan areas.

Expenditures per pupil for school libraries. The rapid increase in dollar expenditures for library services since 1940 is shown in Table 81. The meagre sum of $0.24 per pupil was spent in 1940, but this figure had been raised to $0.75 by 1952. The increase amounted to 212 per cent of the 1940 expenditure, which is less than the 246 per cent increase in over-all current expenditures for the period. Expenditures among the county classifications were very close in 1940, but significant gaps had developed by 1952: rural county expenditures were lowest, rural-urban next, and metropolitan counties were considerably above the other counties and the regional level.

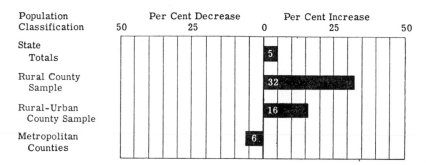

CHART 11. *Changes from 1940 to 1952 in the actual white-over-Negro difference between the number of library books per white and per Negro pupil.*

TABLE 81

PUBLIC SCHOOL LIBRARY EXPENDITURES PER PUPIL
IN SOUTHERN STATES *

Population	Library Expenditures Per Pupil in ADA			Change Per Pupil 1940–1952	
Classification	1939–40	1949–50	1951–52	Actual	Per Cent
State Totals (9 states)	$0.24	$0.62	$0.75	$0.51	212
Rural County Sample (9 states)	0.28	0.49	0.67	0.39	139
Rural-Urban County Sample (9 states)	0.26	0.51	0.76	0.50	192
Metropolitan Counties (9 states)	0.34	1.05	1.01	0.67	197

* See Table 99, Appendix B, for states included.

An analysis of expenditures by white and Negro pupils is given in Table 82. The $0.09 per Negro pupil spent in 1940 could hardly have come close to providing adequate library services for Negro children. Library expenditures per Negro pupil did, however, keep pace with those for white pupils during the two following years, but the dollar gap was not reduced.

Expenditures for white pupils were about the same for the three county classifications in 1940, but expenditures for Negro pupils in metropolitan counties were twice those in rural counties. By 1952, expenditures for Negro pupils in rural counties had gained considerably on expenditures for white pupils; a marked lag still existed in rural-urban counties; and the gap in metropolitan counties had been converted into a Negro-over-white difference.

TABLE 82

PUBLIC SCHOOL LIBRARY EXPENDITURES PER WHITE AND NEGRO PUPIL
IN SOUTHERN STATES *

Population Classification	Library Expenditures Per Pupil in ADA			Change Per Pupil 1940–1952	
	1939–40	*1949–50*	*1951–52*	*Actual*	*Per Cent*
State Totals (7 states)					
White	$0.29	$0.45	$0.86	$0.57	197
Negro	0.09	0.21	0.66	0.57	633
Rural County Sample (9 states)					
White	0.36	0.56	0.68	0.32	89
Negro	0.09	0.38	0.66	0.57	633
Rural-Urban County Sample (9 states)					
White	0.33	0.58	0.85	0.52	158
Negro	0.08	0.33	0.56	0.48	600
Metropolitan Counties (9 states)					
White	0.40	1.03	0.98	0.58	145
Negro	0.18	1.10	1.12	0.94	522

* See Table 99, Appendix B, for states included.

An additional analysis of differences in expenditures and trends in the differences between races is presented in Chart 12. Expenditures for Negro pupils are presented as a percentage of expenditures for white pupils. The data revealed that only 31 per cent as much per Negro pupil was being spent for library services in 1940 as for white pupils but by 1952 this percentage had increased to 77. The trends in county classifications have been touched upon in previous analyses but are portrayed more vividly by the percentage comparison, which clearly shows that expenditures for Negro pupils in rural counties almost reached the level of that for white pupils and surpassed it in metropolitan counties.

A comparison of the gap between library expenditures per pupil in Negro and white schools is shown in the data presented in Chart 13. The seven states which keep separate records by races showed no change in the dollar difference in expenditures for white and Negro pupils from 1940 through 1952. Looking at the picture by county classifications, however, reveals some important variations. The difference was reduced to less than $0.05 in rural counties; it increased slightly in rural-urban counties; and metropolitan counties reported $0.14 more per Negro pupil than per white pupil.

OPPORTUNITIES FOR VOCATIONAL EDUCATION. Vocational education is the one service included in this chapter which may be considered a part of the school curriculum under the most narrow definition of the term. Preparation for vocational competence became

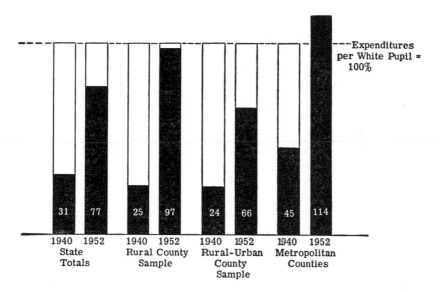

CHART 12.   *Percentage ratio of library expenditures per Negro pupil to those per white pupil.*

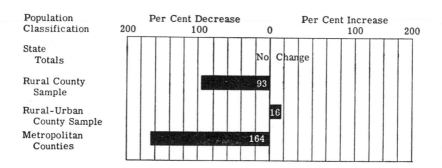

CHART 13.   *Changes from 1940 to 1952 in the actual white-over-Negro difference between library expenditures per white and per Negro pupil.*

a responsibility of the school with the extension of education to the masses and the rise of a culture dependent upon technical know-how. The utilitarian motive gained new impetus late in the nineteenth century and was quickly translated into educational reality. This movement attained such importance in the United States that the Federal government itself became committed to a program of vocational education which went beyond its commitments to any other area of public education. This is still true.

This section undertakes to analyze vocational education in terms of its purpose and function in the program of public education, to present a brief overview of its development in the United States, and to analyze recent vocational education enrollment and expenditure trends in the Southern region.

Broadening the purposes of education required its adaptation to diversified human needs and problems and made possible the emergence of vocational education. Its special function is the development of material and human assets.

Students of the curriculum have incorporated the purpose of vocational education in the general purposes of the school program. One author wrote:

General education and vocational education must remain inseparable if this nation is to continue to have one system of free public education, and since that system was able to meet, adequately, the greatest demand ever put on it, there seems little reason to argue for two systems of education — one for those who would climb the ladder to college entrance and the professions, and another for those who leave school at the secondary level (or before) to enter the fields of business, industry, skilled and unskilled labor.[9]

Much has been done to remove the class stigma formerly attached to vocational education. Three collaborators, writing on the curriculum, said:

Only in societies where certain vocations are associated with particular social classes will this tend to be true. Social systems that emphasize an open-door policy for all occupations — making it possible for every individual irrespective of race, creed, or social background to acquire the knowledge and skills he is capable and desirous of obtaining — will be those societies that reduce the chances that some occupations will be monopolized by privileged classes. In these societies vocational education will be least associated with class education.[10]

The development of vocational education in the United States has, therefore, been a part of the larger pattern of social and economic change. Publicly supported programs of vocational education did not appear until it was evident that such training would make a significant contribution to American prosperity. As long as there was a new plot of land for every man who needed it and few machines for producing goods in quantity, there was little need for men to become specialists.

---

[9] George H. Fern, *What Is Vocational Education?*, written in the foreword by the author (Chicago: American Technical Society, 1944).

[10] B. Othanel Smith, William O. Stanley, and J. Harlan Shores, *Fundamentals of Curriculum* (New York: World Book Company, 1950), p. 12.

Early vocational education in the United States came about either as a normal part of family living, or by studious observation and practice under the supervision of a master workman. Three major conditions were primarily responsible for this situation. First, the economy was founded largely on an agrarian base; second, England controlled the industrial development of the colonies; and third, the American frontier provided a mode of living which was revered by those seeking refuge in the new country. It was not until a new pattern of living emerged in American society that needs for vocational training became evident, and plans were advanced for making such training a responsibility of the educational program.

Benjamin Franklin, a product of the colonial apprentice system, was quick to sense the need for vocational training in the new world. In his "Proposals Relating to the Education of Youth in Pennsylvania," issued in 1749, he suggested provisions for training in surveying, navigation, and agriculture, in addition to the usual academic training. His proposals, however, did not gain widespread recognition before the middle of the nineteenth century.

The economy of colonial days, based primarily on agriculture and commerce, was modified greatly by the time the Civil War ended. The era of the apprentice was over and experimentation with numerous types of industrial schools had proven that no one type of program was adequate for industrial training needs. The pace of industrial advancement quickened and, in the drive for greater efficiency, processes, methods, and machines were steadily perfected. Industrial engineers became necessary, leisure craftsmen disappeared, local industry gave way to national industries, the artisan gave way to the machine, and tools were no longer owned by the individual.

In efforts to find solutions to the complex problem growing out of the industrial revolution, industrial education assumed greater importance. Some states began to institute plans of vocational education, commissions were formed for the study of vocational needs, and by 1917 vocational education surveys had been conducted in many states in anticipation of national provision for vocational training in the public schools. By 1911 five states had adopted some form of state system of vocational education. Within two years, five other states had established similar systems. Almost every state was the seat of some commission or investigation of vocational training needs, and twenty-two national organizations echoed the sentiments of their states and local branches in the support of vocational training for the youth of America.[11] Sentiment for support of vocational education

---

[11] Layton S. Hawkins, Charles A. Prosser, and John C. Wright, *Development of Vocational Education* (Chicago: American Technical Society, 1951), pp. 50–51.

was consolidated as early as 1906 when the National Society for the Promotion of Industrial Education was organized.

Interest of the Federal government in the problem of vocational education is shown by the fact that seven Federal acts had been passed concerning this problem by 1914. During this year, Congress appointed a Commission on National Aid to Vocational Education and charged it with investigating the status of vocational education in the United States and reporting on the desirability and the feasibility of national aid for the promotion of vocational training.[12]

The report of this commission stimulated Congress to pass legislation providing Federal support for a national program of vocational education. The resultant Smith-Hughes Act, passed in February of 1917, was the first of five acts designed to assist states in their promotion of vocational education. The George-Reed Act was passed in 1929, followed by the George-Ellzey Act in 1934, the George-Deen Act in 1936, and the George-Barton Act in 1946.

Following the recommendations of the Commission on National Aid to Vocational Education, the Smith-Hughes Act provided for a Federal board of vocational education consisting of the Secretary of Agriculture, the Secretary of Commerce, the Secretary of Labor, and the Commissioner of Education, and three citizens to be appointed by the President of the United States. The three citizens were to represent manufacturing, agriculture, and commerce. The Act further provided that states, in accepting provisions of the Act, should designate or create a state board of not less than three members empowered to execute the provisions of the Act. This board could be the same as an existing board, such as the state board of education, if the state so elected. The Act provided financial support for the training of vocational teachers, teacher salaries, supervision of the program, the administration of expenditures, and study and investigation in the fields of agriculture, home economics, and trades and industries. Federal subsidies were to be matched equally by the participating states. The George-Deen Act first provided for assistance in instruction in the fields of distributive occupations.

Former patterns of agriculture which depleted the soil in the South, the biracial culture of the region, and rapid industrialization have combined to make Federal provisions for vocational education of particular significance to the region. Formulas for the distribution of funds, taking into account the rural population and farm population, gave the region an advantage in terms of total funds coming to the states. The inferior economic status of the Negro race compared to

---

[12] Elwood P. Cubberly, *Public Education in the United States* (Boston: Houghton-Mifflin Company, 1919), p. 415.

that of the white clearly indicated vocational education as a way to help the Negro become a more productive worker.

According to Horace Mann Bond, four important beliefs of the white race have controlled the provision of vocational education for Negroes in the South. On the theory that Negroes should be "hewers of wood and drawers of water," vocational education was held to be the solution to educational needs of Negroes. The second belief, which was closely related to the first, was a psychological one and held that the Negro was not able to learn tasks calling for the exercise of abstract intelligence. The third belief insisted that a program for Negro vocational training should produce craftsmen; this belief persisted long after the critical need for skilled machine operators developed. The final belief was social in nature and was rooted in the conviction that the old aristocracy of the South would return and that white intellectual work would again rest upon a foundation of Negro artisans and laborers.[13]

The pattern of education that accompanied these beliefs was very interesting. Men of good will toward the Negroes urged the complete discontinuance of all education for Negroes that was not vocational in nature; whereas, in fact, by 1934 all Negro high schools could offer a full curriculum of the classics, since they required no expensive equipment or facilities. The large appropriations for the installation of machinery went to the white schools.[14]

Gunnar Myrdal contributed a similar analysis. As was pointed out earlier in this volume, he observed that in theory white Southerners could propose vocational education for Negroes and keep within the American creed without upsetting the caste system. When the lines were drawn a little more distinctly, however, the Negro could not be provided vocational training and take the bread from the white man's mouth.[15]

A regional study in 1935 of the status and trends of vocational education in eighteen Southern states with segregated schools supported the preceding points of view. For example, the study shows that for each $1.00 spent for each white pupil in vocational education, only $0.58 was expended for each Negro pupil.[16] Summarizing the conditions that have existed in vocational training for Negroes in

[13] Horace Mann Bond, *The Education of the Negro in the American Social Order* (New York: Prentice-Hall, Inc., 1934), pp. 402–404.

[14] *Ibid.*, p. 404.

[15] Gunnar Myrdal, *An American Dilemma,* II (New York: Harper and Brothers, 1944), pp. 897–898.

[16] Doxey A. Wilkerson, *Special Problems of Negro Education,* Staff Study Number 12 of the Advisory Committee on Education (Washington: Government Printing Office, 1939), pp. 92–102.

the South, E. Franklin Frazier writes ". . . when the United States entered World War II Negroes lacked training in industrial skills which an equitable distribution of federal funds for vocational education in trades and industries would have provided."[17]

Numbers of pupils enrolled in vocational education. The unit of measure of pupils enrolled in vocational education is the number per thousand students in high school enrolled for each of four fields of vocational education: agriculture, home economics, trades and industries, and distributive occupations. Obviously, this unit cannot take into account the need for vocational education, but it does provide a common unit of measure for all groups and all types of vocational education included in this study.

The enrollment figures are found in Table 83. The greatest number of pupils per thousand enrolled in any area of vocational education in the Southern states, both in 1940 and 1952, was in home economics. This holds true of all population classifications except for metropolitan counties in 1952. The table also shows that the greatest increase between 1940 and 1952 was in the same field, a condition that held

TABLE 83

VOCATIONAL EDUCATION ENROLLMENT PER THOUSAND PUPILS ENROLLED
IN PUBLIC HIGH SCHOOLS OF SOUTHERN STATES *

Areas of Vocational Education by Population Classifications	Number Enrolled Per Thousand Enrolled in High School			Change Per Thousand 1940–1952
	1939–40	1949–50	1951–52	Actual
State totals				
Agriculture (13 states)	94	120	130	36
Home Economics (12 states)	139	208	212	73
Trades and Industries (9 states)	36	73	63	27
Distributive Occupations (13 states)	1	6	6	5
Rural County Sample				
Agriculture (11 states)	171	221	213	42
Home Economics (11 states)	200	269	268	68
Trades and Industries (8 states)	9	8	9	0
Distributive Occupations (9 states)	0	0	1	1
Rural-Urban County Sample				
Agriculture (11 states)	140	182	218	78
Home Economics (11 states)	177	269	279	102
Trades and Industries (8 states)	43	55	63	20
Distributive Occupations (9 states)	1	2	3	2
Metropolitan Counties				
Agriculture (11 states)	22	29	30	8
Home Economics (11 states)	82	122	136	54
Trades and Industries (8 states)	70	185	145	75
Distributive Occupations (9 states)	2	8	8	6

* See Table 99, Appendix B, for states included.

[17] E. Franklin Frazier, *The Negro in the United States* (New York: The Macmillan Company, 1949), p. 439. With the permission of the publisher.

true for all population classifications except metropolitan counties, where the largest increase was in trades and industries.

The field of agriculture drew the second largest number of pupils per thousand in each of the three years for which figures are presented. The highest rate of enrollment, as would be expected, was in rural counties for all years except in 1952, when enrollment in rural-urban counties exceeded that in rural counties by five per thousand. Enrollment in trades and industries was almost negligible for both years in rural counties, remaining at nine per thousand pupils. Distributive occupations are not represented in rural counties in 1940, and by 1952 only one student per thousand was enrolled in this field.

Looking directly at rural and rural-urban counties, one is struck by rather large increases in both home economics and agriculture that occurred in the twelve-year period. Essentially the same pattern is to be found in rural-urban counties as in rural counties, but total enrollment in vocational education was slightly higher in rural-urban counties than in any other classification. This condition seems to prevail because of offerings in each of the fields of vocational education in rural-urban counties as opposed to limited offerings in some fields in other types of counties.

The pattern of vocational education in the metropolitan counties naturally shows a much heavier emphasis on training for trades and industries. The increase is from seventy per thousand in 1940 to 145 per thousand in 1952. In like manner, the highest enrollment in distributive occupations would be expected in metropolitan counties, although the rate of only eight per thousand shows the opportunity for expansion in this field. Why enrollment in home economics should be so much less in metropolitan counties than in other classes of counties is not known. It may be related, in part, to the broader curricula offerings usually found in the metropolitan schools, whereas in rural and rural-urban schools frequently the only variations from traditional academic subjects are in home economics and agriculture.

Enrollments by Negro and white pupils are shown in Table 84 for the four fields of vocational education included in this analysis. It is interesting to note that Negro enrollment in 1940 exceeded that of white pupils in three out of four fields of vocational education, the exception being in distributive occupations where even white enrollment was extremely low. Changes in the region, however, by 1952 were such that Negro enrollment exceeded that of white in home economics only. As yet, Negroes are barely represented in the field of distributive occupations.

Shifts in population as well as the attraction of Negro pupils to the classic curriculum may be evident in the data presented for county

TABLE 84

VOCATIONAL EDUCATION ENROLLMENT OF WHITE AND NEGRO PUPILS PER THOUSAND ENROLLED IN PUBLIC HIGH SCHOOLS OF SOUTHERN STATES *

Areas of Vocational Education by Population Classifications	Number Enrolled Per Thousand Enrolled in High School						Change Per Thousand 1940–1952	
	1939–40		1949–50		1951–52		1940–1952	
	White	Negro	White	Negro	White	Negro	White	Negro
State Totals								
Agriculture (12 states)	92	126	122	122	135	117	43	– 9
Home Economics (12 states)	128	210	198	253	202	252	74	42
Trades and Industries (7 states)	43	85	101	77	83	74	40	– 11
Distributive Occupations (12 states)	1	0	7	1	7	1	6	1
Rural County Sample								
Agriculture (11 states)	156	296	231	188	218	196	62	–100
Home Economics (11 states)	203	179	289	197	284	216	81	37
Trades and Industries (8 states)	10	0	8	9	8	11	– 2	11
Distributive Occupations (9 states)	0	0	0	0	1	0	1	0
Rural-Urban County Sample								
Agriculture (11 states)	126	222	181	186	203	265	77	43
Home Economics (11 states)	159	291	252	333	255	364	96	73
Trades and Industries (8 states)	39	64	54	59	63	63	24	– 1
Distributive Occupations (9 states)	1	0	3	0	4	0	3	0
Metropolitan Counties								
Agriculture (11 states)	22	24	30	29	29	32	7	8
Home Economics (11 states)	67	151	113	153	130	160	63	9
Trades and Industries (8 states)	70	69	197	142	149	131	79	62
Distributive Occupations (9 states)	2	0	10	2	10	3	8	3

* See Table 99, Appendix B, for states included.

classifications. Negro enrollments ran high in agriculture and home economics in 1940, especially in rural and rural-urban counties. Actual increases in these two fields are notable, being significantly higher for white pupils than for Negro pupils. A similar trend is revealed for distributive occupations and trades and industries, but, of course, they are concentrated primarily in urban counties. A few white pupils are being trained in distributive occupations in rural and rural-urban counties, but opportunities for training Negro pupils in the field seem to be limited to counties with very large cities.

In terms of quantity alone, it appears that vocational education opportunities are more evenly distributed between the two races than school library services. The distribution generally favored Negroes in 1940, but by 1952 the picture had changed considerably. This analysis is pursued in Chart 14, where Negro enrollment is measured as a percentage of white enrollment in each of the four fields of vocational education and by each of the population classifications.

For the states as a whole, the trend is quite evident in all fields. The chart reveals that enrollment for Negroes measured as a percentage of white enrollment was declining in almost every field for all classifications. In agriculture and in trades and industries Negro enrollment in the region decreased from considerably above 100 per cent of the white in 1940 to less than the white in 1952. The trend generally prevailed in the county classifications. This comparison purposely excludes analyses in distributive occupations because of the absence of such programs for Negroes in 1940.

Chart 15 presents another picture of the number of white and Negro pupils enrolled in the four fields of vocational education. Here are found the changes that occurred from 1940 through 1952 in the actual differences that existed between the number of white and Negro pupils enrolled in vocational education per thousand pupils enrolled in high school.

Checking through the county classifications reveals five instances where the Negro enrollment in 1940 exceeded the white enrollment in the four fields of vocational education. In one of these cases, agriculture in rural counties, the gap was completely closed and a new one opened of white-over-Negro. In the trades and industries in rural-urban counties, the gap was completely closed. In the other three cases, agriculture in rural-urban counties, home economics in rural-urban counties, and home economics in metropolitan counties, the 1940 Negro-over-white differences were decreased.

A further examination of the differences which existed in 1940 among the county classifications reveals that there were six instances where there were white-over-Negro differences. One of these six dispari-

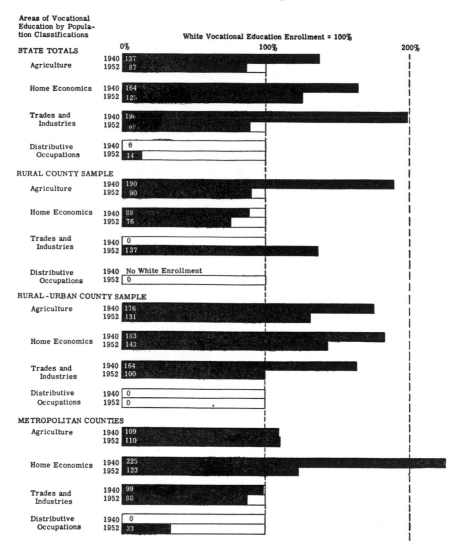

Areas of Vocational Education by Population Classifications

White Vocational Education Enrollment = 100%

CHART 14. *Negro pupils enrolled in vocational education per thousand enrolled in high school as a percentage of white pupils enrolled in vocational education per thousand enrolled in high school.*

ties, trades and industries in rural counties, was reduced during the period. It was completely closed and a Negro-over-white difference was opened by 1952 which was 30 per cent as large as the 1940 gap. The other five white-over-Negro differences which existed in 1940 were widened, ranging from 50 per cent in agriculture in metropolitan

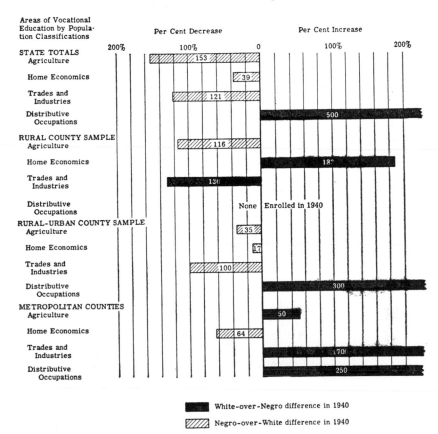

CHART 15. *Changes from 1940 to 1952 in the actual difference between the number of white and Negro pupils enrolled in vocational education per thousand pupils enrolled in high school.*

counties to 1700 per cent in trades and industries in metropolitan counties. The latter is exceptionally high because the difference was extremely small in 1940.

Per pupil expenditures for pupils enrolled in vocational education. Perhaps a more discriminating analysis of vocational education opportunities is one based on expenditures per pupil rather than upon enrollment. This is particularly true in the matter of comparisons between the races. While both measures are gross, the one on expenditures has a qualitative aspect not possible in considering enrollment figures only.

Table 85 presents cost data based on pupils enrolled in the four fields of vocational education under scrutiny. According to these figures, the most expensive of the four types of vocational education is distributive occupations. In 1940 costs were nearly twice those of the next most costly field, agriculture. The two fields also received the largest proportional increases in expenditures during the following twelve years. In 1952 home economics training was costing a little less than one-half as much as agriculture, and training in trades and industries was costing less than one-half as much as distributive education. The actual difference between expenditures for agriculture and home economics almost doubled in the twelve years, while a gap slightly larger than $50.00 between trades and industries and dis‑ tributive occupations increased by better than 79 per cent. Cost per pupil by the three county classifications is also shown in Table 85.

TABLE 85

VOCATIONAL EDUCATION EXPENDITURES PER PUPIL ENROLLED IN VOCATIONAL
EDUCATION IN PUBLIC HIGH SCHOOLS OF SOUTHERN STATES *

Areas of Vocational Education by Population Classifications	Instructional Expenditures Per Pupil Enrolled			Change Per Pupil
	1939–40	1949–50	1951–52	1940–1952
State Totals				
Agriculture (13 states)	$ 41.87	$ 90.64	$ 89.43	$47.56
Home Economics (11 states)	17.88	41.24	43.80	25.92
Trades and Industries (7 states)	29.59	43.59	51.54	21.95
Distributive Occupations (10 states)	82.24	114.75	118.05	35.81
Rural County Sample				
Agriculture (7 states)	46.15	80.50	84.55	38.40
Home Economics (8 states)	19.42	45.96	47.32	27.90
Trades and Industries (7 states)	32.10	59.99	76.40	44.30
Distributive Occupations (8 states)	n.e.ᵃ	n.e.	82.35	—
Rural-Urban County Sample				
Agriculture (7 states)	40.97	90.23	70.32	29.35
Home Economics (8 states)	17.39	39.78	40.26	22.87
Trades and Industries (7 states)	22.22	55.52	49.52	27.30
Distributive Occupations (8 states)	105.55	109.79	107.77	2.22
Metropolitan Counties				
Agriculture (7 states)	44.12	70.32	75.80	31.68
Home Economics (8 states)	12.11	32.87	36.82	24.71
Trades and Industries (7 states)	19.68	38.30	50.95	31.27
Distributive Occupations (8 states)	78.30	119.46	118.51	40.21

* See Table 99, Appendix B, for states included.
ᵃ None enrolled.

The higher expenditures for agriculture in rural counties seem significant. Likewise, training in home economics seems more expensive in rural counties. These levels of expenditures no doubt represent high degrees of educational effort for rural counties. Urban counties seemed to have concentrated more on improving vocational training in distributive occupations and trades and industries; the most improvement was made and higher quality was achieved, if expenditure is indicative of quality, in counties with larger cities.

It may be observed that, with the exception of the expenditures for distributive occupations, the gain from 1940 to 1952 in cost was usually about equal to or slightly in excess of the total amount expended per pupil in 1940. In each case the expenditures seem high when compared to expenditures per pupil for total instruction.

Per pupil expenditures for the four fields of vocational education are analyzed by races in Table 86. Beginning with the regional figures, the cost of Negro vocational education in 1940 was only slightly more than half the cost of vocational education for white students in the three fields for which comparisons were possible. During the next twelve years, increases followed an uneven pattern, total gains favoring Negroes in two out of three instances. Costs were more nearly equalized during these years; agriculture costs reached $85.46 for white students and $65.24 for Negro students; costs of distributive education for Negroes at the end of the period exceeded costs for white students by approximately $46.00 per pupil; and trades and industries costs were also greater for Negroes by about $5.00 per pupil. Costs of vocational education were, therefore, more nearly equalized between races than were total instructional costs.

The same kind of analysis is presented for rural, rural-urban, and metropolitan counties. The general pattern of variations found on the regional level prevails in each of these classifications. It should be noted that cost increases during the twelve years were much more nearly equal than actual costs at either the beginning or the end of the period. A more meaningful comparison is the percentage ratio of expenditures per Negro pupil to expenditures per white pupil (Chart 16).

The regional figures show that expenditures for agriculture, home economics, and trades and industries increased as a percentage of white per pupil expenditures from 1940 to 1952. For trades and industries and distributive occupations expenditures in 1952 for Negro pupils exceeded the expenditures for white pupils. Looking further at the comparisons by county classification, it will be noted that expenditures for Negro pupils increased as a percentage of expenditures for white pupils from 1940 to 1952. In eight cases where comparisons can be made, the percentage increased, but expenditures per Negro pupil exceeded those per white pupil in 1952 for only trades and industries and distributive occupations in metropolitan counties.

A further analysis of equities in expenditures between races per pupil enrolled in vocational education is presented in Chart 17. On the regional level, all white per pupil expenditures in 1940 exceeded

TABLE 86

VOCATIONAL EDUCATION EXPENDITURES PER WHITE AND NEGRO PUPIL ENROLLED IN VOCATIONAL EDUCATION IN PUBLIC HIGH SCHOOLS OF SOUTHERN STATES

Areas of Vocational Education by Population Classifications	Instructional Expenditures Per Pupil Enrolled						*Change Per Pupil*	
	1939–40		*1949–50*		*1951–52*		*1940–1952*	
	White	*Negro*	*White*	*Negro*	*White*	*Negro*	*White*	*Negro*
State Totals								
Agriculture (7 states)	$ 42.20	$ 27.27	$ 84.91	$ 54.81	$ 85.46	$ 65.24	$ 43.26	$ 37.97
Home Economics (7 states)	18.33	8.21	43.61	29.62	42.08	32.64	23.75	24.43
Trades and Industries (6 states)	22.63	13.31	37.38	42.50	46.75	51.92	24.12	38.61
Distributive Occupations (10 states)	82.24	n.e.ᵃ	113.99	154.05	117.09	163.11	34.85	—
Rural County Sample								
Agriculture (7 states)	51.98	26.34	87.47	55.56	91.69	62.47	39.71	36.13
Home Economics (8 states)	20.68	9.96	48.88	33.01	49.26	39.64	28.58	29.68
Trades and Industries (7 states)	32.10	n.e.	63.92	48.00	83.40	58.90	51.30	—
Distributive Occupations (8 states)	n.e.	n.e.	n.e.	n.e.	82.35	n.e.	—	—
Rural-Urban County Sample								
Agriculture (7 states)	47.30	19.98	97.90	63.17	83.57	38.13	36.27	18.15
Home Economics (8 states)	19.27	8.63	42.90	31.24	44.28	29.92	25.01	21.29
Trades and Industries (7 states)	25.00	10.59	57.04	50.72	49.79	48.56	24.79	37.97
Distributive Occupations (8 states)	105.55	n.e.	109.79	n.e.	107.77	n.e.	2.22	—
Metropolitan Counties								
Agriculture (7 states)	48.63	27.85	78.85	48.81	82.58	59.05	33.95	31.20
Home Economics (8 states)	15.00	6.22	34.20	29.50	37.74	34.76	22.74	28.54
Trades and Industries (7 states)	20.41	14.58	37.72	41.02	50.11	54.07	29.70	39.49
Distributive Occupations (8 states)	78.30	n.e.	119.73	112.05	118.09	125.96	39.79	—

* See Table 99, Appendix B, for states included.
ᵃ None enrolled.

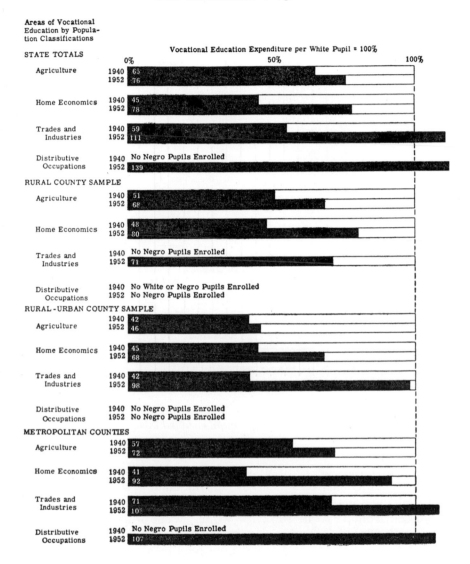

Areas of Vocational Education by Population Classifications

Vocational Education Expenditure per White Pupil = 100%

STATE TOTALS

Agriculture — 1940: 65, 1952: 76

Home Economics — 1940: 45, 1952: 78

Trades and Industries — 1940: 59, 1952: 111

Distributive Occupations — 1940: No Negro Pupils Enrolled, 1952: 139

RURAL COUNTY SAMPLE

Agriculture — 1940: 51, 1952: 68

Home Economics — 1940: 48, 1952: 80

Trades and Industries — 1940: No Negro Pupils Enrolled, 1952: 71

Distributive Occupations — 1940: No White or Negro Pupils Enrolled, 1952: No Negro Pupils Enrolled

RURAL-URBAN COUNTY SAMPLE

Agriculture — 1940: 42, 1952: 46

Home Economics — 1940: 45, 1952: 68

Trades and Industries — 1940: 42, 1952: 98

Distributive Occupations — 1940: No Negro Pupils Enrolled, 1952: No Negro Pupils Enrolled

METROPOLITAN COUNTIES

Agriculture — 1940: 57, 1952: 72

Home Economics — 1940: 41, 1952: 92

Trades and Industries — 1940: 71, 1952: 10?

Distributive Occupations — 1940: No Negro Pupils Enrolled, 1952: 107

CHART 16. *Percentage ratio of the expenditure per Negro to that per white pupil enrolled in vocational education.*

those of Negro pupils. Regional statistics reveal that only the white-over-Negro gap that existed in expenditures for agriculture in 1940 was increased by 1952, while a Negro-over-white difference was created in trades and industries and distribute occupations.

Looking next at the county classifications, it may be seen that each

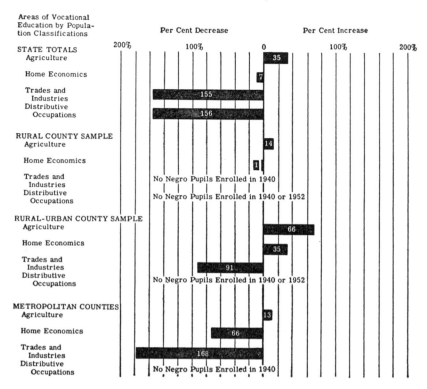

CHART 17. *Changes from 1940 to 1952 in the actual white-over-Negro difference between expenditures per pupil enrolled in vocational education.*

white expenditure in 1940 exceeded that of expenditure per Negro pupil in each county classification. Of the eight possible comparisons in the changes in the amount of actual difference, four differences were increased from 1940 to 1952 for whites, while four decreased. The gap was widened in agriculture in all three types of counties. The gap was narrowed for trades and industries in urban and rural-urban counties, being completely erased and converted into a Negro-over-white gap in metropolitan counties.

SCHOOL LUNCH SERVICE

Probably no service which has been added to the public school enterprise has had such widespread and rapid growth as the lunch program. It is national in scope and is designed to reach all children in the public schools.

School lunches were first conceived as a means of providing nutritious meals for masses of undernourished children, first prominent in America's urban industrial society, but later more widespread in the paradoxical depression period of starvation and plenty. It was during this latter era that the school lunch program was recognized as a potential consumer of surplus foods and a means of supporting food prices. The great influx of mothers into industry during World War II provided additional impetus to the school lunch movement. Perhaps even more fundamental in the long run than the above causes was the effort to create school programs exemplifying good daily living practices, thus making mealtime at school a part of the essential training of the child.

The purpose of this section is to describe the lunch program as a part of the school program, to trace its growth and development, and to analyze recent trends of the service in the Southern region.

The function of the school lunch program has not been the subject of extensive attention in professional literature. One authoritative statement of purposes was expressed as follows:

The principal educational outcomes to be sought through the school lunch include:

1. Outcomes affecting the pupil's nutrition —
   a. Establishment of good habits of food selection.
   b. Understanding the importance of storing, handling, and preparing food in such a way as to protect its nutritive values and safeguard it against contamination.
   c. Cooperation of parents in helping pupils to apply what they have learned about food.
2. Outcomes related to citizenship —
   a. Appreciation of and responsibility for making the lunch at school a social situation.
   b. An increasing ability to share in the direction and the work of operating the lunchroom.
   c. A sense of responsibility for the lunchroom.
   d. A realization that good food practices contribute to family and community health and well-being.[18]

School feeding had its beginning in the countries of the Old World, but the idea was not adopted in the United States until the closing

---

[18] *The School Lunch: Its Educational Contribution*, Nutrition Education Series, Pamphlet No. 6 of the U. S. Office of Education (Washington: Government Printing Office, 1954), p. vi.

frontier checked the spread of population, and the shift from an agrarian to an urbanized industrial society brought about home situations which did not provide adequate breakfast for children and often no noon meal at all. As had been true in Europe, lunch programs were first undertaken as charitable projects for the underprivileged.

Public awakening to the need for school feeding came early in the twentieth century. In 1904 Robert Hunter attacked the system which permitted wealth to accumulate in the hands of a few while other men fell heir to the physical and moral ruin caused by extreme poverty; he pointed out that poverty could no longer be attributed purely to individual causes. He vividly described conditions in industrial New York and their social implications, pointing out that thousands of children arrived daily at school hungry, and added: "These problems of child life are school problems. . . . Are we to have the school ignore this larger work of education and remain a sort of dispensary of learning—an inflexible missionary of the three R's?"[19]

Concern aroused over these conditions was evident in many lunch programs which sprang up to replace outright charitable operations. Progress was such that by 1918 the Bureau of Municipal Research in New York revealed that 76 per cent of 86 cities of 50,000 population or more provided lunches in high school that year. Only 25 per cent of the same cities, however, provided lunches in elementary schools. In either case, the service was looked upon as a convenient accessory to the school system and not a means of improving nutrition. During the decade beginning with 1920 the Federal government showed much interest in the school lunch movement. The Bureau of Human Nutrition and Home Economics and the extension service of the Department of Agriculture worked with land grant colleges to extend the movement to rural areas. Later, the danger of malnutrition among school children during the Great Depression became a matter of national concern. Partial solution of this problem was linked to the solution of another problem of great concern—the utilization of surplus farm products.

Provision was made in 1933 for the establishment of the Federal Surplus Relief Corporation, which was changed in name to the Federal Surplus Commodities Corporation in 1935. Meanwhile, the Department of Agriculture had initiated a program of direct purchase and distribution of surplus crops, some of which were distributed through state welfare agencies in the school lunch program. This corporation worked very closely with various Federal agencies concerned with

19 Robert Hunter, *Poverty* (New York: Grosset & Dunlap, 1904), p. 209.

the problem of improving the economy of the country. Although numerous changes have been made in the laws and provisions concerning the Federal subsidy to the school lunch program and the distribution of surplus commodities, the principle has remained intact. Thus, the Federal government has had a very important hand in the rapid expansion of school lunch programs. The period from 1943 through 1952 saw the number in the nation eating in Federally aided lunch programs more than doubled. While the number participating in lunch programs was increasing, the quality of meals served was also improving.[20] Total expenditures for school lunches in the United States were about 415 million dollars in 1952. The Federal government provided approximately ninety-five million dollars of this amount, a slight increase over Federal support in 1947. State and local sources supplied the remaining 320 million dollars, a sum amounting to about three times their support in 1947.

The school lunch program and provisions for supporting it are of particular importance to the Southern region because of the prevalence of conditions the program is designed to ameliorate. Despite the fact that the South was an agrarian region, it long failed to produce sufficient food for its own uses, and the dietary deficiencies of its people have been widely publicized. The low economic level of the Negro has intensified unfavorable conditions. No section of the country could expect to profit more from a program of school feeding than the South.

Policies governing apportionment of Federal funds favor the Southern states, since the allocation of funds is on the basis of need for assistance as indicated by per capita income in the states. Of the thirteen states in the United States with the lowest per capita income, eleven are in the South. Of the two remaining Southern states, Florida is ranked fourteenth and Texas seventeenth. The South also has more children per thousand population of the total population than the average for the nation. Eight of the thirteen states with the largest number of children ages 5-17 per thousand of the total population are in the South. A widely quoted description of the South's educational problem is this: The Southern states have approximately one-third of the nation's children, one-eighth of the nation's tax paying ability, and one-sixth of the nation's school income.[21]

A provision of the basic law creating the Federal support plan stated:

---

[20] See Appendix B for further information on the expansion of the lunch program.

[21] *Improving Education in the Southern States: School Lunch Policies and Standards,* A Handbook of the Committee on School Lunch Programs, edited by Edgar L. Morphet (Tallahassee, Florida: Southern States Work-Conference on Educational Problems, 1947), Front Cover.

If a State maintains separate schools for minority and for majority races, no funds made available pursuant to this Act shall be paid or distributed to it unless a just and equitable distribution is made within the State, for the benefit of such minority races, of funds paid to it under this Act.[22]

Various organizational plans for administering school lunch programs are in use in the Southern states. Oklahoma is the only state in the region which maintains a school lunch program as a separate division under the State Board of Education. Other procedures followed by the Southern states are: Georgia and Texas maintain separate divisions under the chief state school officer; Arkansas, Kentucky, Louisiana, North Carolina, and Virginia have made the program a subdivision under the Division of Vocational Education; Alabama, Florida, and Mississippi maintain the program as a subdivision under the Division of Instruction; South Carolina includes the program under the Division of School Administration; in Tennessee it is a subdivision of the Division of Health.

Average daily participation in school lunch programs in the Southern region. For purposes of this inquiry, average daily participation is defined as the average number of children eating daily in school lunchrooms per thousand pupils in average daily attendance. Hereafter, the abbreviation ADP will denote average daily participation.

Table 87 is a summary of statistics for state totals and the county classifications, covering the school years ending in 1950 and 1952. It will be noted that in both years the highest rate of participation was in rural-urban counties, with metropolitan counties ranking second and rural counties last.

Although only one school year elapsed between the dates, a very substantial increase in each population classification occurred. As yet, 50 per cent participation has not been achieved in any county classification.

An analysis of the same statistics in terms of the participation rate by white and Negro pupils is shown in Table 88. Ten states maintaining separate records for white and Negro pupils reported that 478 white pupils and 226 Negro pupils per thousand in ADA were eating daily in Federally aided lunchrooms in 1950. During the next two years there was an increase of forty-eight white pupils to two Negro pupils; thus the gap was widened. These figures represent a 10 per cent increase in the number of white pupils and only 1 per cent increase of Negro pupils.

---

[22] *United States Statutes at Large,* LX, Part I — Public Laws Reorganization Plans (Washington: Government Printing Office, 1947), pp. 233–234.

TABLE 87

AVERAGE DAILY PARTICIPATION IN FEDERALLY AIDED LUNCHROOMS PER THOUSAND
PUPILS IN AVERAGE DAILY ATTENDANCE IN PUBLIC SCHOOLS
OF SOUTHERN STATES *

Population Classification	Average Daily Participation Per Thousand in ADA		Change Per Thousand 1950–1952	
	1949–50	*1951–52*	*Actual*	*Per Cent*
State Totals (12 states)	413	445	32	8
Rural County Sample (12 states)	338	445	57	17
Rural-Urban County Sample (12 states)	398	471	73	18
Metropolitan Counties (12 states)	354	399	45	13

* See Table 99, Appendix B, for states included.

TABLE 88

AVERAGE DAILY PARTICIPATION OF WHITE AND NEGRO PUPILS IN FEDERALLY
AIDED LUNCHROOMS PER THOUSAND PUPILS IN AVERAGE DAILY
ATTENDANCE IN PUBLIC SCHOOLS OF SOUTHERN STATES *

Population Classification	Average Daily Participation Per Thousand in ADA		Change Per Thousand 1950–1952	
	1949–50	*1951–52*	*Actual*	*Per Cent*
State Totals (10 states)				
White	478	526	48	10
Negro	226	228	2	1
Rural County Sample (11 states)				
White	498	566	68	14
Negro	176	208	32	18
Rural-Urban County Sample (11 states)				
White	516	586	70	14
Negro	178	255	77	43
Metropolitan Counties (11 states)				
White	395	451	56	14
Negro	193	224	31	16

* See Table 99, Appendix B, for states included.

A more vivid comparison of ADP for Negro and white pupils is
in terms of the percentage Negro ADP is of white ADP. Chart 18
shows this relationship. It is easily seen that in neither 1950 nor 1952
was the ADP of Negro pupils more than 50 per cent of that for white
pupils The regional percentage for Negro pupils actually decreased
from 47 per cent in 1950 to 43 per cent in 1952. Inspection of the
statistics for county classifications shows that ADP of Negro pupils

measured as a percentage of that for white pupils was smallest in rural counties, higher in rural-urban counties, and highest in metropolitan counties.

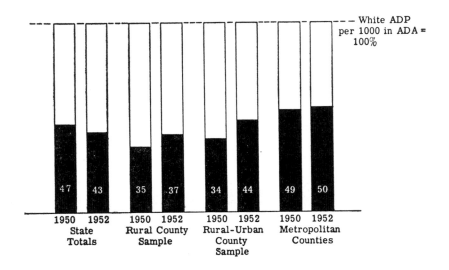

CHART 18. *Percentage ratio of average daily participation of Negro pupils to that of white pupils in Federally aided lunchrooms per thousand pupils in average daily attendance.*

The real differences in ADP between white and Negro pupils computed in terms of numbers of pupils is shown in Chart 19. The 1950 white-over-Negro gap was increased by forty-six pupils by 1952, which created a 20 per cent greater gap. In the county classifications a white-over-Negro difference in 1950 increased in both rural and metropolitan counties, but slightly decreased in rural-urban counties.

Expenditures for school lunch services in the Southern region. Annual expenditures per pupil in average daily participation in Federally aided lunchrooms is reported in Table 89. The $43.37 annual expenditure per pupil in metropolitan counties is substantially higher percentagewise than similar expenditures in the other county classifications and for the region as a whole. Changes during the two years range from a decline of $3.16 per pupil per year in rural counties to an increase of $4.82 in metropolitan counties. Thus, the difference between the two classifications widened.

A similar analysis for white and Negro pupils is shown in Table 90. In every case during both years for which figures are given, expenditures per Negro pupil were quite substantially lower than expenditures

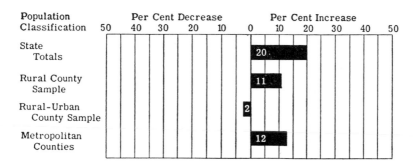

CHART 19.   *Changes from 1950 to 1952 in the actual white-over-Negro difference between the number of white and Negro pupils eating daily in Federally aided school lunchrooms per thousand pupils in average daily attendance.*

TABLE 89

ANNUAL EXPENDITURES PER PUPIL IN AVERAGE DAILY PARTICIPATION IN FEDERALLY
AIDED LUNCHROOMS IN PUBLIC SCHOOLS OF SOUTHERN STATES *

Population Classification	Expenditures Per Pupil in Average Daily Participation 1949–50	1951–52	Change Per Pupil 1950–1952 Actual	Per Cent
State Totals (12 states)	$36.69	$41.72	$5.03	14
Rural County Sample (12 states)	34.29	31.13	−3.16	− 9
Rural-Urban County Sample (12 states)	35.62	40.07	4.45	12
Metropolitan Counties (12 states)	43.37	48.19	4.82	11

* See Table 99, Appendix B, for states included.

per white pupil. Metropolitan counties show the least difference, which was reduced to $6.31 by 1952. Differences in rural counties increased from $15.55 to $17.55. The rural-urban differential also increased. Expenditures for both races were higher in metropolitan counties during both years.

Expenditures per Negro pupil are reported as a percentage of expenditures per white pupil in Chart 20. Little variation occurred in the two years on a regional basis, the 79 per cent figure in 1950 reaching 80 per cent in 1952. More significant changes in the percentage relationships occurred within the county classifications.

A further measure of the degree of equity of expenditures between

TABLE 90

ANNUAL EXPENDITURES PER WHITE AND NEGRO PUPIL IN AVERAGE DAILY
PARTICIPATION IN FEDERALLY AIDED LUNCHROOMS IN PUBLIC SCHOOLS
OF SOUTHERN STATES *

Population Classification	Change Per Pupil 1950–1952		Expenditures Per Pupil in Average Daily Participation	
	Actual	Per Cent	1949–50	1951–52
State Totals (9 states)				
White	$38.65	$42.96	$4.31	11
Negro	30.59	34.57	3.98	13
Rural County Sample (10 states)				
White	35.69	34.66	−1.03	− 3
Negro	20.14	17.11	−3.03	−15
Rural-Urban County Sample (10 states)				
White	39.63	42.90	3.27	8
Negro	26.99	25.14	−1.85	− 7
Metropolitan Counties (10 states)				
White	45.71	48.91	3.20	7
Negro	38.37	42.60	4.23	11

* See Table 99, Appendix B, for states included.

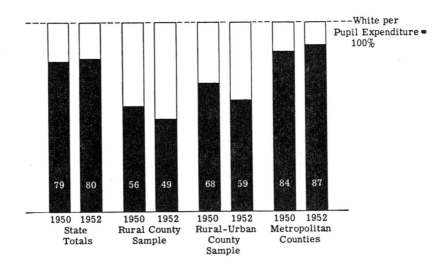

CHART 20. *Percentage ratio of expenditures per Negro to those per white pupil in average daily participation in Federally aided lunchroom.*

the races is shown in Chart 21. This Chart shows that the actual white-over-Negro difference in the states increased slightly from 1950 through

1952. The actual difference increased by 33 cents, or 4 per cent. The chart also shows that the actual difference increased in rural and rural-urban counties, while it decreased in metropolitan counties.

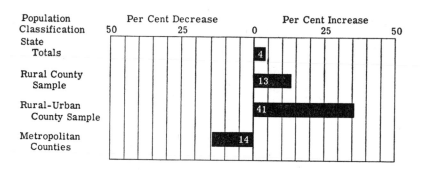

CHART 21. *Changes from 1950 to 1952 in the actual white-over-Negro difference between the expenditure for school lunches per white and per Negro pupil eating in Federally aided school lunchrooms.*

The number of Federally aided lunchrooms per hundred schools. In twelve Southern states there were on the average 38.5 schools per hundred with lunch programs in 1950. By 1952 the number had increased to 44.3 per hundred, a 15 per cent gain (Table 91). Examination of the figures by county classifications shows some interesting variations. Rural schools had the fewest lunchrooms, with rural-urban second, and metropolitan highest. Almost twenty more metropolitan schools per hundred had lunchrooms than rural schools per hundred.

TABLE 91

NUMBER OF SCHOOLS WITH FEDERALLY AIDED LUNCHROOMS PER HUNDRED PUBLIC SCHOOLS IN SOUTHERN STATES *

Population Classification	Number of Lunchrooms Per Hundred Schools		Change Per Hundred 1950–1952	
	1949–50	*1951–52*	*Actual*	*Per Cent*
State Totals (12 states)	38.5	44.3	5.8	15
Rural County Sample (12 states)	33.7	36.8	3.1	9
Rural-Urban County Sample (12 states)	37.5	44.7	7.2	19
Metropolitan Counties (12 states)	53.4	59.3	5.9	11

* See Table 99, Appendix B, for states included.

Table 92 is devoted to a comparison of the number of Federally aided lunch programs per hundred schools for white and Negro pupils. Reports from 11 states in 1950 show that 48.6 schools for white pupils out of each hundred had lunch programs, while only 23.1 out of a hundred schools for Negro pupils had them. By 1952 an increase of seven per hundred had raised the number of schools for white pupils with lunch programs to 56.6, while the program for Negro pupils stood at 25.6, a gain of only 2.5.

Less than half as many Negro schools as white schools per hundred had lunchrooms in rural counties in both 1950 and 1952, with the gap being greater in the latter year. A similar pattern prevails in rural-urban counties, although the number of lunchrooms was considerably larger in 1952 for white schools, and only slightly larger for Negro schools. The gain in white schools for the two years was almost three times that for Negro schools. In metropolitan counties, Negro lunchrooms per hundred were little more than half the number in white schools, with the differential becoming less during the latter year.

TABLE 92

NUMBER OF WHITE AND NEGRO SCHOOLS WITH FEDERALLY AIDED LUNCHROOMS
PER HUNDRED PUBLIC SCHOOLS IN SOUTHERN STATES *

Population Classification	Number of Lunchrooms Per Hundred Schools		Change Per Hundred 1950–1952	
	1949–50	*1951–52*	*Actual*	*Per Cent*
State Totals (11 states)				
White	48.6	56.6	7.0	14
Negro	23.1	25.6	2.5	11
Rural County Sample (12 states)				
White	45.6	50.6	5.0	11
Negro	20.1	20.2	0.1	1
Rural-Urban County Sample (12 states)				
White	52.3	62.6	10.3	20
Negro	20.5	24.2	3.7	18
Metropolitan Counties (12 states)				
White	63.6	69.0	5.4	8
Negro	35.4	40.9	5.5	16

* See Table 99, Appendix B, for states included.

Chart 22 presents a more meaningful comparison of these differences. The number of schools for Negro pupils with lunch programs out of each hundred schools is presented as a percentage of the number of schools for white pupils out of each hundred with lunch programs. It may be noted that the number of schools for Negro pupils with lunch programs as a percentage of those found in white schools decreased from 48 to 46 from 1950 through 1952. Using the same measurement, rural counties increased the inequality, rural-urban counties remained the same, and metropolitan counties increased the schools for Negro pupils with lunch programs by 3 per cent of the number of white schools with such programs.

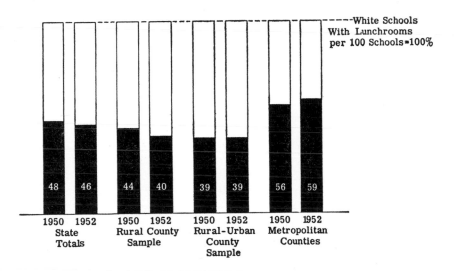

CHART 22. *Percentage ratio of Negro schools with Federally aided lunchrooms per hundred schools to white schools with Federally aided lunchrooms per hundred schools.*

A final analysis of the inequality between the two races is presented in Chart 23. Based on the reports from eleven states, the white-over-Negro difference that existed in 1950 was increased by almost five schools per hundred in the two following years, or by about 18 per cent of the actual difference that existed in 1950. Rural and rural-urban counties likewise increased the white-over-Negro gap, while the metropolitan difference remained about the same.

SUMMARY

Determining educational adequacy must depend ultimately upon the objectives to be sought through education, which are in turn deeply rooted in the values which give direction to a society. Means provided for achieving goals, such as physical facilities, curricula, personnel, supplies, etc., determine the extent to which objectives can be

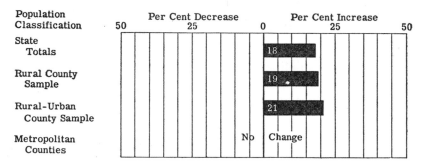

Population Classification	Per Cent Decrease		Per Cent Increase	
	50 25	0	25	50
State Totals			18	
Rural County Sample			19	
Rural-Urban County Sample			21	
Metropolitan Counties		No Change		

CHART 23. *Changes from 1950 to 1952 in the actual white-over-Negro difference between the numbers of Federally aided school lunchrooms per hundred white and of those per hundred Negro schools.*

attained. In a society which gives allegiance to self-improvement, objectives undergo constant revision, thus requiring new interpretations in terms of curricula facilities, teaching abilities, etc.

Educational development in the region has by no means been static; rather it has improved and expanded in keeping with the general development of the region. Levels of teacher training are rising, administration and supervision are taking on higher levels of leadership qualities, constant efforts to improve instruction in the schools through various in-service education programs, extensive use of free textbooks and other instructional materials, and the addition of new services, such as guidance, health, and special education, are evidences of the dynamic quality of education.

Adequacy, as defined by the proportion of those of public school age who are in attendance, has steadily improved. The average number of years spent in school has increased. This means, assuming that all educable children should finish high school, that great progress has been made toward this goal. The task that remains to be done is enormous, however, for the number who actually finish high school is only a small percentage of those who enroll in the first grade. Negroes lag behind whites in this measure of adequacy as they do in others, but the numbers of Negroes who graduate from high school are rapidly increasing.

Intensive studies of the status and trends in three parts of the school program — library service, vocational education, and school lunch service — indicate that educational experiences are improving and are being extended to more and more pupils for longer periods of time. It appears that the extensiveness and quality of services vary among counties with different population characteristics, with urban counties generally exceeding rural counties in quantities of the services available and the amount of support for them, and metropolitan counties usually making greater and greater improvements in services.

Services which determine the quality of educational adequacy are usually provided in greater quantities and at greater cost for white pupils than for Negro pupils; for the period covered in this inquiry, increases in services and expenditures were usually greater for white pupils than for Negro pupils. In some cases the margin in favor of white schools was substantial.

The amounts of service and the increases in the amounts of service during the twelve-year period which was covered in this investigation were more nearly equal for white pupils in rural and metropolitan counties than were amounts and increases of similar services for Negroes in rural and metropolitan counties.

Increases in expenditures for the three services were consistent and occurred in all county classifications. These increases widened the gap between rural and metropolitan counties in terms of both percentages and dollar differences. Differences between the races were also widened but to a lesser extent.

The Issues Redefined—
Looking Ahead

TEN

Taking Stock

In the preceding chapters the public school systems of the South have been described and analyzed as a part of the very complex picture of a region in transition. Attention has been given to the great creative forces which are characteristic of American society in order to suggest that the currents of change in the South and the nation are in many respects expressions of those forces and a product of their impact. A sense of historical perspective has been sought in which the segregation issue can be viewed in its proper relationship to other phases of cultural change, many if not all of which have a long history of development for they appear to be the result of forces set in motion generations ago, forces which are perhaps more active in present society than they have been during any other period of history.

In seeking to establish the present status of education in the region for both whites and Negroes, it was necessary to collect, analyze, and interpret the same kinds of data on the schools of each race. These procedures made possible comparisons which revealed the character and extent of existing differences in schools according to race. On occasion, comparisons were made between Southern and national averages. These undertakings required exhaustive factual analyses of those areas of public education that are of major concern in any general appraisal of school systems.

It was deemed important to make another kind of comparison. Bench marks were established by ascertaining the status of the schools with respect to the various factors studied at three different periods, 1940, 1950, and 1952. This made it possible to identify and measure current trends in educational change. In many cases trends thus identified and measured were traced back to the beginning of the twentieth century. Thus, not only could the directions of change be ascertained but also its nature and extent. According to the thesis subscribed to earlier in this inquiry to the effect that the present often reveals the characteristics of the future, the trends identified may be projected into the future as one basis of planning. On this basis the educational problems of the region may be defined more clearly and goals for the near future may be established with greater confidence.

A substantial body of data on the public schools of the region has been presented. These data have been handled so that their relevance to the segregation issue is obvious, but a determined effort has been made to view education in a comprehensive sense; the race problem, therefore, was considered in proper perspective. The educational scene has at various points been related to certain cultural patterns of the region. Since the test of investigations of this type lies in the application of the findings to the solution of the problems with which they deal, the task at this point is to indicate the guides to such an application by delineating the nature and scope of the problems.

What generalizations are warranted from the previous chapters which should form the basis for intelligent action? What great unfinished tasks lie ahead in public education in the region? What important trends are underway which should be taken into account? What is the setting for continued progress in education? These are among the questions to which this chapter is addressed. The first concern is with the redefinition of the educational problems of the region in the light of the segregation and other issues. This is followed by a brief discussion of some of the factors which may determine the nature of progress in the future.

TASKS WHICH LIE AHEAD

In defining a problem or unfinished task in education it is necessary to refer again to the value commitments which are accepted by American society, since problems exist only in relation to goals. The American commitment to education as a means for achieving a better life continues. A quality of schooling is, therefore, demanded which is adequate to this high purpose. The value ascribed to the individual makes it mandatory that Americans hold to the goal of equal educational opportunity for all. Belief in the capacity of an individual to forge his own destiny compels society to make available to him the tools with which to realize this achievement. It is in the light of all these considerations that the great unfinished tasks in education must be defined. Three major phases of the problem of developing a better educated citizenry merit careful examination.

EQUALIZING THE SCOPE AND QUALITY OF EDUCATIONAL PROGRAMS. The magnitude of the problem of equalizing educational programs is far greater than is realized by many persons otherwise well informed about school needs. While the great issue of current concern is how to provide an education for Negroes as good as that which is provided for the whites, another problem of great magnitude is the difference between rural and urban schools. Serious program inequalities also exist among states, among school districts within states, among schools within districts, and among the classrooms within attendance centers.

Negro and white equalization. A pronounced trend in the direction of bringing the quality of Negro schools more nearly in line with that of white schools has been conspicuous in recent years. Perhaps the greatest effort has centered on providing better physical plants for Negro schools. Despite these efforts, in 1952 absolute equalization of school buildings and equipment on a racial basis would have required an additional expenditure of $264 per Negro pupil in average daily attendance, the values of school buildings and equipment per pupil being $454 for whites and $190 for Negroes. In 1940 the figures were $200 and $50, respectively. The gap in per pupil expenditures for instructional purposes remained substantial in 1952, when the figures were $132.38 per white pupil as contrasted to $90.20 per Negro pupil. Twelve years earlier only $16.29 per Negro pupil in average daily attendance was spent annually, while the sum for whites was $41.99.

Differences in teacher load as measured by pupil-teacher ratio were in favor of white teachers except in Kentucky and Oklahoma, states in which the proportion of Negro population is small. On a regional level the Negro teacher averaged 2.7 pupils more than the white teacher, the averages being 28.0 and 25.3, respectively, as contrasted to 31.2 and 26.0 in 1940. In 1952 the number of books per pupil in school libraries for Negroes was 47 per cent as compared to only 24 per cent in 1940, of the number of books per pupil in white school libraries. Efforts toward equalization of libraries are indicated by expenditure figures; 77 per cent as much money was spent per Negro pupil for library books as was spent per white pupil in 1952 as contrasted to 31 per cent in 1940.

In the fields of vocational education in 1952, 76 per cent as much was spent per Negro pupil as per white pupil in agriculture, 78 per cent in home economics, 111 per cent in trades and industries, and 139 per cent in distributive occupations, with enrollments in the latter two fields very low. Participation of Negroes in Federally aided lunchroom programs in 1952 per thousand pupils in average daily attendance was only 43 per cent of that of white students. In the same year, expenditures for lunch services for Negroes averaged only 80 per cent of those for white students. The number of lunchrooms in Negro schools averaged only 46 per cent as many per hundred as for white schools.

It should be emphasized that these differences are on regional levels.

Extreme variations occur within states and among states. Negro schools in metropolitan areas tend to be superior to white schools in rural areas. Differences between white and Negro schools are greatest in rural counties and least in metropolitan counties. The smallest difference in schools of the two races is found in the number of days in the school term. Almost complete equalization has been achieved in this factor. Great strides have been made in equalizing salaries and levels of teacher preparation as measured by years completed in college. It is now commonplace for state salary schedules to make no distinction with respect to race. It will be noted that, in spite of the rapid improvement of Negro schools within recent years, substantial further progress is necessary before equalization can be achieved.

This discussion has been concerned only with differences in white and Negro schools, not with possible methods of eliminating the differences.

Rural and urban equalization. Generally speaking, metropolitan schools have always been superior to rural schools. Despite marked improvement in public education within recent years, some of the differences between rural and urban schools seem to be increasing. School buildings and equipment in metropolitan counties were valued at $546 per pupil in average daily attendance in 1952 as compared to a value of $253 per pupil in rural counties. In 1940, the figures were $218 and $100, respectively. Expenditures per pupil in average daily attendance for instruction amounted to $138.08 per metropolitan pupil and $94.03 per rural pupil. Corresponding figures for 1940 were $46.51 and $26.63, respectively.

Teacher load as determined by the number of pupils in average daily attendance per secondary teacher favored the rural over the metropolitan teacher, the figures being 18.5 and 21.1. The greater prevalence of small schools in rural areas may account for much of this difference. Teachers in metropolitan schools are better trained than those in rural schools; in 1952, 81 per cent had four or more years in college as compared with 62 per cent in rural counties. Sixty-three per cent of all metropolitan teachers and 35 per cent of all rural teachers had four or more years of college training in 1940. The percentage of teachers with less than two years of training in 1952 was approximately twice as great in rural counties as in metropolitan counties. The number of books per pupil in school libraries was virtually the same for the two county classifications. Expenditures per pupil for library books were substantially higher, however, in metropolitan counties. No important differences exist in expenditures per pupil for vocational education.

One of the greatest differences found was in average salaries of metropolitan and rural teachers. In 1952 the metropolitan teacher received an average salary of $3,085, while the rural teacher received only $2,285. Differences in levels of training account for a part of the higher salaries of metropolitan teachers, but higher salary schedules account for the rest. There was little variation in the average length of school terms but what little did exist favored the metropolitan schools. It should not be overlooked that the range of differences within metropolitan school systems is also very considerable. The range among rural school systems is even greater.

Elementary and secondary school equalization. No statistics have been marshaled to validate this point, but available data show that secondary school facilities are more adequate than elementary school facilities as measured by dollar value per pupil in average daily attendance. In 1952 the elementary teacher had an average of 10.8 more pupils than her secondary counterpart, a slightly larger gap than existed in 1940. The average training of secondary teachers continues to exceed that of elementary school teachers; in 1952, 95 per cent of secondary teachers had four or more years of college compared to 75 per cent of elementary teachers. Salaries also favored secondary teachers, the average being $2,932 as compared to an average of $2,585 for elementary teachers, a slightly smaller dollar difference than that of 1940. The higher level of training of secondary teachers explains most of the salary differential.

The gap between elementary and secondary schools as measured by most of these factors has been decreasing within recent years but the differences are still substantial. The length of school term differential has been eliminated. In most cases, salary scale differentials are nonexistent. But the fact remains that a considerable task lies ahead in equalizing programs in secondary and elementary schools. For one thing, educational authorities generally agree that the best curriculum and teaching practices are found more often in elementary schools than in secondary schools.

Equalization among states. States differ in many important ways which affect their school programs. As a consequence, some states have much better school systems than others. This is difficult to justify in terms of the value commitments of the American people. Some variations among state school systems in 1952 are indicated by the figures which follow. In seven Southern states the value of buildings and equipment per pupil in average daily attendance varied from $278 to $480. Expenditures per pupil in average daily attendance for instruction ranged from $61.89 to $160.85. The range of expenditures per pupil in average daily attendance for current expense other than instruction was from $26.24 to $85.35.

Teacher load ranged from 24.4 to 29.4 pupils, a significant difference. Variations in teacher training were also substantial, ranging from an average of 2.9 to an average of 4.2 years of college training. The lowest state average for teachers' salaries was $1,587 as compared to $3,186 for the highest state average. Inequalities among the states are narrowing somewhat, but it seems virtually impossible under present conditions to equalize educational opportunity among the states. This is one of the arguments commonly used in favor of a program of financial support for the public schools by the Federal government.

Equalization among school districts within states. Financial support from the state level through foundation programs has done much to reduce inequalities among school districts within states. The task of eliminating remaining differences which are not defensible is formidable. Conclusions drawn from the data upon which this inquiry is based indicate quite clearly that in addition to the extreme differences between rural and urban schools already pointed out, school systems within these classifications vary in important degrees in every state in the region. Differences are reflected in school facilities, the level of teacher training, pupil-teacher ratio, salaries paid teachers, and in other important respects. Factors accounting for the differences are uneven distribution of wealth, cost of other governmental services, varying levels of efficiency in public administration, and the differences among communities in the interest people have in good schools.

Equalization among school attendance areas within school districts. No particular effort was made in the study to investigate this phase of educational opportunity. Some observations are possible, however, which may be pertinent. It is on the level of attendance areas that questions of equalization have their real focus. It has been found that expenditures per pupil in different schools within a district sometimes vary as much as $3 spent in one school for each dollar spent in another. Differences in school plants are frequently extensive, also. The better trained teachers tend to concentrate in better socio-economic communities, even though salaries may be no higher than they are in other schools of the district. Interest in schools varies from community to community, which is an important factor in the effectiveness of the local school.

Equalization within attendance areas. The ultimate test of whether different educational programs are of equivalent quality lies in the actual instruction received by children in the various grades of a school. One of the chief differences here, as at other levels, is in the competence of the individual teacher. Relatively equal facilities may be provided by a school but without all groups of children in the school profiting equally; the greatest problem of all is to provide a teacher for each group of the competence desired for every child. Until this can be done there will be no real equalization of educational opportunity.

EXTENDING THE AVAILABILITY OF EDUCATION. A comparison of four statistics tells a remarkable story of how educational opportunity has been extended to larger and larger proportions of the school-age population during the twentieth century. Between 1900 and 1940 there was a 41 per cent increase in school population, an 86.7 per cent increase in school enrollment, a 134.7 per cent gain in school attendance, and a gain of 163.6 per cent in the number of teachers. Both school-age population and enrollment figures were relatively stable during the next ten years, with each showing a slight decline. Attendance, however, increased slightly. Since 1950 school-age population, enrollment, and attendance have all been increasing at a rapidly accelerating pace.

Two major considerations are involved in the problem of making educational opportunities available to all eligible children and youth. The first has to do with the total school population to be educated, and the second is concerned with the number of years it is profitable for each pupil to remain in school.

School-age population. The continuation of high birth rate trends, which began immediately after World War II, can only mean a heavy increase in the educational load as reflected by enrollment and attendance statistics. According to conservative estimates, there will be a 28.3 per cent increase in the number of children of school age in the region in 1960 over the figure in 1952. If present trends in school enrollment are continued this will mean an increase of 23.3 per cent in the number of pupils on school rolls. Current attendance trends, if maintained, will result in an increase of 25.2 per cent pupils in average daily attendance by 1960. This enormous increase in the number of children to be educated has no parallel in the nation's history. Table 93 shows the projected school population, enrollment, and attendance for 1960 by races, states, and the region.

The additional financial outlay required to educate these children at levels of present quality is staggering. To maintain the present pupil-teacher ratio will require 69,000 additional teachers by 1960. Based on costs of instruction in 1950, an increase of $183,000,000 in the annual budget will be needed for instruction alone. Should present trends in costs continue until 1960, the cost of instruction will increase to $351,000,000. A further substantial cost item will be to provide the necessary classrooms in which to house and teach the additional children. Use of the common measure of thirty pupils

TABLE 93

School-Age Population (6-17 Years), Public School Enrollment (Grades 1-12), and Public School Average Daily Attendance (Grades 1-12) for 1950 and 1960 (Projected) by Races in the Southern States

State and Race *	School-Age Population			Enrollment			Attendance		
	Number 1950 (Add 000)	Projected 1960 (Add 000)	% Change 1950 to 1960	Number 1950 (Add 000)	Projected 1960 (Add 000)	% Change 1950 to 1960	Number 1950 (Add 000)	Projected 1960 (Add 000)	% Change 1950 to 1960
Alabama									
White	462	544	17.5	444	486	9.4	388	433	11.5
Negro	254	293	15.7	243	273	12.5	207	240	16.3
Total	716	837	16.9	687	759	10.5	595	673	13.2
Arkansas									
White	335	347	3.6	322	315	− 2.3	272	271	− 0.3
Negro	106	113	7.0	103	107	4.1	83	90	7.9
Total	441	460	4.4	425	422	− 0.7	355	361	1.6
Florida									
White	366	674	84.1	358	620	73.3	308	537	74.4
Negro	124	206	66.0	118	198	66.9	105	175	66.8
Total	490	880	79.5	476	818	71.7	413	712	72.5
Georgia									
White	497	654	31.5	463	577	24.7	413	520	25.7
Negro	269	312	16.0	251	284	13.1	206	249	20.9
Total	766	966	26.1	714	861	20.6	619	769	24.1
Kentucky									
White	615	693	12.8	527	581	10.2	449	450	11.3
Negro	39	50	28.9	37	48	32.3	32	42	33.5
Total	654	743	13.8	564	629	11.6	481	542	12.8

TABLE 93 (Continued)

State and Race *	School-Age Population			Enrollment			Attendance		
	Number 1950 (Add 000)	Projected 1960 (Add 000)	% Change 1950 to 1960	Number 1950 (Add 000)	Projected 1960 (Add 000)	% Change 1950 to 1960	Number 1950 (Add 000)	Projected 1960 (Add 000)	% Change 1950 to 1960
Louisiana									
White	363	505	39.1	296	403	36.2	263	358	36.1
Negro	217	283	30.7	182	259	41.9	157	225	43.1
Total	580	788	36.0	478	662	38.4	420	583	38.7
Mississippi									
White	259	295	13.8	269	284	5.5	246	261	6.0
Negro	267	296	11.0	265	271	2.4	226	236	4.6
Total	526	591	12.4	534	555	4.0	472	497	5.3
North Carolina									
White	654	805	23.1	625	737	17.9	565	667	18.1
Negro	286	351	22.6	269	327	21.8	233	291	24.9
Total	940	1,156	22.9	894	1,064	19.0	798	958	20.1
Oklahoma									
White	417	429	3.0	462	453	− 1.9	371	365	− 1.7
Negro	48	48	0.02	38	39	4.0	31	34	10.2
Total	465	477	2.7	500	492	− 1.5	402	399	− 0.8
South Carolina									
White	285	366	28.4	272	330	21.1	235	287	21.9
Negro	239	265	10.6	222	248	11.6	178	208	16.7
Total	524	631	20.3	494	578	16.8	413	495	19.7
Tennessee									
White	592	716	20.8	553	640	15.8	489	570	16.5
Negro	112	150	33.4	107	139	29.8	94	124	31.0
Total	704	866	22.8	660	779	18.0	583	694	18.9

TABLE 93 (Continued)

State and Race *	School-Age Population			Enrollment			Attendance		
	Number 1950 (Add 000)	Projected 1960 (Add 000)	% Change 1950 to 1960	Number 1950 (Add 000)	Projected 1960 (Add 000)	% Change 1950 to 1960	Number 1950 (Add 000)	Projected 1960 (Add 000)	% Change 1950 to 1960
Texas									
White	1,325	1,951	47.2	1,149	1,650	43.6	983	1,443	46.8
Negro	213	273	27.9	201	245	21.7	169	211	24.9
Total	1,538	2,224	44.5	1,350	1,895	40.3	1,152	1,654	43.6
Virginia									
White	496	716	44.3	446	615	37.9	399	553	38.7
Negro	171	225	31.2	156	200	27.8	138	178	29.1
Total	667	941	40.9	602	815	25.3	537	731	36.2
TOTAL									
White	6,667	8,694	30.4	6,185	7,690	24.3	5,381	6,763	25.7
Negro	2,346	2,865	22.2	2,191	2,637	20.4	1,860	2,304	23.9
Total	9,013	11,559	28.3	8,376	10,327	23.3	7,241	9,067	25.2

*School-age population data listed for Negroes include all persons enumerated as nonwhite by the U.S. Bureau of the Census.

enrolled per classroom means that 65,000 additional classrooms will be needed by 1960. Reliable estimates placed the shortage of adequate classrooms at 100,000 in 1950. To provide total school facilities for 165,000 classroom units at estimated current cost would require a capital outlay of $4,465,000,000 by 1960.

Statistics for the region, while helpful in understanding the magnitude of the increasing problem of extending opportunities for education to the school-age population, can be of only limited value to the actual planning necessary to meet this responsibility until the statistics have been analyzed further. The provision of educational opportunity cannot be achieved until the distribution of the population which is to be educated has been taken into proper account. Three trends are underway which have an important bearing on this problem. They are the declining rural population, the phenomenal urbanization of the region, and the continued out-migration of Negroes.

During the 1940-50 census decade, 714 counties in the region lost in total population, while 592 counties gained in total population. The trend toward more and larger metropolitan centers is continuing at an undiminished rate. These conditions mean that metropolitan counties are faced with rapidly increasing school populations which will require heavy capital outlay and the addition of new teaching personnel, while in many counties it may be difficult to make full use of existing facilities and to retain the needed teaching force.

Present trends in population migration have a special meaning when considered in the light of the segregation issue. The proportion of Negroes in the total population of the region continues to decrease as the out-migration trend remains at its recent high level. This obviously lessens to some degree the problem of carrying out the Supreme Court decision on school segregation. In this connection, it is important to examine the realignment of Negro population within the region.

The Negro is rapidly becoming an urban citizen as he continues to leave the farm to seek more remunerative employment in metropolitan centers. The patterns of Negro housing usually are at opposite extremes in rural and metropolitan areas. In agricultural areas Negro housing tends to be dispersed, while in the cities it is usually concentrated in sections which are inhabited almost exclusively by Negroes. Where the latter situation prevails, school districting powers are likely to be used in an effort to continue all-Negro schools. In such circumstances, it may be expected that a more intensive effort than has been made to date will be centered upon providing educational opportunities in the Negro schools which are in every respect as good as those provided white children.

Such determined effort will also be necessary in order to extend available educational opportunities to all who should be in school. Although trends in enrollment and attendance are rapidly reaching the point at which no further improvements may be expected for either race, the tremendous growth in school population which began after World War II imposes heavier burdens on public finance than have ever been imposed by schools in the history of the nation.

INCREASING THE AVERAGE NUMBER OF YEARS PER PUPIL SPENT IN PUBLIC SCHOOLS. Another really formidable unfinished task of educational responsibility in the region is the extension of available educational opportunities vertically to the larger eligible proportion of school-age population. If it is assumed that the vast majority of children can attend school for twelve years with profit, a monumental task is ahead in achieving this goal.

Data for this inquiry did not make possible an accurate estimate of the additional resources which would be necessary if all children were graduated from high school who were able to profit from a high school education. Some indication of the size of this task may be surmised, however, from the fact that available retention studies show that less than one-fifth of those who enter the first grade in school remain long enough to finish high school. The median grade achievement of persons 25 years of age and above in 1950 in the Southern region, as defined by the Bureau of the Census, was 8.6. Should the achievement level be pushed up to completion of the twelfth grade, the necessary additional personnel and facilities would comprise a very substantial increase over those which are now available.

In view of the fact that the present increases in school enrollment are largely in the six lower grades, the problems of expanding secondary education take on added meaning. Although Negro and white enrollment and attendance no longer seem to vary to any great degree, the secondary education problem for Negroes is more acute, for only within very recent years has the number of Negro students in high school been very substantial. Even in 1952 only 16 per cent of the Negro school enrollment were in the secondary grades as compared to 22 per cent of the white enrollment.

RAISING THE LEVEL OF
EDUCATIONAL QUALITY

Constant concern for the quality of education is to be expected in a democracy. If a society is powered in such a way that it is always in pursuit of goals which serve as ideal, its educational system may be expected to exhibit important characteristics of change. The high premium American society places on education as an instrument for producing social change should compel sensitivity to the quality aspects of school programs. To become complacent about schools is to reject the dynamic nature of the cultural drives and value allegiances which make the nation's citizens ever mindful of the importance of improving the quality of the whole of society.

Serious efforts to improve the quality of education demand that attention be directed at the several factors discussed in the paragraphs which follow.

The problem of adequacy in educational quality. This can be only a relative question for there is no established criterion of perfection toward which we strive. The problems of what constitutes adequacy are philosophical and can be resolved only by the application of measures derived from the values by which men live. It is necessary, therefore, to look closely at what is expected of education and then to determine the adequacy of existing programs in terms of how well they achieve the purposes which have been ascribed to education. This problem is one of constant concern, for what is adequate today may be quite insufficient for the needs of tomorrow.

Evaluating educational outcomes. The only true measure of educational adequacy is the extent to which the person who has been educated reflects in his behavior the objectives which were basic to his school experience. Most evaluative devices in current use are of secondary importance in this kind of measurement. The measurement of subject-matter achievement bears little relationship to the problem of determining the behavioral patterns of a student, and, in the final analysis, these must be the major concern of the school. The satisfactory measurement of attitudes, understandings, motivations, ideals, and the capacity for useful social performance are yet to be attained. Until some degree of success is achieved in such educational measurement, the means are extremely limited for determining whether or not schools achieve the great social and individual objectives that have been set for them in the philosophical realm.

Measuring teacher competence. Much time and effort have been spent in searching for ways to identify and measure in a more objective manner than has heretofore been possible the basic factors of effectiveness in teaching. The success of these efforts has been so limited that teaching competence is still measured largely by the formal education a teacher has had and by his teaching experience. One of the great problems to be solved before education is made a science is the discovery of the critical factors which determine success in teaching and the creation of devices for the measurement of these factors. The apparent intangible nature of competence makes these problems extremely baffling.

Improving teaching methods. Notwithstanding momentous discoveries in the nature of the learning process which have outmoded methods of teaching long held sacred, schools nevertheless continue to reflect in many respects only passing acquaintance with these discoveries. The appalling loss in teacher efficiency due to failure to make use of the best that is now known of teaching method cannot be calculated. Advances in teacher education appear to come very slowly.

Hastening educational change. All studies of the rate of progress in education indicate that change is a very slow and painful process. Paul Mort has said that it takes fifty years for a new invention in education to become diffused throughout the school systems of an area. This indicates that schools are slow indeed to adapt themselves to changing conditions or to take on new practices. One of the great problems in raising the level of educational quality is the discovery of means by which to increase the speed of educational change.

Status of the teacher. One of the strange inconsistencies in American society is the great allegiance to education on the one hand, and the lowly estate of the public school teacher on the other. Strong efforts to change the general social attitude toward teaching and to secure greater cultural status for the teacher have been made in recent years. What the effects will be on the teaching profession is not clear at this time. The position of the teacher in the economy is an important factor in supply and demand. It may be said that in the Southern region the teacher is worse off in an economic sense than he was in 1940, in spite of the fact that the actual dollar increase in his salary amounted to 210 per cent between 1940 and 1952.

It appears that the shortage of well-trained teachers is largely a reflection of the low rating of teaching among the professions. Adequately staffed schools as measured by factors of competence and numbers can scarcely be achieved until the status of the teacher in our society is improved.

More than any other factor discussed as a professional problem in improving the quality of schools, the status of the teacher is a problem of the entire society. It is, however, placed in this section because of its relevance to other professional problems.

The role of educational administration. It has been only within recent years that the more creative functions of educational administration have been generally recognized and their significance understood in improving the quality of school programs. The administration of education is no longer primarily a managerial function. Responsibilities for educational planning, program evaluation, professional growth of the staff, and the improvement of the curriculum are examples of newer professional demands on the school administrator. The need for unremitting efforts to develop schools which are in step with the demands of a changing society pose particularly difficult tasks for educational leadership. It may not be too much to say that success in achieving a continuous improvement of educational offerings will be closely related to the effectiveness of the administrative leadership available in schools and communities.

SOCIAL, ECONOMIC, POLITICAL, AND PSYCHOLOGICAL FACTORS CONDITIONING EDUCATIONAL PROGRESS

Unfinished tasks in Southern education as indicated by value commitments have been defined as the objectives toward which educational efforts in the region should be directed. Major professional problems which have to be considered in coming to grips with these tasks have been discussed. Any realistic appraisal of possibilities for significant improvements in education must take into account a variety of social, economic, political, and psychological factors in the region which, in the final analysis, will be the determinants of the strength and energy which can be utilized in bringing about educational progress. Some of the more important of these factors will be considered briefly.

Control of public education. As was pointed out in Chapter Three, the patterns of educational control which have been developed in the Southern region reflect the political and social doctrines that have prevailed. These patterns, therefore, effectively eliminated the Negro from participation in educational control and the formulation of educational policy, except in very minor capacities. The only place universally found for the Negro in a leadership position has been as principal of the Negro school and there he has largely been under the domination of the majority race. The systems of control which have been developed have not only kept power over education in the hands of the dominant race but they have until recent years rather effectively kept the power in the hands of a minority of the white race, the landed and industrial aristocracy. Control and organization are essential factors to consider in any study of the future of education in the South and of the segregation issue in particular.

Controls which are consistent with principles of democratic government require that power reside in the hands of the people. The appointment of members of the state board of education by the governor, the appointment of members of local boards of education by the various methods listed in Chapter Three, and the dual control plan of having board members and superintendents responsible to different bodies would seem to violate these principles. Schools too often have been subjected to petty and unprofessional interference, especially in county school systems where the superintendent is subject to the popular electorate. No better system of educational control has been advanced than that which allocates the power to select the board of education to the voters, with the board having power to appoint the superintendent.

Reactions to the crisis brought on by the Supreme Court decision on segregation may be said to be indicative of the nature of controls of education in the region. By and large, those occupying positions in the existing organization and admiration of education have been bypassed in the consideration of segregation. Initiative has come from the politician and the legislator rather than from the professionally trained person. In more than one state this initiative has been reflected, first, in threats to abandon the public school system rather than to abide by the Court's decision; and, second, to set out actual legal provisions which are designed to make it possible to abolish the public school system. In no case has such action been predicated upon any serious study of the problem. While courageous school administrators have in some instances spoken out against this method of dealing with the issue, in general the professional services of such leaders have not been sought by those who were making the decisions.

In one sense the politician and the legislator, in bypassing the legal structure of education and its professional leadership, may be said to have usurped their functions. But before condemning this practice, it must be remembered that, in the final analysis, control of education in America is political in nature rather than professional. Such control is perfectly consistent with the nation's concepts of democratic action and political democracy. Certainly the entire pattern of democratic values demands that final authority rest with the people. The American political system is one which provides for the people to speak through their duly elected representatives. Therefore, the way in which such representatives exercise the power entrusted to them becomes extremely important. Should they act in arbitrary and authoritarian ways without regard for the wishes of their constituents and without providing the kind of leadership which helps people decide questions wisely, the fault is with those representatives and not the system.

Two additional related factors stand out in the analysis of control as related to the present crisis. Earlier mention was made of the developing role of the state department of education as a leadership agency. The segregation emergency has provided a splendid opportunity to test this concept of its role in a crisis. Thus far it may be said that it has not been possible for most state departments of education to rise to this challenge. This may be due largely to the fact that state departments of education are frequently subject to political controls and pressures. Where such controls exist, the leadership role is sharply restricted in regard to issues which precipitate violent differences of opinion, for a department can lose some of its effectiveness by becoming too strongly identified with a position which is contrary to popular opinion.

The second factor is the plight of the administrator of the local school system. If he is to be effective in his work, he cannot with impunity violate the mores of the people whom he serves. His status is such that he is not generally looked to for leadership in matters of basic policy in education, and in regard to the segregation issue he has largely remained quiet. Controls imposed by local opinion limit any stand he may personally choose to take unless he is willing to jeopardize his acceptance by the community. For instance, if he should espouse the cause of integration in the typical Southern community, he would undoubtedly precipitate a conflict of opinion which could very possibly cripple or bring to an end his usefulness in the community.

The fact that controls over education are such that its present structure and organization are subject to change by state legislatures has already been discussed. The threat to abolish public school systems and plans already adopted which would seem to make this abolition possible are illustrations of an extreme use of this power. It cannot be denied that the adaptability of structural patterns is consistent with American ideals; but if the principle were stretched to the point of destroying the public school system itself, it could hardly be said that the principle had been wisely practiced. It is to be noted, however, that thus far no state has actually proposed that all responsibility for education be abandoned.

Public understanding of good schools. Implied in the treatment of educational control is the idea that the wise use of the power to control is related to the understandings concerning education upon which the exercise of control is based. Such research as is available indicates a positive correlation between the effectiveness of action taken with reference to education and how much those who take the action really know about good schools.

This indicates that a critically important conditioner of educational progress is the level of the community's capacity to discriminate between good and bad educational practice. Subjective data show that knowledges, attitudes, and beliefs which determine public understandings of good schools can be changed extensively through the use of appropriate processes and materials.

Capacity of financial support. The rapid increase of wealth in the South during recent years shows no sign of slackening. The per capita income of the region was 64.4 per cent of the average for the non-South in 1948, as contrasted to only 51 per cent in 1940. The position of the South in the national economy continues to improve. Between 1940 and 1952, the per capita income of the region increased by 237 per cent, from $339 to $1,143; while revenues per school age child increased from $37 to $117. These figures are not corrected for inflationary trends, but they indicate nevertheless the increasing ability of the region to support public education. The picture is bright on this count.

Changes in the region's economy which are producing this rapid increase in wealth are far-reaching in nature and character. One of these is the continuing industrialization of the region, which is reflected by the increasing concentration of population in metropolitan areas. The decline in rural population has not diminished the importance of the agricultural phase of the Southern economy, for mechanization of farming has made it possible to increase farm income greatly despite the decline in farm population. The continued heavy out-migration of Negroes indicates some decline in the size of the lower income groups. Other important factors in considering the economy are the older median age of the population, the proportionate increase in the oldest and youngest age groups, and the substantial increase in the median grade completed in school. Another significant change has been in occupational patterns, reflected by a proportionate increase in the number of skilled and technical workers.

The diversified industrialization program, which is spreading throughout the South, has already displaced agriculture, forestry, and fisheries as the major phase of the economy. Meanwhile, farm income increased from $2,379,000,000 to $8,951,000,000 during the twelve-year period beginning in 1940. Important changes in farming are reflected by the shift from a row-crop emphasis to emphasis on uncultivated crops and the raising of livestock.

From 1940 to 1952 educational effort actually declined, although the total expenditures for current operation increased by 268 per cent and capital outlay expenditures increased by 717 per cent. When measured by the percentage ratio of school revenue to effective buying income, educational effort declined from 2.98 to 2.85 from 1940 to 1950, but increased to 2.89 by 1952. At the same time, however, the per cent of the state tax dollar spent for education increased from 27.9 to 34.7.

There is little doubt that the wealth of the region has increased so rapidly that problems in education depending on finance can be handled more satisfactorily now than at any other time in the history of the South.

The segregation issue. The completion of unfinished tasks in education depends, as does the very definition of what constitutes an unfinished task, in many respects on factors which are difficult to analyze because of their subjective nature. Nevertheless, some identification and discussion of them are necessary, for in times of a crisis in public education, such as the one faced at present, they become extremely important. The most significant of these intangible factors in the current situation is obviously the segregation issue.

The Court decision adds a new dimension to the educational problems of the Southern region, that of mixing the two races in public schools. This is, of course, an entirely different problem from the one involved in invoking the doctrine of separate but equal facilities and programs, since it calls into play a new set of reactions, most of which are emotional in character. Although students of national history have recognized the ultimate inevitability of the decision, and even though previous court decisions have been powerful levers in the struggle to equalize educational opportunities that have resulted in important improvements in Negro education, the South, nevertheless, was not ready for the segregation decision. The typical Southerner finds it very difficult to substitute the more radical doctrine of placing Negroes and whites in the same school for the doctrine he only recently accepted of providing equal educational programs for the two races.

The average Southerner's reaction to the Court decision creates great turmoil within himself. He wishes to be a law-abiding citizen and he believes himself to be loyal to the great values which have made this nation what it is; but when he applies the test of his basic value commitments as an American to the race problem, he is made very uncomfortable and unhappy. The inner conflict which is brought on has sometimes caused him to shed his objectivity and to surrender to emotionalism. It is hardly conceivable, however, that he will pursue this course for long. He will eventually find a way to reconcile the conflict and retain his fidelity to American values. Strangely enough, he seems generally willing to serve on a jury with Negroes, to work beside them from day to day, to help them when they are in need, but as yet he has not reconciled himself to sending his children to school with Negro children.

Strong dedication to public education. Throughout all the stress of this period there has been no apparent decrease in the faith people have in the power of education. Despite plans in some states to abandon the public school system, these efforts are aimed primarily at the control and administration of schools rather than efforts actually to destroy education. The devices for circumventing the decision of the Court are no more than devices, they represent no decline in the conviction that schools are important. As yet, no evidence exists that there is any willingness to abandon education as an alternative to mixing the races in the schools. In the long run this faith in education will no doubt serve the region well in the difficult days ahead.

A confident South. The region is no longer apologetic and oversensitive. The South believes in itself and in its future. The optimistic spirit which this self-assurance has generated is being translated into a willingness to grapple with problems and the capacity to deal with them effectively. This is a priceless asset.

The current surge of progress. It can scarcely be doubted that the many evidences of substantial social and economic gain in the region reflect the spirit of confidence referred to and, at the same time, serve as a source of strength for developing further confidence. There is no reason to doubt that the present progressive trends will continue. Perhaps they may be further intensified. Momentum has already been built up. This is a great advantage in coming to grips with the difficult problems that must be faced.

Adequacy of leadership. There are many able men of good will of both races who are willing to join together in preserving and strengthening the march of progress which is now characteristic of the region. Voices of these leaders were in the majority during the days immediately following the announcement of the Court's decision. Subsequently, other voices seemed to dominate the scene, voices which showed less understanding of the nature of the vast changes underway in the South. There is no reason to believe that the strong leadership of the region will not assume its proper place in the days ahead.

One clear sign of the effects of the more objective leadership is seen in the disposition, when the chips are down, to keep the segregation issue in its proper context. In recognition of the evolutionary nature of American values and the inevitability of social and economic change, there has been no appreciable decline in efforts throughout the region to continue and expand programs of school improvement. Given time, a sense of balance and proper perspective undoubtedly will prevail; should the ultimate choice be between continuing the present trend toward a greater region, of which developing better public education is an essential part, and joining the forces which would circumvent the law of the land, the choice is surely clear. It would be folly not to recognize that differences of opinion on the segregation issue and other issues are very substantial and that the relative emphasis on values is not the same for all citizens. Indeed, active expression of a value does not result in the same kind of behavior for everyone. But there are substantial areas of public welfare and action upon which there is fairly common agreement. Commonly accepted beliefs and methods make it possible for divergent factions to join hands in these areas while seeking a resolution of differences in other areas.

SUMMARY

On the basis of the recapitulation and interpretation of data in this chapter, great unfinished tasks in education seem to stand out. These tasks may be classified under three headings: first, equalizing the scope and quality of educational programs in the region; second, extending the availability of present educational programs to all children and youth who can profit from them; and third, raising the level of quality of educational programs.

The identification and evaluation of current trends in education reveal none of any substance which run counter to American ideals and the pursuit of objectives reflected by definitions of unfinished tasks. Fortunately, the great changes in Southern public school systems which have been traced in this study are largely on the positive side and are, therefore, moving the region toward the completion of unfinished tasks. The problem in the main is not, then, the inauguration of new trends but the strengthening and the speeding of the tempo of those already underway.

Certain critical professional needs stand out as the educational tasks ahead are faced. These include the necessity of defining educational adequacy, evaluating educational outcomes, measuring teacher competence, improving teaching methods, speeding up the tempo of educational change, raising the status of teaching, and developing more creative educational administrators. It hardly seems likely that continuing progress can be expected in completing the educational tasks of this era unless these problems are faced successfully.

Strong social, economic, political, and psychological factors are present which will condition the future course of education in the region. Some of these factors are positive, others are negative, still others may be considered to be neither at present. Whether forces are positive or negative depends to some extent on how they are used. Segregation is the most critical of all current issues. At present it may be considered to be a negative factor as it affects the whole of education, but in the end the attention it draws to schools and their needs may be a compensating influence. Wealth, strong faith in education, and the current optimism of the region are positive factors. It remains to be seen whether control and leadership are to be as positive in their influence as should be expected.

Unwillingness to permit the segregation issue to divert long-time efforts to develop better schools is a wholesome sign. This indicates

some willingness to consider the entire complex of educational problems as they exist in the social, economic, and cultural setting of the
region for the purpose of developing a unified body of policy with
respect to education which will be consistent with the American way
of handling issues and resolving difficulties.

ELEVEN

Facing The Issues

In the preceding chapter the data which have been presented in this volume were summarized and interpreted to indicate unfinished tasks in making real the American dream of providing adequate and equal educational opportunities for all children and youth; also discussed were the social, economic, political, and psychological factors which may be expected to condition the nature and quality of courses of action designed to resolve the educational issues faced by the region. The region has no choice with respect to these issues if it is to continue its allegiance to the values and ideals which have made this country great; its only course is to face the issues squarely and with the determination to resolve them as effectively as possible.

Fortunately, the way ahead is not uncharted. A society, particularly American society, is always faced by problems and issues as it endeavors constantly to improve itself. In the course of time, some tried and tested means of resolving difficulties are developed and freely used. Such means originate in the complex of basic values and beliefs which govern the society.

The South is thus equipped with certain accepted ways of problem-solving. It was stated early in this volume that confidence in man's ability to solve his own problems and faith in his intelligence to do so are fundamental sources of the nation's cultural drives. Respect for the worth and dignity of the individual requires that man be given the freedom and responsibility of making his own way. Science and the Scientific Method help to give him the necessary tools.

The security which can come from an orientation to problem-solving such as is attempted at this point may be very comforting. In a theoretical sense the task of resolving issues may appear to be relatively easy. The simple fact is, however, that both individuals and groups nearly always find themselves hard pressed to think and act in ways that are completely consistent with the guides developed from philosophical foundations. Conflicting values frequently compete for attention, and the maintenance of necessary balance among the various commitments faced so that unity in direction and effort may be achieved becomes a baffling problem. Some issues are more urgent than others. Sometimes an issue may be less urgent than it seems, but individuals may become so involved that perspective is difficult to achieve and their energies may be consumed in one-sided or tangential efforts.

The segregation issue in public schools is a case in point. No informed person can deny that other critical problems are faced by the schools of the South. Logic dictates that the best interests of public education can be served only if all educational problems are attacked in a unified and comprehensive fashion. There is small chance that this will be done; indeed, it has rarely, if ever, been done. Major effort is usually centered where there is the greatest immediate concern, so we may expect that other educational problems will be relatively overshadowed in the near future.

Success in employing problem-solving approaches consistent with cultural values varies according to the nature and intensity of the issue to be faced. The segregation issue has attracted such attention that it will not only tend to monopolize the formation of educational policy but it will make more difficult the task of putting into practice the best methods of problem-solving. The conflict the Supreme Court decision evokes in the South because of its threat to traditional cultural practices arouses feelings which make it extremely hard to retain fidelity to methods of objectivity and reason. Attitudes, mores, and behavior affected by the decision reach into almost every avenue of community living. What is done with reference to the public school problem will be determined on the basis of feelings and beliefs which transcend the bounds of any single institution or agency. Likewise, the effects of whatever decision a given community puts into practice will be felt on a community-wide basis. This, of course, is true in a limited sense of any issue that touches a community or group of people.

Perhaps taking stock should always be followed by planning a course of action. The determination of goals or objectives is a necessary step in this process. If the completion of unfinished tasks is acceptable as an objective, it is now possible to turn to the consideration of guides to follow in this undertaking. The nature of these guides has been indicated—they are inherent in the nation's value dedications. Upon the assumption that these values are clear and their import recognized, what remains to be done? For one thing, the assumptions upon which action will be predicated need to be clearly understood; these assumptions become apparent when basic values are applied to the current social scene.

BASIC ASSUMPTIONS

When individuals and groups make decisions they act in terms of beliefs and judgments which they accept as valid. Unfortunately, such assumptions are not always clearly stated. Sometimes they are not recognized by those who act upon them. The wisdom of courses of action is strengthened when responsible persons are aware of the fundamental assumptions which govern their behavior and act consistently on the basis of these assumptions. With respect to guides which seem defensible as a foundation for considering the educational needs of the Southern region and for formulating decisions which must be made, five assumptions which seem reasonable are set forth.

Present trends in the Southern region will continue. This means that the South will retain its dedication to public education and will continue to provide for the educational needs of its children and youth. It means that other school problems will not be neglected while the segregation issue is being considered. Current developments substantiate these points. Trends beginning soon after World War II of providing more new buildings, higher salaries for teachers, and additional support of other kinds for schools continue. There is evidence to indicate that the region will treat the racial problem in schools as but one of many educational problems and, in some degree at least, in relation to these problems.

Efforts to equalize educational opportunity will continue. The median grade achievement of the population will continue to increase. Efforts to secure more competent teachers and to pay them better will not cease. A continuation of concern for improving the quality of education, for providing more and better instructional materials, and for the general welfare of students can be expected.

Social and economic changes which are underway in the region will undoubtedly continue. The economy will become stronger, better balanced, and a more substantial part of the national economy. Present trends toward extending the advantages and responsibilities of citizenship to all people in the region will continue. Current conflicts in values concerning practices in the public schools with respect to the races will not result in less adequate public education.

Problems will be solved by use of the method of intelligence. American value commitments admit of no other method of resolving issues. There is no other way to safeguard the rights and privileges of all. In the long run, people will not be satisfied with the use of a substitute method. The method of intelligence was characterized in Chapter One as Science and the Scientific Method.

It is assumed that all problems will be approached in the same way, whether or not they are emotional in character. Obviously, the validity of this assumption is seriously strained when a high degree of emotionalism is involved. In a case of this kind, the assumption becomes a goal to be sought.

If the method of intelligence is used in facing unfinished tasks, a particular frame of mind is required. This frame of mind may be characterized as a desire to achieve a solution to a problem which is best for all concerned. This rules out ready-made answers to questions and ready-made decisions on courses of action based upon feelings and emotions alone. Also ruled out is the making of decisions without due consideration of all who might be concerned and without giving appropriate attention to their points of view. The relevance of this approach to problem-solving to the value commitments defined by Counts needs no elaboration.

The substantial body of responsible leadership will courageously and conscientiously seek a resolution of issues that will serve the best interests of all. As is true of the assumption previously stated, the greater the degree of feeling involved in an issue, the more difficult it is to behave as this assumption dictates. Arbitrary and authoritarian uses of power are out of place where these assumptions prevail; but respect for the institutions of our society which has been developed through experience is strong and it is habitual to heed decisions they make. Thus, the Supreme Court's decision, although depriving a traditional Southern practice of its legal sanction, commands the respect of all.

Responsible leadership reacts to such challenges with sincere efforts to reconcile differences and to find ways of acting within the limits prescribed by the established Rule of Law. Leaders usually take their responsibilities seriously and act in what they consider to be the best interests of the people.

Decisions on all issues and problems will be made through established agencies and institutions which are duly authorized to render decisions on matters of public policy. The structures through which opinions are formed and judgments made on educational issues will be the same as those through which such matters are habitually settled. Processes used in policy-making through the use of these structures will likewise be those traditionally used. How effective the structures and processes can be depends to a considerable extent upon the issue at stake and the degree of emotion the issue involves. It should be repeated that the intensity of feeling surrounding an issue conditions the effective use of processes and instrumentalities of decision-making in keeping with democratic values and traditions.

Emotionalized issues bring to the forefront individuals who have ready-made decisions which may be products of their prejudices rather than their objectivity. Such individuals then seek to exploit existing structures and processes to the promulgation of their particular points of view. Unfortunately, the segregation issue is tinged with such emotion that responsible leaders will find it difficult to obtain objectivity and reason in its consideration. Value conflicts are such that hasty and emotional decisions may be reached which subsequent action will need to modify. Under such circumstances a greater than normal premium may be placed on sound and responsible leadership.

Despite these difficulties, it is hardly conceivable that existing educational structures will be superseded for long, if at all, in efforts to escape responsibilities imposed by the decision on segregation.

The many substantial variations among local communities throughout the region will be taken into proper account in resolving the segregation issue. Procedures based on this assumption would be in keeping with long established principles of home rule and local initiative. No standard solution to the segregation issue is, therefore, possible. Each local community must assume some responsibility for working out its own solution. Essential factors related to the problems of segregation as well as other issues in education vary markedly from state to state and from community to community within states. For example, in one community attitudes may be based almost wholly on emotion, while in another a considerable degree of objectivity may be achieved. Abrupt changes which run contrary to deep-seated beliefs and practices in a local community may lead to tense, explosive situations which can accomplish no good for either race. However, the freedom of local communities to chart and put into effect their own plans of action may be limited to positive application. Undoubtedly, some means will be set up of making sure that such freedom is exercised with the intent of ultimately complying with the law.

THE FORMULATION OF POLICY

Acceptance of the assumptions which have been postulated in the previous section will be reflected in the nature and kinds of steps taken to meet educational problems. These assumptions will not permit a *laissez-faire* attitude. In a society which is based on the belief that people are intelligent and can solve their own problems, patterns of change bear the imprint of deliberate design. Belief in the ability of man to chart his own course requires that positive action be taken to meet the problems that have arisen. Acting in terms of accepted assumptions requires the formulation and execution of policy with respect to the situations which must be met.

As pointed out in Chapter Two, legally constituted agencies answerable in the final analysis to the people have been allocated legal control over public schools. Powers are fairly well distributed among agencies on the state, district, and local levels, although there is some overlapping and duplication. Educational policy is formed by these agencies.

THE ROLE OF ESTABLISHED AGENCIES. In theory, ultimate control over education rests with the state, for state constitutions place responsibility for public education squarely in the hands of the state. No state, however, has actually exercised complete control over education. Traditionally it has allocated much of its power to local school districts which were created to assume much of the control and operation of schools in local communities. Therefore, state agencies, including the legislature, the courts, the state board of education, and the state department of education, may exercise a wide range of choices with respect to the extent and nature of controls over education. In practice these powers have usually been confined to the definition of broad general policies and the provision of implementation services, although from time to time specific and highly detailed controls are instituted and enforced.

In the period immediately following the Supreme Court decision, the executive and legislative branches of state government exhibited two types of behavior toward the segregation problem. Characteristic of the first type was a refusal to take any positive action whatsoever, with the idea of waiting until the court had made known its decrees concerning implementation. Under this principle, proposed legislation designed to circumvent the Court's decision was defeated. The second type of state action was an aggressive effort to use the state's power to forestall any important change in the relationship of the two races in the public schools. Conspicuous among such examples were constitutional and legislative action purportedly designed to abandon the public school system and thus free the state, supposedly, of any responsibility for carrying out the Court's decision.

It is clear that the choices a state may exercise with reference to any educational problem are legion. Obviously, the manner in which the state exercises its authority will go far toward determining what is done about the segregation issue or any other problem in education. Should the assumptions which have been listed be acceptable as a foundation upon which state policy is formulated, the nature of this policy becomes clear. If fidelity to the basic American value commitments is maintained, potential policy is further clarified. In short, each state would adopt broad policy guides which would help school districts live within the law and assist them in solving their school problems so that the traditional goal of equal educational opportunity for all could be pursued as effectively as possible.

The local school district, being a creature of the state, can function only within the limits of power which it is granted from the state. Legally, the district board of education is responsible for policies concerning the maintenance and operation of the local schools in accordance with state provisions. The superintendent of schools is responsible for execution of board policy. Traditionally, local school districts have operated with a great deal of freedom, the amount varying from state to state and from one type of school district to another. This is, of course, compatible with the American conviction that home rule is important. If present issues in the public schools are handled in accordance with assumptions and value judgments consistent with American democratic ideals, local school districts will have a great deal of authority in the resolution of these issues under the broad concept that ultimate compliance with the law is to be achieved.

In this event, local school boards and administrative staffs will be placed under great compulsion to use their powers wisely. In times of great stress and tension, it might be more comfortable to have the state hand down a ready-made pattern to which all should conform. This, however, would deny local communities the responsibility and privilege of solving their own problems within the broad outlines of policy designated by the state. Long-established traditions of local initiative and home rule will make it possible to take into proper account the great range of differences among communities so that the most sensible course of action for any given community may be determined in the light of its own particular conditions. Under this concept, responsibilities of local school boards and superintendents are greatly increased.

All school districts consist of one or more attendance centers, a designation for each school within a district. Certain basic administrative and supervisory functions take place in each of these attendance centers. The principal and the faculty of a school are in a very real sense arms of the state and of the local district insofar as educational matters are concerned. It is in the schools of a district that policy and plans from state and local sources ultimately are expressed in the program of education provided children. School personnel in the attendance center may exercise considerable control over policy and its implementation; however, their control is primarily of an operational nature. Varying choices may exist with respect to how a given educational policy or plan is actually carried out. It is in this area that the school principal and his staff have the greatest freedom of operation and may bring to bear their greatest initiative and inventiveness in the conduct of the educational program. Their behavior is frequently the final test of the adequacy of plans and, therefore, the real test of educational policy and planning is on this level.

Perhaps the most difficult tasks growing out of the assumptions upon which this discussion is predicated will come in the school attendance center. People do not go to school on district and state levels, but in the school attendance center. Therefore, the real impact of change can be felt only at this level. It is in this setting that the differences in attitudes and understandings and the willingness objectively to face problems and issues will be most keenly felt. As important as wise leadership is on state and district levels, it is of equally critical importance in the school attendance center.

STEPS IN POLICY FORMULATION. Use of the method of intelligence provides clear-cut procedures and means through which decisions can be reached and these decisions become the policy upon which action is based. Frequently such procedures and means are formally organized into a sequential pattern known as the steps of the Scientific Method. There are different ways of stating the steps and they vary in number according to preference. The essential elements involved in actual decision-making are three.

Understanding and defining the problem or issue. This may seem to be an easy step but it is generally a very difficult one. Too often opinions as to the real nature of an issue are formed on the basis of false assumptions, misleading information, hearsay, and feelings rather than reason.

The Supreme Court decision on segregation serves as an illustration. Perhaps few judicial pronouncements have been so widely misunderstood. The essence of the decision seems to be that compulsory separation of the races in public schools solely on the basis of race is unconstitutional. This can hardly be taken to mean that all-Negro or all-white schools are illegal. Obviously, sociological factors such as housing patterns and accidents of geography and normal districting procedures have considerable bearing on the make-up of a particular school. But the decision does mean that the inflexible and arbitrary separation of the races in schools on the basis of color alone is no longer legal. Apparently, a major concern of the Court was the effect of compulsory segregation on the minority race. The decision takes the position that enforced separation of the races in public schools under sanction of the law has harmful effects on Negro children, since it implies that the Negro group is inferior.

It is not the purpose here to analyze the Court decision but rather to emphasize the fact that a clear understanding of what the Court said would seem to be a prerequisite to any consideration of plans to be made in light of this decision. In other words, an adequate definition of the issue of segregation demands a clear understanding of the Court decision.

The difficulty of maintaining objectivity is sometimes greatest at the initial point of searching out an essential understanding of a problem. Careful study and analysis at this stage may avoid a great deal of misspent time and effort later.

It should be emphasized that problems always exist in relation to aims, aspirations, and objectives. This is as true for groups as it is for individuals. Thus, any issue should be defined in the perspective of ultimate goals.

Collecting, analyzing, and interpreting relevant information. These constitute the second step in the Scientific Method. It is clear that this process may result in important redefinitions of the issue at stake, for as pertinent data are brought to bear on the problem it may take on different dimensions.

It hardly seems necessary to state the case for taking into account all facts which bear on a problem. The unfortunate fact remains that an individual or group may need to be on constant guard not to accept only data that support a preconceived opinion while rejecting or minimizing data of contrary significance. This demands that investigators hold in abeyance their judgments until enough facts are in and have been interpreted to justify taking a position.

Interpretation is the more difficult phase of this step for facts carry different meanings to different persons, depending upon their orientation. It is not unusual for two individuals to study the same facts and come out with opposite conclusions. What is the test of accuracy in the interpretation of factual information? At this point, further reference to the values which underlie American society is in order. Facts become meaningful only in terms of one's beliefs and values. Facts must be interpreted by means of criteria growing out of basic value dedications such as the Hebraic-Christian Ethic, the Humanistic Spirit, and the Democratic Faith. When this is done, guides to the wise use of facts begin to become apparent. Decisions made as a result of the use of these methods are more objective and they are not likely to conflict with established trends.

The problem of segregation in the public schools affords a timely illustration of how this step could be carried out. What sorts of data should be collected, analyzed, and interpreted with reference to this issue? A wide range of information is called for because of the many community-wide factors involved. Intangible factors important to recognize and understand are represented in such studies as were authorized in Florida in the summer of 1954 and carried out under the auspices of the attorney general's office. Extensive interviews were conducted in selected communities and counties for the purpose of determining citizen attitudes with respect to the segregation issue and community acceptance of various points of view concerning it. Such information would seem almost indispensable to the projection of wise plans.

Other important kinds of knowledge may be needed. For example, the problem posed by the decision is quite different in a community where the Negroes are largely illiterate, unskilled workers of low income and a community where the Negroes occupy a higher social and economic position. The simple fact of the ratio of white to Negro population is very important. The need for developing adequate understanding of the characteristics of a given community's populations cannot be over-emphasized. Included in the kinds of data needed would be an analysis of present patterns of race relations and attitudes in the community and their recent development.

Any comprehensive study to be used as a basis for developing policy on the segregation issue would call for community studies of factors such as those treated in the research reported in this volume. Similar state and district studies would obviously be in order.

Such studies as indicated are imperative if the real nature and dimensions of the problem are to be understood, if discrepancies between present status and expectation are to be grasped, and if a plan of action consistent with objectives and making the best possible use of resources is to be projected.

Formulation of policy. This is the third step in the approach to decision-making under discussion. As used in this connection, policy is a stated plan of action which has been designed to resolve an issue or problem. The two previous steps are valuable only insofar as they pave the way for wise plans of action. Alternative solutions to a given problem are considered and a choice made of the plan most reasonable in terms of the objectives sought and consistency with accepted values.

THE EXECUTION OF POLICY

As previously implied, policy can be justified only insofar as it provides a design for meeting an issue or problem. Therefore, the test of policy is in its application. In short, does it actually result in the improvement of conditions it was designed to ameliorate?

Of course, one set of assurances on this point comes from following the steps in decision-making which have been suggested. But other safeguards are needed.

Responsibilities for policy execution have to be defined and clearly understood by all who are concerned. Each person who has a part to play has a right to know precisely what is expected of him.

One phase of execution is the administration and supervision of plans and of responsible personnel. This is of greater than ordinary importance in educational fields because of the unique nature of educational responsibilities, dealing as they do with people, ideas, beliefs, and so forth.

Another important responsibility in connection with policy execution is evaluation of outcomes. Measures of the extent to which objectives are being met is the heart of evaluation. Only then can the adequacy of policy be ascertained and revisions, if needed, be undertaken. In like manner, issues may be redefined and objectives modified.

AN OPERATIONAL PRINCIPLE. Specific reference to certain other processes which further exemplify the basic values Americans hold as they may be expressed in behavior should be mentioned. It can be inferred from these writings that use of the method of intelligence is limited by value commitments to the pursuit of objectives which are wholesome for the individual and for society.

In like manner, how intelligence is used is conditioned by the regard and respect entertained for others. Thus, in connection with policy formulation and execution an important principle may be stated, to wit: all who are affected by a policy should be meaningfully and appropriately involved in the formulation and execution of the policy.

That principle may be illustrated by one further reference to the segregation issue. If the principle were applied to this issue, it would mean that action taken at state, district, and community levels would include the participation of both white and Negro persons at all possible stages. On the community level, study groups might be formed representing interested parties. Reports of studies might provide the material for community forums and panel discussions. In this way, various points of view could be taken into account and greater community understanding reached for the benefit of all.

Decision-making bodies would not abrogate their responsibilities, but they would act in the open and on the basis of reasons known to all. If there is one lesson which seems clear from experience thus far in facing the segregation issue, it is that decisions are more palatable, whatever they are, if reached on the basis of positive action made in terms of considerations generally made known to all. Half-hearted and furtive actions arouse suspicion and distrust.

TOWARD A GREATER SOUTH

A point of view has been expressed in this chapter as a suggested basis for the consideration of educational problems and issues, with the current segregation issue serving as an illustration of how the point of view may be used in determining courses of action. The American value system is the source of this point of view. Its presumed application to the problems of white and Negro schools in the South is predicated on certain basic assumptions concerning conditions in the region, assumptions which appear to be reasonable in the light of the great cultural drives of American society.

In view of these considerations, an effort has been made to show how policy should be formed and how it should be carried out in the face of current issues and problems in education. In stressing the role of duly constituted agencies, it was implied that a mutually supporting relationship among the three levels of responsibility—the state, the school district, and the attendance center—should be achieved in order that a comprehensive, unified body of policy would evolve which would assure the maximum productive use of available resources in meeting educational needs.

The execution of policy is the test of its value, execution as measured by success in resolving issues and problems.

Both value commitments and outcomes desired require observance of the principle of wide involvement of persons concerned in efforts to continue educational progress in the Southern region.

The broad assumption of the authors is that the South will go ahead with the further development of the present trends which are making it a more mature society. No internal issue will long divert the region from this course. The authors acknowledge the touch of idealism which appears, especially in this chapter. Their conviction is that the general direction of the region will be toward a society which will constantly improve in its capacities to express in its behavior the ideals to which all Americans are dedicated. That mistakes will be made is certain, but the region will learn from its mistakes. Problems will not always be attacked according to the design that has been suggested, but directions will be toward a more faithful and frequent use of the design. The authors are convinced that the cultural drives which have been discussed are a part of the American heritage and that the society of this region and this nation will continue to reach newer understandings of their significance for individual and group behavior. Undoubtedly, the role of the public schools in the South's effort to achieve this lofty destiny will be one of greater importance than has generally been recognized in the past.

Appendix

Sources of Data

The fact that education is a state function and consequently there is wide variability in the records kept from state to state caused problems in the collection of data for this investigation. Comparable state level statistics from the various states are available in such places as the reports of the United States Office of Education and various educational organizations. The nature of this study, however, necessitated consistent statistics not only at the state level but at the school district level as well. Such statistics are available only in the records and reports of individual state departments of education.

In no state in the South were all the statistics readily available in the form required by the nature of this study. Hence, it was necessary in some instances to combine, realign, and adjust several records and reports to get the desired data. In many cases it was necessary to go to original records of the individual districts to obtain information. Obviously, detailed sources for these statistics cannot be given. The source for all the data used in this inquiry unless otherwise designated is the records and reports of state departments of education of the Southern states.

Because of variations among the states, it was not always possible to obtain data on a particular item from all states for all years which were studied. Analysis of trends requires that the data used have the same source for both the beginning and ending of the period. Statistics from states which had incomplete records for any year of the period covered were infrequently used. Therefore, some discussions are based on less than thirteen states.

In order to achieve the purposes of the study, a span of twelve years was used to establish trends. The school years 1939-40 and 1949-50 were employed in order to relate school statistics to population and other data of the United States Bureau of the Census. Statistics were collected for 1951-52, the last year for which school data were available. Data were collected from all states for these three years except North Carolina where figures for 1950-51 were substituted for 1951-52.

A concerted effort was made by the research staff to procure consistent, accurate data from and within the states. The same definitions of terms, data collection forms, and processing procedures were employed by all personnel. After the data were collected and tabulated, reports were submitted to the individual state departments for any check which they could make for accuracy. If inaccuracies exist, however, the research staff assumes full responsibility.

An important aspect of this study was an investigation of the differences existing among counties with different racial and urbanization population characteristics. Obviously, all of the counties which were contained in the thirteen states could not be analyzed, and a sampling procedure was necessary.

The counties of the region were classified into three groups according to the degree of urbanization which prevailed in 1950. These groups were designated rural, rural-urban, and metropolitan. A county designated rural had no urban population. A rural-urban county had some urban population and some rural population, while a metropolitan county contained a city of 50,000 or more, or was contiguous to such a county and met certain criteria defined by the Census Bureau. Of the 1,306 counties in the region in 1950, 496 were rural, 737 were rural-urban, and 73 were metropolitan.

After the counties in each state had been classified, they were arranged in rank order in each classification by the percentage of Negro population in the county in 1950. The distributions obtained of rural and rural-urban counties in each state were divided into quarters. The median of each quarter, or as near the median of each quarter as possible was selected to insure a representative geographical and population-size distribution for the state. All of the metropolitan counties were selected except in Texas where a sample was made using the same process of selection as was used in rural and rural-urban counties.

Although the county is the basic school administrative unit in practically all Southern states, there are frequently separate city or independent districts in these states. All public school statistics were brought to the county level by aggregating the statistics for school districts within the county.

Additional Statistical Data

TABLE 94

PER CENT OF STATE GOVERNMENT REVENUES FROM VARIOUS SOURCES
IN THE SOUTHERN STATES

State	From Sales Taxes			From Property Taxes		
	1940	1950	1952	1940	1950	1952
Alabama	37.5	40.8	37.0	9.5	3.9	3.4
Arkansas	45.4	45.2	44.7	8.3	0.2	0.2
Florida	44.5	54.4	54.1	3.8	2.1	1.6
Georgia	39.7	40.6	49.9	7.1	3.7	2.4
Kentucky	32.4	37.6	34.0	9.1	5.5	5.1
Louisiana	34.7	38.3	35.7	10.2	3.3	2.8
Mississippi	49.9	46.9	46.2	6.5	0.9	0.8
North Carolina	35.8	41.4	37.7	4.4	1.6	1.4
Oklahoma	36.6	39.4	37.7	0.8	0.0	0.0
South Carolina	45.2	41.7	48.5	3.5	1.1	0.7
Tennessee	35.1	48.0	47.8	4.3	0.8	0.0
Texas	30.2	29.8	28.1	13.8	4.4	5.1
Virginia	24.8	30.4	27.7	5.1	4.0	3.5
TOTAL	35.7	39.8	39.2	7.5	2.7	2.4

State	From Severance Taxes			From Federal Grants-in-Aid		
	1940	1950	1952	1940	1950	1952
Alabama	0.6	0.5	0.4	13.4	17.2	22.4
Arkansas	1.4	2.6	2.1	18.1	25.2	24.4
Florida	0.0	0.0	0.0	10.3	18.5	16.7
Georgia	0.0	0.0	0.0	16.0	24.7	19.8
Kentucky	0.0	0.1	0.1	13.2	21.6	21.5
Louisiana	10.7	14.4	13.8	12.0	21.7	19.8
Mississippi	0.0	4.7	3.5	18.5	22.8	23.2
North Carolina	0.0	0.0	0.0	13.2	14.5	13.8
Oklahoma	10.1	8.5	8.8	17.3	26.4	23.0
South Carolina	0.0	0.0	0.0	15.4	19.3	15.2
Tennessee	0.0	0.0	0.0	16.5	21.1	18.1
Texas	9.4	21.5	19.6	13.5	22.9	19.7
Virginia	0.0	0.1	0.1	11.7	9.8	10.8
TOTAL	3.7	6.2	5.8	14.1	20.4	18.8

TABLE 94 (*Continued*)

From State Liquor Monopoly

	1940	1950	1952
Alabama	3.0	5.4	4.9
Virginia	7.0	7.2	6.4

State	From Unemployment Compensation Taxes			From Charges for Current Services		
	1940	1950	1952	1940	1950	1952
Alabama	13.2	6.9	7.0	4.2	6.5	7.2
Arkansas	7.6	4.0	5.8	4.2	4.3	4.0
Florida	9.4	3.9	3.4	3.3	3.2	3.6
Georgia	10.8	7.5	5.4	5.0	5.4	3.9
Kentucky	15.2	10.3	10.4	8.1	4.8	4.7
Louisiana	7.8	4.8	5.0	2.8	1.7	3.7
Mississippi	5.8	3.9	3.5	5.0	6.3	5.8
North Carolina	10.2	7.4	6.5	3.6	3.7	4.1
Oklahoma	7.9	3.4	3.2	2.9	5.4	6.7
South Carolina	8.4	6.5	6.5	5.8	4.8	6.4
Tennessee	12.3	6.5	7.4	5.2	3.9	3.3
Texas	11.1	6.4	3.6	3.6	5.0	4.4
Virginia	12.4	4.8	4.7	7.7	9.4	9.6
TOTAL	10.4	5.9	5.3	4.4	4.7	5.0

State	From Motor Vehicle Licenses			From Other Licenses		
	1940	1950	1952	1940	1950	1952
Alabama	5.1	3.6	3.2	6.1	3.2	2.9
Arkansas	7.7	5.6	5.9	3.7	2.8	2.6
Florida	11.0	9.3	8.1	13.4	5.7	5.3
Georgia	4.0	2.4	1.8	3.5	2.4	1.2
Kentucky	5.1	4.4	4.1	7.4	3.1	3.0
Louisiana	5.0	1.7	1.7	5.9	3.1	2.8
Mississippi	2.2	2.1	2.0	5.7	2.8	2.5
North Carolina	7.8	6.0	5.2	8.7	5.2	4.4
Oklahoma	7.5	7.5	7.4	3.4	2.4	2.3
South Carolina	4.1	3.2	2.4	8.0	3.5	2.1
Tennessee	7.7	5.2	4.7	8.4	6.0	5.7
Texas	4.8	5.2	5.1	4.7	3.2	2.9
Virginia	8.8	5.8	5.6	10.8	5.4	5.3
TOTAL	6.2	4.9	4.4	6.7	3.8	3.3

TABLE 94 (*Continued*)

State	From Individual Income Taxes			From Corporation Income Taxes		
	1940	1950	1952	1940	1950	1952
Alabama	1.9	8.0*	7.2*	1.9	0.0	0.0
Arkansas	0.9	3.4	2.7	0.7	6.1	5.5
Florida	0.0	0.0	0.0	0.0	0.0	0.0
Georgia	3.5	5.4	4.6	4.4	7.2	7.0
Kentucky	3.3	6.6	8.6	2.8	4.9	5.1
Louisiana	2.5	5.2*	5.0*	3.0	0.0	0.0
Mississippi	1.8	3.4	3.1	2.2	5.8	5.8
North Carolina	3.0	8.5	9.1	7.8	10.5	10.6
Oklahoma	2.9	3.0	3.2	4.7	3.2	3.0
South Carolina	3.2	8.0	5.6	4.6	11.2	8.1
Tennessee	2.1	1.4	1.4	2.6	4.7	6.4
Texas	0.0	0.0	0.0	0.0	0.0	0.0
Virginia	2.4	11.1	9.1	3.4	8.5	8.3
TOTAL	2.0	4.4	4.2	2.8	4.0	4.0

* Individual and corporation income taxes combined.

TABLE 95

PER CENT OF STATE GOVERNMENT EXPENDITURES DEVOTED TO VARIOUS
SERVICES IN THE SOUTHERN STATES

State	Public Welfare			Highways			All Education *		
	1940	1950	1952	1940	1950	1952	1940	1950	1952
Alabama	6.0	14.1	14.7	29.1	21.3	20.2	28.9	33.4	41.0
Arkansas	6.8	20.1	17.0	21.7	23.2	24.1	24.6	28.8	31.8
Florida	11.6	21.3	15.3	34.6	19.6	29.1	23.1	31.7	29.1
Georgia	6.9	18.0	18.4	35.8	22.9	20.7	29.1	33.3	38.0
Kentucky	9.8	15.8	17.9	32.9	34.0	28.6	24.9	22.3	24.4
Louisiana	14.0	29.3	25.4	15.4	15.6	17.8	25.5	25.2	25.6
Mississippi	4.0	14.9	12.3	50.4	26.0	25.8	16.1	27.7	30.7
North Carolina	6.1	7.1	6.1	26.1	29.7	29.7	38.0	37.0	40.9
Oklahoma	25.2	31.1	26.3	26.3	25.6	24.9	25.2	26.6	29.6
South Carolina	8.5	12.5	11.4	28.2	25.1	19.8	28.9	29.6	39.8
Tennesse	14.5	17.9	15.8	32.3	25.1	24.4	20.1	29.9	31.8
Texas	9.9	21.7	17.6	30.9	23.2	23.1	36.1	34.6	42.7
Virginia	5.0	5.3	5.0	35.1	27.2	28.1	23.8	27.5	33.8
TOTAL	10.2	18.5	15.9	30.1	24.0	24.3	27.9	30.4	34.7

TABLE 95 (*Continued*)

State	General Control 1940	1950	1952	Public Safety 1940	1950	1952	Natural Resources 1940	1950	1952
Alabama	4.6	3.0	2.4	2.8	1.8	1.8	3.8	3.6	3.2
Arkansas	4.3	2.6	2.0	2.7	1.1	1.2	3.4	4.1	4.0
Florida	3.4	2.5	2.7	2.4	2.1	1.6	5.9	5.7	6.1
Georgia	4.7	2.1	2.0	2.0	1.4	1.7	2.5	3.3	3.8
Kentucky	7.6	4.3	3.5	2.8	2.2	2.3	2.6	3.3	5.2
Louisiana	5.4	2.1	1.9	2.3	1.1	1.2	2.4	2.9	3.2
Mississippi	3.2	3.6	2.3	1.1	1.2	1.7	2.6	4.8	4.4
North Carolina	2.5	1.4	1.2	2.1	1.6	1.8	2.4	2.8	2.7
Oklahoma	3.5	1.8	1.6	1.7	1.1	1.7	2.2	2.1	3.1
South Carolina	4.5	2.0	2.1	2.8	1.7	1.8	3.3	3.5	5.9
Tennessee	3.3	1.8	1.9	2.2	1.3	2.1	2.6	2.4	3.1
Texas	3.3	2.1	1.6	3.5	1.8	1.8	2.5	2.1	2.4
Virginia	5.8	3.8	2.8	2.8	2.6	4.0	2.7	3.7	3.3
TOTAL	4.2	2.4	2.0	2.5	1.6	1.9	2.9	3.2	3.6

State	Health and Hospitals 1940	1950	1952	Unemployment Compensation Benefits and Administration 1940	1950	1952
Alabama	5.1	6.1	6.6	8.2	10.0	4.8
Arkansas	15.3	6.9	6.3	7.4	6.9	5.2
Florida	4.9	7.2	7.5	8.9	5.7	3.3
Georgia	10.5	7.9	8.1	6.6	7.9	4.4
Kentucky	5.6	5.2	6.6	8.8	11.2	7.0
Louisiana	9.0	7.3	7.4	7.3	7.1	4.1
Mississippi	4.2	9.8	9.1	3.8	6.7	4.6
North Carolina	6.8	7.3	6.4	5.3	7.3	5.9
Oklahoma	4.8	5.4	7.3	5.3	4.7	2.5
South Carolina	5.5	8.1	5.8	5.9	9.5	5.2
Tennessee	4.2	6.7	5.8	10.6	11.5	8.2
Texas	4.1	4.3	6.2	7.4	3.1	2.1
Virginia	9.9	13.4	10.8	7.9	7.7	3.2
TOTAL	6.3	7.0	7.1	7.2	7.1	4.3

* All education includes state institutions of higher education, vocational rehabilitation, veterans' training reimbursed through the State Department of Education, state institutions for deaf, blind, and handicapped, expenditures for the State Department of Education, as well as state funds allocated to local districts for public schools. In 1952, it includes state expenditures for libraries. *The per cent which state aid to school districts would be of total state expenditures would be much less than that for all education.* For example, in 1952, expenditures for state institutions of higher education accounted for 25.2 per cent of all educational expenditures of state governments in the region.

TABLE 96

RANK OF SOUTHERN STATES ACCORDING TO THE RATIO BETWEEN EXPENDITURES
FOR INSTRUCTION IN WHITE AND NEGRO SCHOOLS AND ACCORDING
TO PERCENTAGE OF NEGRO POPULATION

State	1940 Ranks Percentage of Negro Population	Ratio of Expend-itures	1950 Ranks Percentage of Negro Population	Ratio of Expend-itures	1952 Ranks Percentage of Negro Population	Ratio of Expend-itures
Alabama	5	5	6	2	6	2
Arkansas	2	3	3	7	3	7
Florida	3	4	2	3	2	3
Georgia	6	6	5	5	5	4
Louisiana	7	8	7	8	7	8
Mississippi	9	9	9	9	9	9
North Carolina	4	1	4	1	4	1
South Carolina	8	7	8	6	8	6
Texas	1	2	1	4	1	5

TABLE 97

RANK OF SOUTHERN STATES ACCORDING TO THE RATIO BETWEEN EXPENDITURES FOR
INSTRUCTION IN RURAL AND METROPOLITAN COUNTIES AND ACCORDING TO
PERCENTAGE OF REVENUE FROM LOCAL SOURCES

State	1940 Rank Local Revenue Percentage	Ratio of Expend-itures	1950 Ranks Local Revenue Percentage	Ratio of Expend-itures	1952 Ranks Local Revenue Percentage	Ratio of Expend-itures
Alabama	2	3	1	3	1	1
Arkansas	7	10	5	8	7	7
Florida	5	2	9	2	9	3
Georgia	4	9	4	6	4	6
Kentucky	9	11	11	11	11	11
Louisiana	3	5	3	1	3	2
Mississippi	8	4	8	9	8	9
North Carolina	1	1	2	4	2	5
South Carolina	6	6	6	5	5	4
Tennessee	10	7	7	7	6	8
Virginia	11	8	10	10	10	10

TABLE 98

NATIONAL TRENDS IN THE NUMBER OF PUPILS IN AVERAGE DAILY PARTICIPATION,
NUMBER OF SCHOOLS PARTICIPATING, AND THE ESTIMATED RETAIL
VALUE OF FOOD DISTRIBUTED, 1937–1943 *

Year (March of Each Year)	Number in Average Daily Participation	Number of Schools	Estimated Retail Value of Food Distributed
1937	342,031	3,839	$ 85,062
1938	567,000	11,021	201,318
1939	892,259	14,075	408,804
1940	2,483,578	35,658	1,177,233
1941	4,715,311	66,783	4,368,371
1942	6,164,799	93,076	6,100,000
1943 †	4,366,829	58,368	2,739,123

* Taken from "The Community School Lunch Program," A Report of the War Food Administration Office of Distribution (Washington: U.S. Government Printing Office, 1944), p. 7.

† March of 1943 was not the usual peak month of participation because of the gradual disappearance of national abundance coupled with mounting transportation and warehousing difficulties.

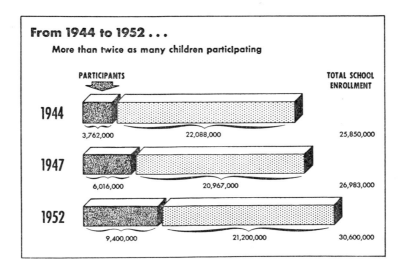

From 1944 to 1952 ...

More than twice as many children participating

PARTICIPANTS   TOTAL SCHOOL ENROLLMENT

1944   3,762,000   22,088,000   25,850,000

1947   6,016,000   20,967,000   26,983,000

1952   9,400,000   21,200,000   30,600,000

CHART 24. *National trends in the number of children eating in Federally aided lunchrooms.*

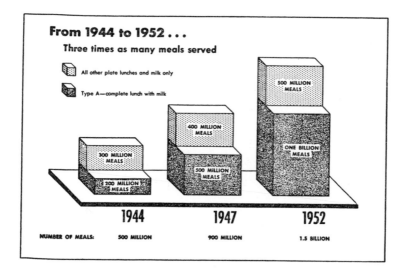

CHART 25. *National trends in the types of school lunches served in Federally aided lunchrooms.*

TABLE 99

Southern States for Which Data Were Available for the Study of School Libraries, Vocational Education, and School Lunch Programs by State Totals and County Classifications*

Southern States	School Libraries — Volumes		School Libraries — Expenditures		Vocational Education — Enrollment — Ag.		— H.E.		— T.&I.		— D.O.		Vocational Education — Expenditures — Ag.		— H.E.		— T.&I.		— D.O.		School Lunch Programs — ADP		— Expenditures		— Number Programs	
	State	County	State	County	State	County	State	County	State	County	State	County	State	County	State	County	State	County	State	County	State	County	State	County	State	County
Alabama			⊗	⊗	⊗	⊗	⊗	⊗	⊗	⊗	⊗	⊗	⊗	⊗	⊗	⊗	⊗	⊗	⊗	⊗	⊗	⊗	⊗	⊗	⊗	⊗
Arkansas			⊗		⊗	⊗	⊗	⊗	⊗	⊗	⊗	⊗	⊗	⊗	⊗	⊗	⊗	⊗	⊗	⊗	⊗	⊗	⊗	⊗	⊗	⊗
Florida	⊗	⊗	⊗	⊗	⊗	⊗	⊗	⊗	⊗	⊗	⊗	⊗	x		x	⊗	⊗	⊗	⊗	⊗	⊗	⊗	⊗	⊗	⊗	⊗
Georgia	⊗	⊗	⊗	⊗	⊗	⊗	⊗	⊗	⊗	⊗	⊗		x							⊗	x	x	x	x	x	⊗
Kentucky	⊗	⊗	⊗	⊗	⊗	⊗	⊗	⊗	x		x	⊗	⊗	⊗	⊗	⊗					⊗	⊗	⊗	⊗	⊗	⊗
Louisiana	⊗	⊗	⊗		⊗	⊗	⊗	⊗	⊗	⊗	⊗	⊗	⊗	⊗	⊗	⊗	⊗	⊗	⊗	⊗	⊗	⊗	⊗	x	⊗	⊗
Mississippi			x		⊗	⊗	⊗	⊗	⊗	(⊗)	⊗	⊗	⊗	⊗	⊗	⊗	⊗	⊗			⊗	⊗	⊗	⊗	⊗	⊗
North Carolina	⊗	⊗	⊗	⊗	⊗		⊗	⊗	⊗	⊗	⊗	⊗	x		x	⊗	⊗	⊗	⊗	⊗	⊗	⊗	⊗	⊗	⊗	⊗
Oklahoma		⊗		⊗	x	⊗		⊗			⊗	⊗	x		x		⊗	⊗			⊗	⊗	⊗	x	⊗	⊗
South Carolina	⊗	⊗	⊗	⊗	⊗	⊗	⊗		x	⊗	⊗		⊗	⊗	⊗	⊗			⊗		⊗	⊗	⊗	⊗	⊗	⊗
Tennessee	⊗	⊗	⊗	⊗	⊗	⊗	⊗	⊗	⊗	⊗	⊗	⊗	⊗	⊗	⊗	⊗			⊗	⊗	⊗	x	⊗	x	⊗	⊗
Texas	⊗	⊗	x	⊗	⊗	⊗	⊗	⊗	x	⊗	⊗	⊗	x		x	⊗	x	⊗			x	x	x	x		
Virginia	⊗	⊗	⊗	⊗	⊗	⊗	⊗	⊗	⊗	⊗	⊗	⊗	x	x	x	⊗	⊗	⊗	⊗	⊗	⊗	⊗	⊗	⊗	⊗	⊗

*Data available and used for states and counties are indicated by x; if also broken by races they are indicated by ⊗.

INDEX